NUTRITION

in infancy and childhood

NUTRITION
in infancy and childhood

PEGGY L. PIPES, R.D., M.P.H.

Assistant Chief, Nutrition Section, Clinical Training Unit,
Child Development and Mental Retardation Center;
Lecturer, School of Nutritional Sciences and Textiles,
University of Washington, Seattle, Washington

SECOND EDITION

with 34 illustrations

The C. V. Mosby Company

ST. LOUIS • TORONTO • LONDON   1981

MOSBY

1906 **75** 1981
YEARS

A TRADITION OF PUBLISHING EXCELLENCE

SECOND EDITION

Copyright © 1981 by The C. V. Mosby Company

Previous edition copyrighted 1977

Printed in the United States of America

The C. V. Mosby Company
11830 Westline Industrial Drive, St. Louis, Missouri 63141

Library of Congress Cataloging in Publication Data

Pipes, Peggy L
    Nutrition in infancy and childhood.

    Bibliography: p.
    Includes index.
    1. Children—Nutrition. I. Title. [DNLM:
1. Child nutrition. 2. Infant nutrition.
3. Nutrition—In adolescence. WS115 N985]
RJ206.P56 1981   618.92'39   80-25068
ISBN 0-8016-3941-7

GW/VH/VH 9 8 7 6 5 4 3 2 1   03/D/335

Contributors

JUDITH BUMBALO, M.S.

Lecturer, School of Nursing; Chief, Nursing Section, Child Development and Mental Retardation Center, University of Washington, Seattle, Washington

†PAULA CARMAN, M.O.T.

Instructor, School of Rehabilitation Medicine; Occupational Therapist, Child Development and Mental Retardation Center, University of Washington, Seattle, Washington

MIRIAM E. LOWENBERG, Ph.D.

Professor Emerita, Pennsylvania State University; Consultant, Seattle, Washington

BETTY LUCAS, M.P.H.

Lecturer, School of Nutritional Sciences and Textiles; Nutritionist, Child Development and Mental Retardation Center, University of Washington, Seattle, Washington

SALLY M. O'NEIL, Ph.D.

Chairman, Maternal and Child Nursing; Professor, School of Nursing, University of Washington, Seattle, Washington

JANE REES, M.S.

Lecturer, School of Nutritional Sciences and Textiles; Nutritionist, Child Development and Mental Retardation Center, University of Washington, Seattle, Washington

CRISTINE M. TRAHMS, M.S.

Lecturer, School of Nutritional Sciences and Textiles; Nutritionist, Child Development and Mental Retardation Center, University of Washington, Seattle, Washington

BONNIE WORTHINGTON-ROBERTS, Ph.D.

Professor, School of Nutritional Sciences and Textiles; Chief, Nutrition Section, Child Development and Mental Retardation Center, University of Washington, Seattle, Washington

---

†Deceased.

Preface

The second edition of *Nutrition in Infancy and Childhood* has been prepared for use by students whose career goals are focused on the provision of health care services to children and their parents. The contributors and I have again drawn on our clinical experience and have focused on information that we believe is relevant to the service arena. The case illustrations used in the book have been based on our clinical experience at the Child Development and Mental Retardation Center. Questions from parents and students in our unit guided the decisions as to what kind of information was suitable for inclusion.

The first four chapters again focus on nutrition in growth and development and energy and nutrient needs of children. Students who have received this information in other classes may wish to omit these chapters. We find, however, that most students consider a review necessary and that all students need information on what foods and how much food children should reasonably be expected to eat. A new chapter on collecting and assessing food intake information, with contributions from our feeding clinic nurse and occupational therapist, provides screening tools to identify children with motor and psychosocial problems that may compromise a child's nutrient intake. This material should prepare students to collect a more comprehensive data base on which to make recommendations for change.

The remainder of the book concerns the many aspects of feeding and eating during infancy and childhood that must be considered when planning with parents as to what and how to feed their children. Information on the vegetarian diet, the hyperactive child, and nutrition and athletics has been expanded from the first edition, and new chapters on each of these subjects are presented by contributors chosen because of a research interest or considerable practical experience with the subject discussed.

This book has become a reality only because of the continuing support of the staff of the Child Development and Mental Retardation Center at the University of Washington and because of the interest of our students and the cooperation of the parents of the children seen in the center. The staff of the feeding clinic has been particularly helpful in expanding our view of feeding children by focusing on the broad spectrum of influences on children's food intake and by providing support for us and our students when we assumed the role of case manager and found it necessary to identify appropriate referrals and counseling methods for children and their parents.

Many friends and family members have been most helpful during the revision of the book. I am particularly grateful to our section secretary, Ruth Boyd, whose efficiency and patience left me the energy to stay with my task, to Janell Douglas, who maintained her pleasant personality and positive outlook as she typed our manuscript in the face of short deadlines, and to my parents, whose continuous encouragement and support made completion of the effort possible.

Peggy L. Pipes

Contents

NUTRITION

in infancy and childhood

1

Nutrition
growth and development

A normal, healthy child grows at a genetically predetermined rate that can be compromised or accelerated by undernutrition, imbalanced nutrient intake, or overnutrition. Progress in physical growth is one of the criteria used to assess the nutritional status of populations and of individual children. It is, therefore, important that persons concerned with nutrition and feeding of infants and children be familiar with the process and parameters of growth as well as the charts and grids used to measure it.

There are many excellent reviews on growth and development. For a comprehensive review, the reader is referred to a standard textbook.[1,2] Although every aspect and component of growth is thought to be influenced by nutrition, this discussion will be focused on those parameters with which persons concerned with a child's food intake will be dealing.

NUTRITION AND PHYSICAL GROWTH

Children subjected to undernutrition are shorter and weigh less than their well-nourished peers. The rate of gain in weight is more affected than is gain in height, but if the nutritional deficit is severe enough and continues long enough, linear growth will be retarded or may even cease.

Overnutrition results in taller, heavier, more mature children.

During and after World War II a number of studies were conducted in Europe to determine the effect of war-induced shortages of food on the growth of children.[3-5] Prewar heights of children were found to be consistently greater than those recorded during the war years. The differences were most pronounced in adolescents, except in the case of 16-year-old females in Paris. The average heights of this age group were greater during the war than before it because most of the girls in this age group had worked on farms during vacations and had obtained better food.

Children from low-income families consume less food and, therefore, less energy and total nutrients than children from families with greater financial resources. Nutritional status studies have shown that children from these families are shorter and weigh less than children whose families are more affluent. Differences in stature are greater than those in weight. In fact, several studies have found that children living under conditions of marginal food supplies are shorter yet appear fatter than those who have an abundant supply of food available.[6,7] One study has shown that children who were known to be undernourished and whose diets were supplemented with milk experienced increases in height, weight, and skeletal maturity as compared with a control group whose diets were not supplemented.[8] The same observations have been made for children who were known to be receiving only minimal food supplies and whose diets were increased in energy.

The provision of supplemental food to low-income families of preschool children in Memphis, Tennessee, resulted in a higher percentage of children who were taller. Heights of the population shifted to a more normal distribution.[9] Children at nutritional risk who have received Womens, Infants, and Childrens (W.I.C.) supplemental food packages that include iron-fortified cereal, iron-fortified infant formula or milk, cheese, eggs, and fruit and vegetable juices have experienced increased rates of growth in height and weight.[10]

Growth patterns of children of racial groups whose members have been believed genetically small have been found to increase under conditions of improved nutrition. Especially striking is the change in the growth pattern of Japanese children born since World War II. In 1962 males at age 14 years were found to be 7.6 cm taller and females at age 11 years 6.6 cm taller than prewar children of the same ages. The change in growth patterns has been credited to an increase in the intake of animal protein.[11] A 1960 survey of children in Japanese orphanages whose food budgets were limited found heights to be significantly less than those of the national averages for children of the same age and sex. Adolescents were shorter as compared to their age group average than were younger children. During the subsequent 10 years the provision of 180 gm milk and one egg daily and increases in food budgets resulted in improvements in the quality and quantity of protein as well as in the amount of total nutrients consumed. Increases in average stature were greater than expected. A 1970 survey found that only teenage males were significantly below the national averages for height.[12]

CHARACTERISTICS OF GROWTH

Growth may be defined as an increase in the physical size of the body as a whole or as an increase in any of its parts associated with an increase in cell number and/or cell size. Development is defined as the acquisition of function associated with cell differentiation and maturation of individual organ systems. Growth and development are affected by genetic, hormonal, environmental, and behavioral factors that interact to determine an individual's growth pattern. Individual children have their own genetically predetermined growth patterns. Growth and development, however, proceed in an orderly and predictable sequence. Each organ and organ system has its own period of rapid growth marked by rapid cell differentiation, changes in form, and susceptibility to physical and environmental influences.

Critical periods of growth

Increases in physical size are achieved by increases in both the number and size of cells. Cell growth in any organ proceeds in three stages: *hyperplasia*, in which an increase occurs in cell number; *hypertrophy* and *hyperplasia*, in which increases occur in both the size and number of cells; and *hypertrophy*, in which only the size of the cells increases. Since deoxyribonucleic acid (DNA) is found almost entirely in the cell nucleus and is constant in the diploid nucleus of each cell, it is possible to determine both the number and size of cells.

Enesco and Leblond determined the number of cells in each organ of the rat at different ages throughout growth by measuring the DNA content of the organ. Knowing the weight of the organ, they then estimated the size of the cells.[13] Winick and Noble, using the same method for rat studies, found that there is a time when cell division stops before the organ attains its final size. There is a phase when cell number is not increasing but cell size is. This was found to be true in all nonregenerating organs, including the brain.[14]

It was also found that rats malnourished by restriction of total food intake during the period of increase in cell number but given normal diets during later growth had a reduction in the number of brain cells, while those malnourished in later life and rehabilitated had a normal number as well as size of cells.[15] Elliott and Cheek, in studies of muscle and liver cells of rats, found that restriction of calories resulted in fewer cells, whereas restriction of protein and calories resulted in a decrease in cell size and number.[16] Winick and Noble have also found that overnutrition during a period of hyperplasia resulted in larger animals with a larger number of cells in the organs.[17] The period of hyperplasia, the time when cell number is increasing, is the time the organ is most vulnerable to compromised nutrition and can be considered *critical* to an individual's acquisition of a normal complement of cells.

Growth in height and weight

The birth weight is determined by the mother's prepregnancy weight and weight gain during pregnancy. After birth genetic influences are "target seeking." A period of "catch-up" or "lag-down" growth may occur. The majority of infants who are genetically determined to be longer shift channels of growth during the first 3 to 6 months. However, many infants born at or below the tenth percentile who are determined to be of average height may not achieve a new channel until a year of age. Larger infants whose genotypes are for smaller size tend to grow at their fetal rates for several months before the lag-down in growth becomes evident. Often a new channel is not apparent until the child is 13 months of age.[18]

Low birth weight premature infants catch up in size with full-term infants by 3 years of age. Small for date infants also show catch-up growth, but only until 18 months. They do not catch up with full-term infants by 3 years of age.[19]

Immediately after birth there is a weight loss, but birth weight is usually regained by the tenth day. Thereafter, weight gain in infancy proceeds at a rapid but decelerating rate. By 4 months of age most infants have doubled their birth weights, and by 12 months of age their birth weights have usually tripled. Males double their birth weights earlier than do females, and smaller newborns double their birth weights sooner than do heavier infants. The weight increment during the second year is slightly less than the birth weight. The normal newborn infant who weighs 3.5 kg at birth, for example, can be expected to weigh 7 kg at 4 to 6 months, 10.5 kg at 1 year, and 13 kg at 2 years of age. Thereafter, the yearly increments in weight proceed at a slower but constant rate averaging 2.3 kg/year until the ninth or tenth year, when the rate of gain shows a steady increase. This continues until adolescence, when a rapid increase in the rate of gain occurs.

As shown in Tables 1-1 and 1-2, annual increments in height decrease from birth until adolescence, when a spurt in growth occurs. Infants usually increase their lengths by 50% the first year, double them by 4 years of age, and triple them by 13 years of age. The average birth length of 50 cm increases to 74 to 76 cm at 1 year of age, 100 to 105 cm at 4 years of age, and 150 to 155 cm in the preadolescent years. During adolescence the rapid rate of linear growth is most pronounced in the earliest period of acceleration prior to menarche in females. Acceleration of growth generally occurs 2 years later in males than in females. The adolescent growth spurt occurs in every individual; however, it varies in age of onset, intensity, and duration. Growth continues after adolescence but at a very slow rate until the epiphyses close and linear growth ceases.

Racial differences have been noted in rates

Table 1-1. NCHS percentiles for length and weight

Age	Percentiles, boys			Percentiles, girls			Measurement
	10th	50th	90th	10th	50th	90th	
Birth	47.5	50.5	53.4	46.5	49.9	52.0	Length (cm)
	2.8	3.3	3.8	2.6	3.2	3.6	Weight (kg)
4 months	60.2	63.7	67.1	58.7	62.0	65.3	Length (cm)
	5.4	6.7	7.9	5.1	6.0	7.1	Weight (kg)
8 months	67.7	71.0	74.5	65.7	69.1	72.6	Length (cm)
	7.6	8.8	10.1	7.0	8.2	9.4	Weight (kg)
12 months	72.8	76.1	79.8	70.8	74.3	78.0	Length (cm)
	8.8	10.2	11.5	8.2	9.5	10.9	Weight (kg)
18 months	78.7	82.4	86.6	77.2	80.9	85.0	Length (cm)
	9.9	11.5	13.0	9.3	10.8	12.3	Weight (kg)
24 months	83.5	87.6	92.2	82.5	86.5	90.8	Length (cm)
	10.9	12.6	14.3	10.3	11.9	13.6	Weight (kg)
30 months	88.2	92.3	97.0	87.0	91.3	95.6	Length (cm)
	11.8	13.7	15.5	11.2	12.9	14.8	Weight (kg)
36 months	92.4	96.5	101.4	91.0	95.6	100.0	Length (cm)
	12.7	14.7	16.7	12.1	13.9	16.0	Weight (kg)

From National Center for Health Statistics, Health Resources Administration, Department of Health, Education, and Welfare, Hyattsville, Md. 20782.

of growth. American black males and females are smaller than caucasians at birth. They grow more rapidly during the first 2 years and from that age through adolescence are taller than American white boys and girls of the same age groups. Asian children tend to be smaller than black children and white children.[2]

Body composition

Changes occur not only in height and weight during growth but also in the components of the tissues. Increases in height and weight and skeletal maturation are accompanied by changes in body composition—in adiposity, lean body mass, and hydration. Estimates of the changes in body composition have been made from chemical analysis of human bodies and of individual tissues, from indirect measurements of water and electrolyte levels, from excretions of creatinine and hydroxyproline, and from estimates of fatness. Indirect measurements of body fat have been attempted by a number of methods, including measurements of the density of the whole body, measurements of total body weight minus lean body mass, the use of fat-soluble gases, measurement of the thickness of fat by roentgenographic studies, and measurement of subcutaneous fat layers. Although there is much yet to be learned about body composition, there is an important body of data that can be related to physical growth and nutrient needs.

Determinations of total body water alone or in combination with other measurements such as density or potassium have been used as a basis for estimations of lean body mass. Total body water as a percentage of body weight decreases throughout infancy from approximately 75% at birth to 60% at 1 year of age, which is the adult value. Reduction

Table 1-2. NCHS percentiles for length and weight

Age	Percentiles, boys			Percentiles, girls			Measurement
	10th	50th	90th	10th	50th	90th	
2 years	83.5	86.8	92.0	82.1	86.8	92.0	Stature (cm)
	10.96	12.34	14.38	10.3	11.80	13.58	Weight (kg)
3 years	90.3	94.9	100.1	89.3	99.1	99.0	Stature (cm)
	12.58	14.62	16.95	12.26	14.1	16.54	Weight (kg)
4 years	97.3	102.9	108.2	96.4	101.6	106.1	Stature (cm)
	14.24	16.69	19.32	13.84	15.96	18.93	Weight (kg)
5 years	103.7	109.9	115.4	102.7	108.4	113.8	Stature (cm)
	15.96	18.67	20.14	15.26	17.66	21.23	Weight (kg)
6 years	107.7	116.1	121.9	106.6	114.6	120.8	Stature (cm)
	16.93	20.69	24.31	16.05	19.52	23.89	Weight (kg)
7 years	115.0	121.7	127.9	113.6	120.6	127.6	Stature (cm)
	19.53	22.85	27.36	18.39	21.84	27.39	Weight (kg)
8 years	118.1	127.0	133.6	118.7	126.4	134.2	Stature (cm)
	20.4	25.3	31.06	20.45	24.84	32.04	Weight (kg)
9 years	125.2	132.2	139.4	123.9	132.2	140.7	Stature (cm)
	23.33	28.13	35.57	22.92	28.46	37.6	Weight (kg)
10 years	130.1	137.5	145.5	129.5	138.3	147.2	Stature (cm)
	25.52	31.44	40.80	25.76	32.55	43.7	Weight (kg)
11 years	135.1	143.3	152.1	135.6	144.8	153.7	Stature (cm)
	28.17	35.30	46.57	28.9	36.95	49.96	Weight (kg)
12 years	140.3	149.7	159.4	142.3	151.5	160.0	Stature (cm)
	31.46	39.78	52.73	32.53	41.53	55.99	Weight (kg)
13 years	145.8	156.5	167.0	148.0	157.1	165.3	Stature (cm)
	35.6	44.95	59.12	36.35	46.10	61.45	Weight (kg)
14 years	148.8	163.1	173.8	151.5	160.4	168.7	Stature (cm)
	38.22	50.77	65.57	40.1	50.28	66.04	Weight (kg)
15 years	158.2	169.0	178.9	153.2	161.8	170.5	Stature (cm)
	46.06	56.71	71.91	43.38	53.68	69.54	Weight (kg)
16 years	163.9	173.5	182.4	154.1	162.4	171.1	Stature (cm)
	51.16	62.1	77.97	45.78	55.89	71.68	Weight (kg)
17 years	167.7	176.2	184.4	155.1	163.1	171.2	Stature (cm)
	55.28	66.31	83.58	47.04	56.69	72.38	Weight (kg)
18 years	168.7	176.8	185.3	156.0	163.7	173.6	Stature (cm)
	57.89	68.88	88.41	47.47	56.62	82.47	Weight (kg)

From National Center for Health Statistics, Health Resources Administration, Department of Health, Education, and Welfare, Hyattsville, Md. 20782.

of body water is almost entirely extracellular. Extracellular water decreases from 44% of body weight at birth to 26% of body weight at 1 year of age. This results from decreases in the water content of adipose tissue, increases in adipose tissue, and relative increases in lean body mass.[20] The percentage of weight of water in lean body mass at any age is relatively stable. In other words, there is a direct relationship between total body water and lean body mass. Water is responsible for 84.3% of the weight of fat-free mass at birth and 72% to 73% of the weight of fat-free mass of the adult. Fomon estimated the percentage of water in fat-free mass of the reference infant as 81.7% at 4 months, 77.5% at 12 months, 76.8% at 2 years, and 75.9% at 3 years of age[21,22] (see Table 1-3).

Since potassium is found predominantly within the cells of lean tissue and K^{40} in a fixed relationship to total body potassium, measurements of K^{40} give an estimate of lean body mass in older children and adults. The concentration of potassium in lean body mass of newborn infants is less than in the adult, and it increases during infancy and early childhood. Because of these changes K^{40} is not, at present, considered a reliable indicator of lean body mass in young children. It is considered, however, to be a valid measure of lean body mass in the older child and adolescent.

Anderson and Langham found that potassium concentration (gram per kilogram of body weight) increases from the first year of life, reaches a maximum at 8 or 9 years of age, and then declines sharply. After this decline sex differences become apparent. Potassium concentration showed a second increase in males between 14 and 16 years of age and another decline at age 16 years. The potassium concentration in the female continued to decline during adolescence.[23]

Table 1-3. Body water of male reference infant

Age	Water content, whole body (gm/100 gm)	Fat-free mass (gm/100 gm)
Birth	75.1	84.3
4 months	60.2	81.7
12 months	59.0	77.5
36 months	62.0	75.9

From Fomon, S. J.: Infant nutrition, Philadelphia, 1974, W. B. Saunders Co.

At any age taller children of the same sex have a greater amount of lean body mass than their shorter peers. During adolescence the rate of deposition of lean body mass per centimeter of height is much greater than during the preadolescent years; adolescent males accumulate lean body mass at a much faster rate than do females. The height at which one enters the adolescent growth spurt and the rate of gain in length influence the rate at which lean body mass is acquired.

Forbes, in studies of children 7.5 to 20.5 years of age, found, with a K^{40} counter, a linear relationship between height and lean body mass at any age and an exponential relationship between lean body mass, height, and age groups. Sex differences in lean body mass and height ratios were noted in the earlier years, although they were not found great enough to be significant. Males had greater amounts of lean body mass per centimeter of height than did females. After 12.5 years of age the lean body mass:height ratio increased rapidly in the male, whereas the increase was more gradual in the female. The female's lean body mass:height ratio maximum, which was about two-thirds that of the male maximum value, appeared to be attained at age 16 years, 3 years earlier than in the male. At age 20 years males had one and a half times more lean body mass per centimeter of height than did females.[24]

Fat is found in adipose tissue, in sites in the bone marrow, in phospholipids in the brain and the nervous system, and as a part of cells. It is the component of the body in which the greatest differences between children, age groups, and sexes are seen. The fat content of the body increases slowly during early fetal development, then increases rapidly in the last trimester. Widdowson and Spray found total body fat of the newborn infant to have a mean value of 16%.[25] Fat accumulates rapidly during infancy until approximately 9 months of age. Between 2 and

6 months of age the increase in adipose tissue is more than twice as great as the increase in the volume of muscle.[22] Sex-related differences appear in infancy, the female depositing a greater percentage of weight as fat than the male.

During childhood the yearly increments for fat show a steady decrease. In many children there is a prepubertal fat spurt occurring before the true growth spurt. When growth proceeds most rapidly in height, adipose tissue increases least rapidly in the female. In the male there is an actual decrease and loss of fat during high velocity periods of growth.[26]

Examples of growth in special systems

Brain and adipose cellular development have been intensively studied in relation to nutrition and nutrient intake. Although the long-term physiologic effects have yet to be clarified, events during early growth of these two systems are thought by many investigators to be important to an individual's growth and development.

Brain growth. The most rapid and critical period of brain growth in humans begins 9 months before birth and continues into the second year. During this time there is rapid cell multiplication and increasing differentiation. In the human, brain cell number increases until 12 to 15 months of age. Thereafter, there continues to be an increase in cell size and a resulting increase in mass. A study comparing brain growth of marasmic and normal infants who died in the first year of life demonstrated significant reductions in wet weight, dry weight, total protein content, and total DNA in the cerebrum, cerebellum, and brain stems of marasmic children. The brain stem was less affected. It appears that each region of the brain may have its own critical period of growth.[27] Brains of children thought to be adequately fed in the first year of life but malnourished

at an older age have been found to have a normal complement of DNA but reduced brain weight. This indicates a normal cell number but reduced cell size, further defining the critical period of increase in cell number of the brain.[28]

Dobbing has hypothesized that the period of the brain growth spurt, which includes not only an increase in cell number but (among other things) the establishment of the synaptic connections between them and myelination as well, may be the critical or vulnerable period. He has identified this period of growth as beginning in midgestation and extending into the second postnatal year, five-sixths of the period being postnatal. He believes that brain growth may have a single opportunity and that an insult during the critical stage of development will not delay but will lessen brain growth.[29,30]

The rapid increase in brain mass is accompanied by rapid increases in head circumference. The head grows rapidly prenatally and during the first year. Head circumference achieves two thirds of its postnatal growth by 24 months of age.[31] Head circumferences of malnourished children have been found to be smaller than those of their well-nourished peers.[32]

Malnourished children have been reported to perform less well on a variety of intelligence tests than those who are well nourished. But it must be recognized that children who are so nutritionally deprived that they experience brain growth retardation usually come from environments that may also compromise a child's development. The interaction of these two variables make the permanent effects of nutrition on mental development difficult to ascertain.

It has been well documented that children who have been subjected to malnutrition prenatally because of war-induced famine or during infancy because of disease or anomalies and who have been discharged to middle class families that provided sufficient food and stimulating environments were able to make up any nutritionally induced intellectual deficits.[33-35] The fact still remains that some children who were malnourished in later life who have returned to environments of poverty, questionable sanitation, limited stimulation, and undernutrition have performed as well or almost as well on intelligence tests as their peers, while some children who were malnourished at earlier stages of development who have returned to the same type of environments have not been able to perform as well.

Adipose cell size and number. Studies of obesity in adults have shown that obesity may be associated with an increase in adipose cell number and in cell size or with only an increase in the size of the cell. Weight reduction in adults results only in a decrease in the size of adipose cells, not a reduction in the number of adipose cells. Studies of 21-year-old obese subjects who had a history of childhood obesity before and after weight reduction showed a larger number of adipose cells as compared to nonobese adults. Reduction in weight of the subjects was associated with a reduction only in cell size, not in cell number.[36]

Brook found that the number of adipose cells of children who became obese in the first year of life was higher than the number of adipose cells of children who became obese in later childhood. He also found that those children who were light for their age and who had suffered an insult to growth in infancy had a profound deficit in adipose cell number.[37] Knittle, in a study of obese and nonobese subjects ranging in age from 2 to 26 years, found that at all ages studied obese children have a greater number of adipose cells and that on the average these cells are larger than in nonobese children. He believes that in some obese children a rapid increase begins in cellularity between 5 and 7

years of age or even earlier, while nonobese children experience a similar event between age 9 and 12 years.[36] There is insufficient information at the present time to define a critical period of development in relation to adipose cellular development. Excessive numbers of adipose cells at any stage of development should be discouraged on the basis of their immediate and long-term consequences.

Doubt about the validity of studies on adipose cellularity has been expressed on the basis that many adipose cells of children and adults after weight reduction may contain insufficient fat to be stained and counted, whereas every adipose cell of obese adults will contain sufficient fat to be stained and counted.[22]

METHODS OF ASSESSMENT

It is important that persons concerned with a child's nutrient intake be aware of how growth is progressing. Assessments are made by periodic determinations of height, weight, and head circumference. The measurements must be determined accurately, and they must be interpreted in relation to the child's current stage of growth. Individual children whose growth does not appear to be proceeding normally may require additional methods of assessment such as bone age and fat-fold measurements.

Growth standards

Growth standards for height, weight, and head circumference make it possible to visualize how a child's growth is proceeding. Standards for bone age permit an estimate of physiologic maturity. Fat-fold and arm circumference standards provide a basis for determining obesity versus overweight.

Height, weight, and head circumference. Standards for growth have been devised from studies in which large numbers of healthy, normal children of the same race and socioeconomic group were carefully measured at various ages. For some norms large numbers of children at various ages were studied (a cross-sectional study), from which mean heights and weights and standard deviations were calculated.[38] Other norms are based on measurements of children as they grew (a longitudinal study) and data ranked in percentiles, the number in the percentile indicating the position that a measurement would hold in a series of one hundred.[39-42] Data from these studies have been presented in tables, charts, and graphs. Growth curves and grids have been designed to measure how far the child has grown (distance curves) or how fast the child has grown (velocity curves). These growth grids are used in health evaluation to give some indication of how a child is growing, and they are often used in the assessment of nutritional status.

The grids are prepared so that age values lie along the axis, whereas height or weight values or changes in height or weight values are plotted along the abscissa. Height and weight values plotted for one age give information as to how children rank in size in relation to other children of the same sex, age, and ethnic background and information as to the relationship of weight to height as compared to other children. Several measurements of height and weight at different ages plotted on the grids enable one to visualize if the child's growth is progressing as might be expected. Most children stay in approximately the same percentile during growth. Growth, however, does not proceed in a smooth curve as the charts might be interpreted to indicate. Children grow in spurts, and changes may not adhere to the normal curve. A child may have no gain one month but considerable gain the next. During adolescence the growth patterns of many individuals will change in percentile, the early maturer moving to a higher percentile and the later maturer to a lower percentile. Both patterns usually return to the original percentiles by the time growth is complete. It is for this reason that maturational stages become important in adolescence.

Velocity grids give an indication of how fast a child is growing.[41,42] Children tend not to stay at a given velocity percentile nearly as closely as they do to a distance percentile. However, change does signal an important acceleration or deceleration. These grids are particularly useful in adolescence when children and parents often become concerned about height and weight in relation to peers and about final stature.

The most commonly used growth grids in North America are those prepared by an expert committee for the National Center for Health Statistics.[38] Data from the Fels Research Institute was used to determine the standards for children from birth to 36 months of age. The committee used data from the Health Examination Surveys and the Health and Nutrition Examination Survey to prepare grids for children from 2 to 18 years of age.

In addition to graphs that reflect gains in weight and height, the committee constructed body weight for length or stature graphs that are appropriate for plotting values for prepubescent boys and girls.

Appropriate use of these charts requires that measurements be made in the same manner in which the reference data were secured. Weight values for the child less than 36 months of age should be obtained while the child is nude on calibrated beam balance scales. Length values should be of recumbent length, not of upright height. The charts for children between the ages of 2 and 18 years use measurements of children in stocking feet and standard examination clothing.

Fig. 1-1 shows the effect of undernutrition on a female infant subjected to inade-

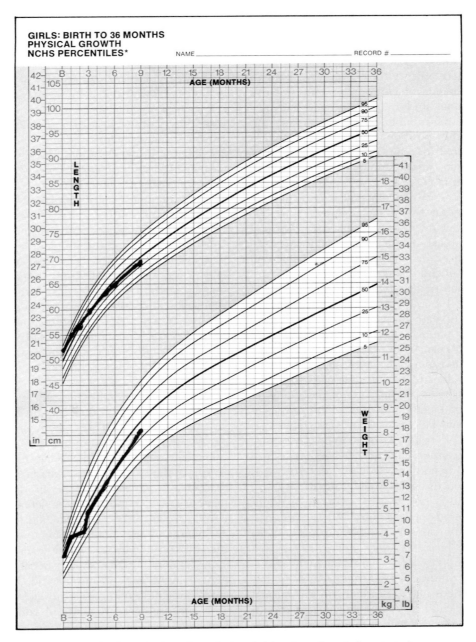

Fig. 1-1. Growth chart for infant girls (Courtesy Ross Laboratories).

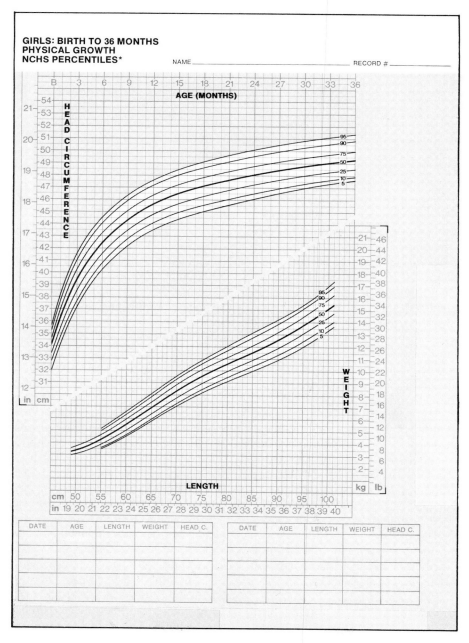

Fig. 1-1, cont'd. For legend see opposite page.

quate calorie intake because of a dilute formula. The mother of this infant was concerned because the baby was spitting up. A neighbor suggested that she add additional water. When the baby continued to spit up, the mother diluted the formula even more. When a nutrition evaluation was requested at age 10 weeks it was found that the child had gained only 460 gm since birth. Her weight was increasing at a very slow rate, dropping from the tenth to the third percentile. Her linear growth continued in the fiftieth percentile. She was consuming an incredible amount of formula, but only 190 to 225 kcal/day, approximately 50 kcal/kg. A change to a concentrated formula that provided 24 kcal/oz resulted in a gain of 500 gm the first week and 240 gm the second week. The rapid rate of gain continued until she reached the twenty-fifth percentile, where she has remained.

Fig. 1-2 shows the effect of a restriction in food intake on the growth of a preschool male because of a sudden change in income and the parents' inability to buy the quantity of food they had previously provided. Catch-up occurred when the family applied for and received food stamps and the child was given his normal ration of food.

Fig. 1-3 shows the drop in weight channel of an obese adolescent who was sufficiently motivated to lose weight that she adhered to a low-calorie diet. This grid, prepared by Tanner and associates in England, is frequently used in clinics serving adolescents. The graphs shown differ in that the first two examples present data on children living in the United States, whereas the last graph presents data on children living in England. [41,42]

Growth grids for premature and low birth weight infants have been prepared by Gairdner and Pearson[43] (Fig. 1-4). These grids utilize the concept of conceptual age—that is, chronological age as corrected to the expected date of delivery.

Measurements of head circumference are made in health examinations by passing a metal, cloth, or paper tape measure over the most prominent part of the occiput and just above the supraorbital ridges. Nellhaus has prepared a graph of head circumference measurements during growth.[31] The graph reflects weighted averages of variance from records of fourteen reports in the world literature and shows standard deviations. Sequential measurements plotted on this graph (Fig. 1-5) can be used to identify children whose cranial growth is deviating from normal. A rapid increase in the rate of growth may indicate hydrocephalus. A slowdown or arrest in the rate of growth may indicate a condition that will cause developmental delays. Such slowdowns and arrests have been noted in children subjected to severe undernutrition.[32]

Skeletal maturation. Fusion of the epiphyses and the appearance of ossification centers occur first in one bone and then in others in a predictable order. As a result, skeletal maturation can be assessed by observation of the various centers of ossification and the fusion of the epiphyses on roentgenographic studies. Standards of bone age have been devised from longitudinal roentgenographic studies of hands and wrists of children. The most commonly used standards are those of Greulich and Pyle, which were based on 100 hand films of children who were examined periodically from birth to age 18 years.

Bone age is often used to assess the physiologic maturity of a child whose linear growth appears to be proceeding at a very slow or very rapid rate. It is an especially useful tool in adolescence when parents and/or children become concerned about late and early maturation. Bone age correlates with secondary sex characteristics and with mature height.

Undernutrition will retard skeletal ossification. Insufficient calorie intakes slow bone growth and delay calcification of the ossifica-

Text continued on p. 19.

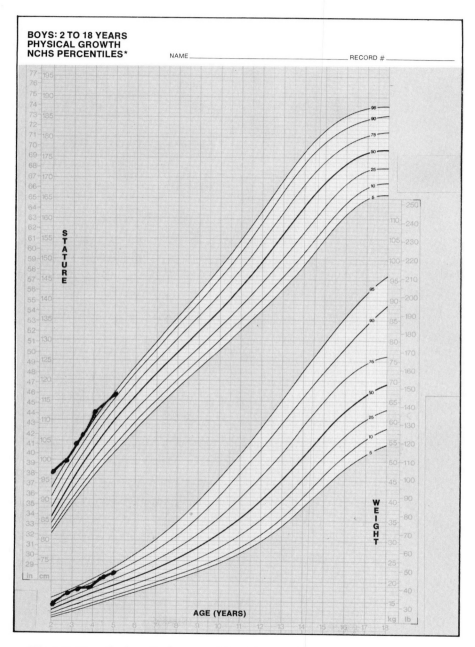

Fig. 1-2. Growth chart for boys aged 2 to 18 years (Courtesy Ross Laboratories).

Continued.

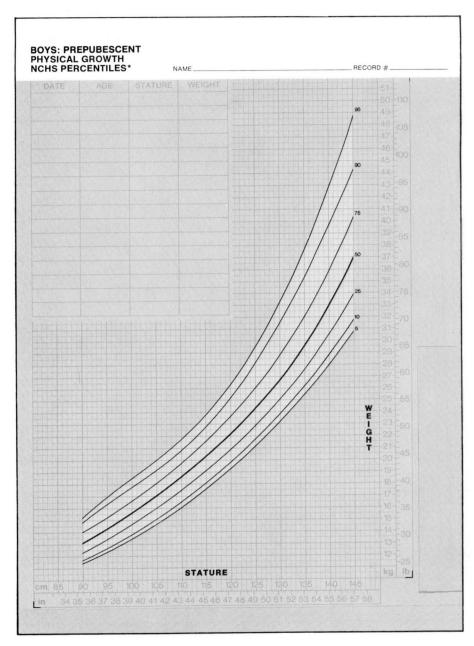

Fig. 1-2, cont'd. For legend see p. 13.

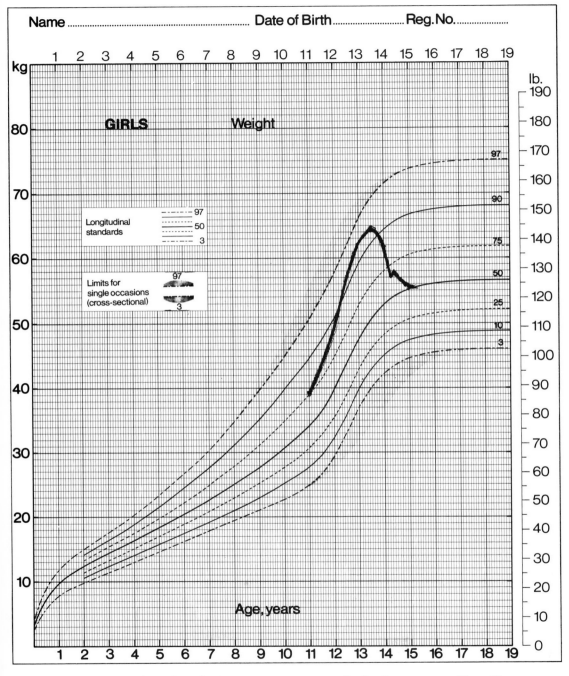

Fig. 1-3. Growth charts for girls. (From Tanner, S. M., and Whitehouse, R. N.: Clinical longitudinal standards for height, weight, height velocity, and stages of puberty, Arch. Dis. Child. **51**:170, 1976.)

Continued.

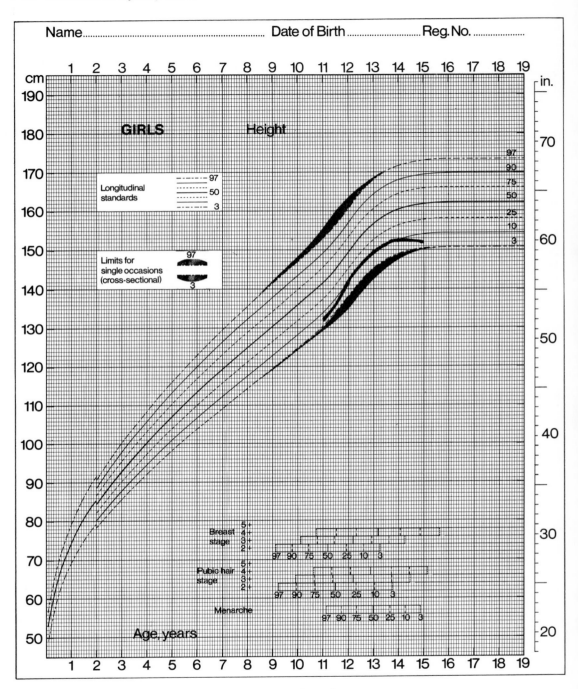

Fig. 1-3, cont'd. For legend see p. 15.

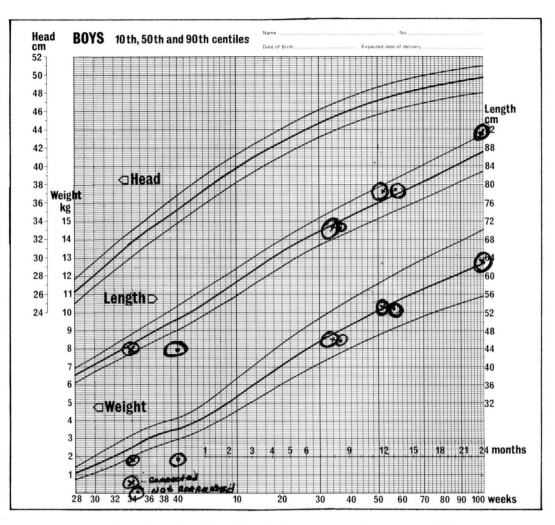

Fig. 1-4. Heights and weights of a male infant born at 34 weeks gestation; (x) denotes plottings when corrected for gestational age. (·) denotes plottings by chronologic age. The infant caught up to the ninety-fifth percentile by age 24 months. (From Gairdner, D., and Pearson, J.: A growth chart for premature and other infants, Arch. Dis. Child. **46:**783, 1971. Copyright Castlemead Publications.)

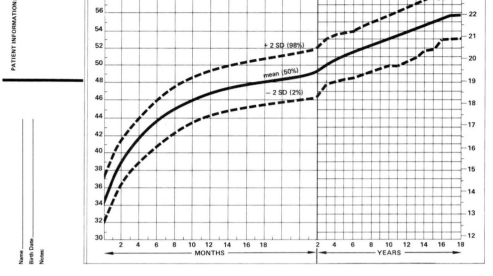

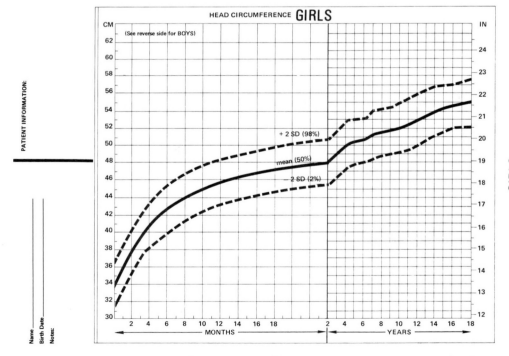

Fig. 1-5. Head circumference charts. (From Nellhaus, G.: Composite international and inter-racial graphs, Pediatrics **41:**106, 1968.)

tion centers. Also, the bone appears normal but often is thinner. Protein malnutrition, caused by either an insufficient intake of protein or an intake of poor quality protein or both, results not only in a reduction in bone growth but also in delays in the appearance of ossification centers and possibly alterations in the sequence of ossification.[45] Obese children have been found to have advanced skeletal ages.

Fat-fold thickness. Since approximately half of the total body fat is deposited in subcutaneous adipose tissue, the fatness of an individual can be estimated by measuring the thickness of the fat fold at selected sites with special calipers that have been calibrated to provide a constant tension (Fig. 1-6). In general one truncal (subscapular) measurement and one limb (triceps) measurement are advised. If only one measurement is to be used, measurement of the triceps is preferred. The triceps is the easiest site to measure and is representative of body fatness.

The triceps measurement is taken midway between the acromion and olecranon processes on the back of the upper arm. The arm should hang freely. The person making the measurement grasps the skin fold firmly with the thumb and forefinger about 1 cm from the site to be measured, so that the fold runs parallel to the length of the arm. The fat fold is pulled away from the underlying muscle and the jaws of the caliper are permitted to exert full pressure as the trigger lever of the caliper is released. The dial is read to the nearest 0.5 mm.

Standards for triceps fat-fold measurements have been published by a number of researchers.[46,47] Triceps fat-fold measurements have been compiled from a cross-sectional study of white subjects from birth to 44 years of age included in the ten-state nutrition survey of 1968-1970, and these measurements have been published in percentiles[48] (Table 1-4). Such measurements are

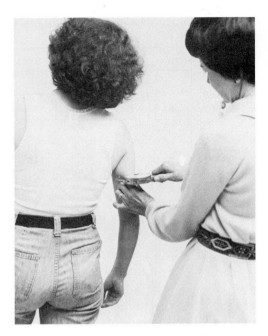

Fig. 1-6. Fat-fold measurements define obesity versus overweight.

very useful as a complement to standard growth charts in the evaluation of children's growth and in the decision as to the necessity to modify calorie and/or nutrient intake. Athletic, muscular children may appear overweight or obese if only height and weight are used as criteria for judgment. On the other hand, handicapped children with poor muscle tone often plot in a lower percentile for weight than height, even though they have an adequate padding of adipose tissue.

Racial differences have been noted in measured fat thicknesses. Puerto Ricans have greater fat measurements than North American whites and blacks. Black children have a greater deposition of adipose tissue from infancy through 4 years of age than do their white age group peers. After age 4 years, the differences are reversed. White children are fatter through adolescence than are those of the black race.[49] Group norms and genetic

Table 1-4. Percentiles for triceps skin folds for whites of the ten-state nutrition survey of 1968-1970

| Age group (years) | Triceps skin fold percentiles (mm) | | | | | | | | | |
| | Males | | | | | Females | | | | |
	5th	15th	50th	85th	95th	5th	15th	50th	85th	95th
0.0-0.4	4	5	8	12	15	4	5	8	12	13
0.5-1.4	5	7	9	13	15	6	7	9	12	15
1.5-2.4	5	7	10	13	14	6	7	10	13	15
2.5-3.4	6	7	9	12	14	6	7	10	12	14
3.5-4.4	5	6	9	12	14	5	7	10	12	14
4.5-5.4	5	6	8	12	16	6	7	10	13	16
5.5-6.4	5	6	8	11	15	6	7	10	12	15
6.5-7.4	4	6	8	11	14	6	7	10	13	17
7.5-8.4	5	6	8	12	17	6	7	10	15	19
8.5-9.4	5	6	9	14	19	6	7	11	17	24
9.5-10.4	5	6	10	16	22	6	8	12	19	24
10.5-11.4	6	7	10	17	25	7	8	12	20	29
11.5-12.4	5	7	11	19	26	6	9	13	20	25
12.5-13.4	5	6	10	18	25	7	9	14	23	30
13.5-14.4	5	6	10	17	22	8	10	15	22	28
14.5-15.4	4	6	9	19	26	8	11	16	24	30
15.5-16.4	4	5	9	20	27	8	10	15	23	27
16.5-17.4	4	5	8	14	20	9	12	16	26	31

From Frisancho, A. R.: Triceps skin fold and upper arm muscle size norms for assessment of nutritional status, Am. J. Clin. Nutr. **27**:1052, 1974.

differences must be considered in interpreting fat-fold measurements.

Mid–upper arm circumference. Measurement of mid–upper arm circumference combined with triceps fat fold is one method used to estimate muscle and fat bulk.

The measurement, as the triceps fat fold, is made at the midpoint of the upper part of the left arm. A flexible steel, fiberglass, or paper insertion measuring tape is placed around the whole arm but not so tight that it causes indentation. Arm circumference is measured to the nearest 0.1 cm. Arm muscle diameter may be estimated by the following formula:

Arm muscle diameter (mm) =

$$\frac{\text{Arm circumference (mm)} - \text{triceps fat fold (mm)}}{\pi}$$

Standards for arm muscle diameter and arm circumference have been derived from the ten-state nutrition survey.[48]

Potassium-40. Research centers may be equipped to estimate body composition by measuring the amount of K^{40} emitted from an individual by radioactive counting. The gamma rays of K^{40} are counted by using NaI crystals as detectors or in a liquid scintillation chamber. Both of these instruments, which measure K^{40}, must be accurately calibrated, are relatively expensive, and are rarely available for clinical evaluation of individual children. Neither instrument offers the potential for any hazard or trauma to the individual other than claustrophobia, which may be experienced in the steel chamber used when K^{40} radiation is measured with NaI. The length of time the individual must remain in the counter ranges from several minutes to several hours.

When the K^{40} content of the body has been determined, the fat-free or lean body mass is calculated by dividing the total K^{40} content of the body by the known K^{40} content of lean body mass.

$$LBW = \frac{K^{40} \ (gm)}{gm \ of \ K^{40}/kg \ of \ lean \ body \ weight}$$

Forbes and Lewis estimated that there are 2.66 gm of K^{40}/kg of lean body weight.[50] Behnke calculated the K^{40} content of lean body weight to be 2.46 gm/kg for males and 2.28 gm/kg for females.[51]

FAILURE TO THRIVE

If inadequate growth in height or weight occurs in the absence of disease or other medical concerns, environmental and/or nutritional deprivation is suspected. Some researchers believe that nonorganic failure to thrive results from endocrinologic changes in children who do not have adequate mothering. Others believe that mothers with unmet needs of their own have distorted perceptions of how much food their children need to eat and do not offer their children sufficient food. These children are often viewed as having had feeding problems in infancy and difficulty in accepting semisolid foods. They frequently will consume more food for their fathers than for their mothers. When placed in an environment that provides adequate mothering and stimulation, such as a foster home, the children consume large quantities of food. They catch up in height and weight and their rates of growth become appropriate.

Therapy for this failure to thrive must be directed to correction of the psychosocial difficulties that caused the disturbed mother-child relationship.

CATCH-UP GROWTH

During recovery from undernutrition or illness that has ceased or depressed growth, a child grows at a rate above that expected for his or her age. As the more rapid growth proceeds, the child catches up toward his or her growth curve. Prader, Tanner, and von Harnack have termed this developmental canalization.[52] Gain in weight proceeds very rapidly until the child reaches the correct weight for height, then proceeds at a slower rate as height and weight increase together. During the second phase growth proceeds at a height-expected rather than age-expected rate.[53]

When an insult such as malnutrition occurs to growth, the timing, severity, nature, and duration of the insult will influence the degree of deficit observed in growth and has been thought to influence the potential for catch-up. Early researchers reported that malnutrition sufficient to cause hospitalization during the first year of life results in permanent stunting in linear growth and head circumference of these children when compared to children of their same age and racial group.[32,54]

However, a number of studies of children rehabilitated from malnutrition have shown that catch-up growth is possible. Garrow showed that Jamaican children who were malnourished in infancy caught up or grew larger than their siblings on examination 2 to 8 years after discharge from the hospital.[55] Children in Peru who had been hospitalized for malnutrition between 3 and 15 months of age and were then discharged to foster homes, adoptive parents, or relatives of higher socioeconomic status than their parents were able to catch up in both height and head circumference at a time when catch-up growth of most malnourished children had decelerated.[56]

Stoch and Smythe found that African adolescents nutritionally deprived in infancy caught up in height by 15 to 18 years of age when compared with age group controls. Differences in head circumference increased over time.[57]

Although there is evidence that low birth weight infants are at a greater risk for short stature than are other infants, the premature infant seems to have a better chance to catch up to his or her normal growth channel than does the infant who is small for gestational age. Cruise has shown that children small because of prematurity at birth were more likely to catch up with their peers at age 5 years than were infants small for gestational age.[58]

Several researchers have studied catch-up growth in children known to be malnourished in infancy because of illness or physical anomalies that had been corrected by medical therapy or surgery or were uncorrectable. Barr, Shmerling, and Prader studied patients with celiac disease for 3 years after the institution of a gluten-free diet between the ages of 9 and 15 months. At the time of diagnosis height, weight, bone age, metacarpal cortex, and diameter were all retarded significantly. In 3 years all parameters except metacarpal diameter demonstrated complete catch-up.[59]

Ellis and Hill found that children with cystic fibrosis under adequate medical care who had and had not suffered from severe malnutrition in infancy caught up in height and weight for age when evaluated at 7 to 10 years of age.[60] On the other hand, Eid conducted a follow-up study on children with failure to thrive in the first year of life because of chronic disease or physical anomalies to determine if a treated group and an untreated group were able to achieve heights and weights equal to siblings who were used as controls. He found that failure to thrive in the first year caused significant growth retardation in both treated and untreated children. His conclusion was that the duration of illness and undernutrition and the interac-

tion of these factors were the most significant causes of permanent growth retardation.[61] There is much yet unknown about the ability of an undergrown child to catch up. The initial period of rapid gain in weight and height is common among all children during rehabilitation. It appears that some children almost or do completely catch up, whereas some do not catch up but remain stunted.

REFERENCES

1. Lowrey, G. H.: Growth and development of children, Chicago, 1973, Year Book Medical Publishers, Inc.
2. Smith, D. W.: Growth and its disorders, Philadelphia, 1977, W. B. Saunders Co.
3. Stuart, H. C.: Studies of the nutritional state of children in unoccupied France in the fall of 1942, J. Pediatr. **25**:257, 1944.
4. LaPorte, M.: Effects of war-imposed dietary limitations on growth of Paris school children, Am. J. Dis. Child. **71**:244, 1946.
5. Ellis, R. W. B.: Growth and health of Belgium children during and after German occupation, Arch. Dis. Child. **20**:97, 1945.
6. Committee to Review the Ten-State Nutrition Survey, American Academy of Pediatrics: The ten-state survey: a pediatric perspective, Pediatrics **51**:1095, 1973.
7. Adrianzen, T. B., Baertl, J. M., and Graham, G. G.: Growth of children from extremely poor families, Am. J. Clin. Nutr. **26**:926, 1973.
8. Dreizen, S., Currie, C. C., Gilley, E. J., and Spies, T. D.: The effect of milk supplements on the growth of children with nutritive failure. II. Height and weight changes, Growth **14**:189, 1950.
9. Kafatos, A. G., and Zee, P.: Nutritional benefits from federal food assistance, Am. J. Dis. Child. **131**:265, 1977.
10. Edozien, J. C., Switzer, B. R., and Bryan, R. B.: Medical evaluation of the special supplemental food program for women, infants, and children, Am. J. Clin. Nutr. **32**:677, 1979.
11. Mitchell, H. S.: Nutrition in relation to stature, J. Am. Diet. Assoc. **40**:521, 1962.
12. Mitchell, H. S., and Santo, S.: Nutritional improvement in Nokkaido orphanage children—1960-1970, J. Am. Diet. Assoc. **72**:506, 1978.
13. Enesco, M., and Leblond, C. P.: Increase in cell numbers as a factor in the growth of the organs of the young male rat, J. Embryol. Exp. Morphol. **10**:530, 1962.
14. Winick, M., and Noble, A.: Quantitative changes

in DNA, RNA, and protein during prenatal and postnatal growth in the rat, Dev. Biol. **12**:451, 1965.

15. Winick, M., and Noble, A.: Cellular growth in rats during malnutrition at various ages, J. Nutr. **89**:300, 1966.
16. Elliott, D. A., and Cheek, D. B.: Muscle and liver cell growth in rats with hypoxia and reduced nutrition. In Cheek, D. B.: Human growth, body composition, cell growth, energy and intelligence, Philadelphia, 1968, Lea & Febiger, p. 326.
17. Winick, M., and Noble, A.: Cellular response with increased feeding in neonatal rats, J. Nutr. **91**:179, 1967.
18. Smith, D., and others: Shifting linear growth during infancy: illustration of genetic factors in growth from fetal life through infancy, J. Pediatr. **89**:225, 1976.
19. Falkner, F.: Normal growth and development, Postgrad. Med. **62**:58, 1977.
20. Owens, G. M., and Brozek, J.: Influence of age, sex and nutrition on body composition during childhood and adolescence. In Falkner, F., editor: Human development, Philadelphia, 1966, W. B. Saunders Co.
21. Fomon, S. J.: Body composition of the male reference infant during the first year of life, Pediatrics **40**:863, 1967.
22. Fomon, S. J.: Infant nutrition, Philadelphia, 1974, W. B. Saunders Co.
23. Anderson, E. C., and Langham, W. H.: Average potassium concentration of the human body as a function of age, Science **130**:713, 1959.
24. Forbes, G. B.: Relation of lean body mass to height in children and adolescents, Pediatr. Res. **6**:32, 1972.
25. Widdowson, E. M., and Spray, C. M.: Chemical development in utero, Arch. Dis. Child. **26**:205, 1951.
26. Tanner, J. M.: Growth at adolescence, Oxford, 1962, Blackwell Scientific Publications Ltd.
27. Winick, M., Rosso, P., and Waterlow, J.: Cellular growth of cerebrum, cerebellum and brain stem in normal and marasmic children, Exp. Neurol. **26**:393, 1970.
28. Winick, M.: Nutrition and nerve cell growth, Fed. Proc. **29**:1510, 1970.
29. Dobbing, J.: Undernutrition and the developing brain, Am. J. Dis. Child. **120**:411, 1970.
30. Dobbing, J., and Sands, J.: Quantitative growth and development of the human brain, Arch. Dis. Child. **48**:757, 1973.
31. Nellhaus, G.: Head circumference from birth to eighteen years, Pediatrics **41**:106, 1968.
32. Stoch, M. B., and Smythe, P. M.: The effect of undernutrition during infancy on subsequent brain growth and intellectual development, S. Afr. Med. J. **41**:1027, 1967.
33. Stein, Z., and others: Nutrition and mental performance, Science **178**:708, 1972.
34. Valman, H. B.: Intelligence after malnutrition caused by neonatal resection of ileum, Lancet **1**:425, 1974.
35. Lloyd-Still, J. D., and others: Intellectual development after severe malnutrition in infancy, Pediatrics **54**:306, 1974.
36. Knittle, J. L.: Obesity in childhood: a problem in adipose tissue cellular development, J. Pediatr. **81**:1048, 1972.
37. Brook, C. G. D.: Cell growth in man, Am. Heart J. **86**:571, 1973.
38. National Center for Health Statistics: NCHS growth charts, 1976, Monthly vital statistics report, vol. 25, no. 3, Suppl. (HRA) 76-1120, Rockville, Md., 1976, Health Resources Administration.
39. Reed, R. B., and Stuart, H. C.: Patterns of growth in height and weight from birth to eighteen years of age, Pediatrics vol. 24, suppl. 904, part II, 1959.
40. Tanner, J. M., and Whitehouse, R. H.: Standards of height and weight of British children from birth to maturity, Lancet **2**:1086, 1959.
41. Tanner, J. M., Whitehouse, R. H., and Takaishi, M.: Standards from birth to maturity for height, weight, height velocity, and weight velocity: British children, 1965. Part I: Arch. Dis. Child. **41**:454, 1966. Part II: Arch. Dis. Child. **41**:613, 1966.
42. Tanner, J. M., and Whitehouse, R. H.: Clinical longitudinal standards for height, weight, height velocity, and stages of puberty, Arch. Dis. Child. **51**:170, 1976.
43. Gairdner, D., and Pearson, J.: A growth chart for premature and other infants, Arch. Dis. Child. **46**:783, 1971.
44. Greulich, W. W., and Pyle, S. I.: Radiographic atlas of skeletal development of the hand and wrist, Stanford, Calif., 1959, Stanford University Press.
45. Garn, S. M.: Malnutrition and skeletal development in the preschool child. In Pre-school child malnutrition, primary deterrent to human progress, Publication No. 1282, Washington, D.C., 1966, National Academy of Sciences, National Research Council.
46. Seltzer, C. C., and Mayer, J.: A simple criterion of obesity, Postgrad. Med. **38**:A-101, 1965.
47. Tanner, J. M., and Whitehouse, R. H.: Standards for subcutaneous fat in British children, Br. Med. J. **1**:446, 1962.
48. Frisancho, A. R.: Triceps skin fold and upper arm muscle size norms for assessment of nutritional status, Am. J. Clin. Nutr. **27**:1052, 1974.

49. Garn, S. M., with Clark, D. C., and Guire, K. E.: Growth, body composition and development of obese and lean children. In Winick, M., editor: Childhood obesity, New York, 1975, John Wiley and Sons, Inc., p. 23.

50. Forbes, G. B., and Lewis, A. M.: Total sodium, potassium and chloride in adult man, J. Clin. Invest. 35:596, 1956.

51. Behnke, A. R., and Wilmore, J. H.: Evaluation and regulation of body build and composition, Englewood Cliffs, N.J., 1974, Prentice-Hall, Inc.

52. Prader, A., Tanner, J. M., and von Harnack, G. A.: Catch-up growth following illness or starvation, J. Pediatr. 62:646, 1963.

53. Davies, T. F., and Parkin, J. M.: Catch-up growth following childhood malnutrition, East Afr. Med. J. 49:672, 1972.

54. Graham, G. G.: Effect of infantile malnutrition on growth, Fed. Proc. 26:139, 1967.

55. Garrow, J. S.: The long-term prognosis of severe infantile malnutrition, Lancet 1:1, 1967.

56. Graham, G. G., and Adrianzen, T. B.: Late "catch-up" growth after severe infantile malnutrition, Johns Hopkins Med. J. 131:204, 1972.

57. Stoch, M. B., and Smythe, P. M.: 15-year developmental study on effects of severe undernutrition on subsequent physical growth and intellectual functioning, Arch. Dis. Child. 51:327, 1976.

58. Cruise, M. O.: A longitudinal study of growth of low birth weight infants. 1. Velocity and distance growth, birth to 3 years, Pediatrics 51:620, 1973.

59. Barr, D. G. D., Shmerling, D. H., and Prader, A.: Catch-up growth in malnutrition, studied in celiac disease after institution of gluten-free diet, Pediatr. Res. 6:521, 1972.

60. Ellis, C. E., and Hill, D. E.: Growth, intelligence, and school performance in children with cystic fibrosis who have had an episode of malnutrition during infancy, J. Pediatr. 87:565, 1975.

61. Eid, E. E.: A follow-up study of physical growth following failure to thrive with special reference to a critical period in the first year of life, Acta Paediatr. Scand. 60:39, 1971.

ADDITIONAL READINGS

Baertl, J. M., Adrianzen, T. B., and Graham, G. G.: Growth of previously well-nourished infants in poor homes, Am. J. Dis. Child. 130:33, 1976.

Birch, H. G.: Malnutrition, learning and intelligence, Am. J. Public Health 62:773, 1972.

Birch, H. G., and others: Relation of kwashiorkor in early childhood and intelligence at school age, Pediatr. Res. 5:579, 1971.

Brozek, J.: Human body composition, Oxford, 1965, Pergamon Press, Ltd.

Cheek, D. B.: Human growth, body composition, cell growth, energy, and intelligence, Philadelphia, 1968, Lea & Febiger.

Fancourt, R., and others: Follow-up study of small-for-dates babies, Br. Med. J. 1:1435, 1976.

Graham, G. G.: Environmental factors affecting the growth of children, Am. J. Clin. Nutr. 25:1184, 1972.

Graham, G. G., and others: Growth standards for poor urban children in nutrition studies, Am. J. Clin. Nutr. 32:703, 1979.

Hamill, P. V. V., and others: Physical growth: National Center for Health Statistics percentiles, Am. J. Clin. Nutr. 32:607, 1979.

Klein, P. S., Forbes, G. B., and Nadar, P. R.: Effect of starvation in infancy (pyloric stenosis) on subsequent learning abilities, J. Pediatr. 87:8, 1975.

Krzywicki, H. J., and others: A comparison of methods for estimating human body composition, Am. J. Clin. Nutr. 27:1380, 1974.

Mann, M. D., Bowie, M. D., and Hansen, J. D. L.: Total body potassium estimations in young children: the interpretations of results, Pediatr. Res. 8:879, 1974.

McCance, R. A.: Food, growth, and time, Lancet 2:621, 1962.

McGowan, A., Jordan, M., and MacGregor, J.: Skinfold thickness in neonates, Biol. Neonate 25:66, 1975.

Neumann, C. G., and Alpaugh, M.: Birthweight doubling time: a fresh look, Pediatrics, 57:469, 1976.

Novak, L. P., Hamamoto, K., Orvis, A. L., and Burke, E. C.: Total body potassium in infants, Am. J. Dis. Child. 119:419, 1970.

Owen, G. M.: The assessment and recording of measurements of growth of children: report of a small conference, Pediatrics 51:461, 1973.

Sheng, H. P., and Huggins, R. A.: A review of body composition studies with emphasis on total body water and fat, Am. J. Clin. Nutr. 32:630, 1979.

Tanner, J. M.: Growth at adolescence, Oxford, 1962, Blackwell Scientific Publications Ltd.

Williams, J. P. G., Tanner, J. M., and Hughes, P. C. R.: Catch-up growth in female rats after growth retardation during the suckling period, comparison with males, Pediatr. Res. 8:157, 1974.

Williams, J. P. G., Tanner, J. M., and Hughes, P. C. R.: Catch-up growth in male rats after growth retardation during the suckling period, Pediatr. Res. 8:149, 1974.

Wingerd, J., and Schoen, E. J.: Factors influencing length at birth and height at five years, Pediatrics 53:737, 1974.

Winick, M.: Malnutrition and brain development, New York, 1976, Oxford University Press, Inc.

2

Energy and energy-producing nutrients
proteins, fats, and carbohydrates

Children must consume sufficient energy and protein of high quality in their diets to facilitate acceptable growth. Energy generated from the metabolism of fats, carbohydrates, and proteins provides the fuel that supports the maintenance of bodily functions and covers the cost of activity and growth. Protein provides amino acids for the synthesis of new tissues and nitrogen for the maturation of existing tissue in early childhood.

ENERGY

The unit that has been used to measure food energy and that has been reported in tables of food values is the kilocalorie (kcal), the amount of heat necessary to raise 1 kg of water 1° C. The Bureau of Standards in the United States has adopted the recommendation of the International Organization for Standardization that all energy be expressed in the metric system as joules, the energy expended when 1 kg is moved 1 m by a force of 1 newton.[1] It may be important to remember that 1 kcal is equal to 4.184 kilojoules. One may anticipate that food energy as well as requirements will in the future be expressed as kilojoules. However, since food values currently are expressed as calories, (kcal), this unit will be used in this discussion.

Energy requirements. The energy expended by any child is determined primarily by body size and composition, physical activity, and the rate of growth. In infancy a higher basal metabolic demand is thought to be caused by a larger loss of heat because of a relatively greater body surface and by a larger proportion of metabolic tissue.[2] Measurements of basal metabolic rates in older children have determined that males expend greater amounts of basal energy than do females. The differences are small during the preadolescent years and become pronounced during adolescence.

Maintenance requirements approximate 1.5 the basal metabolic expenditure, since some movement occurs even during sleep, and the specific dynamic action is estimated to be 6% of ingested energy. Energy costs of growth have been estimated to approximate 4.4 to 5.7 kcal/gm of tissue gained.[3-5] Decreasing rates of growth result in decreasing requirements for energy per unit of size (kcal/kg). In other words, as children grow older they need greater numbers of calories because of larger body sizes, but their need for energy per unit of size decreases.

The contribution of physical activity to total energy expenditure is quite variable among children and in individual children from day to day. At all ages, activity patterns among children show wide ranges both in the time spent in the various activities and the intensity of the activities. Some infants, for

25

example, may be quiet, cuddly, and satisfied to explore their environment with their eyes, while others may expend more energy in crying, kicking, and physical movement to see the world around them. Some older children may engage in such sedentary activities as looking at books or watching television, whereas their peers may be engaged in physical activities that demand running, jumping, and general body movements.

Energy requirements, which are greatest per unit of size in infancy, decline until adolescent growth is complete. During adolescence the energy expenditure will be a reflection of the adolescent growth spurt. Since adolescents enter the growth spurt at different ages, requirements established for a given age must be applied with caution.

During a period of catch-up growth, the requirement for energy and nutrients will be greatly increased.

Intakes of 150 to 250 kcal/kg of body weight have been recommended for children of preschool age. An intake of 200 kcal/kg/day should produce a weight gain of 20 gm/kg/day.[6,7]

The energy needs of individual children of the same size, age, and sex vary. Reasons for these differences remain unexplained. Differences in physical activity, in the metabolic cost of minimal and excessive protein intakes at equivalent levels of energy intake, and in the efficiency with which individuals utilize energy have all been hypothesized to exert an influence.[8] Recommended daily dietary allowances established by the Food and Nutrition Board are shown in Table 2-1. Since few children exactly fit the definition of average, the recommended intakes are listed as kcal/kg. It is hypothesized that 50% of these calories will be expended for maintenance, 25% for activity, and 25% for growth during infancy. Wide ranges of energy intakes including amounts both above and below the recommended intakes are known to be ap-

Table 2-1. Recommended energy intakes for children of various ages

	Age (years)	Energy (kcal/kg)
Infants	0-0.5	115
	0.5-1	105
Children	1-3	100
	4-6	85
	7-10	85
Males	11-14	60
	15-18	42
Females	11-14	48
	15-18	38

From Food and Nutrition Board: Recommended daily dietary allowances, ed. 9, Washington, D.C., 1980, National Academy of Sciences, National Research Council.

propriate for individual children. The recommended allowances are often used to establish energy needs of groups. In combination with growth data, the allowances can provide a basis for estimations of appropriate ranges of energy intakes of individual children.

In 1930 an expert committee, after reviewing energy intake data in relation to physical parameters, stated that height appeared to be the most appropriate criterion on which to base studies of energy needs.[9] The observation was never used. In estimating energy needs of children, body surface or weight has continued to be used as a reference for suggested energy intakes of children. Energy per cm of height has been proven clinically, however, to be a useful reference in estimating energy needs and designing diets for individual children. It is an especially useful reference for children who are genetically short. For example, preschool children with Prader-Willi syndrome maintain their weight in growth channel consuming 10 to 11 kcal/cm of height as compared to 14.7 to 15.4 kcal/cm of height, the 50th percentile of intake of normal males, and 12.9 to 13.8 kcal/cm of height, the fiftieth percentile of intake

Table 2-2. Selected foods as sources of energy

Food	Energy	
	kcal/oz	kcal/tbsp
Milk		
Human milk	24	12
Commercially available infant formula	20	10
Whole cow's milk	20	10
Commercially available infant foods (average value)		
Dry infant cereals	105	9
Strained and junior fruits	16	8
Strained and junior vegetables	11	5
Strained and junior meats	32	16
Strained egg yolks	58	29
Strained and junior dinners		
Vegetables with meat	15	7.5
High meat dinners	24	12
Strained and junior desserts	22	10

Adapted from Gebhardt, S. E., Cutrufelli, R., and Matthews, R. H.: Composition of foods, baby foods, raw, processed, prepared, Agriculture Handbook No. 8-3, Washington, D.C., 1978, U.S. Department of Agriculture.

of normal females of the same age.[10,11] Culley and others found that although children with Down's syndrome consumed considerably less energy than their age group peers to maintain their weight in growth channel, their intakes per cm of height were similar. Males with Down's syndrome consumed 16.1 kcal/cm of height and females 14.3 kcal/cm of height.[12]

Food sources. Three nutrients provide energy: proteins, fats, and carbohydrates, in approximate amounts of 4, 9, and 4 kcal/gm, respectively. Total calorie intakes will depend on the provision of the above nutrients by the food consumed. Energy values of foods commonly consumed during infancy and early childhood are shown in Tables 2-2 and 2-3.

To demonstrate food intakes that support appropriate energy intakes for several age groups, data for a hypothetical 2-month-old, 10-month-old, and 4-year-old child are shown in Table 2-4.

Deficient intakes. If intakes of energy are less than those required, children will grow at a less than normal rate or they will lose weight. If reductions in energy intake are severe and continue over time, linear growth will cease. Macy and Hunscher estimate that a reduction of 10 kcal/kg below the requirement can limit growth.[13]

Excessive intakes. Intakes of energy in excess of requirements result in heavier, more mature children. Over time this leads to obesity.

PROTEIN

Protein provides calories but also serves a more important and complex function. Protein, the basic component of the protoplasm in the cells, is important in the synthesis of purines and pyrimidines and is part of the deoxyribonucleic acid (DNA) and ribonucleic acid (RNA) molecules. Cell walls and various membranes are composed mainly of protein.

Table 2-3. Selected foods as sources of energy

Food	Portion size	Average kcal
2% milk with 2% nonfat milk solids	½ cup	72
Meat, poultry, or fish	1 oz	80
Egg	1 medium	80
Peanut butter	1 tbsp	94
Cheese	½ oz	57
Legumes, cooked	¼ cup	90
Enriched bread	½ slice	35
Ready-to-eat cereals (not sugar coated)	¾ cup	70
Cooked cereal	½ cup	55
Saltine crackers	1	12
Rice, macaroni, spaghetti, cooked	¼ cup	50
Potato (boiled)	½ medium	45
Potato chips	5	55
Green beans	¼ cup	6
Carrots		
Cooked	¼ cup	15
Raw	2 medium sticks	14
Apple	1 small	80
Banana	1 small	80
Orange	1 small	50
Orange juice	½ cup	60
Sugar	1 tsp	16
Jam or jelly	1 tsp	20
Butter, margarine, oil, mayonnaise	1 tsp	35
Cookies, assorted	1	40-50
Ice cream	¼ cup	70

Adapted from Adams, C. F.: Nutritive value of American foods in common units, Agriculture Handbook No. 456, Washington, D.C., 1975, U.S. Department of Agriculture.

$$NH_2 - \underset{\underset{R_1}{|}}{\overset{\overset{H}{|}}{C}} - \boxed{\underset{}{\overset{\overset{O}{\|}}{C}} - \underset{}{\overset{\overset{H}{|}}{N}}} - \underset{\underset{R_2}{|}}{\overset{\overset{H}{|}}{C}} - COOH$$

Amino   **Peptide**
group   **linkage**

Basic structure of protein molecule

Amino acids joined by peptide linkage. R_1 and R_2 designate amino acid molecules as side chains.

Enzymes, hormones, and antibodies are proteins.

Structure. Proteins are large molecules that contain specific amino acids joined by peptide linkages in a particular sequence. In addition to carbon, hydrogen, and oxygen, all amino acids contain nitrogen and some contain sulfur.

Amino acids. Amino acids have been classified as essential—amino acids that must

Table 2-4. Foods that provide appropriate energy for various age groups

Age	Weight (kg)	Recommended energy intake (kcal)	Examples of foods that provide R.D.A. for energy
2 months	5	575	28-32 oz human milk or infant formula
10 months	9.5	1000	24 oz homogenized milk or infant formula
			8 tbsp dry infant cereal
			14 tbsp junior fruit
			8 tbsp junior vegetable
			4 tbsp junior meat
			½ slice toast
			1 oz chopped chicken
			1 tbsp mashed green beans
			1 small banana
			2 tbsp ice cream
			2 arrowroot biscuits
4 years	18	1530	24 oz milk
			6-8 oz fruit juice
			3 slices bread
			½ to ¾ cup dry cereal
			2 tbsp peanut butter
			1 tsp jelly
			1 frankfurter
			¼ cup macaroni and cheese
			¼ cup green beans
			⅓ cup ice cream
			1 graham cracker
			1 medium apple
			1 small banana

be provided preformed in the diet—and nonessential—amino acids that may be synthesized by the body at a rate that will support maintenance and normal growth. Tyrosine is formed from phenylalanine, cystine from methionine. The other nonessential amino acids are produced by transfer of amino groups to carbon skeletons that result from the metabolism of fats and carbohydrates.

Naturally occurring amino acids are shown in Table 2-5. As will be noted there are nine amino acids that are essential during infancy and early childhood. There is evidence that the sulfur-containing amino acids taurine and

Table 2-5. Essential and nonessential amino acids

Essential amino acids	Nonessential amino acids
Threonine	Glutamic acid
Leucine	Glycine
Isoleucine	Aspartic acid
Valine	Proline
Methionine	Cystine
Phenylalanine	Tyrosine
Tryptophan	Glutamine
Lysine	Arginine
Histidine	Alanine
	Serine
	Asparagine

cystine may also be essential for premature infants.[14]

Digestion and absorption. During digestion the large protein molecules from the diet are broken down into individual amino acids and a few chains containing a small number of amino acids. This breakdown occurs in the acidic medium of the stomach and alkaline medium of the small intestine, which provide the optimum pH for activity of specific enzymes.

Pepsin secreted into the stomach breaks the protein molecule into the smaller polypeptides. In the duodenum the proteases trypsin, chymotrypsin, and elastase attack the interior peptide linkage and the carboxypeptidases attack the terminal peptide linkages. Although the peptide bonds are identical, the various enzymes are specific as to the amino acids whose peptide bonds they split. The products of the action of these enzymes—free amino acids, dipeptides, and small peptides—are hydrolyzed in the intestinal mucosal cells by peptidase enzymes.

The amino acids are then absorbed by active transport into the portal bloodstream and they enter the metabolic pool.

The proteolytic activity of duodenal juice is as great in infancy as in adulthood. However, the total quantity of protein that can be digested per hour is less during infancy and childhood and increases with age. It has been hypothesized that this results from a lesser volume of duodenal juice.[15]

Functions. Amino acids from protein consumed in the diet are continually mixed with amino acids derived from the degradation of body protein to form a pool from which essential compounds are synthesized. Amino acids are incorporated with other nutrients into body proteins that replace tissue that has been broken down and form new tissue during growth. They are synthesized into enzymes that act as catalysts and permit the reactions of intermediary metabolism. Hormones such as insulin and adrenalin that regulate body function are proteins. Antibodies, the compounds that combat infection, are synthesized from the amino acid pool in response to infective agents.

Protein in the blood functions with other elements to regulate water balance. Because proteins are buffers, they react with acids and bases and maintain neutrality of body fluids.

In addition to a requirement for amino acids, infants and children have a requirement for nitrogen. This requirement can be met from a variety of sources, including amino acids, ammonia, and urea. The body at birth contains about 2% nitrogen as compared with a little more than 3% in the nonobese adult. The shift toward mature body composition takes place during the first 4 years.[16] There is also a need for nitrogen for the formation of nonprotein nitrogenous substances required by the body, such as creatine, choline, etc.

Amino acid requirements of infants and children. Amino acid requirements of infants have been estimated by Holt and Snyderman from studies in which pure amino acids were supplied in proportions of amino acids of human milk.[17] The requirement of an amino acid was defined as the least amount required to maintain satisfactory nitrogen retention and weight gain when nitrogen levels and other amino acids were held constant. Fomon and Filer[18] and Fomon and associates[19] have estimated amino acid requirements from intakes of infants between the ages of 8 and 112 days who were fed whole protein in cow's milk formulas and soy formulas. Satisfactory linear growth and weight gain, nitrogen balance, and serum concentrations of albumin equivalent to those of normal breast-fed infants were used as criteria of adequacy.

The FAO/WHO expert committee has suggested that a composite of the lower estimates of the data from the studies of Holt and Snyderman[17] and from Fomon and

Table 2-6. Estimated amino acid requirements of infants

Amino acid	Estimated requirements		Composite of lower values (mg/kg/day)‡
	Holt and Snyderman[17] (mg/kg/day)*	Fomon and Filer[18] (mg/kg/day)†	
Histidine	34	28	28
Isoleucine	119	70	70
Leucine	229	161	161
Lysine	103	161	103
Methionine plus cystine	45 plus cys	58§	58
Phenylalanine plus tyrosine	90 plus tyr	125§	125
Threonine	87	116	87
Tryptophan	22	17	17
Valine	105	93	93

From Energy and Protein Requirements, Report of a Joint FAO/WHO Ad Hoc Committee, World Health Organization Technical Report Series No. 522, FAO Nutr. Meet. Rep. No. 52, Geneva, 1973, World Health Organization.
*Requirements estimated when amino acids were fed or incorporated in basal formulas. The values represent estimates of maximal individual requirements to achieve normal growth.
†Calculated intakes of amino acids when formulas were fed in amounts sufficient to maintain good growth in all the infants studied; the amino acids were not varied independently.
‡Based on a safe level of 2 gm protein/kg/day, the average of suggested levels for the period of ages 0 to 6 months.
§The values for cystine and tyrosine were estimated on the basis of the methionine:cystine and phenylalanine:tyrosine ratios in human milk.

Table 2-7. Estimated amino acid requirements of schoolchildren 10 to 12 years of age

Amino acid	Observed requirement* (mg/kg/day)
Histidine	0
Isoleucine	30
Leucine	45
Lysine	60
Methione plus cystine	27
Phenylalanine plus tyrosine	27
Threonine	35
Tryptophan	4
Valine	33

From Energy and Protein Requirements, Report of a Joint FAO/WHO Ad Hoc Committee, World Health Organization Technical Report Series No. 522, FAO Nutr. Meet. Rep. No. 52, Geneva, 1973, World Health Organization.
*Based on Nakagawa, I., and others. The values represent estimates of the upper range of individual requirements for the achievement of positive nitrogen balance in boys.

Filer[18] would provide estimates of the upper range of the requirement of infants aged 0 to 6 months[20] (see Table 2-6).

Estimates of amino acid requirements of 10- to 12-year-old preadolescents based on studies by Nakagawa and associates[21] are shown in Table 2-7. These investigators found amino acid requirements for 10- to 12-year-old children to be two to three times greater than those for adults. Requirements of males in all cases exceeded those of females.

Protein needs for growth expressed as percentages of requirement decrease as rates of growth decline. The 50% of protein need utilized for growth in the first 2 months of life declines to 11% at 2 to 3 years of age and is gradually reduced to 0% after an increase during the adolescent growth spurt. Amino acids required for growth differ from those required for maintenance. Factorial calculations based on patterns of growth indicate that the suggested amino acid requirements after infancy have been overestimated.[22]

Recommended intakes. The recommendations for daily protein intakes for infants and children shown in Table 2-8 assume in adequate intake of energy. These recommendations are based on ingestion of milk protein in infancy and a mixed diet that provides protein, which has an efficiency of utilization of 75% in older children. During periods of catch-up growth protein requirements increase. Intakes of 3.2 gm of milk protein/kg when energy intakes are adequate have been suggested.[23]

Fomon and associates have suggested that during infancy amino acid and protein requirements expressed per unit of calories consumed reflecting both size and rate of growth would be more meaningful than expressions of requirements on the basis of body weight alone.[19] They estimate the protein requirement to be 1.6 gm/100 kcal for children 1 to 4 months of age and 1.4 gm/100 kcal for children 8 to 12 months of age.

The American Academy of Pediatrics has set minimum standards for infant formula of 1.8 gm/100 kcal with a protein efficiency ratio equal to that of casein.[24]

The protein requirement for any child will depend on the rate of growth and the quality of protein in the diet. This implies that evaluation of a child's protein intake must be approached on the basis of the adequacy of the rate of growth, the quality of protein in the foods ingested, the combinations of foods that provide amino acids consumed together, and the adequacy of those nutrients (minerals and vitamins) and energy that are necessary for protein synthesis to proceed.

Food sources. Protein of high quality is available to most infants in developed countries as human milk and modified cow's milk formula. Infants whose parents are unwilling to feed them cow's milk formulas or infants who have allergic reactions to cow's milk are often fed formulas prepared from water-soluble soy isolates. As discussed in Chapter 7, commercially prepared formulas are prepared so that all nutrients are provided in the appropriate amounts. Home

Table 2-8. Recommended daily intakes of protein for children

	Age (years)	Protein (gm/kg)
Infants	0-0.5	2.2
	0.5-1	2.0
Children	1-3	1.8
	4-6	1.5
	7-10	1.2
Males	11-14	1.0
	15-18	0.8
Females	11-14	1.0
	15-18	0.8

From Food and Nutrition Board: Recommended daily dietary allowances, ed. 9, Washington, D.C., 1980, National Academy of Sciences, National Research Council.

Table 2-9. Approximate protein contents of various milks and foods fed to infants

Food	Protein (gm/oz)
Human milk	0.3
Commercial formulas	0.5
Homogenized milk	1.1
Evaporated milk prepared 1:1	1.1
Infant cereals, high protein	10.2
Infant cereals, rice	2.0
Strained chicken noodle dinners	0.6
Strained split pea, vegetable, and ham or bacon dinners	1.1
Strained beef and vegetable dinners	1.6
Strained turkey and vegetable dinners	1.6
Strained egg yolk	2.8
Strained beef	3.9
Strained veal	3.8

From Gebhardt, S. E., Cutrufelli, R., and Matthews, R. H.: Composition of foods, baby foods, raw, processed, prepared, Agriculture Handbook No. 8-3, Washington, D.C., 1978, U.S. Department of Agriculture.

preparation of soy formulas should be discouraged because parents may not be careful to heat the milk sufficiently to achieve inactivation of the trypsin inhibitor and may discard the residue of soy material from which the milk was made. In so doing, much of the protein and many of the other essential nutrients are discarded.

Table 2-9 lists foods commonly consumed in infancy that contribute protein.

As children grow older and accept table food they receive additional foods that provide high-quality protein. Examples of foods acceptable to preschoolers that provide high-quality protein are shown in Table 2-10.

Examples of combinations of foods that meet the recommended allowances for 2-month-old, 10-month-old, and 4-year-old children are shown in Table 2-11.

The examples given include much less protein than most children consume. In fact, it would be very difficult to provide sufficient energy in the diet if protein intakes were restricted to only the recommended amounts and milk and small amounts of other animal protein were included in the diet.

One will, however, encounter some children whose protein intakes will be a matter of concern. Kwashiorkor (severe protein deficiency) has been reported in infants whose parents purposely withheld milk after episodes of vomiting and/or diarrhea treated

Table 2-10. Selected foods as sources of protein for preschool children

Food	Portion size	Protein (gm)
Yogurt, made from whole milk	½ cup	3.7
Cheddar cheese	1 oz	7.1
Hamburger patty	2 oz	15.4
Chicken drumstick	1	12.2
Peanut butter	1 tbsp	4.0
Egg	1 medium	5.7
Liverwurst	1 oz	4.6
Tuna fish	¼ cup	11.5
Frankfurter, 5" by ¾"	1	5.6
Nonfat milk solids, dry	1 tbsp	1.52

From Adams, C. F.: Nutritive value of American foods in common units, Agricultural Handbook No. 456, Washington, D.C., 1975, U.S. Department of Agriculture.

Table 2-11. Foods that provide recommended protein for children

Age	Weight (kg)	Recommended protein intake (gm)	Examples of foods that provide RDA for protein
2 months	5	11	33 oz human milk *or* 22 oz commercially manufactured infant formula
10 months	9.5	19	18 oz homogenized milk
4 years	18	27	16 oz milk 1 tbsp peanut butter 1 medium egg

with clear liquids.[25] Children with multiple allergies who have learned to control parents by refusing all protein-rich foods have been known to experience catch-up growth when their parents learned to reinforce their acceptance of the meats and soy milk to which they had no allergic reactions. Children hypersensitive in the oral area frequently refuse all meat and eggs and will consume very limited amounts of milk and dairy products if unlimited amounts of carbohydrates such as starches and sugars are available to them. Limited financial resources restrict the amounts of high-quality protein parents can purchase for their children. Without very careful planning the quality of a child's protein intake may be compromised.

Interrelationship of protein and energy. Unless fat and carbohydrate supply sufficient calories, protein will be used to provide energy. Protein consumed at low levels of calorie intake will be deaminated and used for energy and will not enter the amino acid pool.

In addition, protein is utilized more efficiently when energy intakes are adequate. It has been suggested that a safe level of protein:energy ratio in the diets of children 2 to 3 years of age is close to 5%.[26] Carbohydrate has a sparing effect on protein because it releases insulin to take glucose in the cell and this facilitates muscle synthesis. Protein is more efficiently utilized when carbohydrate and/or fats are consumed at the same time or soon after.

Evaluation of quality of protein. The quality as well as quantity of protein must be considered when diets for children are being evaluated and planned. A number of complex methods have been used to evaluate food protein. Amino acid patterns of diets can be calculated for children who restrict their intakes of animal protein; these patterns can then be compared to a standard as an aid in evaluating the quality of protein in the diet. The determined biologic value and net protein utilization are used when planning diets for children who consume vegetarian diets.

Amino acid patterns for evaluating protein have been proposed by the FAO/WHO Committee and the Food and Nutrition Board of the National Research Council[20] (Table 2-12). The amino acid score of a pro-

Table 2-12. Proposed amino acid pattern for scoring quality of protein

Amino acid	FAO/WHO pattern	FNB/NRC (mg/gm of protein)	Egg	Human milk
Histidine		17	24	22
Isoleucine	40	42	66	55
Leucine	70	70	91	91
Lysine	55	51	66	66
Methionine plus cystine	35	26	55	41
Phenylalanine plus tyrosine	60	73	101	95
Threonine	40	35	50	45
Tryptophan	10	11	18	16
Valine	50	48	74	62

From Williams, H. H., and others: Nitrogen and amino acid requirements. In Committee on Amino Acids, Food and Nutrition Board: Improvement of protein nutriture, Washington, D.C., 1974, National Academy of Sciences, National Research Council. And from Energy and protein requirements. Report of a Joint FAO/WHO Ad Hoc Expert Committee, World Health Organization Technical Report Series No. 522, FAO Nutr. Meet. Rep. No. 52, Geneva, 1973, World Health Organization.

tein or mixture of proteins is calculated by using the amino acid in shortest supply in the following formula:

Amino acid score =

$$\frac{\text{mg of amino acid per gm of test protein}}{\text{mg of amino acid in reference pattern}} \times 100$$

The *biologic value* of food protein is a measure of nitrogen retention in relation to nitrogen absorbed. It is determined by the following formula:

$$BV = \frac{\text{Food N} - (\text{fecal N} + \text{urinary N})}{\text{dietary N} - \text{fecal N}}$$

Net protein utilization is used to express both digestibility of protein and biological value of the amino acids absorbed. It is an expression of nitrogen retained divided by nitrogen intake.

$$NPU = \frac{\text{N retained} \times 100}{\text{N intake}}$$

The *protein efficiency ratio* (PER) has been employed in studies of infants. It is determined by dividing the weight gain of a growing animal by its protein intake when energy intake is adequate.

Deficient intakes. Deficient intakes of protein result in reduction in rates of growth. If the deficiency is severe and continues over time, a cessation of linear growth and a loss of body protein occur.

Severe protein deficiency, as has been identified in developing countries, results in a condition called kwashiorkor. Symptoms of this deficiency disease include failure to thrive, edema, enlarged liver, coarse, pluckable hair, anemia, apathy, and irritability.

Excessive intakes. Protein intakes greater than 20% of total calories during infancy increase solutes and, as a result, increase the requirement for water. Dehydration may occur.

Excessive protein intakes in older children

may present no physiologic difficulties. This is, however, an economically and metabolically inefficient method of providing calories.

FAT

Fat, the most calorically concentrated nutrient, supplies between 40% and 50% of the energy consumed in infancy and approximately 40% of the energy consumed by individuals in developed countries thereafter. Fats, which are chemically named lipids, include a group of compounds that are insoluble in water but that dissolve in organic solvents such as alcohol and ether. Biologically, they appear in adipose tissue, function as vitamins and hormones, and are important components of membrane structures.

Structure. Lipids in the diet are derived from both animal and vegetable sources. Triglycerides comprise the major portion of dietary lipids, small amounts of phospholipids are found in foods. Animal fats contain cholesterol.

Triglycerides are neutral fats and include one molecule of glycerol to which three fatty acids are attached by an ester linkage. The positions of the fatty acids on the glycerol molecule are numbered in sequence, the exterior positions being designated as 1 and 3, as shown.

Triglyceride molecule

The fatty acids that occupy the three positions may be different fatty acids or the same.

They may be long or short chain and saturated or unsaturated.

Fatty acids are carbon chains that contain from 4 to 24 carbon atoms; they are classified according to the number of double bonds in the molecule.

Positions of the carbon atoms on the fatty acid molecule are numbered beginning at the carboxyl chain,, making it possible to identify fatty acids and the position of the double bonds by shorthand. The position of the double bond is expressed as the first carbon atom to which it is attached. Linoleic acid, for example, is commonly seen expressed as $18:2$ or as $18\Delta_{9,12}$, indicating that it contains 18 carbon atoms with double bonds between the ninth and tenth and the twelfth and thirteenth carbon atoms.

$$H-\underset{\underset{H}{|}}{\overset{\overset{H}{|}}{C}}-(CH_2)_7-\overset{\overset{H}{|}}{C}=\overset{\overset{H}{|}}{C}-(CH_2)_7-COOH$$

Monoenoic-oleic acid ($18:1$ or $18\Delta_9$)

The most common saturated fats found in animals and plants are stearic and palmitic acids, which contain 16 and 18 carbon atoms, respectively. The monounsaturated (monoenoic) fatty acid oleic acid is the most widely distributed fatty acid in nature and contains 18 carbon atoms and 1 double bond between the ninth and tenth carbon atoms.

Phospholipids contain glycerol, fatty acids, a nitrogenous compound, and phosphate. The largest group of phospholipids are lecithins, which contain glycerol, two fatty acids, choline, and phosphoric acid.

Cholesterol is a steroid, a compound with a characteristic cyclopentanophenanthrene nucleus and a free hydroxyl group.

Digestion and absorption. A greater percentage of fat is absorbed in later life than in infancy. Approximately 95% of ingested fat is absorbed by adults. Newborn infants absorb approximately 85% to 90% of the fat provided by human milk. Many infants absorb less than 70% of cow's milk fat.[27] Mixtures of vegetable oils in commercially prepared infant formulas are absorbed well, although the reason for the degree of absorption of those containing oleo oil remains unclear.[27] Absorption of fat begins to reach adult levels between the ages of 6 and 9 months.

The major portion of the digestion of fats takes place in the small intestine. A limited amount of lypolysis occurs in the stomach by a lipase secreted from the serous gland located at the base of the tongue. The activity is higher on short and medium chain triglycerides than on long chain triglycerides and produces mainly free fatty acids and partial glycerides.[29]

The amount of fat in the stomach controls its emptying rate; the more fat in the food mixture, the longer it remains. It enters the duodenum in regulated amounts where it is mixed with bile and pancreatic juice. When fats interact with bile, an emulsion is formed that functions to get the dietary lipids into mixed micelles. The micelles are both fat and water soluble, and in this form lipids are dispersed in the aqueous intestinal chyme and are acted on by pancreatic and intestinal lipase. Pancreatic lipase activity is low in the newborn infant, especially the premature infant.

The bile acid pool, although present, is reduced in the newborn. When compared on the basis of surface area, the newborn, although able to synthesize bile, has a bile acid pool one-half that of the adult.[28]

Pancreatic lipase attacks the fatty acid at the outer primary ester bond of the triglyceride. The reaction produces first 1,2-diglycerides and free fatty acids, then 2-monoglycerides and fatty acids. Unsaturated fatty acids are released more rapidly than saturated fatty acids.

Phospholipase A hydrolyzes the phospholipids into their component parts. Much of dietary cholesterol is present in the unesterified form. Esterified cholesterol is hydrolyzed by cholesterol esterase, which frees fatty acids and cholesterol.

Lipids are absorbed in the jejunum. Absorption is thought to be by passive diffusion. Bile salts are not absorbed with the lipids but reenter the intestine and are absorbed in the terminal ileum, are transported to the liver, and are then resecreted.

During infancy the position the saturated fatty acids occupy on the glycerol molecule influences absorption. Stearic acid is poorly absorbed in any position. Free palmitic acid, hydrolyzed from positions 1 and 3, is poorly absorbed, whereas palmitic acid, which occupies the position 2 on the glycerol molecule, remains as a monoglyceride and appears to be well absorbed.[30]

In the intestinal mucosal cells, lipids are reesterified to triglycerides, phospholipids, and cholesterol esters and synthesized to chylomicrons and low-density lipoproteins. The chylomicrons are discharged into intracellular space and appear in the lacteals, where they are collected into the thoracic duct and enter the bloodstream through the left subclavian vein.

Short chain and medium chain fatty acids do not form micelles, nor are they reesterified. They are bound to albumin and enter the portal circulation.

Functions. Energy provided by fats spares protein for tissue synthesis. Fats serve as carriers of the fat-soluble vitamins A, D, E, and K, give a pleasing taste to food, and provide satiety because the rate at which a meal is emptied from the stomach is related to its fat content.

The concentrated source of energy provided by fats per unit of volume is an asset during periods of rapid growth when the volume that an infant or child can consume is limited. Phospholipids are important components of membrane structure, are constituents of all cells, and are involved in the absorption and transport of fat, as has been described. Cholesterol serves as a precursor for the production of bile salts, vitamin D, and a number of hormones. It is a component of a number of tissues, including the myelin sheath covering the brain.

Essential fatty acids. Polyunsaturated linoleic acid has been conclusively proven to be an essential nutrient for both children and adults. Although arachidonic acid performs some of the same functions, it is not essential because it can be synthesized from linoleic acid.

Some investigators consider linolenic acid also essential even though no specific deficiency of linolenic acid has been reported in humans.

One of the earliest manifestations of fatty acid deficiency recognized in animals was an increased basal metabolic rate.[31] Infants who are fed formulas low in the essential fatty acid consume greater numbers of calories than do those who consume adequate quantities of linoleic acid to maintain normal growth. Caloric utilization has been reported to vary with intakes of linoleate up to 4% to 5% of the calories.[32] It has been suggested that the ratio of triene:tetraene fatty acids in the blood serum can be used in assessing nutritional status of linoleic acid. A triene:tetraene ratio of 0.4 or less is considered indicative of normal fatty acid status, and a ratio greater than 0.4 is indicative of an insufficient intake of essential fatty acid.[32] Such biochemical evidence of deficiency appears when linoleic acid is fed as less than 1% of the total calories. On this basis the minimal requirements for linoleic acid are considered to be approximately 1% of the calories consumed, and an optimal intake is thought to be 4% to 5% of the calories consumed.

Table 2-13. Lipids in milks

	Human milk	Cow's milk	Commercial formulas
Fat (gm/100 ml)	4.5	3.7	3.4-3.7
Percent of total calories from fat	54	48	46-50
Linoleic acid (gm/100 ml)	10.6	2.1	23-35
Percent of total calories from linoleic acid	4	1.01	11.4-22.3
Cholesterol (mg/100 ml)	20	14	1.5-3.0

From Schubert, W. K.: Fat nutrition and diet in childhood, Am. J. Cardiol. 31:581, 1973.

Table 2-14. Foods as sources of fat for infants

Food	Fat (gm/oz)
Infant cereal, dry (11-13 tbsp/oz)	.8-2.2
Vegetable and meat dinners	0.1-1.1
Meat and vegetable dinners	0.6-1.6
Strained and junior meats	1.1-2.7
Strained egg yolks	4.9

From Gebhardt, S. E., Cutrufelli, R., and Matthews, R. H.: Composition of foods, baby foods, raw, processed, Agriculture Handbook No. 8-3, Washington, D.C., U.S. Department of Agriculture.

Table 2-15. Foods as sources of fat for preschool children

Food	Portion size	Fat (gm)
Cooking fat	1 tbsp	12.5
Mayonnaise	1 tbsp	11.2
Butter	1 tsp	3.8
Cheddar cheese	1 oz	7.1
Peanut butter	1 tbsp	8.1
Frankfurter, 5" by ¾"	1	11.5
Broiled hamburger patty	2 oz	15.4
Chicken drumstick	1	12.2
Egg	1 medium	5.1
Tuna, drained	¼ cup	3.3
Ice cream	¼ cup	3.5
Potato chips	10	8.0

From Adams, C. F.: Nutritive value of American foods in common units, Agriculture Handbook No. 456, Washington, D.C., 1975, U.S. Department of Agriculture.

Linoleic and linolenic acid, as well as arachidonic acid, are direct precursors of the fatty acid–containing compounds prostaglandins, hormone-like substances that have many functions including activation of the adenyl cyclase enzyme system, which catalyzes the formation of cyclic AMP from ATP.[33] Lack of precursor necessary to synthesize prostaglandins may be responsible for a portion of the symptoms of essential fatty acid deficiency.

Recommended intakes. No recommendations for intakes of fat have been made. However, if less than 30% of energy intakes are derived from fat, a dry and unpalatable diet may result.

Fomon suggests that diets that provide less than 30% of total calories or greater than 50% of total calories as fat should be avoided.[27]

Food sources. Human milk, cow's milk, and commercially available infant formulas provide approximately 50% of the calories as fat (Table 2-13). Approximately 4% of the total calories in human milk and 1% of the calories in cow's milk are provided by linoleic acid. Commercially available infant formulas contain blends of vegetable oils and contribute greater amounts of linoleic acid.

The Committee on Nutrition of the American Academy of Pediatrics has recommended that infant formulas contain a minimum of 300 mg of 18:2 fatty acids/100 kcal (1.7% of the energy content).[24]

Prepared infant foods are relatively low in fat as compared to foods consumed by older children. Tables 2-14 and 2-15 list the amounts of fat provided by foods commonly consumed by infants and children.

Deficient intakes. The only clinical symptoms that result from diets devoid of fat are those of linoleic acid deficiency. Essential fatty acid deficiency results in dry, thickened skin with desquamation as well as increased energy requirements. Animal experiments have shown that essential fatty acid deficiencies are also associated with susceptibility to infection, diminished immunologic competence, and high neonatal mortality.

If fat provides less than 30% of the total calories in a child's diet, intakes of both protein and carbohydrate will be increased sufficiently that hypernatremia or diarrhea may result.

Excessive intakes. Excessive intakes of fat satiate children and limit their appetite for other foods. Very high fat intakes may produce ketosis.

CARBOHYDRATES

Carbohydrates supply between 40% and 50% of the energy consumed by most infants and children in North America. Biologically, carbohydrates occur as glycogen in the liver and in cardiac, skeletal, and smooth muscles and as glucose in the blood and extracellular fluids. They are constituents of mucopolysaccharides, mucoproteins, galactolipids, and nucleoproteins.

Structure. Carbohydrates in food occur primarily as monosaccharides, disaccharides, amylose, amylopectin, and cellulose. Glucose, fructose, and galactose are classified as monosaccharides. These carbohydrates contain six carbon atoms to which the hydrogen and oxygen are attached alone and in alcohol or aldehyde groups. The carbohydrates sucrose, maltose, and lactose are disaccharides and are made up of two monosaccharides linked together. Sucrose contains one molecule each of glucose and fructose; lactose contains one molecule each of glucose and galactose; and maltose contains two molecules of glucose.

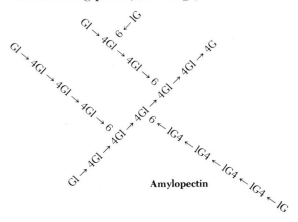

Lactose

The more complex carbohydrate, starch, is made up of many molecules of glucose arranged in straight or branched chains. The straight chain amyloses contain between 25 and 2,000 glucose units joined by an oxygen linkage between the first carbon atom of one glucose unit and the fourth carbon atom of the next (1,4 linkage). Amylopectin, a branch-chained starch, is a much larger molecule containing straight chains joined as amyloses and also containing an oxygen bridge between the first carbon of one glucose unit and sixth carbon atom of the next at the branching point (1,6 linkage).

Amylopectin

From Montgomery, R., Dryer, R. L., Conway, T. W., and Spector, A. A.: Biochemistry: a case-oriented approach, ed. 2, St. Louis, 1977, The C. V. Mosby Co.

Digestion and absorption. Digestion of carbohydrate begins in the mouth when the salivary amylase ptyalin begins to break the larger starch molecules into smaller units by hydrolyzing the straight chain starches at the 1,4 linkage. As the carbohydrates are moved through the digestive tract, amylose and amylopectin are broken down in the small intestine by the action of pancreatic amylase into the disaccharides maltose and maltotriose (a trisaccharide) and into dextrins (branched chains of an average of eight molecules of glucose).[34]

The products of starch digestion and the disaccharides lactose and sucrose are further broken down to monosaccharides by the enzymes lactase, maltase, isomaltase, and sucrase located in the outer fuzzy coat of the brush border and in the microvillar membrane when sugars make contact with the mucosal cell surface of the intestine (jejunum). The enzymes are specific and hydrolyze only those sugars that have appropriate structures. The monosaccharides glucose and galactose are actively transported into the portal system while fructose is absorbed by facilitated diffusion. The monosaccharides are then metabolized for energy, synthesized to glycogen or fat, and stored as such.

Maltase, isomaltase, and sucrase activity reach adult levels by 28 to 32 weeks gestation. Lactase present at low levels at 28 weeks gestation increases near term and reaches adult levels at birth.[35] Salivary and pancreatic amylase are low during the first months after birth. Concentrations of salivary amylase rise to adult values between the ages of 6 months and 1 year.[36] Concentrations of pancreatic amylase increase from birth through the preschool years. Hadorn and associates found that output of amylase per kg in children less than 6 months of age was two to four times less than in children 1 year of age. There appears also to be an increase in output of amylase from preschool to school-age years.[37]

Because pancreatic amylase is low in infancy, the early introduction of large quantities of starches may result in loss of calories provided by those foods in the stools or in abnormally loose stools. A 4-month-old infant who failed to gain normally and who had copious, loose, frequent stools as a result of absent amylase activity has been reported by Lillibridge and Townes. When starch was removed from the diet, the infant experienced catch-up growth despite a reduction in calorie intake. There was improvement in stool consistency, volume, and frequency. At 12 months of age the child had low amylase activity but was able to consume a completely liberalized diet and maintain normal growth.[38]

DeVizia and associates concluded from balance studies on infants 1 and 3 months old who were feed cooked wheat, corn, tapioca, potato, and rice starch, and of children 1 to 2 years old who were fed cooked wheat and potato starch, that although pancreatic amylases are low in infancy there may be sufficient amounts ot digest 10 to 23 gm of dietary starch per day in infants 1 and 3 months old or that digestion of starch may be provided at least in part by the activity of maltase, splitting starch and dextrins directly into glucose.[39] Fomon suggested, however, that bacterial digestion of starch in the colon could explain the absence of starch in the feces. He believes increases in blood glucose after starch feeding are more reliable for determining digestion of starch.[40]

Measurements of blood glucose of infants 2½ to 3½ days old who were fed starch orally showed only small increases in blood sugar that were delayed in timing of occurrence when compared to rises in blood glucose of the same infants fed glucose, maltose, and dextrimaltose.[41] Husband, Husband, and Mallinson showed that starch empties more rapidly from the stomachs of infants 4 to 60 days old than does an equal amount of glucose.[42] A slow but sustained rise in blood glucose over 2½ hours further suggested that starch hydrolysis was slow.

Functions. Metabolism of carbohydrate produces energy. If carbohydrate is not provided preformed in the diet, protein and fat are degradated and metabolized to serve this function. They are also used to synthesize glycogen, the storage form of carbohydrates. Carbohydrates, therefore, spare protein for tissue synthesis.

Glycogen reserves serve as an ever-present source of energy to all systems in the body. They are especially important to the cardiac muscle and in the maintenance of normal levels of blood glucose.

Recommended intakes. Since carbohydrate can be synthesized from amino acids and the glycerol moiety of fat, no specific recommendation for intake has been made. The Food and Nutrition Board of the National Research Council suggests minimum intakes of 50 to 100 gm/day.

Food sources. The predominant carbohydrate in the young infant's diet is lactose, found in human milk and cow's milk. It has

Table 2-16. Carbohydrates in foods for infants

Food	Carbohydrate (gm/oz)
Human milk	2.9
Prepared infant formulas	2.1
Homogenized milk	1.5
Infant cereals, dry	16.4-22.8
Strained and junior desserts	3.7-6.1
Strained and junior vegetable and meat dinners	1.9-3.2
Strained and junior meat and vegetable dinners	1.2-5.3
Strained and junior fruit	2.9-6.1
Strained and junior vegetables	1.6-4.6

From Gebhardt, S. E., Cutrufelli, R., and Matthews, R. H.: Composition of foods, baby foods, raw, processed, prepared, Agriculture Handbook No. 8-3, Washington, D.C., U.S. Department of Agriculture.

become a common practice for parents to add starch (in the form of prepared cereals and ingredients of commercially prepared infant foods) and sucrose (which they add to fruits and vegetables) to the infant's diet at 4 to 6 months of age.

Some foods contain carbohydrate and few other nutrients, whereas others contribute carbohydrate and, in addition, other essential nutrients. Candy, cookies, and potato chips, for example, provide primarily calories, whereas cereal grains are important sources of the B vitamins; potatoes contribute vitamin C; and legumes offer amino acids, iron, and B vitamins as well as carbohydrates. Therefore, careful attention to the nutrients carried by the carbohydrate-containing foods is important in planning diets for children.

Most children prefer "sweet foods." In fact, infants at birth appear to distinguish sugar water from water. They accept larger quantities of sugar-sweetened solutions than unsweetened mixtures.[43] Indiscriminate consumption of candy, cookies, carbonated beverages, and other sweetened drinks dulls the appetite for other foods and should be discouraged. The impact of these sucrose-containing foods on the incidence of dental caries is discussed in Chapter 13.

Deficient intakes. If intakes of carbohydrate are low, amino acids and fats are metabolized for energy and converted to glycogen. When this happens, there is a risk of ketosis from the breakdown of fat. Urea formed from the breakdown of protein will obligate additional water for excretion.

A syndrome that results in symptoms similar to those of starvation has been described in individuals who consume diets that completely eliminate carbohydrate. Symptoms include dehydration, ketosis, loss of body protein, fatigue, and loss of energy.

Excessive intakes. Excessive intakes of carbohydrate may load the enzyme system at least temporarily, and diarrhea may result.

Table 2-17. Carbohydrates in foods commonly consumed by preschool children

Food	Portion size	Carbohydrate (gm)
Bread, whole wheat	1 slice	13.0
Corn flakes	½ cup	10.7
Sugar-coated corn flakes	½ cup	18.3
Oatmeal	½ cup	11.7
Potato, diced	¼ cup	6.6
Potato chips	10	10.0
Noodles	¼ cup	9.3
Spaghetti	¼ cup	8.0
Rice	¼ cup	10.0
Corn, whole kernel	¼ cup	7.8
Navy beans, cooked	¼ cup	10.1
Saltine cracker	1	2.0
Graham cracker	2 squares	10.4
Cookie, oatmeal	1	9.5
Apple	1 small	20.0
Applesauce, sweetened	½ cup	15.0
Banana	1 small	21.1
Orange	1 medium	15.0
Sugar	1 tsp	4.0
Carbonated beverages, cola	3 oz	9.3
Jelly beans	1 oz (10)	26.4

Adapted from Adams, C. F.: Nutritive value of American foods in common units, Agriculture Handbook No. 456, Washington, D.C., 1975, U.S. Department of Agriculture.

REFERENCES

Energy

1. Ames, S. R.: The joule-unit of energy, J. Am. Diet. Assoc. **57:**415, 1970.
2. Snyderman, S. E.: Nutrition in infancy and adolescence. In Goodhart, R. S., and Shils, H. E., editors: Modern nutrition in health and disease, ed. 6, Philadelphia, 1980, Lea & Febiger.
3. Brooke, O. G., Alvear, J., and Arnold, M.: Energy retention, energy expenditure, and growth in healthy immature infants, Pediatr. Res. **13:**215, 1979.
4. Ashworth, A.: Growth rates in children recovering from protein-calorie malnutrition, Br. J. Nutr. **23:** 835, 1969.
5. Spady, D. W., and others: Energy balance during recovery from malnutrition, Am. J. Clin. Nutr. **29:** 1073, 1976.
6. Spady, D. W., Hill, A. A., and Waterlow, J. C.: Energy cost of catch-up growth in malnourished children, Nutr. Metab. **21:**224, 1977.
7. Ashworth, A.: Ad lib feeding during recovery from malnutrition, Br. J. Nutr. **31:**109, 1974.
8. Hegsted, D. M.: Energy needs and energy utilization, Nutr. Rev. **32:**33, 1974.
9. White House Conference on Child Health and Protection: Growth and development of the child. III. Nutrition, Report of the Committee on Growth and Development, New York, 1932, Century House, Inc., p. 532.
10. Pipes, P., and Holm, V. A.: Weight control of children with Prader-Willi syndrome, J. Am. Diet. Assoc. **62:**520, 1973.
11. Beal, V. A.: Nutritional intake. In McCammon, R. W.: Human growth and development, Springfield, Ill., 1970, Charles C Thomas Publisher.
12. Culley, W. J., and others: Calorie intake of children with Downs syndrome (mongolism), J. Pediatr. **66:**772, 1965.
13. Macy, I. G., and Hunscher, H. A.: Calories—a limiting factor in the growth of children, J. Nutr. **45:**189, 1951.

Protein

14. Alfin-Slater, R. B., and Jelliffe, P. B.: Nutritional requirements with special reference to infancy, Pediatr. Clin. North Am. **24**:3, 1977.
15. Lindberg, T.: Proteolytic activity in duodenal juice in infants, children and adults, Acta Paediatr. Scand. **63**:805, 1974.
16. Holt, L. E., Jr., and others: Protein and amino acid requirements in early life, New York, 1960. New York University Press.
17. Holt, L. E., Jr., and Snyderman, S. E.: The amino acid requirements of infants, J.A.M.A. **175**:100, 1961.
18. Fomon, S. J., and Filer, L. J.: Amino acid requirements for normal growth. In Nyhan, W. L.: Amino acid metabolism and genetic variations, New York, 1967, McGraw-Hill Book Co.
19. Fomon, S. J., and others: Requirements for protein and essential amino acids in early infancy, Acta Paediatr. Scand. **62**:33, 1973.
20. Report of a Joint FAO/WHO Ad Hoc Expert Committee: Energy and protein requirements, World Health Organization Technical Series No. 522, FAO Nutr. Meet. Ser. No. 52, Geneva, 1973, World Health Organization.
21. Nakagawa, I., and others: Amino acid requirements of children: nitrogen balance at the minimal level of essential amino acids, J. Nutr. **83**:115, 1964.
22. Lozy, M., and Hegsted, D. M.: Calculation of the amino acid requirements of children at different ages by the factorial method, Am. J. Clin. Nutr. **28**:1052, 1975.
23. Whitehead, P. G.: Protein and energy requirements of young children living in developing countries to allow for catch-up growth after infections, Am. J. Clin. Nutr. **30**:1545, 1977.
24. Committee on Nutrition, Academy of Pediatrics: Commentary on breastfeeding and infant formula, Pediatrics **57**:278, 1976.
25. John, T. J., and others: Kwashiorkor not associated with poverty, Pediatrics **90**:730, 1977.
26. Payne, R. P.: Safe protein-calorie ratios in diets. The relative importance of protein and energy intake as a causal factor in malnutrition, Am. J. Clin. Nutr. **28**:281, 1975.

Fat

27. Fomon, S. J.: Infant nutrition, Philadelphia, 1974, W. B. Saunders Co.
28. Watkins, J. B.: Bile acid metabolism and fat absorption in newborn infants, Pediatr. Clin. North Am. **21**:501, 1974.
29. Hamosh, M.: A review. Fat digestion in the newborn: role of lingual lipase and preduodenal digestion, Pediatr. Res. **13**:615, 1979.
30. Filer, L. J., Mattson, F. H., and Fomon, S. J.: Triglyceride configuration and fat absorption by the human infant, J. Nutr. **99**:293, 1969.
31. Wesson, L. G., and Burr, G. O.: The metabolic rate and respiratory quotients of rats on a fat deficient diet, J. Biol. Chem. **91**:525, 1931.
32. Holman, R. J., Caster, W. O., and Weise, H. F.: The essential fatty acid requirement of infants and the assessment of their dietary intake of linoleate by serum fatty acid analysis, Am. J. Clin. Nutr. **14**:70, 1964.
33. Crawford, M. A., Hassam, A. G., and Rivers, J. P. W.: Essential fatty acid requirements in infancy, Am. J. Clin. Nutr. **31**:2181, 1978.

Carbohydrate

34. Gray, G. M.: Carbohydrate digestion and absorption, N. Engl. J. Med. **292**:1225, 1975.
35. Bayless, T. M., and Christopher, N. L.: Disaccharidase deficiency, Am. J. Clin. Nutr. **22**:181, 1969.
36. Rossiter, M. A., and others: Amylase content of mixed saliva in children, Acta Paediatr. Scand. **63**:389, 1974.
37. Hadorn, B., and others: Quantitative assessment of exocrine pancreatic function in infants and children, J. Pediatr. **73**:39, 1968.
38. Lillibridge, C. B., and Townes, P. L.: Physiologic deficiency of pancreatic amylase in infancy: a factor in iatrogenic diarrhea, J. Pediatr. **82**:279, 1973.
39. DeVizia, B., and others: Digestibility of starches in infants and children, J. Pediatr. **86**:50, 1975.
40. Fomon, S. J.: Infant nutrition, Philadelphia, 1974, W. B. Saunders Co.
41. Anderson, T. A., Fomon, S. J., and Filer, L. J.: Carbohydrate tolerance studies with 3-day-old infants, J. Lab. Clin. Med. **79**:31, 1972.
42. Husband, J., Husband, P., and Mallinson, C. N.: Gastric emptying of starch meals in the newborn, Lancet **2**:290, 1970.
43. Maller, O., and Desor, J. A.: Effect of taste on ingestion by human newborns. In Bosma, J. F., editor: Oral sensation and perception, Publication No. (NIH) 73-546, Bethesda, Md., 1973, Department of Health, Education, and Welfare.

ADDITIONAL READINGS
Energy

Ashworth, A.: Energy balance and growth experience in treating children with malnutrition, Kidney Int. **14**:301, 1978.
Fomon, S. J., and others: Food consumption and growth of normal infants fed milk based formulas, Acta Paediatr. Scand. Suppl. 223, 1971.

Food and Agriculture Organization of the United Nations: Calorie requirements report of the Second Committee on Calorie Requirements, FAO, Italy, 1972.

Lindquist, B.: Nutritional needs in preschool and school age. In Blix, G., editor: Nutrition in preschool and school age, Symposium of the Swedish Nutrition Foundation VII, Uppsala, 1969, Almqvist & Wiksell, p. 50.

Moore, T.: The calorie as the unit of nutritional energy, World Rev. Nutr. Diet. 26:1, 1977.

Wait, B., Blair, R., and Roberts, L. J.: Energy intakes of well nourished children and adolescents, Am. J. Clin. Nutr. 22:1383, 1969.

Protein

Abernathy, R. P., and Ritchey, S. J.: Position paper on R.D.A. for protein for children, Adv. Exp. Med. Biol. 105:1, 1978.

Assessment of protein nutritional status, a committee report, Am. J. Clin. Nutr. 23:807, 1970.

Beaton, G. H., and Swiss, L. D.: Evaluation of the nutritional quality of food supplies: prediction of "desirable" or "safe" protein: calorie ratios, Am. J. Clin. Nutr. 27:485, 1974.

Block, R. J., and Mitchell, H. H.: The correlation of the amino acid composition of proteins with their nutritive value, Nutr. Abstr. Rev. 16:249, 1946.

Chopra, J. G., Forbes, A. L., and Habicht, J. P.: Protein in the US diet, J. Am. Diet. Assoc. 72:253, 1978.

Clark, H. E., and others: Nitrogen retention and plasma amino acids of men consuming isonitrogenous diets containing egg albumin or mixture of amino acids, Am. J. Clin. Nutr. 28:316, 1975.

Committee on Amino Acids, Food and Nutrition Board: Improvement of protein nutriture, Washington, D.C., 1974, National Academy of Sciences, National Research Council.

Evans, E., and Whitty, R.: An assessment of methods used to determine protein quality, World Rev. Nutr. Diet. 32:1, 1978.

Gallina, D. L., and Dominquez, J. M.: Human utilization of urea nitrogen in low calorie diets, J. Nutr. 101:1029, 1971.

Hegsted, D. M.: Theoretical estimates of protein requirements of children, J. Am. Diet. Assoc. 33:225, 1957.

Hegsted, D. M.: Protein needs and possible modifications of the American diet, J. Am. Diet. Assoc. 68:317, 1976.

Irwin, M. I., and Hegsted, D. M.: A conspectus of research on amino acid requirements of man, J. Nutr. 101:535, 1971.

Irwin, M. I., and Hegsted, D. M.: A conspectus of research on protein requirements of man, J. Nutr. 101:385, 1971.

Kishi, K., Miyatani, S., and Iroue, G.: Requirement and utilization of egg protein by Japanese young men with marginal intakes of energy, J. Nutr. 108:658, 1978.

Miller, D. S., and Payne, P. R.: Assessment of protein requirements for nitrogen balance, Proc. Nutr. Soc. 28:225, 1969.

Munro, H. N.: Energy balance and protein intakes as determinants of nitrogen balance, Kidney Int. 14:313, 1978.

Nicol, B. M.: Protein and calorie concentration, Nutr. Rev. 29:83, 1971.

Snyderman, S. E., and others: Unessential nitrogen: a limiting factor for human growth, J. Nutr. 78:57, 1962.

Sukhatme, P. V., and Margen, S.: Models for protein deficiency, Am. J. Clin. Nutr. 31:1237, 1978.

Ziegler, E. E., and others: Nitrogen balance studies with normal children, Am. J. Clin. Nutr. 30:939, 1977.

Fat

Alfin-Slater, R. B., and Aftergood, L.: Essential fatty acids reinvestigated, Physiol. Rev. 48:758, 1968.

Barltrap, D., and Oppe, T. E.: Absorption of fat and calcium by low birthweight infants from milk containing butterfat and olive oils, Arch. Dis. Child. 43:496, 1973.

Barnes, L. A., and others: Calcium and fat absorption from infant formulas with different fat blends, Pediatrics 54:217, 1974.

Bozkowa, K., and Gornicke, B.: Studies on the influence of diets on the metabolism of infants, Bibl. Nutr. Dieta 20:114, 1974.

Fomon, S. J., and others: Excretion of fat by normal full-term infants fed various milks and formulas, Am. J. Clin. Nutr. 23:1299, 1970.

Galli, C., Jacini, G., and Pecile, A., editors: Dietary lipids and post natal development, New York, 1973, Raven Press.

Hahn, P.: Lipid metabolism and nutrition in the prenatal and postnatal period. In Winick, M., editor: Nutrition and development, New York, 1972, John Wiley and Sons, Inc., p. 99.

Hanna, F. M., Navarrete, D. A., and Hsu, F. A.: Calcium-fatty acid absorption in term infants fed human milk and prepared formulas simulating human milk, Pediatrics 45:216, 1970.

Himan, J. A.: Prostaglandins, Annu. Rev. Biochem. 41:161, 1972.

Holman, R. T.: Essential fatty acid deficiency in humans. In Galli, C., Jacini, G., and Pecile, A., editors:

Dietary lipids and post natal development, New York, 1973, Raven Press, p. 127.

Jensen, R. G., Hagerty, M. M., and McMahon, E.: Lipids of human milk and infant formulas: a review, Am. J. Clin. Nutr. **31**:990, 1978.

Soderhjelm, L., Weise, H. F., and Holman, R. T.: The role of polyunsaturated fatty acids in human nutrition and metabolism, Prog. Chem. Fats Other Lipids **9**:555, 1970.

Williams, M. L., and others: Calcium and fat absorption in neonatal period, Am. J. Clin. Nutr. **23**:1322, 1970.

3

Vitamins

Vitamins are essential organic substances required for normal metabolism of amino acids, fat, and carbohydrate to produce energy and synthesize tissue, enzymes, hormones, and other vital compounds. Some of the vitamins act as coenzymes and participate as components of enzymatic reactions; others are thought to regulate the synthesis of compounds at the ribosomal level. The vitamins have been classified according to their solubility in lipids and in water.

Fat-soluble vitamins are absorbed and transported in a manner similar to that described for lipids; therefore, malabsorption of fat may result also in malabsorption of the fat-soluble vitamins. Intakes in excess of requirement of fat-soluble vitamins are not excreted but are stored. Therefore, reserves of these nutrients can be accumulated. It is not to a child's advantage, however, to receive large amounts of fat-soluble vitamins. Vitamins A and D consumed in large amounts are toxic.

Water-soluble vitamins are not stored in appreciable amounts; excesses are excreted in the urine. When adequate amounts are consumed in the diet, the use of vitamin supplements "just in case" is not only unnecessary but is an expensive method of enriching the urine. There are instances, however, when the use of vitamin supplements is appropriate; for example, children with food allergies who must restrict their intake of many foods may need vitamin supplements. In cases of conflict between parents and children about what the children shall eat, the temporary use of vitamin supplements may permit time to resolve a basic conflict without compromising the child's nutritional status. In such cases the use of vitamin supplements should not be encouraged indiscriminately but should be based on careful evaluation of the nutrients supplied by the food available to and ingested by the child. Appropriate supplementation of an infant's diet with vitamins is important.

FAT-SOLUBLE VITAMINS

The recommended dietary allowances for fat- and water-soluble vitamins are shown in Tables 3-1 and 3-4.

Because available information is not sufficient to make recommendations for daily intakes of vitamin K, biotin, and pantothenic acid, amounts that are safe and adequate have been estimated.

Vitamin A

Several biologically active compounds are collectively known as vitamin A. Retinol and 3-dehydroretinol are alcohols. Retinal is the aldehyde. Retinoic acid is the vitamin A acid.

Retinol and retinal can be reversibly oxidized and reduced and can perform all functions of vitamin A. Retinoic acid once formed cannot be metabolized to retinal or retinol. The acid does not prevent night blindness and is not stored.

Several carotenoids, precursors of vitamin A, are found in plants: α-, β-, and γ-carotene

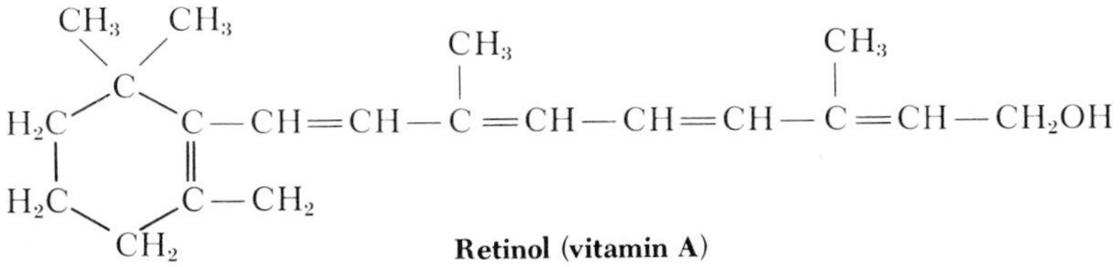

Retinol (vitamin A)

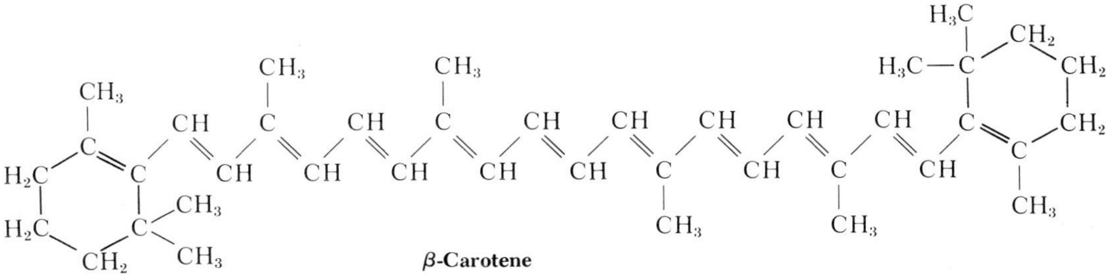

β-Carotene

and lycopene. Of these, β-carotene is the most predominant and active form, the biopotency of α- and γ-carotene being about half that of β-carotene. Absorption of β-carotene is only about one-third of intake. During the conversion of β-carotene to retinol, losses of approximately another 50% occur. Therefore, 1 μg β-carotene in the diet has activity equal to 0.16 μg retinol. β-Carotene is an asymmetrical molecule containing two β-ionone rings. The blood levels of the vitamin are independent of liver reserves and do not reflect current dietary intake as long as there are small reserves in the liver.

Liver reserves are low in the newborn infant, varying from less than 1 to 5.0 μg/gm of fresh tissue. The concentration of vitamin A in fetal blood approximates one half of that in the mother's plasma.[1]

Functions. Retinal is essential for visual adaptation to changes in light. Rhodopsin (visual purple), the light-sensitive pigment of the rods of the retina, is a compound that contains retinal and a protein, opsin. When light hits the retina, retinal is isomerized and rhodopsin splits into opsin and retinene. In darkness retinene is isomerized to the original retinal and again combines with opsin to regenerate rhodopsin so that night blindness, the first appearing symptom in vitamin A deficiency, is prevented.

Vitamin A fulfills many other functions as yet undescribed at the metabolic level. It interacts metabolically with fat-soluble vitamins D and E and with other vitamins and hormones and plays a role in the protection and regulation of the cell membrane structure. Because it plays a role in the stability of membrane structure, it aids in resistance to infection. It affects growth of the skeleton and soft tissue by influencing synthesis of protein. It is necessary for reproduction.

Interrelationships. Vitamin E appears to spare vitamin A by protecting it from oxidation and increasing absorption, utilization, and storage. Protein influences both absorption and utilization. Absorption is impaired in severe protein malnutrition. Since vitamin A is transported bound to a carrier protein, transport to and mobilization from liver storage are reduced when plasma protein levels are low.

Recommended intakes. Vitamin A activity has been expressed until recently as international units, 1 IU being equivalent to 0.3 μg of retinol and 0.6 μg β-carotene. The FAO/WHO Committee has proposed that vitamin A activity be stated as equivalent weights of retinol: 1 retinol equivalent is equal to 1 μg of retinol, 6 μg β-carotene, and 12 μg of other provitamin A carotenoids. As international units, 1 retinol equivalent is

Table 3-1. Recommended daily dietary allowances for fat-soluble vitamins

	Age (yr)	Vitamin A RE* (μg)	Vitamin D (μg)	Vitamin E (mg α-TE)
Infants	0.0-0.5	420	10	3
	0.5-1.0	400	10	4
Children	1-3	400	10	5
	4-6	500	10	6
	7-10	700	10	7
Males	11-14	1000	10	8
	15-18	1000	10	10
Females	11-14	800	10	8
	15-18	800	10	8

From Food and Nutrition Board: Recommended dietary allowances, rev. ed. 9, Washington, D.C., 1980, National Academy of Sciences, National Research Council.
*Retinol equivalent.

Table 3-2. Selected foods as sources of vitamin A

Food	Household measure	Vitamin A (IU)
Cow's milk	8 oz	350
Human milk	8 oz	560
Cheddar cheese	1 oz	370
Egg	1 medium	520
Liver, beef	1 oz	15,112
Liver, chicken	1 liver	3080
Liverwurst	1 slice, ⅓ oz	650
Butter	1 tsp	160
Apricots, canned	¼ cup	1125
Orange	1 medium	280
Peach	1 medium	1330
Watermelon	½ cup diced	470
Carrots	¼ cup	3808
Acorn squash	¼ cup baked and mashed	718
Sweet potatoes, mashed	¼ cup	5038
Green peas	¼ cup	280
Spinach	¼ cup cooked	3645
Tomotoes, canned	¼ cup	542

From Adams, C. F.: Nutritive value of American foods in common units, Agriculture Handbook No. 456, Washington, D.C., 1975, U.S. Department of Agriculture.

equal to vitamin A activity from 3.33 IU of retinol equivalents.[2]

The recommended allowance of vitamin A for infants is based on the average retinol content of human milk. For older children, allowances are interpolated from the infant and male adult allowances based on body weight and arbitrary amounts needed to satisfy growth needs (see Table 3-1).

Food sources. Preformed vitamin A occurs only in animal products such as dairy products, eggs, and organ meats. A number of foods such as infant formulas, skim milk, margarine, and some cereals are fortified with the vitamin. The carotenoids are found chiefly in the deep orange, yellow, and green fruits and vegetables.

In the United States usual foods available are estimated to provide about half the total vitamin A activity in the form of retinol and half in the form of provitamin A. Foods commonly consumed by infants and children that contribute vitamin A are listed in Table 3-2.

Deficient intakes. Night blindness is the first symptom of inadequate vitamin A nurture. In cases of continued inadequate intakes of the vitamin there is in addition generalized drying up and scale formation, keratinization of the epithelial cells and connective tissue, decreased resistance to infection, and a retardation of bone growth and tooth formation. Appetite is depressed because of loss of taste and smell. Increased pressure in cerebrospinal fluid may cause bulging of the fontanel. Nerve lesions have been reported. Severe deprivation of vitamin A results in xerophthalmia and loss of sight.

Although clinical symptoms of vitamin A deficiency are rarely seen in developed countries, there are indications that members of certain age groups have greater vitamin A reserves in the liver than others. Mitchell, Young, and Seward analyzed liver specimens obtained from hospitals and the coroner's office in Washington, D.C., from individuals who died of acute, traumatic means and chronic disease, and found very low mean liver concentrations of vitamin A and carotene in infants less than 2 months of age and high concentrations in children 2 months to 10 years of age. They hypothesized that low levels in early infancy reflected limited reserves at birth and the higher levels in children 2 months to 10 years of age were caused by wide use of vitamin supplements, vitamin-fortified formulas, and baby foods.[3] Raica and associates studied vitamin A and carotenoid concentrations of human tissues collected at autopsies from five areas in the United States and found an incidence of 27% of low liver reserves in infants under 1 year of age, no low liver reserves in children 1 to 10 years of age, but an incidence of 35% of low liver reserves in children 11 to 20 years of age.[4]

Excessive intakes. Hypervitaminosis A is a well-defined clinical entity the etiology of which is ingestion of excessive amounts of vitamin A. Acute hypervitaminosis A occurs after ingestion of a single large dose of vitamin A: 300,000 IU for infants and 1,000,000 to 7,000,000 IU for older children and adults. The clinical picture in infants is one of acute hydrocephalus or bulging fontanel accompanied by vomiting and agitation or drowsiness. Older children will experience headaches, nausea, vomiting, spinal fluid pressure, and notable desquamation of the skin.

Chronic hypervitaminosis A, the result of ingestion of lesser but excessive intakes of the vitamin over a period of months, results in symptoms of anorexia; dry, itchy skin; alopecia; sparse coarse hair; and swelling of the extremities. Infants may experience a bulging fontanel.

Vitamin D

Vitamin D, the antiricketic vitamin necessary for normal bone formation, includes a group of steroids. The most important are ergocalciferol (vitamin D_2) and cholecal-

Cholecalciferol (vitamin D_3)

ciferol (vitamin D_3). Ergocalciferol is formed by the irradiation of the provitamin ergosterol found in ergot and yeast. Cholecalciferol occurs naturally in fish liver oil and is formed by the conversion of the provitamin 7-dehydrocholesterol in the skin by sunlight. The vitamin can thus be obtained both by ingestion and/or irradiation of the skin and is considered to be both a vitamin and a hormone.

Functions. With parathyroid hormone and calcitonin, vitamin D maintains normal serum calcium levels and facilitates mineralization of the bone.

The vitamin concentrates in the liver where it is hydroxylated to 25-hydroxycholecalciferol. Synthesis of 25-OHD$_3$ is regulated by a feedback mechanism dependent on the liver level of 25-OHD$_3$. The 25-OHD$_3$ is transported to the kidney. Parathyroid hormone secreted in response to low serum calcium levels stimulate synthesis of 1,25-dihydroxycholecalciferol, the active form of the vitamin. When serum calcium levels rise, calcitonin is secreted. This hormone causes a reduction in the renal synthesis of 1,25-OHD$_3$ and synthesis of alternate metabolites of vitamin D. Low serum levels of phosphorus also stimulate synthesis of 1,25-OHD$_3$, and high serum phosphorus levels function to reduce synthesis of the active form of the vitamin. The 1,25-OHD$_3$ is carried to the target organs.

In the intestine 1,25-OHD$_3$ acts with a calcium-binding protein to facilitate the transport of calcium across the intestinal barrier. It increases renal reabsorption of calcium. With parathyroid hormone the active form of vitamin D mobilizes calcium and phosphorus from the bone. The result of these regulatory effects on calcium is the maintenance of normal serum levels of calcium and phosphorus. It has been suggested that normal serum levels are supersaturated and that normal calcification of bone is thus possible.[5]

Some researchers have suggested that the improvement in muscle strength in rachitic children and patients suffering from renal osteodystrophy when treated with vitamin D and 1,25 OHD$_3$ indicates a function in muscle metabolism. Others believe that the evidence is not convincing. Another suggested function of vitamin D for which many researchers believe there is insufficient evidence is that of suppressing the size and hormone secretion of the parathyroid gland.[6]

A postgestational age of 36 to 38 weeks appears to be necessary for homeostasis of 25-OHD$_3$. Serum levels of 25-OHD$_3$ in premature infants given oral doses of vitamin D are decreased; infants given intravenous doses of vitamin D maintain but do not increase serum concentrations of 25-OHD$_3$. Full-term infants with normal concentrations of 25-OHD$_3$ maintain levels, and those with low concentrations increase the levels of 25-OHD$_3$ circulating in the plasma when they are fed formulas containing 10 μg vitamin D/quart.[7]

Recommended intakes. The National Research Council recommends an intake of 10 μg cholecalciferol, which is equivalent to 400 IU vitamin D daily, an amount that will cover the requirements of infants and children who are never exposed to sunlight[2] (Table 3-1).

Food sources. Evaporated milk, infant formulas, powdered skim milk, and most homogenized milks are fortified with 10 μg of cholecalciferol/quart. Human milk contains 2 IU of fat-soluble vitamin D/dl and 1.78 ± .39 μg of water-soluble vitamin D sulfate/dl.[8] Many cereals, margarines, and diet foods are also fortified.

Vitamin preparations and fortified milks are major sources of vitamin D for infants and preschool children. As children grow older and consume a wider variety of foods, they consume greater amounts of the other fortified foods. The contribution of natural food sources of vitamin D is small at all ages.

Deficient intakes. Vitamin D deficiency results in low levels of serum inorganic phosphorus and plasma calcium and elevated levels of alkaline phosphatase. Rickets, the deficiency disease, results when the organic matrix of the bones is not mineralized; bones are soft as a result. Rickets caused by dietary deficiency usually occurs in the first 2 years of life but may also occur in adolescence, when growth is rapid. Although cases of rickets are rare in North America, there are children who are at risk for inadequate intakes of vitamin D.

It appears that premature infants are vulnerable to deficiencies of fat-soluble vitamins. They have less time in utero to accumulate reserves. They absorb a lesser percentage of fat, and therefore fat-soluble vitamins, than full-term infants. Because they are small and immature the volume of vita-

min-fortified formula they can consume may be limited. Premature and low birth weight babies are at risk for a variety of medical complications that may further reduce the volume of milk they can consume. Studies have found rickets in premature infants who consumed a limited volume of formula as the only source of vitamin D and in those who consumed the recommended 10 μg cholecalciferol daily; requirements for vitamin D in the rapidly growing premature infant may therefore be in excess of 10 μg.[9,10] Such infants should be monitored for symptoms of vitamin D deficiency.

Even though human milk contains a vitamin D sulfate, rickets continues to be reported in breast-fed infants whose diets are not supplemented. Those infants who have dark skin and are exposed to little sunlight are at greatest risk.[11] Rickets has also been known to occur in children allergic to milk who received a calcium supplement but no additional vitamin D and in children who receive anticonvulsant medications (Chapter 14). Diets of infants who are breast fed, of children with lactose intolerance (Chapter 13), of others who appreciably reduce their intake of milk, and of those who consume raw milk should be carefully monitored for sources of vitamin D, both provided by food and by the effect of sunlight. They should receive supplementary vitamin D in cases where foods fortified with vitamin D are consumed in limited amounts.

Excessive intakes. Large doses of vitamin D consumed over long periods of time result in symptoms of toxicity. The toxic effects have generally been credited to hypercalcemia, although toxic effects in the absence of hypercalcemia have been reported.[12] Symptoms include anorexia, nausea, excessive thirst, polyuria, weight loss, and calcification of soft tissues. Irreversible renal damage resulting from calcification is possible. Since an intake of 10 μg of cholecalciferol allows for a margin of safety for the normal child, supplementation in excess of this amount should be discouraged.

Vitamin E

Several substances, four tocopherols and four tocotrienols exhibiting qualitatively biologic activity of α-tocopherol, are collectively known as vitamin E. They are all derivatives of 6-hydroxychroman and contain a thirteen-carbon isoprenoid side chain differing only in number and position of the methyl groups in the ring structure. The side chain is saturated in the tocopherols, triply unsaturated in the tocotrienols. α-Tocopherol is the most active of the compounds, the activity of the β-, ζ-, and γ-tocopherols decreasing in the order listed.

Functions. Researchers agree that vitamin E is an essential nutrient for human beings, but its specific functions are not understood as yet. There is strong evidence that the vitamin functions as a biologic antioxidant.[13] However, some researchers believe that it may be a constituent of an enzyme system.[14] Polyunsaturated fatty acids are components of the structure of cellular and subcellular membranes. Antioxidants prevent damage to the membranes by limiting peroxidation of the polyunsaturated fatty acids in tissue lipids. The antioxidant properties of vitamin E protect the tissue lipids from excessive oxidation. They also protect vitamins A and C against oxidative destruction.

Other functions of vitamin E have been suggested but remain to be proven. A role in the synthesis of heme has been suggested. In vitamin E deficiency the synthesis of two enzymes necessary for heme synthesis is reduced.[15] Researchers, however, have not found a reduced synthesis of heme in vitamin E deficiency states.[16,17]

Recommended intakes. Researchers agree that the requirement for vitamin E is related to the polyunsaturated content of cellular tissue, a result of the type of fat consumed in the diet and of that synthesized by the organism and incorporated into vital compounds.[17] Satisfactory levels of vitamin E have been reported in the plasma of infants receiving formulas with a ratio of vitamin E to polyunsaturated fatty acids of 0.4 and in an adult receiving similar ratios, indicating adequate intakes of the vitamin.[18,19] The Food and Nutrition Board of the National Research Council has used these ratios in expressing the recommended allowances for vitamin E (Table 2-1). Increases in intake of polyunsaturated fatty acids will increase an individual's need for vitamin E.[2]

Antioxidants other than vitamin E substitute for or spare vitamin E. Selenium as a constituent of glutathione peroxidase protects cells against oxidative destruction and has reversed some of the effects of vitamin E deficiency in experimental animals. It is hypothesized that selenium can fulfill part but not all of the vitamin E requirements.

The presence of oxidants such as iron increases the requirements for vitamin E.

Tocopherol reserves are low in the tissues of the fetus and newborn infant and are es-

d-α-Tocopherol (vitamin E)

pecially limited in the premature infant. Dju, Mason, and Filer found the total body content of tocopherol of a 3500 gm full-term infant to be approximately 25 mg, whereas that of a 1000 gm premature infant was only 3 mg.[20] Premature infants do not absorb fat-soluble vitamin E as well as do full-term infants, absorption increasing as the infants reach gestational age. It has been documented that such infants absorb a water-miscible vitamin well.[21] The Committee on Nutrition of the American Academy of Pediatrics has recommended that premature infants receive vitamin E supplements of 0.5 mg/kg of body weight/day.[22]

Children who malabsorb fat-soluble vitamin E, such as children with cystic fibrosis, should receive a water-miscible vitamin. A recommendation has been made that such children receive vitamin E supplements of 1 mg/kg of body weight/day.[23]

Food sources. Tocopherol is widely distributed in food and occurs in highest concentrations in cereal grain oils. Vegetable oils are important sources of the tocopherols. Other foods that contribute tocopherols to the diet are milk, eggs, fish, muscle meat, leafy vegetables, and cereal. Human milk contains considerably more tocopherol than does cow's milk, and colostrum is a much richer source than later human milk. Infant formulas are fortified with vitamin E (Table 3-3).

Plasma tocopherol levels of newborn infants are low, ranging from one-third to one-fifth of those of the mother.[24] There is, however, a direct relationship between the plasma level of the mother and those of both the premature and full-term infants.[25]

Deficient intakes. Children with cystic fibrosis of the pancreas and biliary atresia who have low plasma vitamin E levels because of malabsorption of fat have been found to have no clinical symptoms of vitamin E deficiency. Life span of the red cell is often shortened, but anemia has not been found.[26]

Table 3-3. Selected food sources of vitamin E

Food	Household measure	Vitamin E (mg)
Cow's milk	8 oz	0.16
Human milk	8 oz	0.29
Egg	1 medium	0.71
Ground beef, pan fried	2 oz	0.35
Beef liver, broiled	1 oz	0.46
Salmon steak	2 oz	1.02
Chicken breast	2 oz	0.33
Potato, boiled	½ medium	0.05
Whole wheat bread	1 slice	0.6
Butter	1 tsp	0.05
Corn oil margarine	1 tsp	2.19
Corn oil	1 tbsp	14.28
Green beans, cooked	¼ cup	0.15
Strawberries	½ cup	0.22
Orange juice	½ cup	0.25

Adapted from Bunnell, R. H., Keating, J., Quaresimo, A., and Parman, G. K.: alpha-Tocopherol content of food, Am. J. Clin. Nutr. 17:1, 1965; and Herting, D. C., and Drury, E. J. E.: Vitamin content of milk, milk products and simulated milk: relevance to infant nutrition, Am. J. Clin. Nutr. 22:145, 1969.

Other symptoms of vitamin E deficiency noted in children with malabsorption similar to those found in animals depleted of vitamin E include creatinuria, ceroid pigmentation of the smooth muscle, and multifocal degeneration of the striated muscle.[27]

Premature infants who weigh less than 1500 gm seem to be particularly vulnerable to vitamin E deficiency. In addition to the limited reserves with which they are born and the lesser percentage of fat-soluble substances they absorb, many of these infants have in past years been offered formulas rich in polyunsaturated fats and iron and have often been exposed to high concentrations of oxygen, which increase their need for vitamin E.

In 1967 Oaski reported that premature infants often developed hemolytic anemia at 4 to 6 weeks of age. All of the infants studied had been fed a formula containing iron, which acts as an oxidant, and a high concentration of linoleic acid.[28] Laboratory studies showed a decrease in plasma concentrations of vitamin E and an increased sensitivity of erythrocytes to hemolysis in dilute solutions of hydrogen peroxide. Other symptoms of vitamin E deficiency included irritability and edema.[29] Subsequent increases in the vitamin E content of formula and the recommendation that iron-containing formulas not be introduced to children less than 2 months old have essentially resolved this concern.

Graeber, Williams, and Oaski have shown

that the very small premature infant who receives intramuscular injection of 100 to 125 mg of vitamin E during the first 8 days of life has a normalization of the hydrogen peroxide hemolysis test and maintains high serum levels of vitamin E. Intramuscular injection of iron does not negate the effects of vitamin E when given in the above dosage.[30]

Intramuscular injection of vitamin E has been shown to reduce the incidence and severity of retrolental fibroplasia and to lessen the toxicity of high concentrations of oxygen required to treat respiratory distress syndrome in premature infants.[31,32] Therefore, a vitamin E supplement or intramuscular injection of vitamin E is offered to many premature infants during the first month of life.

Excessive intakes. Vitamin E appears to be the least toxic of the fat-soluble vitamins. No beneficial or pathologic effects were noted in adults ingesting 600 IU/day for one month or 800 IU/day for 3 years.[33,34]

Vitamin K

Vitamin K refers to a group of compounds known as quinones. Phylloquinone (vitamin K_1) and farnoquinone (vitamin K_2) occur in nature. Menadione (vitamin K_3) is prepared synthetically. Natural vitamin K is available in water-soluble and water-miscible preparations. Menadione is available in fat- and water-soluble preparations.

Function. Vitamin K epoxide is a major

Phylloquinone (vitamin K_1)

metabolite in both humans and rats. Vitamin K functions in the maintenance of normal prothrombin and three other clotting factors—VII, IX, and X. It performs this function by participating in the conversion of a precursor protein to prothrombin[36] by playing a role in the carboxylation of the glutamic acid residue of the prothrombin precursor.[37] Another suggested function of vitamin K is that of a role in calcium metabolism.[38]

Recommended intakes. Minimum requirements for newborn infants have been estimated to be 0.15 to 0.25 μg/kg/day of vitamin K_1 or its equivalent.[39]

A safe and adequate daily intake of vitamin K is estimated to be 12 μg/day in early infancy, increasing to 50 to 100 μg/day in adolescence.[2] Children who malabsorb fat may have secondary vitamin K deficiency and may require water-miscible vitamin K supplements. Intakes of 50 to 100 μg/day have been recommended.[40]

Food sources. Green leafy vegetables are the richest food sources of vitamin K. Lesser amounts are found in meats and dairy products. Human milk contains 15 μg/liter, cow's milk, 60 μg/liter. Many species of bacteria (including those in the gut) synthesize vitamin K.

Deficient intakes. Vitamin K deficiency results in increased coagulation time and hemorrhage. Deficiency is uncommon after infancy; the infant, however, is born with a sterile gut and the prothrombin level of the newborn infant is 20% to 50% of that of the adult. In breast-fed infants the prothrombin level falls often to hemorrhagic levels during the first few days of life, and hemorrhagic disease of the newborn infant may occur. In artificially fed infants the fall of the prothrombin level is less and is of shorter duration.[41] Breast-fed infants are at risk for vitamin K deficiency in early life.[42,43] Vitamin K administered at birth causes prothrombin

levels to rise in 1 to 2 hours. Therefore, a prophylactic dose of 0.5 to 1.0 mg is usually given parenterally to infants at birth as a preventive measure.

Excessive intakes. Phylloquinone (vitamin K_1) produces no toxic symptoms after oral administration. Ingestion of menadione causes vomiting.

Toxicity of vitamin K_3 preparations has been reported in premature and newborn infants. Hyperbilirubinemia, kernicterus, and hemolytic anemia have been reported after parenteral administration of the vitamin K analogues.[39]

WATER-SOLUBLE VITAMINS

In contrast to vitamins A, D, E, and K, the water-soluble vitamins are stored in small amounts and deficiencies can be expected to occur in a relatively short period of time if the nutrient is absent from dietary intake. Many but not all of the metabolic functions of the B complex vitamins have been described, whereas the manner in which the vitamins function to fill other roles is yet to be defined.

Recommended dietary allowances of water-soluble vitamins for children, as prepared by the Food and Nutrition Board of the National Research Council, are given in Table 3-4.

Ascorbic acid

Ascorbic acid, vitamin C, is a simple six-carbon compound with a structure similar to that of the monosaccharides. *l*-Ascorbic acid is considered to be the active form. Metabolically, ascorbic acid exists both in the reduced and oxidized forms, both with the same biologic activity. Ascorbate-3-sulfate is a metabolically active derivative. Ascorbic acid is present in the body in extracellular fluids and is in the greatest concentration in glandular tissue such as the adrenal cortex, pituitary gland, pancreas, liver, and spleen.

Table 3-4. Recommended daily dietary allowances for water-soluble vitamins

	Age (years)	Thiamine (mg)	Riboflavin (mg)	Niacin (mg)	Vitamin B$_6$ (mg)	Folacin (μg)	Vitamin B$_{12}$ (μg)	Ascorbic acid (mg)
Infants	0-0.5	0.3	0.4	6.0	0.3	30	.5	35
	0.5-1.0	0.5	0.6	8.0	0.6	45	1.5	35
Children	1-3	0.7	0.8	9.0	0.9	100	2.0	45
	4-6	0.9	1.0	11	1.3	200	2.5	45
	7-10	1.2	1.4	16.0	1.6	300	3.0	45
Males	11-14	1.4	1.6	18.0	1.6	400	3.0	50
	15-18	1.4	1.7	18	1.8	400	3.0	60
Females	11-14	1.2	1.3	15	1.8	400	3.0	50
	15-18	1.1	1.3	14.0	2.0	400	3.0	60

From Food and Nutrition Board: Recommended daily dietary allowances, rev. ed. 9, Washington, D.C., 1980, National Academy of Sciences, National Research Council.

Ascorbic acid
(vitamin C)

Functions. Ascorbic acid has many functions as yet undefined at the metabolic level. It is a reactant in a number of enzyme systems and is believed to have multiple functions.[44] It serves as a coenzyme or cofactor in many reactions in which the rate of reaction is important and may function in the regulation of intracellular oxidation-reduction potentials. It aids in the conversion of folic acid to folinic acid and is involved in the degradation of some amino acids, e.g., tyrosine. Vitamin C facilitates the gastrointestinal absorption of iron and calcium and inhibits the absorption of copper. As an antioxidant it protects vitamins A and E and the polyunsaturated fatty acids. It is necessary for the formation of ground substance that cements the cells of the bones, teeth, connective tissues, and capillaries. It functions in the synthesis of collagen from proline and in the metabolism of the amino acids tyrosine and tryptophan. The claim that vitamin C is effective in the prevention and treatment of colds remains a subject of controversy.

Recommended intakes. The recommended intake of ascorbic acid in infancy, 35 mg/day, has been based on the amount ingested by a breast-fed infant consuming 850 ml/day of milk produced by an adequately fed lactating mother. An intake of 45 to 50 mg/day is recommended for children between the ages of 1 and 11 years, after which the recommended intake increases to the adult level of 60 mg/day considered sufficient to produce tissue satuation (Table 3-4).

Food sources. Many artificially flavored and colored fruit drinks as well as natural fruit juices are fortified with varying amounts of vitamin C. Examples of natural food sources are given in Table 3-5.

Deficient intakes. Deficiencies of ascorbic acid result in impaired bone formation, dis-

Table 3-5. Selected food sources of vitamin C

Food	Household measure	Vitamin C (mg)
Human milk	8 oz	16
Cow's milk	8 oz	2
Broccoli	1 spear	22
Brussels sprouts	¼ cup	31
Cabbage, raw, chopped	¼ cup	11
Cabbage, cooked, wedge	¼ cup	10
Cantaloupe, diced	½ cup	27
Grapefruit	½	37
Orange	1 medium	66
Orange juice	½ cup	62
Potato, boiled (2½ inch)	½	11
Strawberries	1 cup	88
Tomato, raw (2⅛ inch)	1	42
Tomatoes, canned	½ cup	20
Tomato juice	½ cup	20

From Adams, C. F.: Nutritive value of American foods in common units, Agriculture Handbook No. 456, Washington, D.C., 1975, U.S. Department of Agriculture.

rupted metabolism of tyrosine and tryptophan, formation of glycoproteins, and conversion of proline to collagen. Wound healing is impaired and hemorrhagic manifestations occur. Subperiosteal bleeding and petechial hemorrhages are early sumptoms of deficiency of this vitamin. Scurvy, the deficiency disease, results in tender, painful muscles, joints, and bones, muscle cramps, and loss of appetite.

Thiamine

Thiamine, vitamin B_1, contains both a pyrimidine and a thiazole moiety.

Thiamine (vitamin B_1)

Functions. Thiamine functions in metabolic systems as the coenzyme thiamine pyrophosphate. It participates in at least 24 different reactions, playing a role in glycolysis and the glycolytic pathways, the citric acid cycle, and the hexose monophosphate shunt. It serves as a coenzyme in the decarboxylation of pyruvic acid, which is necessary for the formation of active acetyl, and is involved in the decarboxylation of ketoglutaric acid to succinic acid in the citric acid cycle. It is necessary for the enzymatic action of transketolase in the pentose pathway. Phosphoric esters of thiamine are involved in the metabolism and function of excitable membranes. It is therefore thought to have a role in neurophysiology.[46] Thiamine itself undergoes metabolism in the body; over 20 metabolites of thiamine have been found in urine.[47]

Recommended intakes. Because it is so intimately involved in the metabolism of carbohydrate and because of its participation in the citric acid cycle, the requirement for thiamine is determined by the carbohydrate and caloric intake. The National Research Council has recommended an intake of 0.5 mg/1000 kcal for all ages[45] (Table 3-4). The 2-month-old infant who consumes 585 calories per day, for example, will need to consume 0.3 mg of thiamine, and 0.8 mg of thiamine will be needed by the 4-year-old child who consumes 1600 calories per day.

Food sources. Important food sources of thiamine are listed in Table 3-6.

Deficient intakes. The deficiency disease beriberi is almost nonexistent in North America. Deficiencies have been produced experimentally in adult males. Symptoms of deficiency include anorexia, vomiting, fatigability, aching muscles, ataxia of gait, and emotional disturbances such as moodiness and depression. In thiamine deficiency there is an accumulation of pyruvic acid in the blood, lowered erythrocyte activity, and decreased excretion of thiamine and its metabolites in the urine.[47]

Riboflavin (vitamin B₂)

The chemical formula of riboflavin, originally identified as the prosthetic group of the yellow enzyme, is shown below.

Riboflavin (vitamin B₂)

Functions. Riboflavin is a precursor of two enzymes, flavin mononucleotide (FMN) and flavin adenine dinucleotide (FAD), which are essential to a number of oxidative enzyme systems. These enzymes are involved in the

Table 3-6. Selected foods as sources of thiamine

Food	Household measure	Thiamine (mg)
Human milk	8 oz	0.04
Cow's milk	8 oz	0.09
Infant cereals, high protein	1 tbsp	0.06
Infant cereals, rice	1 tbsp	0.06
Farina, enriched	½ cup	0.05
Oatmeal	½ cup	0.1
Rice, enriched	¼ cup	0.06
Bread, whole wheat	1 slice	0.03
Bread, enriched white	1 slice	0.07
Macaroni, enriched	¼ cup	0.06
Strained pork	1 oz	0.05
Pork, cooked	1 oz	0.26
Hamburger	2 oz	0.05
Liver, beef, cooked	1 oz	0.07
Liver, chicken, cooked	1 liver	0.04
Green peas	¼ cup	0.04
Great northern beans	¼ cup	0.06

From Adams, C. F.: Nutritive value of American foods in common units, Agriculture Handbook No. 456, Washington, D.C., 1975, U.S. Department of Agriculture.

transfer of hydrogen atoms and in this role they function in many reactions of intermediary metabolism involving protein, fat, and carbohydrate. They also function in the deaminization of certain amino acids, in the oxidation of fatty acids, and in the citric acid cycle and play a role in hydrogen transfer in cellular oxidation.

Recommended intakes. The Food and Nutrition Board of the National Research Council recommends an intake of 0.6 mg riboflavin/1000 kcal at all ages[45] (Table 3-4).

Food sources. Milk and dairy products provide significant amounts of riboflavin. Organ meats are rich sources. Enriched cereal grains and green vegetables are also important sources for infants and children (Table 3-7).

Deficient intakes. Symptoms of deficiency include corneal vascularization of the eye; seborrheic dermatitis, especially in the skin folds, including the nasolabial folds and scrotum; cheilosis and angular stomatitis; and glossitis (inflammation and reddening of the tongue). Riboflavin deficiencies rarely occur alone but occur most often in combination with other vitamin deficiencies.

Recent reports suggest that phototherapy, used in the treatment of neonatal jaundice, can induce biochemical riboflavin deficiency as a result of photodecomposition of riboflavin by the blue light.[48]

Niacin

Niacin, nicotinic acid, is 3-pyridinecarboxylic acid. It is active both as the acid and as nicotinamide. The amino acid tryptophan can be converted to niacin and fulfill a portion of the body's requirement for niacin. Sixty milligrams of tryptophan are converted to 1 niacin equivalent.

Niacin (nicotinic acid)

Table 3-7. Foods as sources of riboflavin

Food	Household measure	Riboflavin (mg)
Human milk	8 oz	0.08
Cow's milk	8 oz	0.41
Prepared infant formula	8 oz	1.48-2.80
Cheddar cheese	1 oz	0.13
Infant cereals, high protein	1 tbsp	0.06
Infant cereals, rice	1 tbsp	0.06
Farina	½ cup	0.035
Oatmeal	½ cup	0.025
Macaroni, enriched	¼ cup	0.03
Liver, beef	1 oz	1.18
Liver, chicken	1 liver	0.67
Broccoli	1 spear	0.03
Green peas	¼ cup	0.03
Spinach	¼ cup	0.06

From Adams, C. F.: Nutritive value of American foods in common units, Agriculture Handbook No. 456, Washington, D.C., 1975, U.S. Department of Agriculture.

Functions. Niacin functions as an essential component of the coenzymes nicotinamide-adenine dinucleotide phosphate (NADP) and nicotinamide-adenine dinucleotide (NAD), which are necessary for many biochemical reactions. They are essential for the transfer of hydrogen in the intercellular respiratory mechanism of all cells. The coenzymes are necessary for the conversion of lactic acid to pyruvic acid and of β-hydroxybutyric acid to acetyl aldehyde. They are essential for cellular biosynthesis of fatty acids and function in energy release and in amino acid metabolism.

Recommended intakes. The National Research Council has recommended an intake of 8 mg/1000 kcal of niacin for infants, two-thirds of which will ordinarily by provided by tryptophan. Thereafter, the recommended intake for children and adolescents is 6.6 mg/1000 kcal, but no less than 8 mg/day[45] (Table 3-4).

Food sources. Meat, poultry, liver, legumes, and peanut butter contribute significant amounts of preformed niacin. Because tryptophan is converted to niacin, all animal protein, including dairy products and eggs, offers potential sources of niacin. Human milk contains 1.47 mg/liter of niacin, and cow's milk contains 0.94 mg/liter of niacin. Enriched cereal grains and peas are also important sources.

Deficient intakes. Deficiency of niacin produces symptoms of anorexia, nausea, vomiting, weakness, and indigestion, including heartburn. Psychic and emotional changes such as anxiety, irritability, and depression also occur. In advanced stages more severe psychic changes such as those of confusion, disorientation, and hallucinations are noted. Inflammation of the mucous membranes resulting in glossitis and diarrhea occurs, and a dermatitis, especially of the skin surface exposed to sunlight, develops.

Pyridoxine (vitamin B_6)

Vitamin B_6 occurs naturally in food in various forms but mainly as pyridoxal, pyridoxamine, pyridoxine, pyridoxamine 5-phosphate, and pyridoxal 5-phosphate. Pyridoxine, pyridoxal, and pyridoxamine are all effective in human nutrition and are all designated as vitamin B_6.

Pyridoxine (vitamin B_6)

Functions. As the coenzyme pyridoxal 5-phosphate, vitamin B_6 is involved in a large number of enzyme systems associated with nitrogen metabolism. The action of the transaminases, decarboxylases, and desulfhydrases is pyridoxal dependent. Pyridoxal phosphate is essential for the conversion of tryptophan to niacin. The action of phosphorylase, the enzyme catalyzing glycogen to glucose 1,6-phosphate, is dependent on the coenzyme pyridoxal phosphate. Pyridoxyl phosphate is also required for the synthesis of δ-aminolevulinic acid, a precursor of heme. Pyridoxine is involved in lipid metabolism; its function, however, has not been established.

Recommended intakes. The Food and Nutrition Board of the National Research Council has stated that metabolic requirements for vitamin B_6 will be adequately met if the vitamin is present in amounts of 0.15 mg/gm of protein or 0.04 mg/100 kcal. An intake of 0.3 mg of vitamin B_6 in the first 6 months of life, gradually increasing to an intake of 2.0 mg in adolescence, has been recommended by the Board[45] (Table 3-4).

Food sources. Food sources of vitamin B_6 are shown in Table 3-8. Muscle and organ

Table 3-8. Selected food sources of vitamin B_6

Food	Household measure	Vitamin B_6 (mg)
Cow's milk	1 cup	0.1
Human milk	1 cup	0.02
Infant cereals, high protein	1 tbsp	0.01
Infant cereals, rice	1 tbsp	0.007
Infant dinners, split peas and bacon	1 oz	0.014
Infant dinners, vegetables and liver	1 oz	0.036
Strained beef	1 oz	0.056
Strained liver	1 oz	0.227
Beef liver, uncooked	3½ oz	0.84
Chicken liver, uncooked	3½ oz	0.75
Beef, uncooked	3½ oz	0.33
Chicken, canned	1 oz	0.084
Peanut butter	1 tbsp	0.053
Egg	1 medium	0.055
Whole wheat bread	1 slice	0.05
White bread	1 slice	0.011
Green peas, canned	¼ cup	0.008
Tomatoes, canned	¼ cup	0.054
Squash, frozen	¼ cup	0.055
Banana	1 small	0.71
Orange juice	½ cup	0.05
Strawberries	½ cup	0.040

Adapted from Orr, M. L.: Pantothenic acid, vitamin B_6 and vitamin B_{12} in foods, Home Economics Research Report No. 36, Washington, D.C., 1969, U.S. Department of Agriculture.

meats are excellent sources, and whole grains and bananas also supply significant amounts of vitamin B_6.

Deficient intakes. Clinical deficiencies of pyridoxine have been produced in two infants fed vitamin B_6–deficient diets. These infants failed to gain weight after several months, and the ability to convert tryptophan to niacin was lost. Convulsions occurred in one of the infants, and hypochromic anemia developed in the other. Both children responded quickly to therapy with vitamin B_6.[49] In the early 1950's infants fed an autoclaved commercial formula found subsequently to be deficient in vitamin B_6 were reported to have epileptiform convulsions unassociated with any form of illness. Every case responded to therapy with vitamin B_6.[50,51]

Personality changes in adults placed on vitamin B_6–deficient diets who are receiving a pyridoxine antagonist include irritability, depression, and loss of sense of responsibility. Symptoms of deficiency in children include pyridoxine responsive anemia and diarrhea. Seizures may develop.

Folate

Folate is composed of pteridine para-aminobenzoic acid and one or more molecules of glutamic acid. Folacin is the pteroylmonoglutamate.

Functions. With vitamin B_{12} (cyanocobalamin), folate functions in the synthe-

$$HOOC-\overset{\overset{\displaystyle H}{|}}{C}-\overset{\overset{\displaystyle H}{|}}{N}-\overset{\overset{\displaystyle O}{\|}}{C}-\underset{}{\bigcirc}-\overset{\overset{\displaystyle H}{|}}{N}-\overset{\overset{\displaystyle H}{|}}{\underset{\underset{\displaystyle H}{|}}{C}}-\text{(pteridine ring)}-NH_2$$

$$HOOC-CH_2$$

Folacin

sis of thymidylate and, therefore, deoxyribonucleic acid (DNA). It functions as a coenzyme in the metabolism of certain amino acids and as such is necessary for the conversion of serine to glycine and of homocystine to methionine and the degradation of histidine. As a component of tetrahydrofolate it functions in carbon transfer and is involved in the synthesis of heme, the iron-containing protein in hemoglobin, and in the synthesis of purines and thymine. It may also function in the desaturation and hydroxylation of long chain fatty acids in the brain.

Recommended intakes. The folate status of the infant at birth is dependent on the maternal status. Requirements depend on the child's weight and subsequent rate of growth. A dietary intake of 30 μg/day of folacin for the first year of life, gradually increasing to 400 μg/day in the preadolescent years, has been recommended[45] (Table 3-4).

The plasma folacin levels of infants at birth are higher than those of normal adults. After birth plasma and red cell values decline. The fall in the values of premature infants is greater than in full-term babies and minimal values are reached at an earlier age. There is a high incidence of megaloblastic anemia in premature infants. Less severe deficiencies that do not produce megaloblastosis may impair growth. Many infants whose birth weights are less than 2 kg receive 50 μg/day of folacin during the first 3 months to prevent deficiency during this period of rapid growth.[52]

Food sources. Organ meats, green leafy vegetables, yeast, and orange juice are rich sources of folacin.

Many naturally occurring folates are destroyed by heat and assay methods unless they are protected from oxidation by ascorbic acid. Tables of food values using older procedures underestimate the folate content of food.[53] Only a limited number of foods have been analyzed by more accurate procedures.

Folate occurs in food in combination with one, three, or seven molecules of glutamic acid. The monoglutamate and triglutamate compounds are the best absorbed. Total folate, however, is absorbed from some foods, its availability varying from food to food.[54] For example, total folate is absorbed from liver, spinach, and peas. Thirty-one percent of the total folate in orange juice, 39% of folate in egg yolk, and 25% of folate in romaine lettuce have been reported to be absorbed.[55] Table 3-9 shows free and total folate in selected foods determined by microbiologic assay when ascorbic acid was used during extraction to protect labile folates.

Human milk is reported to contain 42 to 51 μg total and 3 to 17 μg free folacin. Sterilizing pooled human milk and evaporated milk formula may yield products that are folate deficient.

Goat's milk contains very little folate. Diets of infants and children who consume goat's milk should be monitored for food sources of folate.

Marked prematurity, congenital heart disease, anticonvulsant drug therapy, and mal-

Table 3-9. Folacin content of selected foods

Food	Folacin (mcg/100 gm)	
	Free	**Total**
Cow's milk	5	5
Human milk	3	5
Yogurt	<.5	11
Eggs, hard cooked	—	49
Liver, beef, lamb, pork, cooked	—	145
Kidney, beef, raw	63	80
Tunafish, canned	8	15
Ground beef, cooked	—	4
Spinach, cooked	60	91
Broccoli, cooked	27	56
Beets, cooked	38	78
Romaine lettuce	60	179
Brewers yeast	175	3909
Bread, white	13	39
Bread, whole wheat	27	58
Orange juice, fresh, frozen reconstituted	34	55
Banana	22	28
Apple	3	8

From Perloff, B. P., and Butrum, R. R.: Folacin in selected foods, J. Am. Diet. Assoc. **70**:161, 1977.

absorption all contribute to the development of folate deficiency.

Deficient intakes. Deficiencies result in growth retardation and megaloblastic anemia indistinguishable from anemia as a result of vitamin B_{12} deficiency. It has also been suggested that folate deficiency may also be associated with neurologic disease. Motor retardation, hyperreflexia, and hypotonia were reported to improve when low serum folate levels in a 7-month-old infant were corrected.[56]

Cobalamin

Vitamin B_{12} is the only vitamin that contains cobalt. Cyanocobalamin is the generic term for all cobalamin-active compounds. The term coenzyme B_{12} designates only 5-deoxyadenosyl cobalamin, whereas vitamin B_{12} coenzyme refers to any coenzyme form of B_{12}.

Functions. The coenzyme forms of cobalamin are involved in many metabolic processes in protein, fat, and carbohydrate metabolism. Coenzyme B_{12} is required for hydrogen transfer and isomerization as methylmalonate is converted to succinate in fat and carbohydrate metabolism. It is necessary for the conversion of homocysteine to methionine. Coenzymes of vitamin B_{12} participate in the formation of red cells. Vitamin B_{12} catalyzes the release of pteroylmonoglutamic acid from conjugated folate and facilitates the synthesis of folate coenzymes. With folate, cobalamin participates in the synthesis of purines and pyrimidine and is, therefore, essential for the synthesis of DNA.

Recommended intakes. The recom-

Vitamin B₁₂

mended intake for vitamin B_{12} in infancy, 0.5 μg, is based on the average daily output of a well-nourished lactating woman. Recommended intakes for children have been gradually increased to 3 μg at 7 years of age,

the amount considered to be an appropriate intake throughout adolescence[37] (Table 3-4).

Food sources. Cobalamin occurs only in animal foods. Lean meat, liver, eggs, and fish are excellent sources of vitamin B_{12}. Human milk contains 0.3 μg/liter, and cow's milk contains 0.43 μg/liter of cobalamin.

Deficient intakes. Deficiencies of vitamin B_{12} resulting from lack of dietary intake are rare and occur almost exclusively in persons on vegan diets who restrict their intake of all animal protein. Deficiency symptoms include dyspepsia, sore tongue, tiredness, breathlessness, nervous lesions, and megaloblastic anemia. Some persons have stiff poker backs, the so-called vegan back.

One case of congenital vitamin B_{12} deficiency in a 6-month-old male infant whose mother had been on a strict vegan diet for 8 years prior to pregnancy has been described. Symptoms observed in the infant included megaloblastic anemia, neurologic anomalies, homocystinuria, and methylmalonic aciduria.[57]

Pantothenic acid

Pantothenic acid is a relatively simple nitrogen-containing compound.

Pantothenic acid

Functions. Pantothenic acid is essential for the synthesis of coenzyme A, which participates in the energy release of protein, fat, and carbohydrate. It participates in the oxidation of pyruvate and acetaldehyde and in the acetylation of choline and certain amino acids and vitamins. Also, it is essential for the synthesis of porphyrin, fat, and cholesterol.

Recommended intakes. The safe and adequate intake of pantothenic acid is 2 mg/day in infancy, 4 to 7 mg/day in adolescence.

Food sources. Pantothenic acid is present in all living matter. Many foods are good sources. Meat, eggs, cereal grain, and many fresh vegetables are excellent sources. Human milk contains 2.2 mg/liter, and cow's milk contains 3.40 mg/liter.

Deficient intakes. Because pantothenic acid occurs so abundantly in food, deficiencies are exceedingly rare. However, volunteers who were maintained on experimentally designed deficient diets and/or who received pantothenic acid antagonists developed symptoms of headache, fatigue, weakness, impaired motor coordination, muscle cramps, emotional lability, and gastrointestinal disturbances such as nausea and vomiting.

Biotin

Biotin is a simple organic ring compound.

Biotin

Functions. Biotin is a constituent of enzymes essential for carboxylation reactions important in the synthesis of fatty acids, in the production of energy from glucose, and in conversion reactions in the synthesis of some amino acids. Biotin stimulates protein synthesis and is necessary for the synthesis of nicotinic acid and pancreatic amylase. It stimulates synthesis of the enzyme responsible for the phosphorylation of glucose.

Recommended intakes. A safe and adequate intake of biotin has been estimated to increase from 35 μg/day in the first 6 months to 100 to 200 μg/day during adolescence.

Food sources. Biotin is synthesized by microorganisms in the intestinal tract and is widely distributed in food. Organ meats, dairy products, and eggs are rich sources. Legumes and cereal grains provide appreciable amounts. Cow's milk contains 0.031 mg/liter; human milk contains 0.008 mg/liter.

Deficient intakes. Natural deficiencies of biotin have not been reported in humans. Raw egg whites contain avidin, a carbohydrate-containing protein that inactivates biotin. Volunteer adults maintained on diets low in biotin that contain 30% of the total calories from egg white developed symptoms including a nonpruritic dermatitis, grayish pallor of the skin, hyperesthesia, anorexia, nausea, depression, sleeplessness, and muscle pains.

VITAMIN SUPPLEMENTATION

The importance of appropriate vitamin supplements for infants is discussed in Chapter 7.

Vitamin supplementation of diets of older children should be recommended only after careful evaluation of the child's food intake. Diets of children who restrict their intake of milk because of real or imagined allergies, lactose intolerance, or for psychosocial reasons should be monitored for riboflavin and vitamin D. Diets of infants and children receiving goat's milk should be carefully monitored for food sources of folacin. Diets of children who consume limited amounts of fruits and vegetables should be checked for sources of vitamins A and C.

Vitamin supplements, especially those that are colored and sugar coated, should be stored in places inaccessible to young children.

REFERENCES
Fat-soluble vitamins

1. Smith, B. M., and Malthus, E. M.: Vitamin A content of human liver from autopsies in New Zealand, Br. J. Nutr. **16**:213, 1962.
2. Food and Nutrition Board: Recommended dietary allowances, rev. ed. 9, Washington, D.C., 1980, National Academy of Sciences, National Research Council.
3. Mitchell, G. V., Young, M., and Seward, C R.: Vitamin A and carotene levels of a selected population in metropolitan Washington, D.C., Am. J. Clin. Nutr. **26**:992, 1973.
4. Raica, N., and others: Vitamin A concentration in human tissue collected from five areas in the United States, Am. J. Clin. Nutr. **25**:291, 1972.
5. DeLuca, H. F.: Vitamin D: the vitamin and the hormone, Fed. Proc. **33**:2211, 1974.
6. DeLuca, H. F.: The vitamin D system in the regulation of calcium and phosphorus, Nutr. Rev. **37**:161, 1979.
7. Hillman, L. S., and Haddad, J. G.: Perinatal vitamin D metabolism II: serial 25-hydroxy-vitamin D concentrations in sera of term and premature infants, J. Pediatr. **86**:928, 1975.
8. Lakdawala, D. R., and Widdowson, E. M.: Vitamin D in human milk, Lancet **1**:167, 1977.
9. Lewin, P. K., and others: Iatrogenic rickets in low birth weight infants, J. Pediatr. **78**:207, 1971.
10. Hoff, N., and others: Serum concentrations of 25-hydroxyvitamin D in rickets of extremely premature infants, J. Pediatr. **94**:460, 1979.
11. O'Connor, P.: Vitamin D deficiency rickets in two breast-fed infants who were not receiving vitamin D supplements, Clin. Pediatr. **16**:361, 1977.
12. Yendt, E. R., and others: Clinical aspects of vitamin D. In DeLuca, H. F., and Suttie, J. W., editors: The fat soluble vitamins, Madison, 1969, University of Wisconsin Press, p. 125.
13. The function of vitamin E as an antioxidant, as revealed by a new method for measuring lipid peroxidation, Nutr. Rev. **36**:84, 1978.
14. Horwitt, M. K.: Vitamin E. In Goodhart, R. S., and Shils, M. E.: Modern nutrition in health and disease, Philadelphia, 1980, Lea & Febiger.
15. Caasi, P. I., Hauswirth, J. W., and Nair, P. P.: Biosynthesis of heme in vitamin E deficiency, Ann. N.Y. Acad. Sci. **203**:93, 1972.
16. Carpenter, M. P.: Vitamin E and microsomal drug hydroxylations, Ann. N.Y. Acad. Sci. **203**:81, 1972.
17. Diplock, A. T.: Possible stabilizing effect of vitamin E on microsomal, membrane bound, selenide-containing protein and drug metabolizing enzyme systems, Am. J. Clin. Nutr. **27**:995, 1974.
18. Horwitt, M. K.: Status of human requirements for vitamin E, Am. J. Clin. Nutr. **27**:1182, 1974.
19. Lewis, J. S.: An E/PUFA ratio of 0.4 maintains normal plasma tocopherol levels in growing children, Fed. Proc. **28**:758, 1969 (abstract).
20. Dju, M. Y., Mason, K. E., and Filer, L. J., Jr.: Vita-

min E (tocopherol) in human fetuses and placentae, Etud. Neonate 1:49, 1952.

21. Gross, S., and Melhorn, D. K.: Vitamin E–dependent anemia in the premature infant. III. Comparative hemoglobin, vitamin E, and erythrocyte phospholipid responses following absorption of either water-soluble or fat-soluble d-alpha tocopherol, Pediatrics **85**:753, 1974.

22. Committee on Nutrition, American Academy of Pediatrics: Vitamin E in human nutrition, Pediatrics **31**:324, 1963.

23. Harries, J. T., and Muller, D. P. R.: Absorption of different doses of fat soluble and water miscible preparations of vitamin E in children with cystic fibrosis, Arch. Dis. Child. **46**:341, 1971.

24. Mason, K. E., and Horwitt, M. K.: Effects of deficiency in man. In Sebrell, W. H., and Harris, R. S., editors: The vitamins: chemistry, physiology, pathology, methods, ed. 2, vol. 5, New York, 1972, Academic Press, Inc., pp. 293-309.

25. Leonard, P. J., Doyle, E., and Harrington, W.: Levels of vitamin E in the plasma of newborn infants and of the mothers, Am. J. Clin. Nutr. **25**:480, 1972.

26. Nitowsky, H. M., Gordon, H. H., and Tildon, J. T.: Studies of tocopherol deficiency in infants and children. IV. The effects of alpha tocopherol on creatinuria in patients with cystic fibrosis of the pancreas and biliary atresia, Bull. Johns Hopkins Hosp. **98**:361, 1956.

27. Blanc, W. A., Reid, J. D., and Anderson, D. H.: Avitaminosis E in cystic fibrosis of the pancreas, Pediatrics **22**:494, 1958.

28. Oaski, F. A., and Barness, L. A.: Vitamin E deficiency: a previously unrecognized cause of hemolytic anemia in the premature infant, J. Pediatr. **70**:211, 1967.

29. Ritchie, J. H., and others: Edema and hemolytic anemia in premature infants. A vitamin E deficiency syndrome, N. Engl. J. Med. **279**:1185, 1968.

30. Graeber, J. E., Williams, M. L., and Oaski, F. A.: The use of intramuscular vitamin E in the premature infant, J. Pediatr. **90**:282, 1977.

31. Johnson, L., Schaffer, D., and Boggs, T. R.: The premature infant, vitamin E deficiency and retrolental fibroplasia, Am. J. Clin. Nutr. **27**:1158, 1974.

32. Ehrenkranz, R. A., and others: Amelioration of bronchopulmonary dysplasia after vitamin E administration. A preliminary report. N. Engl. J. Med. **299**:564, 1978.

33. Farrell, P. M., and Bieri, J. G.: Megavitamin E supplementation in man, Am. J. Clin. Nutr. **28**:1381, 1975.

34. Tsai, A. C., and others: Study on the effect of mega-

vitamin E supplementation in man, Am. J. Clin. Nutr. **31**:831, 1978.

35. Bell, R. G.: Metabolism of vitamin K and prothrombin synthesis: anticoagulants and the vitamin K epoxide cycle, Fed. Proc. **37**:2599, 1978.

36. Suttie, J. W.: Mechanism of action of vitamin K: demonstration of a liver precursor of prothrombin, Science **179**:192, 1973.

37. The functional significance of vitamin K action, Nutr. Rev. **34**:182, 1976.

38. Lian, J. B., Hauschka, P. V., and Gallop, P. M.: Properties and biosynthesis of a vitamin K dependent calcium binding protein in bone, Fed. Proc. **37**:2621, 1978.

39. Committee on Nutrition, American Academy of Pediatrics: Vitamin K supplementation for infants receiving milk substitute infant formulas and for those with fat malabsorption, Pediatrics **48**:483, 1971.

40. Committee on Nutrition, American Academy of Pediatrics: Vitamin K compounds and the water soluble analogues, Pediatrics **28**:501, 1961.

41. Dam, H., and others: The relation of vitamin K deficiency to hemorrhagic disease of the newborn, Adv. Pediatr. **5**:129, 1952.

42. Southerland, J. M., Glueck, H. I., and Gleser, G.: Hemorrhagic disease of the newborn, breast feeding as a necessary factor in the pathogenesis, Am. J. Dis. Child. **113**:524, 1967.

43. Keenan, W. J., Jewett, T., and Glueck, H. I.: Role of feeding and vitamin K in hypoprothrombinemia of the newborn, Am. J. Dis. Child. **121**:271, 1971.

Water-soluble vitamins

44. Baker, E. M.: Vitamin C requirements in stress, Am. J. Clin. Nutr. **20**:583, 1967.

45. Food and Nutrition Board: Recommended dietary allowances, rev. ed. 9, Washington, D.C., 1980, National Academy of Sciences, National Research Council.

46. Barchi, R. L.: The non-metabolic role of thiamine in excitable membrane function. In Gubler, C., Fujiwara, M., and Dreyfuss, P., editors: Thiamine, New York, 1976, John Wiley and Sons, Inc.

47. Sauberlich, H. E.: Biochemical alterations in thiamine deficiency—their interpretation, Am. J. Clin. Nutr. **20**:528, 1967.

48. Gromish, D. S.: Light (phototherapy)-induced riboflavin deficiency in the neonate, J. Pediatr. **90**:118, 1977.

49. Snyderman, S. E., Carretero, R., and Holt, L. E.: Pyridoxine deficiency in the human being, Fed. Proc. **9**:371, 1950.

50. Coursin, D. B.: Convulsive seizures in infants with

pyridoxine deficient diet, J.A.M.A. **154**:406, 1954.

51. Maloney, C. J., and Parmelee, A. H.: Convulsions in young infants as a result of pyridoxine (vitamin B₆) deficiency, J.A.M.A. **154**:405, 1954.

52. Strelling, M. K., Blackledge, D. G., and Goodall, H. B.: Diagnosis and management of folate deficiency in low birthweight infants, Arch. Dis. Child. **54**:271, 1979.

53. Toepfer, E. W., and others: Folic acid content of foods, Agriculture Handbook No. 29, Washington, D.C., 1951, U.S. Department of Agriculture.

54. Retief, F. P.: Urinary folate excretion after ingestion of pteroylmonoglutamic acid and food folate, Am. J. Clin. Nutr. **22**:352, 1969.

55. Tamura, T., and Stokstad, E. L. R.: The availability of food folate in man, Br. J. Haematology **25**:513, 1973.

56. Shapira, Y., Ben, A. B., and Slater, M. S.: Folic acid deficiency: a reversible cause of infantile hypotonia, J. Pediatr. **93**:984, 1978.

57. Higginbottom, L., Sweetman, L., and Nyhan, W. L.: A syndrome of methylmalonic aciduria, homocystinuria, megaloblastic anemia and neurological abnormalities of a vitamin B₁₂–deficient breast fed infant of a strict vegetarian, N. Engl. J. Med. **299**:317, 1978.

ADDITIONAL READINGS
Vitamin A

Bauernfeind, J. C., Newmark, H., and Brin, M.: Vitamin A and E nutrition via intramuscular or oral route, Am. J. Clin. Nutr. **27**:234, 1974.

Committees on Drugs and on Nutrition, American Academy of Pediatrics: The use and abuse of vitamin A, Pediatrics **48**:655, 1971.

Lui, N. S. T., and Roels, O. A.: Vitamin A and carotene. In Goodhart, R. S., and Shils, M. E.: Modern nutrition in health and disease, Philadelphia, 1980, Lea & Febiger.

Owen, G. M., and others: Nutritional status of preschool children: plasma vitamin A, J. Pediatr. **78**:1042, 1971.

Srikantia, S. G.: Human vitamin A deficiency, World Rev. Nutr. Diet. **20**:184, 1975.

Vitamin D

Castile, R. G., Marks, L. J., and Stickler, G. B.: Vitamin D deficiency, rickets, two cases with faulty infant feeding practices, Am. J. Dis. Child. **129**:964, 1975.

Committee on Nutrition, American Academy of Pediatrics: The prophylactic requirement and the toxicity of vitamin D, Pediatrics **31**:512, 1963.

Committee on Nutrition, American Academy of Pediatrics: The relation between infantile hypercalcemia and vitamin D—public health implications in North America, Pediatrics **40**:1050, 1967.

Haussler, M. R., and McCain, T. A.: Basic and clinical concepts related to vitamin D metabolism and action, I and II, N. Engl. J. Med. **297**:974, 1041, 1977.

Rosen, J. F., and others: 25-Hydroxyvitamin D, plasma levels in mothers and their premature infants with neonatal hypocalcemia, Am. J. Dis. Child. **127**:220, 1974.

Vitamin E

Horwitt, M. K.: Vitamin E: a reexamination, Am. J. Clin. Nutr. **29**:569, 1976.

Lake, A. M., Stuart, M. J., and Oaski, F. A.: Vitamin E deficiency and enhanced platelet function: reversal following E supplementation, J. Pediatr. **90**:722, 1977.

McWhirter, W. R.: Plasma tocopherol in infants and children, Acta Paediatr. Scand. **65**:446, 1975.

Muller, D. P. R., and Harries, J. T.: Vitamin E studies in children with malabsorption, Biochem. J. **112**:28P, 1969.

Vitamin K

Poley, J. R., and Humphrey, G. B.: Bleeding disorder in an infant associated with anicteric hepatitis, Clin. Pediatr. **13**:1045, 1974.

Suttie, J. W.: Vitamin K and prothrombin synthesis, Nutr. Rev. **31**:105, 1973.

Water-soluble vitamins

Ariaey-Nejad, M. R., and others: Thiamine metabolism in man, Am. J. Clin. Nutr. **23**:764, 1970.

Asfour, R., and others: Folacin requirements of children. III. Normal infants, Am. J. Clin. Nutr. **30**:1098, 1977.

Baker, E. M., Saari, J. C., and Tolbert, B. M.: Ascorbic acid metabolism in man, Am. J. Clin. Nutr. **19**:371, 1966.

Baker, H., and others: Vitamins, total cholesterol and triglycerides in 642 New York City school children, Am. J. Clin. Nutr. **20**:850, 1967.

Chatterjee, I. B.: Ascorbic acid metabolism, World Rev. Nutr. Diet. **30**:69, 1978.

Coursin, D. B.: Vitamin B₆ (pyridoxine) in milk, Q. Rev. Pediatr. **10**:2, 1955.

Darby, W. J., McNutt, K. W., and Todhunter, E. N.: Niacin, Nutr. Rev. **33**:289, 1975.

Gandy, G., and Jacobson, W. J.: Influence of folic acid on birthweight and growth of the erythroblastic infant. I. Birthweight, II. Growth during the first year. III. Effect of folic acid supplementation, Arch. Dis. Child. **52**:1, 7, 16, 1977.

Herbert, V.: Nutritional requirements for vitamin B₁₂ and folic acid, Am. J. Clin. Nutr. **21**:743, 1968.

Herbert, V.: The five possible causes of all nutrient deficiency: illustrated by deficiencies of vitamins B_{12} and folic acid, Am. J. Clin. Nutr. **26**:77, 1973.

Hodges, R. E., and others: Human pantothenic acid deficiency produced by omega-methyl pantothenic acid, J. Clin. Invest. **38**:1421, 1959.

Hodges, R. E., and others: Clinical manifestations of ascorbic acid deficiency in man, Am. J. Clin. Nutr. **24**:432, 1971.

Holt, L. E., and others: The thiamine requirement of the normal infant, J. Nutr. **37**:53, 1949.

Kinsman, R. A., and Hood, J.: Some behavioral effects of ascorbic acid deficiency, Am. J. Clin. Nutr. **24**:455, 1971.

Knott, E. M., and others: Is breast milk adequate in meeting the thiamine requirement of infants? J. Pediatr. **22**:43, 1943.

Moran, J. R., and Green, H. L.: The B vitamins and vitamin C in human nutrition. I. General considerations and obligatory B vitamins; II. Conditional B vitamins and vitamin C, Am. J. Dis. Child. **133**:308, 1979.

McCormick, D. B.: Biotin, Nutr. Rev. **33**:97, 1975.

Rivlin, R. S., editor: Riboflavin, New York, 1975, Plenum Publishing Corp.

Sterner, R. T., and Price, W. R.: Restricted riboflavin: within subject behavioral effects in humans, Am. J. Clin. Nutr. **26**:150, 1973.

Stevens, D., and others: Folic acid supplementation in low birthweight infants, Pediatrics **64**:333, 1979.

Van der Horst, R. L.: Scurvy in a 4 year old child, Am. J. Dis. Child. **126**:712, 1973.

4

Minerals and water

Minerals are inorganic nutrients that remain as ash when plant or animal tissues are burned. Although they contribute only 3% to 4% of the body weight, they play important roles in the regulation of body fluids, acid base balance, and metabolic processes, where they function as catalysts and are found as constituents of enzymes and hormones. They are structural components of bone and other tissue. Based on the relative amounts in the body, they are classified as either major minerals or trace minerals. Calcium, phosphorus, sulfur, sodium, chloride, and magnesium are designated as major minerals. Iron, copper, molybdenum, iodine, selenium, zinc, chromium, cobalt, and manganese are trace minerals. It has yet to be proved that fluoride, tin, nickel, and vanadium are essential minerals in the human body.

The Food and Nutrition Board of the National Research Council has established recommended allowances for three major and three trace minerals. These recommended daily dietary allowances are shown in Table 4-1.

Insufficient information exists on many of the trace minerals to make recommendations for daily intake. Ranges of intake, however, have been suggested and are shown in Table 4-2.

WATER AND ELECTROLYTES

Even more essential to the body than food is water. It functions as an essential component of body structure and as a solvent for minerals and other physiologically important compounds. It transports nutrients to and waste products from the cells and helps to regulate body temperature.

The percentage of body weight provided by water decreases from approximately 75% at birth to 60% at 1 year of age (see Chapter 1). After age 1 year intracellular water accounts for approximately 60% and extracellular water for 40% of total body water. The minerals and other solutes maintain the osmotic pressure of the fluids, which in turn maintains a balance of water between intracellular and extracellular fluids, and water can pass freely across the semipermeable cell membrane.

The major cations in body fluids are sodium and potassium. The major anions are chloride, sulfate, carbonate, phosphate, and protein. Glucose in the plasma does not conduct electricity but does contribute to plasma osmolality. However, since the end products of its metabolism, carbon dioxide and water, leave during breathing it obligates no water. Sodium and chloride are concentrated in the extracellular fluid. Potassium is found primarily within the cells.

The maintenance of osmolality between 285 and 290 mOsm/liter is achieved by continuous regulation of the volume and osmolality of the urine. As the osmolality of the plasma increases, receptors in the posterior portion of the pituitary gland secrete antidiuretic hormone, which acts on the renal

Table 4-1. Recommended daily dietary allowances for minerals

	Age (years)	Calcium (mg)	Phosphorus (mg)	Iodine (μg)	Iron (mg)	Magnesium (mg)	Zinc (mg)
Infants	0.0-0.5	360	240	40	10	50	3
	0.5-1.0	540	360	50	15	70	5
Children	1-3	800	800	70	15	150	10
	4-6	800	800	90	10	200	10
	7-10	800	800	120	10	250	10
Males	11-14	1200	1200	150	18	350	15
	15-18	1200	1200	150	18	400	15
Females	11-14	1200	1200	150	18	300	15
	15-18	1200	1200	150	18	300	15

From Food and Nutrition Board: Recommended dietary allowances, rev. ed. 9, Washington, D.C., 1980, National Academy of Sciences, National Research Council.

Table 4-2. Estimated safe and adequate daily dietary intakes of selected trace minerals

		Trace minerals					
	Age (years)	Copper (mg)	Manganese (mg)	Fluoride (mg)	Chromium (mg)	Selenium (mg)	Molybdenum (mg)
Infants	0-0.5	0.5-0.7	0.5-0.7	0.1-0.5	0.01-0.04	0.01-0.04	0.03-0.06
	0.5-1	0.7-1.0	0.7-1.0	0.2-1.0	0.02-0.06	0.02-0.06	0.04-0.08
Children	1-3	1.0-1.5	1.0-1.5	0.5-1.5	0.02-0.08	0.02-0.08	0.05-0.1
and	4-6	1.5-2.0	1.5-2.0	1.0-2.5	0.03-0.12	0.03-0.12	0.06-0.15
adolescents	7-10	2.0-2.5	2.0-3.0	1.5-2.5	0.05-0.2	0.05-0.2	0.1-0.3
	11+	2.0-3.0	2.5-5.0	1.5-2.5	0.05-0.2	0.05-0.2	0.15-0.5
		2.0-3.0	2.5-5.0	1.5-4.0	0.05-0.2	0.05-0.2	0.15-0.5

		Electrolytes		
	Age (years)	Sodium (mg)	Potassium (mg)	Chloride (mg)
Infants	0-0.5	115-350	350-925	275-700
	0.5-1	250-750	425-1275	400-1200
Children	1-3	325-975	550-1650	500-1500
and	4-6	450-1350	775-2325	700-2100
adolescents	7-10	600-1800	1000-3000	925-2775
	11+	900-2700	1525-4575	1400-4200
		1100-3300	1875-5625	1700-5100

From Food and Nutrition Board: Recommended dietary allowances, rev. ed. 9, Washington, D.C., 1980, National Academy of Sciences, National Research Council.

tubule and causes reabsorption of water. Conversely, if the plasma becomes dilute, the pituitary gland inhibits secretion of antidiuretic hormone, and diuresis occurs. If plasma osmolality is decreased, the adrenal cortex secretes aldosterone, which causes a reabsorption of sodium. Also, a sensation of thirst, mediated from the ventromedial and anterior hypothalamus, results when there is a decrease in volume of body fluids or an increase in osmolality.

Recommended intakes. Water is lost by evaporation through the skin and respiratory tract (insensible water loss) and through perspiration when the environmental temperature is elevated, and by elimination in the feces and in the urine. During growth a positive water balance is necessary since additional water is obligated as a constituent of tissue and for increases in the volume of body fluids. The amount of water required for growth, however, is very small at all ages.

Water lost by evaporation in infancy and early childhood accounts for more than 60% of that needed to maintain homeostasis, as compared to 40% to 50% in the adult. At all ages approximately 24% of the basal heat loss is by evaporation of water through the skin and respiratory tract.[1] This amounts to 45 ml of insensible water loss per 100 kcal expended. Fomon estimates evaporative water loss at 1 month of age to average 210 ml/day and at age 1 year, 500 ml/day.[2] Adult losses by evaporation average 800 to 1050 ml/day under ordinary circumstances. Evaporative losses increase with fever and increased environmental temperature. Increases in humidity decrease respiratory loss. Loss of water in the feces averages 10 ml/kg/day in infancy.[3]

The volume of urine in general reflects fluid intake. It includes both water required to concentrate the solutes presented to the kidney for excretion and water in excess of body need. The renal water requirement is determined by the diet and by the concentrating power of the kidney. Older children and adults have the ability to concentrate 1200 to 1400 mOsm/liter. The young infant, however, has a functionally immature kidney. The ratio of glomerular surface area to tubular volume in an infant's kidney is high, compared to the kidney of the adult.[4] The glomerular filtration rate is low. The concentrating capacity of some neonates has been reported to be as limited as 700 mOsm/liter and for others it is as great as that of older children.[5,6]

Ziegler and Fomon have developed a method for estimating the renal solute load by calculating the amount of dietary sodium, chloride, potassium, and urea (estimated to be 4 mOsm/gm of protein).[7] The urinary water requirement can then be estimated from the sum of these values. The National Research Council recommends an intake of 1.5 ml/kcal/day for the infant, 1.0 ml/kcal/day for the adult.[8] Balance studies of 5-year-old children showed intakes of 1100 ml/day; metabolic water contributed an additional 200 ml/day. Water intakes averaged 0.7 ml/kcal/day.[9] Ranges of average water requirements of infants and children are shown in Table 4-3.

Food sources. Fluid in liquids and food consumed are the primary source of water. In addition, metabolic water is created from the metabolism of protein, fat, and carbohydrate. One gram of fat produces 1.07 ml water; 1 gm of protein produces 4.1 ml water; and 1 gm of carbohydrate produces 5.5 ml water. Table 4-4 shows the water content of representative foods consumed in infancy and early childhood. When milk is boiled the liquid evaporates and protein and electrolytes are concentrated. Boiled milk is an inappropriate feeding for infants.

Because of a relatively greater demand for insensible water and a renal concentrating capacity that may be less than that of the adult, the infant is vulnerable to water imbalance. Under normal environmental conditions infants do not need additional water. Difficulties arise when formulas are improperly prepared (see Chapter 7), when infants ingest limited volumes of milk during illness, and when extrarenal losses are greater than usual, such as during episodes of vomiting and diarrhea.[7] To ensure adequate water intakes infant formula should not be concentrated to more than 100 kcal/100 ml.

As children grow older the concentrating power of the kidney increases. Children learn to communicate and ask for water when they become thirsty. Difficulties in achieving water balance are unlikely in the absence of vomiting or diarrhea.

CALCIUM AND PHOSPHORUS

Calcium and phosphorus occur in the body in three systems. Ninety-nine percent of body calcium is present in bone, and 1% is found in body fluids and striated muscle. Eighty percent of body phosphorus is found in bone. The remainder is in striated muscle and blood serum.

Calcium is distributed in three forms in body fluids—in combination with protein, ionized and free, and in complex with other substances. Inorganic phosphorus in the serum exists in two forms, as phosphate and as phosphoric acid. Plasma calcium and phosphorus levels are higher in children than in adults. Serum concentrations of the minerals

Table 4-3. Water requirements of infants and children

Age	Water requirement (ml/kg/day)
10 days	125-150
3 months	140-160
6 months	130-155
1 year	120-135
2 years	115-125
6 years	90-100
10 years	70-85
14 years	50-60

From Laupus, W. E.: Nutrition and nutritional disorders. In Vaughan, V. C., McKay, R. J., and Nelson, W. E.: Nelson textbook of pediatrics, ed. 10, Philadelphia, 1975, W. B. Saunders Co.

Table 4-4. Percentage of water in selected foods

Food	Water (%)	Food	Water (%)
Human milk	85.2	Strained carrots	92.3
Cow's milk	87.4	Hamburger patty	68.3
Infant cereals, high protein	6.1	Chicken, cooked, dark meat	64.4
Infant cereals, rice	6.7	Egg, hard boiled	73.7
Strained macaroni and cheese	87.1	Oatmeal, cooked	83.6
Strained chicken with vegetables	90.0	Bread, white, enriched	35.6
Strained beef with vegetables	85.4	Carrots, cooked	91.2
Strained applesauce	88.6	Peas, canned	81.5
Strained peaches	80.1	Banana	75.7
Strained beef	80.6	Pears, canned	91.1
Strained peas	87.5		

From Gebhardt, S. E., Cutrufelli, R., and Matthews, R. H.: Composition of foods, baby foods, raw processed, prepared, Agriculture Handbook No. 8-3, Washington, D.C., 1978, U.S. Department of Agriculture.

are highest during early childhood, then decrease, paralleling decreases in parathyroid hormone. The levels plateau between 6 and 12 years of age and decline during adolescence to adult values.[10]

The calcium content of the body reflects both sex and stature. The body of the adult female contains approximately three-fourths as much calcium as the body of the adult male. The skeletons of blacks tend to be larger than those of whites. The amount of calcium accumulated during growth depends on the rate of growth and final stature attained. It has been estimated that the fetus acquires an average of 97 mg of calcium/day.[11] Shaw estimates the placental transfer at term to be 150 mg/kg/day.[12] The body of the full-term newborn infant has been estimated to contain approximately 27 gm of calcium, that of the adult female 770 to 920 gm of calcium, and that of the adult male 950 to 1290 gm of calcium.

Functions. Both calcium and phosphorus function in the synthesis and remodeling of skeletal tissue. The skeleton is built according to definite morphologic and chemical patterns. Crystalline protein fibers, collagen, form a cellular matrix on which minerals are deposited and are set in a gel of mucopolysaccharides, the ground substance. Bone mineral contains crystals of calcium and phosphate (hydroxyapatite). Magnesium, sodium carbonate, citrate, and small quantities of fluoride are also deposited.

Bone is not an inert tissue but is constantly being remodeled by destruction and renewal of collagen and addition and loss of mineral. Increases in skeletal length are achieved by this process of continuous dissolution and remodeling of bone. Newly formed bone contains less mineral than mature bone. Maturation of bone is achieved by growth of the crystal solution and recrystallization to the stage where space between crystals no longer permits passage of

ions.[13] The constant loss of bone mineral must be replaced at all ages. During growth minerals must be provided for increases in size as well.

The same type of structure is present in the tooth. The crystals are, however, larger and more firmly packed. In contrast to bones there is a very slow exchange of hydroxyapatite. Also, that which is exchanged is confined almost entirely to the dentin. A deficiency of calcium during tooth formation cannot be later reversed.

Skeletal requirements for calcium and phosphorus are dependent on body size and rates of growth. Requirements are greatest for taller, more rapidly growing children at any age.

Garn has estimated gains in skeletal weight and amounts of calcium and phosphorus retained in bone from longitudinal and cross-sectional roentgenographic studies of the second metacarpal.[14]

Christiansen and associates have measured bone density of school-age children at different ages by photon absorption.[15] Other investigators have analyzed skeletal weights and percentages of skeletal ash of individuals from infancy to adulthood.[16]

Leitch and Aitken have estimated skeletal calcium requirements from analysis of the calcium content of analyzed bodies and rates of growth.[17]

Garn estimates an average skeletal retention in males of 90 mg of calcium/day and 43 mg of phosphorus/day in the first year of life. Leitch and Aitken suggest skeletal calcium increments during the same period to average 150 mg/day. Both investigators estimate a decline in skeletal retentions of the minerals between the first and fourth years, after which the skeletal retentions gradually increase. Garn estimates that during the adolescent growth spurt males retain an average of 275 mg of calcium and 132 mg of phosphorus/day. Leitch and Aitken suggested that between ages 15 and 17 years skeletal requirements for calcium average 375 to 400 mg/day. The Committee on Nutrition of the American Academy of Pediatrics estimates a retention of 290 to 400 mg of calcium/day in males and 210 and 240 mg of calcium/day in females during their peak growth spurts.[11] Skeletal retentions of the two minerals are less in females than in males except between the tenth and twelfth years when rates of growth of females are greater than those of males.

Extraskeletal functions of calcium. Calcium is bound to lecithin in cell membranes where it is an activator of several enzymes that influence cell membrane permeability. It controls the uptake of nutrients by the cells and activates enzyme systems responsible for contractile properties of the muscle.

Calcium also functions as a catalyst in many biologic reactions. Serum calcium functions in blood clotting by stimulating the release of thromboplastin and the conversion of fibrinogen to fibrin. It activates pancreatic lipase, which splits fatty acids from the glycerol molecule, and many enzymes that function in the release of energy. The intestinal absorption of cobalamin is calcium dependent. Calcium ions in the extracellular fluids are involved in the synthesis of acetylcholine, the substance required for nerve impulses to be passed from a nerve cell to the cell adjacent to it. Low levels of ionized calcium cause uncontrolled muscle spasms. Calcium in intercellular fluid is necessary for pancreatic secretion of insulin when stimulated by glucose.

Extraskeletal calcium requirements have been estimated to average 100 mg/day in infancy, 50 to 60 mg/day during childhood, and 150 mg/day in adolescence.[17]

Extraskeletal functions of phosphorus. Phosphorus is a necessary constituent of every cell in the body. Phosphorylated compounds function in hundreds of essential metabolic reactions. Glucose and glycerol are phosphorylated during digestion from the intestine. Glucose that has been absorbed by the cell and glycogen that has been removed from storage are phosphorylated as they enter the pathway of glycolysis. Phosphate forms high-energy bonds as it is attached to ADP and forms ATP in the citric acid cycle. Phosphate also serves as an essential constituent in many enzymes. It is a part of many proteins that are enzymes. It is complexed with thiamin when it is active in metabolic processes.

Phosphorus is a component of nucleic acids and nucleoproteins, which determine the genetic code. Also, it is a part of phospholipids, which function in the emulsification and transport of fat.

Phosphate in the plasma serves as buffer ions and functions in control of the acid–base balance.

Recommended intakes. Attempts to establish recommended intakes of calcium have caused considerable controversy for many years. Populations that have adapted to intakes of 200 to 400 mg/day without adverse effects have been identified.[18] The recommended daily dietary allowances (Table 4-1) were planned to meet the needs of formula-fed infants who retain 25% to 30% of the calcium consumed in cow's milk.[8] Although breast-fed infants ingest less calcium, they retain approximately two-thirds of intake. Recommendations for children are set at 800 mg/day, since growing children may need two to four times as much calcium as adults. The higher recommended intakes of 1200 mg/day during preadolescence and puberty were designed to provide for maximum calcium retention.

Recommended intakes of phosphorus are the same as for calcium except during infancy, when a calcium:phosphorus ratio in the diet of 1.5:1 is recommended.

Food sources. Milk and dairy products are

the richest sources of calcium in the North American diet. Table 4-5 shows the contribution of selected milk and dairy products. Egg yolks and most dark green leafy vegetables also contribute appreciable amounts of calcium.

Phosphorus is found in combination with calcium in dairy products but also occurs in foods that contain little calcium. It occurs in most protein-rich foods such as meats, eggs, nuts, and legumes and is also found in grains. Phosphate-containing additives are ingredients of many carbonated beverages, processed meats, cheese, and refrigerated bakery goods.

Interrelationships. Vitamin D is essential for calcium absorption and, along with parathyroid hormone and calcitonin, maintains serum calcium levels (see Chapter 3).

Lactose, the carbohydrate in milk, increases calcium absorption. Phytic acid, found in the outer husk of cereal grains, and oxalic acid, found in rhubarb and spinach, form insoluble compounds with calcium and thus reduce absorption. The effect of these two compounds is not, however, considered to be of practical importance under ordinary circumstances.

Large variations in phosphorus do not appear to affect absorption when intakes of calcium are nutritionally adequate. It has been hypothesized that when dietary intakes of calcium are high, phosphorus may depress calcium absorption by the formation of insoluble calcium phosphate in the gut.[19]

Adults fed diets with a calcium:phosphorus ratio of 0.7:1 to 0.35:1 experienced a decrease of 0.3 mg/dl in serum calcium levels and an increase of 0.7 mg/dl in serum phosphorus levels in 4 weeks. Mild intestinal symptoms were experienced.[20]

A number of investigators have found that the level of dietary protein has an effect on urinary excretion of calcium. As levels of protein consumed increase, levels of urinary calcium increase. When the quantity of protein in the diet is reduced, urinary calcium excretion decreases.[21,22] Spencer and associates, however, found that a high meat intake providing 2 gm of protein/kg did not cause a sustained increase in urinary calcium levels in adult males.[23]

The effect of fat on calcium absorption depends on the fatty acids in the diet. Increased calcium recovered in the feces of infants has been noted to be associated with palmitic and stearic acid in the vegetable oil added to nonfat cow's milk in infant formulas.[24]

Table 4-5. Calcium in milk and dairy products

Food	Household measure	Calcium (mg)
Human milk	4 oz	40
Cow's milk	4 oz	144
Powdered milk, nonfat, instant dry	⅓ cup	293
Cheddar cheese	1 oz	213
Yogurt	½ cup	147
Custard, baked	½ cup	148
Chocolate pudding, cooked with milk	½ cup	133
Chocolate pudding, instant	½ cup	187
Ice cream	½ cup	97

From Adams, C. F.: Nutritive value of American foods in common units, Agriculture Handbook No. 456, Washington, D.C., 1975, U.S. Department of Agriculture.

Deficient intakes. Rickets resulting from an inadequate calcium intake was noted in one full-term infant who for 10 months was fed a lamb base formula deficient in calcium but adequate in vitamins.[25] Inadequate phosphorus intakes have also been suggested as the cause of rickets in some premature and full-term infants.[26,27] It has been reported that human milk contains insufficient amounts of phosphorus for rapidly growing premature infants and that these infants may need phosphorus supplements.[26]

No deficiency disease has been described in older children or adults that can be attributed directly to insufficient dietary calcium intakes. Some studies have suggested decreased rates of growth associated with low intakes of calcium. The diets of those individuals studied have, however, been low in protein and other nutrients as well as calcium. Aykroyd and Krishnan in 1938 observed significantly greater increases in heights and weights of Indian children 2 to 7 years of age who received 500 mg of calcium lactate for 4 months as compared to children of the same age receiving no supplements.[28] Other investigators have been unable to reproduce similar results in children between 6 months and 2½ years of age.[29]

Neonatal hypocalcemia. Plasma concentrations of calcium and phosphorus are greater in cord blood than in maternal blood. During the first 2 to 3 days of life the levels of calcium fall significantly.[30] The decline is greatest in premature infants, infants of abnormal pregnancies and deliveries, infants with asphyxia, and infants of diabetic mothers.[31,32] In normal, full-term infants the decline is greatest in those who are formula-fed and least in those who receive human milk. The fall in plasma calcium levels is accompanied by a rise in plasma inorganic phosphorus levels.[33]

After the initial decline plasma calcium levels stabilize and tend to rise by the tenth day of life, the level being dependent on the phosphorus content or the calcium:phosphorus ratio of milk.[34] Serum calcium concentrations in breast-fed infants are greater than those in formula-fed infants. Serum concentrations of phosphorus reflect the phosphorus content of the milk consumed, being significantly less in breast-fed infants than in formula-fed infants.[33,35] Breast-fed infants generally show an increase in serum calcium concentration by 5 to 7 days of age. Snodgrass and associates noted no increase in levels of plasma calcium in formula-fed infants between the first and sixth to eighth day of life. They noted a fall in serum calcium concentrations in one-third of formula-fed infants during the first week of life; in 9% of infants the levels fell below 7.5 mg/100 ml, a level at which hypocalcemia is defined by many and at which the infant is at risk of tetany.[33]

There are two periods when hypocalcemia is detected in the neonate. Early neonatal hypocalcemia occurs in the first 24 to 48 hours and is thought to be the result of depressed levels of parathyroid hormone as a result of transient functional hypoparathyroidism.[36] It occurs most frequently in infants of diabetic mothers, infants who have experienced asphyxia, and low birth weight infants.[37] Some investigators have suggested that a continuous prophylactic infusion or oral supplements of calcium and magnesium lactate be given to all low birth weight infants.[38,39] Late neonatal hypocalcemia occurs in association with hyperphosphatemia in otherwise normal, full-term infants between the fifth and eighth day of life. It is rarely seen in breast-fed infants but occurs more often in infants who receive a high dietary intake of phosphorus. Phosphorus consumed in excess of that which can be excreted by the kidney elevates serum phosphate levels. It has been hypothesized that elevated serum phosphorus levels depress serum calcium levels by causing deposition of calcium in bone. A normal response would be an increased output of parathyroid hormone, causing solubilization of bone mineral, phosphate diuresis, and blockage of tubular resorption. The neonatal infant with an immature parathyroid gland may not be able to respond with the normal homeostatic mechanism, and serum calcium levels may fall. Irritability and convulsions often, although not inevitably, occur when serum levels fall below 7 mg/100 ml.

One of the striking differences between human milk and cow's milk is the content of calcium and phosphorus. Cow's milk contains more than three times as much calcium and six times as much phosphorus as does human milk. There is less calcium relative to phosphorus in cow's milk than in human milk. Gittleman and Pincus in 1951 found that newborn infants given a high-phosphate diet as represented by evaporated milk or whole cow's milk mixtures responded with hyperphosphatemia and a tendency toward hypocalcemia.[40] In 1952 Gardner suggested that excess dietary phosphorus in the face of limited kidney function had profound effects on the renal tissue as well as on the parathyroid gland, causing hypertrophy of the parathyroid gland and renal lesions.[41]

Manufacturers of infant formulas have reduced the quantity of phosphorus in cow's milk formulas. Isolated cases of neonatal hypocalcemic tetany, however, continue to be reported. Pierson and Crawford reported two cases of neonatal hypocalcemia resulting in tetany that occurred on the eighth and ninth days of life. One infant received a high-phosphate load from a soybean formula preparation, the other from the addition of cereal to the formula.[42] Monitoring the amount of phosphorus consumed by infants in the early neonatal period continues to be important.

MAGNESIUM

Magnesium is the fourth most abundant mineral in the body and the second most abundant intercellular cation. Approximately 50% of the body's magnesium is deposited with calcium and phosphorus in bone, 25% is in muscle, and the remainder is found in soft tissue. Erythrocytes contain 4.4 to 6.0 mEq/liter.[43] Thirty-five percent of plasma magnesium is bound to protein, 13% is complexed to other compounds, and the remainder is free and ultrafilterable.

Functions. Ionized magnesium participates as a cofactor in many metabolic systems. It activates enzymes that hydrolyze and transfer phosphate groups and in this role it participates in reactions involving ATP. It is therefore necessary for the production and transfer of energy. It is involved in protein synthesis because it binds messenger RNA and plays a role in synthesis and degradation of DNA. With calcium it has a complex and interdependent effect on muscle contractility and excitability of nerves. Magnesium in extracellular fluid bathes the nerve cells and helps conduct nerve impulses that relax muscles following contraction.

Magnesium appears to promote calcium retention in tooth enamel and increase resistance to dental caries. It facilitates the release of thyroxine.

Recommended intakes. The recommended daily dietary allowances for infants have been estimated from the magnesium content of human milk and cow's milk (Table 4-1). Allowances for children and adolescents are stated to be only estimates intended to allow for increasing needs during bone growth.[8]

Harris and Wilkinson state that the newborn infant needs to retain 10.2 mg/day of magnesium to satisfy the requirement for growth.[44] Fomon estimates the requirement to be 16.5 mg/day during the first 4 months and suggests an intake of 25 mg/day.[45] Laupus suggests intakes of 40 to 70 mg/day for infants, 100 to 150 mg/day for children 1 to 3 years of age, 200 to 300 mg/day for children ages 3 to 12 years, and 350 to 400 mg/day for adolescents ages 12 to 18 years.[46]

Food sources. Magnesium is relatively widespread in nature. Nuts, soybeans, whole grains, legumes, and shellfish are excellent sources. It exists in all green plants as a component of chlorophyll. Human milk contains approximately 4 mg of magnesium/100 ml and cow's milk contains 12 mg of magnesium/100 ml.

Interrelationships. Magnesium is absorbed in the small intestine, where it shares a common absorptive pathway with calcium. Therefore, the two minerals compete for absorption. Absorption also may be reduced by the presence of fat or phytates. Parathyroid hormone has a regulatory effect on body magnesium similar to but of lesser magnitude than that of calcium. This hormone apparently increases mobilization from bone, increases intestinal transport, and decreases renal excretion when serum levels fall. Protein, calcium, and phosphorus all increase the metabolic requirement for magnesium.

Deficient intakes. Magnesium depletion may result secondary to any disorder that interferes with its absorption from the intestinal tract and/or causes loss of gastrointestinal fluid, such as vomiting or diarrhea. It is commonly encountered when losses of water and other electrolytes have been replaced but no magnesium has been given.[44] Clinical signs of magnesium depletion include apathy, irritability, weakness, tremors, twitching, and seizures.

A rare congenital condition of magnesium malabsorption that results in hypomagnesemia and tetany has been noted in males. Hypocalcemia secondary to magnesium malabsorption has been noted in every case. Oral supplements of magnesium are required indefinitely.[47]

A magnesium deprivation syndrome of growth occurs in children receiving all essential nutrients except magnesium and is most accelerated during catch-up growth following nutritional deprivation. This syndrome, which includes hypomagnesemia, electrocardiographic changes, tetany, and convulsions, is thought to be one reason for the clinical deterioration that occurs when children with protein calorie malnutrition are rehabilitated with high-protein milk and magnesium supplements are not given.[48]

Unusual symptoms of magnesium deficiency noted in adults include vertical nystagmus and dysphagia.[49]

Hypomagnesemia. Decreased serum magnesium levels occur in full-term infants small for gestational age and remain low for 3 to 4 days. This is a manifestation that has been hypothesized to be compatible with the theory that intrauterine growth retardation is a form of intrauterine malnutrition.[47]

Hypomagnesemia often accompanies hypocalcemia during the neonatal period, a phenomenon thought to be caused by depressed activity of the parathyroid gland. Magnesium levels return to normal as hypocalcemia is controlled. In cases of magnesium malabsorption, hypocalcemia will respond to magnesium therapy.[48]

Clinical signs of hypomagnesemia are similar to hypocalcemia and include neuromuscular excitability, muscle twitching, and convulsions. Hypomagnesemia is diagnosed when serum levels are below 1.5 mg/100 ml. Tetany usually occurs when levels fall below 1.2 or 1.3 mg/100 ml.

IRON

Iron is the most abundant trace mineral in the body, accounting for approximately 75 mg/kg of the full-term newborn infant, 50 mg/kg of the adult male, and 35 mg/kg of the adult female.[50] Sixty to ninety percent of total body iron exists as hemoglobin and myoglobin. Fifteen to twenty percent has been estimated to be combined with nonheme protein as storage iron in the liver, spleen, and bone marrow. Less than 1% functions in the iron-dependent enzyme systems present in every living cell.[51]

Iron is transported in the blood bound to the protein transferrin, which both accepts and releases iron. It is stored as ferritin and hemosidirin, both of which can be mobilized for body need. Greater amounts are usually stored as ferritin. As concentrations of storage iron increase, additional iron is deposited as hemosidirin and the ratios may be reversed. Iron stored during growth is present only as ferritin, indicating limited stores.[51]

The concentration of hemoglobin at birth averages 17 to 19 gm/100 ml of blood. During the first 6 to 8 weeks of life it decreases to approximately 10 to 11 gm/100 ml because of a shortened life span of the fetal cell and decreased erythropoiesis. After this age there is a gradual increase in hemoglobin concentration to 13 gm/100 ml at 2 years of age. During adolescence a sharp increase occurs in males at the time of the growth spurt.

Functions. Iron in hemoglobin and myoglobin is stabilized in the ferrous state and can be reversibly bonded to oxygen. In this form it carries oxygen to and carbon dioxide from tissues. Iron is also a component of the cytochrome system, which functions in cellular oxidation-reduction reactions. It acts as a cofactor in many other enzyme systems involved in the formation of high-energy phosphate bonds. It catalyzes the conversion of β-carotene to vitamin A and plays a role in the synthesis of purines and collagen and in antibody production.

Recommended intakes. The recommended dietary allowances of the National Research Council assume 10% absorption and are planned to meet variations in individuals (Table 4-1). Iron requirements of individual children vary with rates of growth and increasing blood volumes, iron stores, varia-

tions in menstrual losses of iron of adolescent females, and the timing of the growth spurt of adolescents. Larger, more rapidly growing children have the greatest requirement for iron at any age.

During menstruation iron loss varies widely among females but is consistent from month to month in individuals. Average losses of blood of 15-year-old girls in a Swedish study were 33.8 ml/period, equivalent to an iron loss of approximately 0.5 mg of iron/day.[52]

Food sources. Diets in North America have been estimated to provide 6 mg of iron/1000 kcal. Organ meats, shellfish, and muscle meats provide the richest and most usable sources. Other food sources include nuts, green vegetables, whole wheat flour, and bread.

Of the iron in pork, liver, and fish, 30% to 40% is in the form of heme iron, and of the iron in beef, lamb, and chicken, 50% to 60% is in the form of heme iron. Obviously, these foods are sources of nonheme iron also, as are greens, vegetables, grains, legumes, and eggs.[53] Human milk and cow's milk contain 0.5 to 1.0 mg of iron/liter. During infancy, iron-fortified formulas and cereals fortified with reduced iron are primary food sources. Table 4-6 lists representative sources of iron for infants and children.

Iron absorption from food. The percentage of iron absorbed from food depends on the presence of heme iron and/or nonheme iron, the combinations of food consumed together, and the iron reserves of the individual. Individuals with inadequate iron stores absorb approximately 35%; those with adequate iron stores absorb 25% of heme iron consumed. Individuals with deficient iron reserves may absorb as much as 20% of nonheme iron, whereas iron-replete individuals may absorb as little as 2%. The presence of meat, which offers heme iron and ascorbic acid, increases the absorption of

Table 4-6. Selected food sources of iron

Food	Household measure	Iron (mg)
Iron-fortified formula	8 oz	3.0
Infant cereals, high protein	1 tbsp	1.8
Infant cereals, rice	1 tbsp	1.8
Strained split peas with ham	1 oz	0.1
Strained chicken with vegetables	1 oz	0.1
Strained beef with vegetables	1 oz	0.1
Strained beef	1 oz	0.4
Strained liver	1 oz	1.5
Hamburger, cooked	2 oz	1.8
Chicken, dark meat	1 oz	0.5
Liver, beef	1 oz	2.5
Liver, chicken	1 liver	2.1
Liverwurst	1 oz	1.7
Frankfurter, 5″ by ¾″	1	0.9
Egg	1 medium	1.0
Pork and beans	¼ cup	1.5
Peanut butter	1 tbsp	0.3
Bread, enriched white	1 slice	0.7
Macaroni, enriched, cooked	¼ cup	0.4
Carrots, cooked	¼ cup	0.2
Orange	1 medium	0.6
Canned pears	¼ cup	0.1

From Adams, C. F.: Nutritive value of American foods in common units, Agriculture Handbook No. 456, Agriculture Research Service, Washington, D.C., 1975, U.S. Department of Agriculture; and Gebhardt, S. E., Cutrufelli, R., and Matthews, R. H.: Composition of foods, baby foods, raw, processed, prepared, Agriculture Handbook No. 8-3, Washington, D.C., 1978, U.S. Department of Agriculture.

nonheme iron. Absorption is decreased by the inclusion of dairy products, eggs, calcium phosphate salts, or tea in the foods consumed at the same time.[53] Forty-nine percent of the iron in human milk, 19% of the iron in cow's milk, and 3% of the iron in iron-fortified formula is absorbed.[54] The addition of strained vegetables to the infant's diet significantly reduces the availability of iron from human milk.[55]

Many foods are fortified with iron salts. Of particular importance to persons concerned with iron intakes of infants and children are those iron salts used to fortify the commercially prepared infant formulas, cereal grains, and cereals consumed so abundantly by chil-dren. Iron-fortified formulas contain 12 mg of iron/quart as ferrous sulfate. Cereals and baked products may be fortified with reduced iron, sodium iron pyrophosphate, or ferric orthophosphate.

Ferrous sulfate is the most available of the iron salts, but it is seldom used to fortify food because of difficulties in manufacturing. The percentage of absorption of reduced iron will depend on the particle size, surface area, and porosity of the salts, which in turn determines the extent to which the particles dissolve in the acid of the stomach.[56]

Cook and associates found that when consumed in baked rolls, an average of 0.3% sodium iron pyrophosphate, 1.1% ferric orthophosphate, and 8.6% of reduced iron ground in particles 5 to 10 μg in size was absorbed. This was 5%, 33%, and 95% of the amount of ferrous sulfate absorbed. The absorption of ferrous sulfate in the rolls ranged from 8.7% to 4.0%, the percentage absorption decreasing as the supplement given at one time increased from 1 to 5 mg. Absorption was increased when the fortified rolls were consumed at a meal with meat and reduced when meat was not a part of the food intake.[57]

Interrelationships. The amino acids histidine and lysine increase absorption of nonheme iron. Calcium phosphate salts will reduce the percentage absorption of nonheme iron. Zinc, cadmium, and copper compete with iron for protein-binding sites in the intestinal mucosa. Their presence in large amounts can reduce the percentage absorbed.

Deficient intakes. Iron deficiency is the most common nutritional deficiency in North America. It occurs most frequently in 4- to 24-month-old infants, in adolescent males, and in females during their childbearing years. It may result from inadequate iron intakes, impaired absorption, a large hemorrhage, or repeated small hemorrhages. Microcytic hypochromic anemia is the final stage of deficiency, occurring only after iron stores are depleted and there has been a fall in plasma iron and transferrin saturation. Iron deficiency is diagnosed when transferrin saturations fall below 16%[51]; anemia is diagnosed when hemoglobin concentrations fall below 11.0 gm/100 ml and hematocrits fall below 33%.[58]

Symptoms of iron deficiency include anorexia, irritability, pallor, and listlessness. Pica has also been reported to be associated with iron deficiency.[59] Gastrointestinal anomalies include impaired absorption, blood loss, and loss of plasma protein into the gut. Naiman and associates described an enteropathy associated with chronic duodenitis and mucosal atrophy in iron-deficient children. After treatment with oral iron, most of the observed abnormalities returned to normal.[60] Some researchers believe anemic individuals have a lower resistance to infection.[61]

Decreased activity of iron-containing enzyme systems has been reported in iron-deficient animals and infants.[62] The effect of reduction of activity of the oxygen-containing enzymes has not been delineated. Suggestions have been made that behavioral changes occur, including reduced motivation to persist in intellectually challenging tasks. Shortened attention spans and diminished intellectual performance may also result.[63] Iron-deficient children often are disruptive, irritable, and restless in classrooms. Iron-deficient infants are listless and uninterested in their surroundings. When replenished with iron, they become more alert and responsive and demonstrate improved gross motor and fine motor coordination.[64]

Iron is accumulated in utero in proportion to body size. Premature and low birth weight infants have limited reserves at birth that are quickly depleted during rapid growth. Even with the advantage of full-term iron stores, the rapidly growing infant is at risk of iron deficiency. The Committee on Nutrition of the American Academy of Pediatrics has recommended that premature infants receive an iron supplement by 2 months of age, full-term infants by 4 months of age.[65] Iron-fortified formula is a reliable source of iron for young infants who are not breast fed. A convenient source of iron for infants at 4 to 6 months of age is iron-fortified dry cereal.

Enteric blood loss as a result of the consumption of homogenized but not evaporated milk has been identified as one of the causes of iron deficiency in infancy. The protein of fresh cow's milk causes bleeding into the gastrointestinal tracts of some infants.

This ceases approximately 48 hours after homogenized milk is replaced by evaporated milk, infant formulas, or soybean milk. The greater the quantity of milk ingested, the greater is the amount of blood lost.[66,67] Many clinicians suggest that fresh cow's milk be introduced only after 6 months and that intakes be limited to 0.75 liter/day.

Adolescents are at risk for iron deficiency because of the high demands for iron during the adolescent growth spurt and the onset of menses.

A desirable iron status can be compromised by a low-calorie diet, poor selection of foods, or any dietary extremes. Assuming that a well-chosen diet contains approximately 6 mg of iron/1000 kcal, adolescents dieting to lose weight will be receiving minimal iron intakes. In addition to this, the common practice of choosing foods such as yogurt and cottage cheese as primary protein foods in a reducing diet results in an even lower dietary iron intake.

Regular monitoring of iron status should ideally be provided for infants and adolescents, especially those having limited high-iron foods available or those practicing various dietary extremes or restrictions.

COPPER

Trace amounts of copper are distributed in all tissues throughout the body. The highest concentrations of the mineral are found in the liver, brain, and kidney.[68]

In the blood, copper occurs in erythrocytes as ceruloplasmin and is also loosely bound to both albumin and amino acids. Erythrocyte copper remains constant regardless of the copper status of the individual. Ceruloplasmin accounts for approximately 90% of total plasma copper.

Newborn infants have concentrations of storage copper in the liver that are five to ten times greater than those of adults.[69] The average plasma copper concentration at birth is 29 μg/100 ml as compared to 106 μg/100 ml in adults. Plasma concentrations gradually rise and reach levels that exceed those of normal adults by 8 months of age.[70]

Functions. Copper is essential for erythropoiesis. It facilitates the absorption and transport of iron. The copper-containing enzyme ceruloplasmin catalyzes oxidation of ferrous iron and promotes the transfer of iron from storage to transferrin. Utilization of iron for hemoglobin synthesis is therefore impaired in copper deficiency, and abnormal erythrocytes with short life spans are produced.

Cytochrome oxidase, another copper-containing enzyme, is essential to cellular metabolism and is important in the release of energy. Copper-containing enzymes function in the synthesis of phospholipids and in the conversion of tyrosine to melanin. They are also involved in the cross-linking of elastin and collagen, and as a result are necessary for the formation of normal bone matrices. Other copper-containing enzymes include monoamine oxidase, ascorbic acid oxidase, laccase, and uricase. In addition, copper activates a number of enzymes, including oxalacetic decarboxylase and lecithinase.

Recommended intakes. Large reserves of copper at birth make requirements for copper low during infancy. However, deficiencies of copper have been described in premature infants maintained on low-copper formulas.[71,72]

It has been estimated that full-term infants require at least 50 μg of copper/kg/day. Recommended intakes of copper for premature infants are 90 μg/kg/day.[73]

Estimates of requirements from balance studies of 3- to 6-year-old children indicate that the requirement of children weighing less than 20 kg averages 1.0 to 1.6 mg/day.[74] It is estimated that 6- to 10-year-old children require 1.3 mg/day or 60 μg/kg/day.[75,76] Suggested safe intakes increase from 0.5 to 0.7

mg/day in early infancy to 2.5 to 5.0 mg/day in adolescence.

Food sources. The copper content of plants reflects the copper content of the soil in which they were grown. The richest sources of copper are shellfish, organ meats, and dried legumes. Milk and dairy products are poor sources. It has been suggested that since human milk has a lower zinc:copper ratio than cow's milk a higher percentage of copper is absorbed from human milk than from cow's milk.[69] Cow's milk contains 0.015 mg/liter, whereas the copper content of human milk ranges from 0.15 to 1.05 mg/liter.[77] Copper in the water supply can contribute significantly to the daily intake, particularly when the water is soft and copper-lined pipes are used.

Interrelationships. Cadmium, mercury, zinc, and silver compete for binding sites in the intestine and reduce absorption. Phytate forms compounds with copper that cannot be absorbed. Sulfide reacts with copper to form nonabsorbable complexes.

Deficient intakes. The requirement for copper is so low and copper occurs in such a large number of foods that deficiencies are unlikely to occur in normal children who consume a variety of foods.

Cases of copper deficiency have been noted in children with generalized malnutrition secondary to malabsorption and prolonged diarrhea followed by rehabilitation with milk-base diets.[78-80]

Copper deficiency has been noted in premature infants who were fed a predominantly milk diet and in infants and adults maintained on copper-deficient hyperalimentation.* Symptoms include pallor, hypochromic anemia unresponsive to iron, neutropenia, retarded bone age, osteoporosis, and scurvy-like bone changes. Premature infants may also experience anorexia, failure to

thrive, skin lesions, and seborrheic dermititis. Central nervous system symptoms of hypotonia, lack of visual responses, and apneic episodes all improve with supplementation.

It has also been suggested that an inadequate dietary intake of copper played a role in the cause of vitamin D–resistant rickets in a 4½-month-old, full-term, small for date female.[83]

Excessive intakes. Copper toxicity is uncommon. Intakes in excess of 15 mg/day in adults result in symptoms of nausea, vomiting, abdominal cramps, diarrhea, headaches, and weakness. Copper poisoning has been reported in a 15-month-old male who consumed water from a copper-lined hot water system for 3 months. The infant had behavioral changes, diarrhea, and progressive marasmus.[84]

IODINE

Seventy to eighty percent of iodine in the human adult is concentrated in the thyroid gland, which synthesizes its only functional compounds, thyroxine and triiodothyronine. The remaining iodine in the body is distributed in the blood, skin, and other tissues.

Functions. The iodine-containing hormones thyroxine and triiodothyronine regulate the rate of oxidation reactions and, therefore, energy metabolism. The hormones also appear to influence synthesis of cholesterol. Hypothyroidism results in hypercholesterolemia, and hyperthyroidism results in hypocholesterolemia. The conversion of carotene to vitamin A, the synthesis of protein, and the intestinal absorption of carbohydrate are all more efficient when there are normal levels of thyroid hormones.

Iodine in the saliva has been hypothesized to inhibit the formation of dental caries.

Recommended intakes. The Food and Nutrition Board of the National Research Council recommends an intake of 40 μg of iodine/

---

*See references 71, 72, 81, and 82.

day during the first 6 months of life, gradually increasing to 150 μg/day in adolescence (Table 4-1). The breast-fed infant will receive 10 to 20 μg of iodine/100 kcal from an adequately fed lactating mother. It has been suggested that requirements for 8- to 16-year-old children may not be much greater than 56 μg/day.[85] Average intakes of iodine in the United States are five to ten times the recommended amounts. However, wide variations in iodine intakes may be experienced by individuals, depending on sources of food and geographic locations.

Food sources. Iodized salt, bread made with iodate as a dough conditioner, milk, and seafood are excellent sources of dietary iodine. The fact that the iodine content of food is determined by the soil in which it is grown is no longer of significance in the etiology of iodine deficiency. Food consumed in one area is often transported from another. The iodine content of milk and dairy products depends on whether the cattle have been given iodine-supplemented feed or iodized salt blocks. Milk iodine may be as high as 450 μg/liter.

The amount of iodine absorbed from environments polluted by the combustion of fossil fuels and organic matter can be significant. Many therapeutic drugs also contain large amounts of iodine.[86]

Goitrogens. Certain foods and drugs that interfere with the synthesis of thyroxine are known as goitrogens. Cabbage, turnips, and other members of the cabbage family are known goitrogens. The quantity of goitrogenic foods usually consumed is unlikely to contribute to manifestations of goiter.

Deficient intakes. The thyroid must trap 70 to 100 μg of iodine daily if requirements for secretion are to be met. If plasma levels of iodide are low the thyroid clearance rate is increased. This is usually associated with increases in gland size, goiter.

Children born to mothers who have very limited intakes of iodine or who have goiter may have hypothyroidism at birth, resulting in cretinism. The syndrome is not identifiable at birth but soon becomes apparent when normal growth and development fail to occur. Symptoms include difficulties in sucking, failure to thrive, constipation, thick skin, protruding abdomen, large tongue, and mental retardation. If diagnosis is made and treatment begun soon after birth, many of the symptoms of cretinism can be prevented.

Excessive intakes. If the iodide in the plasma is suddenly increased by increased dietary intakes, the fraction that enters the gland initially remains constant. Increased amounts enter the gland and are incorporated into hormones and secreted. The increased levels of hormone decrease the secretion of thyroid-stimulating hormone and uptake of iodine. In addition, iodine binding in the thyroid gland is blocked. Usually the block in binding is a transient phenomenon, and adaptation occurs; thyroid iodine transport diminishes. With this decrease in iodide transport, intracellular iodine in the thyroid falls and the block of iodine binding is relieved. Occasionally, adaptations fail to occur and goiter and hypothyroidism occur.[87]

Evidence from studies of 9- to 16-year-old children in areas in the United States with an incidence of 6.8% goiter have indicated adequate and excessive intakes of iodine. Although the etiology of this goiter remains to be defined, it has been suggested that high intakes of iodine may be the cause.[88,89]

ZINC

Zinc is distributed throughout all cells and tissues. The highest concentrations are in the male sex gland, bone, and hair. Tissue concentrations change only slightly throughout growth. The fetus contains approximately 20 mg/kg, whereas the adult has 30 mg/kg of fat-free tissue.[90] In the blood, zinc appears in erythrocytes, leukocytes, and plasma. Erythrocyte zinc accounts for 75% to 85% of whole blood zinc. Twelve to twenty-two percent is in the plasma, and 3% is in the leukocytes. In the body, zinc is in a constant state of movement. The most rapid accumulation and turnover occur in the liver, spleen, kidney, pituitary gland, and testes. The turnover rate is slow in the brain, muscles, and erythrocytes, especially in the bones. Zinc leaves the hair only when hair is shed.

Functions. Zinc functions as an essential constituent of over 40 mettalloenzymes, including pancreatic carboxypeptidase, which hydrolyzes the carboxyl terminal of proteins and peptides in the digestive tract, and carbonic anhydrase, which catalyzes the interconversion of carbonic acid and carbon dioxide and water. It is a constituent of the enzymes alkaline phosphatase, which functions in mineralization of the bone, and alcohol dehydrogenase, which oxidizes methanol and ethylene glycol and serves as a mechanism of detoxification of these compounds. It is also a cofactor in a sizable number of other enzyme systems. For example, dipeptidases and tripeptidases are zinc dependent.

Zinc is firmly bound to RNA and plays a role in the synthesis of DNA and the synthesis of protein from amino acids. Because it plays a role in the incorporation of cystine into proline and glycine and proline into collagen, it is important in wound healing. It also functions in the mobilization of vitamin A from liver stores.

Recommended intakes. Recommendations for intake have been made from studies of zinc intakes of apparently well-nourished individuals and from studies of zinc balance.

The infant is born without zinc stores and rapidly becomes dependent on an adequate supply of biologically available zinc. Normal breast-fed infants have been noted to be in negative balance at age 1 week. Plasma concentrations of 6-month-old infants are similar to those of well-nourished adults, whereas those of formula-fed infants without zinc supplementation are significantly less.[91] Variations in plasma zinc concentrations during growth reflect the continual utilization and depletion of body stores of zinc. Declines occur during periods of most rapid growth. The steepest decline appears to occur at age 10 to 11 years in the female and at age 12 to 13 years in the male.[92] Breast-fed infants receive 0.7 to 5 mg/day, approximately 0.2 to 1.2 mg/kg.[93] Intakes of children 1 to 3 years of age have been estimated to average 5 mg/day, those of children 3 to 5 years of age 5 to 7 mg/day, and those of adolescents 13 mg/day.[94] Balance studies of Engel, Miller, and Price suggest that 6 mg/day is adequate for preadolescent children.[95] Studies by Tribble and Scoular indicate that 12 mg/day is adequate for college students.[96]

The Food and Nutrition Board of the National Academy of Sciences has based its recommended intake on the above studies (Table 4-1).

Food sources. Seafoods and meats are rich sources of available zinc. Cereals and legumes also contain significant amounts.[97] The bioavailability ranges from 20% to 30%. Estimates of zinc in human milk and cow's milk range from 3 to 5 mg/liter.[98] Picciano and Guthrie found ranges of 0.14 to 3.95 mg/liter in milk of 50 lactating women.[99] Colostrum contains 20 mg/liter, three to five times as much as later milk. Levels of zinc in human milk decline after 2 months of lactation and may fall below 1 mg/liter. Infant formulas are supplemented and contain 3 to 4 mg of zinc/liter. Animal studies suggest a bioavailability of 59.2% of zinc in human milk, 43% to 53.9% of zinc in cow's milk, and 26.8% to 39.5% of zinc in infant formula.[100]

Table 4-7 shows the zinc content of representative foods consumed by infants and children.

Interrelationships. Calcium competes with zinc for absorption. Phytates from in-

Table 4-7. Selected food sources of zinc

Food	Household measure	Zinc (mg)
Cow's milk	4 oz	0.5
Ground beef, cooked	2 oz	2.5
Chicken drumstick	1	1.4
Liver, beef, cooked	2 oz	2.9
Liverwurst	1 oz	0.8
Frankfurter	1	0.9
Egg	1 medium	0.5
Oatmeal, cooked	½ cup	0.6
Bread, white	1 slice	0.2
Bread, whole wheat	1 slice	0.5
Green beans, canned	¼ cup	0.2
Spinach	½ cup	0.6
Banana	½ medium	0.2
Orange	1 medium	0.3

Adapted from Murphy, E. W., Willis, B. W., and Watt, B. K.: Provisional tables on the zinc content of food, J. Am. Diet Assoc. **66:**345, 1975.

soluble complexes with zinc and interfere with its absorption.

Deficient intakes. Deficiency of zinc may result from inadequate dietary intake, malabsorption, or ingestion of chelating substances (e.g., phytate) which interfere with absorption. Deficiency results in growth retardation, abnormalities of the sense of taste and smell, roughness of skin, anorexia and disinterest in food, sexual immaturity, and impaired wound healing.[99,100] The absorption of dietary folate may be impaired in zinc deficiency.[101] Severe zinc deficiency was first described in males 18 to 20 years of age in Iran and 16 to 19 years of age in Egypt.[102,103] The men had symptoms of iron deficiency anemia, hepatosplenomegaly, dwarfism, and hypogonadism. Diets of the affected individuals included a high percentage of unleavened bread, which contributed a large amount of phytate and fiber. Anemia responded to iron supplements. Treatment with zinc and an adequate diet resulted in both longitudinal growth and sexual

maturation. The syndrome has since been reported in females as well as in males.[104]

Hambidge and associates reported low concentrations of zinc in hair in 10 of 132 children over 4 years of age from middle- and upper-income families that were studied in Denver, Colorado. The children had histories of poor appetite, consumed small amounts of meat, and had diminished taste acuity. Nine of the ten children had heights that plotted at or below the tenth percentile.[105] Increased appetite, taste acuity, and growth occurred after zinc supplementation.

It appears that many preschool and school-age children from low- and middle-income families may be ingesting inadequate amounts of zinc. Studies in Denver of Headstart children 3.5 to 6 years of age whose heights were less than the third percentile revealed that 40% had low concentrations of hair zinc and 69% had low plasma and/or hair zinc concentrations.[106] Supplements of zinc sulfate that provided 0.2 mg zinc/kg given to five schoolchildren with hypogeusia and low levels of zinc in hair resulted in normalization of taste perception and substantial increases in hair zinc content.[105]

Excessive intakes. Zinc is relatively nontoxic.[76] It has been hypothesized that high zinc:copper ratios in the diet may predispose individuals to hypercholesterolemia.[107] However, acute zinc intoxication has been noted in a 16-year-old male following ingestion of 2 gm of metallic zinc. Symptoms included drowsiness, lethargy, lightheadedness, difficulty in writing, and staggering of gait.[108] Food poisoning after ingestion of food contaminated with zinc resulted in symptoms of nausea, vomiting, diarrhea, and fever.[109]

FLUORIDE

Fluoride in the body is concentrated in the bones and teeth. It is present in soft tissue and body fluids only in minute amounts. The concentration in bones increases linearly with increased intakes.

The role of fluoride as an essential trace mineral lies in its ability to reduce the incidence of dental caries. It has not been proved essential to survival. Female mice consuming low fluoride intakes have exhibited progressive decreases in fertility.[110] Increased rates of growth have been observed in rats fed low-fluoride diets when the mineral was added to their dietary intakes.[111]

Epidemiologic studies have repeatedly proved that there is a close relation between tooth decay and the amount of fluoride ingested during tooth development.[112,113] When the fluoride content of community drinking water has been adjusted to a level of 1 ppm (1 mg/liter), the incidence of dental caries has been reduced 40% to 60%.[114] Although the effect is especially important during tooth development, fluoride has been shown also to be beneficial to adults.[115]

Mottling and fluorosis of tooth enamel. When the fluoride concentrations of drinking water increase above 2 ppm, mottling (a brown stain on the teeth) during tooth development occurs. The incidence and severity of the manifestation increase as the fluoride content of the water increases. At levels of 8 ppm almost all individuals who have consumed water during tooth development have extensively mottled teeth.[114] In areas with a high natural concentration of fluoride, it has become a practice to dilute fluoride to no more than 1.2 ppm. In warmer climates and during periods of elevated environmental temperatures when the intakes of water are increased, suggested levels for fluoridation of water are 0.6 to 0.7 ppm.[116]

Fluorosis, usually manifested as opaque spots or streaks on the enamel of permanent teeth, has been noted in 14% of children who received fluoride supplements in addition to that in formula and food.[117] This is twice as high the incidence reported for children who live in communities with optimally fluoridated water. To prevent this fluorosis, infant

Table 4-8. Supplemental fluorine dosage schedule (mg/day*)

Age	Concentration of fluoride in drinking water (ppm)		
	<.3	0.3-0.7	>0.7
2 weeks to 2 years	0.25	0	0
2 to 3 years	0.50	0.25	0
3 to 16 years	1.00	0.50	0

From Committee on Nutrition: Fluoride supplementation: revised dosage schedule, Pediatrics **63**:150, copyright American Academy of Pediatrics 1979.
*2.2 mg of sodium fluoride contains 1 mg of fluoride.

formulas are no longer manufactured with fluoridated water.

Recommended intakes. The Committee on Nutrition of the American Academy of Pediatrics recommends that supplemental fluoride dosages be adjusted to the fluoride content of the water supply[118] (Table 4-8). In communities with less than 0.3 ppm of fluoride in the water supply supplements of 0.25 mg of fluoride/day are recommended from 2 weeks to 2 years of age, 0.5 mg/day between 2 and 3 years of age, and 1.0 mg/day after 3 years of age. It is suggested that children whose drinking water contains between 0.3 and 0.7 mg of fluoride ppm receive 0.25 mg between 2 and 3 years of age and 0.50 mg between 3 and 16 years of age.

Food sources. All foods and water contain very small amounts of fluoride. Seafood and tea are exceptions and contain greater amounts. Food produced and prepared in fluoridated areas reflect the fluorine content of the water.

Cow's milk contains 0.03 to 0.1 μg of fluoride/liter; human milk contains less than 0.05 mg/liter.[119]

MANGANESE

The normal, healthy adult body contains one-fifth as much manganese as copper and one–one hundredth as much manganese as zinc.[120] It is distributed throughout the body tissues and fluids. The highest concentrations of manganese are found in the bones, liver, kidney, pancreas, and pituitary gland. In contrast to other minerals, the relative concentrations of manganese in tissues are maintained throughout life.

Functions. Manganese functions as an activator of many enzymes, including polysaccharide polymerase and galactotransferase, which catalyze polysaccharide synthesis necessary for normal skeletal and connective tissue development. Manganese appears to play a role in initiating protein synthesis by stimulating RNA polymerase and DNA polymerase activities. It plays a role in the synthesis of cholesterol and fatty acids. The only proved manganese-containing enzyme is pyruvate carboxylase, which plays a role in gluconeogenesis.

Recommended intakes. Safe and adequate intakes of manganese increase from 0.5 to 0.7 mg in infancy to 2.5 to 5.0 mg in adolescence. Daily intakes range from 3 to 7 mg.

Food sources. Nuts, whole wheat cereals, and grains are the foods richest in manganese. Tea and cloves are exceptionally rich. Meat, fish, and dairy products have low concentrations of the mineral.

Human milk is relatively deficient in manganese. During the first weeks of life, intakes of manganese are low and infants are in negative balance.[121,122] As semisolid foods are added to diets, intakes of manganese gradually increase to age 2 years.[121]

Deficient intakes. In 1972 an adult male volunteer in a metabolic unit manifested the first deficiency described in humans, when by error manganese was not added to the diet mixture designed for a study of vitamin K. Symptoms included weight loss, changes in beard and hair color, slow growth of hair, occasional nausea and vomiting, and hypocholesterolemia. No symptoms of deficiency have been reported in infants or children.[123]

Symptoms of deficiency in animals include skeletal abnormalities, suboptimal growth, ataxia of the newborn infant, and decreased testicular and ovarian functions.

Excessive intakes. Manganese is one of the least toxic of the trace elements. Poisoning occurs in miners working manganese ores only after long continued inhalation of the mineral. No cases of manganese toxicity have been reported in infants or children.

MOLYBDENUM

Molybdenum is a constituent of the iron-containing enzymes xanthine oxidase and aldehyde oxidase. Xanthine oxidase catalyzes the oxidation of purines and aldehydes and may play a role in the release of iron from ferritin. It is required for the formation of uric acid from purines. It has been suggested but not proven that molybdenum plays a role in the prevention of dental caries.

Recommended intakes. Safe intakes increase from 0.03 to 0.06 mg/day in infancy to 0.15 to 0.5 mg/day in adolescence.

Interrelationships. Molybdenum interacts with sulfate and copper. Increases in dietary sulfate and copper increase urinary excretion of molybdenum and cause its depletion in blood and tissues. Conversely, excessive intakes of molybdenum result in symptoms of copper deficiency.

Excessive intakes. Excessive intakes of molybdenum alter the activity of alkaline phosphatase, resulting in bone abnormalities. At high levels of intake toxicity occurs, and diarrhea, depressed growth, and anemia result.

COBALT

Cobalt is essential only because it is a constituent of cyanocobalamin, vitamin B_{12}. Requirements for cobalt are met when vitamin B_{12} is consumed and absorbed in sufficient quantities. Deficiencies of cobalt are associated only with deficiencies of vitamin B_{12}, as described in Chapter 3.

SELENIUM

All tissues contain selenium, the highest concentrations being found in the kidneys, hair, and liver. Selenium is a known constituent of one mammalian and avian enzyme, glutathione peroxidase, and two bacterial enzymes, formate dehydrogenase and glycine reductase.[124] Glutathione peroxidase functions as an antioxidant at the cellular level. Therefore, the action of selenium is closely linked to that of vitamin E and selenium has a sparing effect on vitamin E requirements. Other selenium-containing proteins have been identified, but their functions are yet to be defined.

Although selenium has been proven to be an essential trace mineral in animals, neither deficiency nor toxicity has been reported in humans. Decreased blood levels of selenium have been reported in malnourished children as compared to those rehabilitated from malnutrition.[125,126] Significant weight gains were noted in three infants with protein-energy malnutrition when their diets were supplemented with sodium selenite in milk.[127]

Epidemiologic studies in Oregon and Wyoming have suggested that selenium may increase the incidence of dental caries.[128,129] Studies of experimental animals have shown that selenium consumed during the period of tooth development increases the incidence of dental caries in proportion to the quantity of selenium in the diet.[130,131]

Epidemiologic studies have also caused speculation that suboptimal selenium intakes may contribute to certain forms of cancer and cardiovascular disease.[132,133]

The selenium content of food depends on the soil in which the food was grown. Human milk contains an average of 0.02 ppm.[134] The level of selenium in cow's milk reflects the selenium content of the soil in the area in which it was produced and in which the feed consumed by the animals was grown. In localities where the soil content is low, the selenium content of milk is below 0.02 ppm.

Recommended intakes. A safe intake of selenium is estimated to be 0.01 to 0.04 mg/day in early infancy, 0.15 to 0.5 mg/day in adolescence.

CHROMIUM

Extremely small amounts of chromium are distributed throughout the body. The skin, muscle, and fat contain the greatest amounts. Tissue concentrations in all organs other than the lungs decrease with age. Blood and plasma chromium concentrations reflect recent dietary intake and metabolic response to glucose loads; however, they are not meaningful indicators of chromium nutritional status.

Although the specific metabolic functions of chromium are yet to be defined, trivalent chromium has been proved to be an essential nutrient for normal glucose metabolism. It is an essential constituent of glucose tolerance factor, a low molecular weight, water-soluble compound that facilitates the initial tissue insulin interactions. Humans are thought to have a limited ability to synthesize the compound and are probably dependent on an exogenous source.[135]

Recommended intakes. The requirement for chromium is unknown. The average chromium intake of adults in the United States is calculated to be 50 to 80 μg/day. Individual variations range from 5 to 115 μg/day. It has been suggested that 10 to 30 μg of glucose tolerance factor chromium/day will meet daily requirements.[136] Adequate intakes of chromium are estimated to increase from 0.01 to 0.04 mg/day in infancy to 0.05 to 0.2 mg/day in adolescence.

Food sources. Not all chromium in food occurs in the glucose tolerance factor. The highest concentrations of biologically available chromium have been found in brewer's yeast, black pepper, animal meat, and whole grains.

Deficient intakes. The first symptom of chromium deficiency is impaired glucose tolerance. Experimental animals subjected to chromium deficiency experience impaired growth, hypercholesterolemia, glycosuria, and corneal opacities.

Improved rates of glucose removal have been reported in some children with protein-energy malnutrition who have been given chromium supplements during rehabilitation.[137,138] Increased rates of weight gain have also been reported in malnourished children receiving chromium supplements.[139]

It has been suggested also that chromium deficiency may play a role in the etiology of hypercholesterolemia and atherosclerosis.[140]

REFERENCES
Water and electrolytes

1. Hey, E. N., and Katz, G.: Evaporative water loss in the newborn baby, J. Physiol. **200:**605, 1969.
2. Fomon, S. J.: Infant nutrition, ed. 2, Philadelphia, 1974, W. B. Saunders Co.
3. Pratt, E. L., Bienvenu, B., and Whyte, M. M.: Concentration of urine by young infants, Pediatrics 1:181, 1948.
4. Nash, M. A., and Edelmann, C. M.: The developing kidney, Nephron 11:71, 1973.
5. Edelmann, C. M., Barnett, H. L., and Troupkou, V.: Renal concentrating mechanism in newborn infants. Effects of dietary protein and water content, role of urea and responsiveness to antidiuretic hormone, J. Clin. Invest. 39:1062, 1960.
6. Polacek, E., and others: The osmotic concentrating ability in healthy infants and children, Arch. Dis. Child. 40:291, 1965.
7. Ziegler, E. E., and Fomon, S. J.: Fluid intake, renal solute load, and water balance in infancy, J. Pediatr. 78:561, 1971.
8. Food and Nutrition Board: Recommended dietary allowances, rev. ed. 9, Washington, D.C., 1980, National Academy of Sciences, National Research Council.
9. Stolley, H., and Schlage, C.: Water balance and

water requirement of preschool children, Nutr. Metab. **21**(suppl. 1):15-17, 1977.

Calcium, phosphorus, and magnesium

10. Arnaud, S. B., and others: Serum parathyroid hormone and blood minerals: interrelationships in normal children, Pediatr. Res. 7:485, 1973.
11. Committee on Nutrition, American Academy of Pediatrics: Calcium requirements in infancy and childhood, Pediatrics 62:826, 1978.
12. Shaw, J. C. L.: Evidence for defective skeletal mineralization in low birth weight infants: the absorption of calcium and fat, Pediatrics 57:16, 1976.
13. Fourman, P., and Royer, P., in collaboration with Levell, M. J., and Morgan, D. B.: Calcium metabolism and the bone, ed. 2, Oxford, 1968, Blackwell Scientific Publications Ltd.
14. Garn, S. M.: The earlier gain and the later loss of cortical bone in nutritional perspective, Springfield, Ill., 1970, Charles C Thomas, Publisher, p. 87.
15. Christiansen, C., Rödbro, P., Neilsen, C. T.: Bone mineral content and estimated total body calcium in normal children and adolescents, Scand. J. Clin. Lab. Invest. 35:507, 1975.
16. Trotter, M., and Hixon, B. B.: Sequential changes in weight, density, and percentage ash weight of human skeleton from the early fetal period through old age, Anat. Rec. 179:1, 1974.
17. Leitch, I., and Aitken, F. C.: The estimation of calcium requirements: a re-examination, Nutr. Abstr. Rev. 29:393, 1959.
18. Walker, A. R. P.: The human requirement of calcium: should low intakes be supplemented? Am. J. Clin. Nutr. 25:518, 1972.
19. Wills, M. R.: Intestinal absorption of calcium, Lancet 1:820, 1973.
20. Bell, R. R., and others: Physiological responses of human adults to foods containing phosphate additives, J. Nutr. 107:42, 1977.
21. Anand, C. R., and Linkswiler, H. M.: Effect of protein intake on calcium balance of young men given 500 mg. calcium daily, J. Nutr. 104:695, 1974.
22. Chu, J. Y., Margen, S., and Costa, F. M.: Studies in calcium metabolism. II. Effects of low calcium and variable protein intakes on human calcium metabolism, Am. J. Clin. Nutr. 28:1028, 1975.
23. Spencer, H., and others: Effect of a high protein (meat) intake on calcium metabolism in man, Am. J. Clin. Nutr. 31:2167, 1978.
24. Hanna, F. M., Navarrete, D. A., and Hsu, F. A.: Calcium-fatty acid absorption in term infants

fed human milk and prepared formula simulating human milk, Pediatrics **45**:216, 1970.

25. Kooh, S. W., and others: Rickets due to calcium deficiency, N. Engl. J. Med. **297**:1264, 1977.

26. Rowe, J. C., and others: Nutritional hypophosphatemic rickets in a premature infant fed breast milk, N. Engl. J. Med. **300**:293, 1979.

27. Lapatsanis, P., and others: Two types of nutritional rickets in infants, Am. J. Clin. Nutr. **29**:1222, 1976.

28. Aykroyd, W. R., and Krishnan, B. G.: Effect of calcium lactate on children in a nursery school, Lancet **2**:153, 1938.

29. Bansal, P., and others: Effect of calcium supplementation on children in a rural community, Indian J. Med. Res. **52**:219, 1964.

30. David, L., and Anast, C. S.: Calcium metabolism in newborn infants, the interrelationship of parathyroid function and calcium, magnesium, and phosphorus metabolism in normal, "sick," and hypocalcemic newborns, J. Clin. Invest. **54**:287, 1974.

31. Tsang, R. C., and Oh, W.: Neonatal hypocalcemia in low birth weight infants, Pediatrics **45**:773, 1970.

32. Tsang, R. C., and others: Hypocalcemia in infants of diabetic mothers, J. Pediatr. **80**:384, 1972.

33. Snodgrass, G. J. A. I., and others: Interrelations of plasma calcium, inorganic phosphate, magnesium, and protein over the first week of life, Arch. Dis. Child. **48**:279, 1973.

34. Barltrop, D., and Oppe, T. E.: Dietary factors in neonatal calcium homeostasis, Lancet **2**:1333, 1970.

35. Oppe, T. E., and Redstone, O.: Calcium and phosphorus levels in healthy newborn infants given various types of milk, Lancet **1**:1045, 1968.

36. Tsang, R. C., and others: Possible pathogenic factors in neonatal hypocalcemia of prematurity, J. Pediatr. **82**:423, 1973.

37. Schedewh, H. K., and others: Parathormone and perinatal calcium homeostasis, Pediatr. Res. **13**: 1, 1979.

38. Salle, B. L.: Prevention of early neonatal hypocalcemia in low birth weight infants with continuous calcium infusion: effect on serum calcium, phosphorus, magnesium, and circulating immunoreactive parathyroid hormone and calcitonin, Pediatr. Res. **11**:1180, 1977.

39. Moya, M., and Domeneax, E.: Calcium intake in the first five days of life in the low birth weight infant, Arch. Dis. Child. **53**:784, 1978.

40. Gittleman, I. F., and Pincus, J. B.: Influence of diet on the occurrence of hyperphosphatemia and hypocalcemia in the newborn infant, Pediatrics **8**:778, 1951.

41. Gardner, L.: Tetany and parathyroid hyperplasia in the newborn infant: influences of dietary phosphate load, Pediatrics **9**:534, 1952.

42. Pierson, J. D., and Crawford, J. D.: Dietary dependent neonatal hypocalcemia, Am. J. Dis. Child. **123**:472, 1972.

43. Wacker, W. E. C., and Parish, A. F.: Magnesium metabolism, N. Engl. J. Med. **278**:658, 712, 722, 1968.

44. Harris, I., and Wilkinson, A. W.: Magnesium depletion in children, Lancet **2**:735, 1971.

45. Fomon, S. J.: Infant nutrition, Philadelphia, 1974, W. B. Saunders Co.

46. Laupus, W. E.: Nutrition and nutritional disorders. In Vaughan, V. C., McKay, R. J., and Nelson, W. E.: Nelson's textbook of pediatrics, ed. 10, Philadelphia, 1975, W. B. Saunders Co.

47. Tsang, R. C.: Neonatal magnesium disturbances, Am. J. Dis. Child. **124**:282, 1972.

48. Caddell, J. L.: Magnesium in nutrition of the child, Clin. Pediatr. **13**:263, 1974.

49. Clinical signs of magnesium deficiency, Nutr. Rev. **37**:6, 1979.

Iron

50. Widdowson, E. M., and Spray, C. M.: Chemical development in utero, Arch. Dis. Child. **26**:205, 1951.

51. Smith, N. J., and Rios, E.: Iron metabolism and iron deficiency. In Schulman, I., editor: Advances in pediatrics, Chicago, 1974, Year Book Medical Publishers, Inc.

52. Hallberg, L., and others: Menstrual blood loss— a population study, Acta Obstet. Gynecol. Scand. **45**:320, 1966.

53. Monsen, E. R., and others: Estimation of available dietary iron, Am. J. Clin. Nutr. **31**:134, 1978.

54. McMillan, J. A.: Iron absorption from human milk, simulated human milk, and proprietary formulas, Pediatrics **60**:896, 1977.

55. Saarinen, U. M.: Iron absorption from breast milk, cow's milk, and iron-supplemented formula: an opportunistic use of changes in total body iron determined by hemoglobin, ferritin, and body weight in 132 infants, Pediatr. Res. **13**:143, 1979.

56. Waddell, J.: The bioavailability of iron sources and their utilization in food enrichment, Fed. Proc. **33**:1779, 1974.

57. Cook, J. D., and others: Absorption of fortification iron in bread, Am. J. Clin. Nutr. **26**:861, 1973.

58. World Health Organization: Nutritional anaemias, Report of a World Health Organization Scientific

Group Technical Report Series No. 405, Geneva, 1968, World Health Organization.

59. Crosby, W. H.: Food pica and iron deficiency, Arch. Intern. Med. **127**:960, 1971.

60. Naiman, J. L., and others: The gastrointestinal effects of iron-deficiency anemia, Pediatrics **33**:83, 1964.

61. Strauss, R. G.: Iron deficiency infections and immune function: a reassessment, Am. J. Clin. Nutr. **31**:660, 1978.

62. Dallman, P. R., Sunshine, P., and Leonard, Y.: Intestinal cytochrome response with repair of iron deficiency, Pediatrics **39**:863, 1967.

63. Pollitt, E., and Leibel, R. L.: Iron deficiency and behavior, J. Pediatr. **88**:372, 1976.

64. Oski, F. A., and Honig, A. S.: The effects of therapy on the developmental scores of iron-deficient infants, J. Pediatr. **92**:21, 1978.

65. Committee on Nutrition, American Academy of Pediatrics: Iron supplementation for infants, Pediatrics **58**:765, 1976.

66. Wilson, J. F., Heiner, D. C., and Lahey, M. E.: Milk-induced gastrointestinal bleeding in infants with hypochromic microcytic anemia, J.A.M.A. **189**:568, 1964.

67. Woodruff, C. W., Wright, S. W., and Wright, R. P.: The role of fresh cow's milk in iron deficiency. II. Comparison of fresh cow's milk with a prepared formula, Am. J. Dis. Child. **124**:26, 1972.

Copper

68. Evans, G. W.: Copper homeostasis in the mammalian system, Physiol. Rev. **53**:535, 1973.

69. Widdowson, E. M.: Trace elements in foetal and early postnatal development, Proc. Nutr. Soc. **33**:275, 1974.

70. Henkin, R. I., and others: Changes in total, non-diffusible, and diffusible plasma zinc and copper during infancy, J. Pediatr. **82**:831, 1973.

71. Al-Rashid, R. A., and Spangler, J.: Neonatal copper deficiency, N. Engl. J. Med. **285**:841, 1971.

72. Ashkenazi, A., and others: The syndrome of neonatal copper deficiency, Pediatrics **52**:525, 1973.

73. Hambidge, K. M.: Trace elements in pediatric nutrition, Adv. Pediatr. **24**:191, 1977.

74. Scoular, F. I.: A quantitative study by means of spectographic analysis of copper in nutrition, J. Nutr. **16**:437, 1938.

75. Engel, R. W., Price, N. O., and Miller, R. F.: Copper, manganese, cobalt and molybdenum balance in preadolescent girls, J. Nutr. **92**:197, 1967.

76. Price, N. O., Bunce, G. E., and Engel, R. W.: Copper, magnesium and zinc balance in preadolescent girls, Am. J. Clin. Nutr. **23**:258, 1970.

77. Picciano, M. F., and Guthrie, H. A.: Copper, iron, and zinc contents of mature human milk, Am. J. Clin. Nutr. **29**:243, 1976.

78. Graham, G. G., and Cordano, A.: Copper depletion and deficiency in the malnourished infant, Johns Hopkins Med. J. **124**:139, 1969.

79. Cordano, A., Placko, R. P., and Graham, G. G.: Hypocupremia and neutropenia in copper deficiency, Blood **28**:280, 1966.

80. Cordano, A., and Graham, G. G.: Copper deficiency complicating severe intestinal malabsorption, Pediatrics **38**:596, 1966.

81. Karpel, J. T., and Peden, V. H.: Copper deficiency in long term parental nutrition, J. Pediatr. **80**:32, 1972.

82. Dunlap, W. M., James, G. W., III, and Hume, D. M.: Anemia and neutropenia caused by copper deficiency, Ann. Intern. Med. **80**:470, 1974.

83. Sann, L., and others: Copper deficiency and hypocalcemic rickets in a small-for-dates infant, Acta Paediatr. Scand. **67**:303, 1978.

84. Salmon, M. A., and Wright, T.: Chronic copper poisoning presenting as pink disease, Arch. Dis. Child. **46**:108, 1971.

Iodine

85. Fomon, S. J.: Infant nutrition, Philadelphia, 1974, W. B. Saunders Co.

86. Cullen, R. W., and Oace, S. M.: Iodine: current status, J. Nutr. Ed. **8**:101, 1976.

87. DeGroot, L. J., and Stanbury, J. B.: The thyroid gland and its diseases, New York, 1975, John Wiley and Sons, Inc.

88. Trowbridge, F. L., and others: Findings relating to goiter and iodine in the ten-state nutrition survey, Am. J. Clin. Nutr. **28**:712, 1975.

89. Trowbridge, F. L., and others: Iodine and goiter in children, Pediatrics **56**:82, 1975.

Zinc

90. Widdowson, E. M.: Chemical analysis of the body. In Brozek, J., editor: Human body composition, Oxford, 1965, Pergamon Press Ltd., p. 31.

91. Hambidge, K. M., and others: Plasma zinc concentrations of breast fed infants, J. Pediatr. **94**:607, 1979.

92. Butrimovitz, G. P., and Purdy, W. C.: Zinc nutrition and growth in children, Am. J. Clin. Nutr. **31**:1409, 1978.

93. Schlage, C., and Wortberg, B.: Zinc in the diet of healthy preschool and school children, Acta Paediatr. Scand. **61**:421, 1972.

94. Cavell, P. A., and Widdowson, E. M.: Intakes and

excretions of iron, copper and zinc in the neonatal period, Arch. Dis. Child. **39**:496, 1964.

95. Engel, R. W., Miller, R. F., and Price, N. O.: Metabolic patterns of preadolescent children. XIII. Zinc balance. In Prasad, A. S., editor: Zinc metabolism, Springfield, Ill., 1966, Charles C Thomas, Publisher, p. 326.

96. Tribble, H. M., and Scoular, F. I.: Zinc metabolism of young college women on self-selected diets, J. Nutr. **52**:209, 1954.

97. Underwood, E. J.: Trace elements in human and animal nutrition, New York, 1977, Academic Press, Inc.

98. Johnson, P. E., and Evans, G. W.: Relative zinc availability in human milk, infant formulas, and cow's milk, Am. J. Clin. Nutr. **31**:416, 1978.

99. Picciano, M. F., and Guthrie, H. A.: Copper, iron, and zinc contents of mature human milk, Am. J. Clin. Nutr. **29**:242, 1976.

100. Burch, R. E., Hahn, H. K., and Sullivan, J. F.: Newer aspects of the roles of zinc, manganese, and copper in human nutrition, Clin. Chem. **21**:501, 1975.

101. Tamura, T., and others: Absorption of mono and polyglutamyl folates in zinc depleted man, Am. J. Clin. Nutr. **31**:1984, 1978.

102. Prasad, A. S., Halsted, J. A., and Nadimi, M.: Syndrome of iron deficiency, dwarfism, and geophagia, Am. J. Med. **31**:532, 1961.

103. Prasad, A. S., and others: Biochemical studies on dwarfism, hypogonadism and anemia, Arch. Intern. Med. **111**:407, 1963.

104. Halsted, J. A., and others: Zinc deficiency in man, Am. J. Med. **53**:277, 1972.

105. Hambidge, K. M., and others: Low levels of zinc in hair, anorexia, poor growth, and hypogeusia in children, Pediatr. Res. **6**:868, 1972.

106. Hambidge, K. M., and others: Zinc nutrition of preschool children in the Denver Headstart Program, Am. J. Clin. Nutr. **29**:734, 1976.

107. Klevay, L. M.: Coronary heart disease: the zinc/copper hypothesis, Am. J. Clin. Nutr. **28**:764, 1975.

108. Murphy, J. V.: Intoxication following ingestion of elemental zinc, J.A.M.A. **212**:2119, 1970.

109. Hsu, J. M.: Current knowledge of zinc, copper, and chromium in aging. World Rev. Nutr. Diet. **33**:42, 1979.

Fluoride

110. Messer, H. H., Armstrong, W. D., and Singer, L.: Fertility impairment in mice on a low fluoride intake, Science **177**:893, 1972.

111. Schwarz, K., and Milne, D. B.: Fluorine requirement for growth in the rat, Bioinorg. Chem. **1**:331, 1972.

112. Dean, H. T.: Endemic fluorosis and its relation to dental caries, Public Health Rep. **53**:1443, 1938.

113. Dean, H. T., Arnold, F. A., and Elvove, E.: Domestic water and dental caries. V. Additional studies of the relation of fluoride domestic water to dental experience in 4425 white children, Public Health Rep. **57**:1155, 1942.

114. Nizel, A. E.: Nutrition in preventive dentistry: science and practice, Philadelphia, 1972, W. B. Saunders Co.

115. Russell, A. L., and Elvove, E.: Domestic water and dental caries. VII. A study of the fluoride-dental caries relationship in the adult population, Public Health Rep. **66**:1389, 1951.

116. Galagan, D. J., and Vermillion, J. R.: Determining optimum fluoride concentrations, Public Health Rep. **72**:491, 1957.

117. Aasenden, R., and Peebles, I. C.: Effects of fluorine supplementation from birth on human deciduous and permanent teeth, Arch. Oral. Biol. **19**:321, 1974.

118. Committee on Nutrition, American Academy of Pediatrics: Fluoride supplementation: revised dosage schedule, Pediatrics **63**:150, 1979.

119. Dirks, O. B., and others: Total and free ionic fluoride in human and cow's milk as determined by gas-liquid chromatography and the fluoride electrode, Caries Res. **8**:181, 1974.

Manganese

120. Underwood, E. J.: Trace elements in human and animal nutrition, ed. 4, New York, 1977, Academic Press, Inc.

121. Schlage, C., and Wortberg, B.: Manganese in the diet of healthy preschool and school children, Acta Paediatr. Scand. **61**:648, 1972.

122. Widdowson, E. M.: Trace elements in human development. In Barltrop, D., and Burland, W. L., editors: Mineral metabolism in paediatrics, Philadelphia, 1969, F. A. Davis Co., p. 85.

123. Doisey, E. A., Jr.: Micronutrient control on biosynthesis of clotting proteins and cholesterol. In Humphries, D. D., editor: Proceedings of the University of Missouri's 6th annual conference on trace substances in environmental health, Columbia, Mo., 1973, University of Missouri Press. Cited in Burch, R. E., Hahn, H. K. J., and Sullivan, J. F.: Newer aspects of the roles of zinc, manganese and copper in human nutrition, Clin. Chem. **21**:501, 1975.

Selenium

124. Stadtman, T. C.: Biological function of selenium, Nutr. Rev. **35**:161, 1977.
125. Burke, R. F., and others: Blood-selenium levels and in vitro red blood cell uptake of 75 Se in kwashiorkor, Am. J. Clin. Nutr. **20**:723, 1967.
126. Levine, R. J., and Olson, R. E.: Blood selenium in Thai children with protein-calorie malnutrition, Proc. Soc. Exp. Biol. Med. **134**:1030, 1970.
127. Majaj, A. S., and Hopkins, L. L., Selenium and kwashiorkor, Lancet **2**:592, 1966.
128. Hadjimarkos, D. M.: Effect of trace minerals on dental caries, Adv. Oral Biol. **3**:252, 1968.
129. Hadjimarkos, D. M., Storvick, C. A., and Remmert, L. F.: Selenium and dental caries: an investigation among school children in Oregon, J. Pediatr. **40**:451, 1952.
130. Hadjimarkos, D. M.: Selenium: a caries-enhancing trace element, Caries Res. **3**:14, 1969.
131. Bowen, W. H.: The effect of selenium and vanadium on caries activity in monkeys (*M. irus*), J. Irish Dent. Assoc. **18**:83, 1972.
132. Frost, D. V., and Lish, P. M.: Selenium in biology, Annu. Rev. Pharmacol. **15**:259, 1975.
133. Schrauzer, G. N.: Selenium anticarcinogenic action of an essential trace element. In Proceedings of the symposium on selenium-tellurium in the environment, Pittsburg, 1976, Industrial Health Foundation.
134. Hadjimarkos, D. M.: Selenium in mature human milk, Am. J. Clin. Nutr. **26**:583, 1973.

Chromium

135. Hambidge, K. M.: Chromium nutrition in man, Am. J. Clin. Nutr. **27**:505, 1974.
136. Mertz, W.: Chromium occurrence and function in biological systems, Physiol. Rev. **49**:163, 1969.
137. Hopkins, L. L., Ransome-Kuti, O., and Majaj, A. S.: Improvement of impaired carbohydrate metabolism by chromium (III) in malnourished infants, Am. J. Clin. Nutr. **21**:203, 1968.
138. Gürson, C. T., and Saner, G.: Effect of chromium or glucose utilization in marasmic protein-calorie malnutrition, Am. J. Clin. Nutr. **24**:1313, 1971.
139. Gürson, C. T., and Saner, G.: Effect of chromium supplementation on growth in marasmic protein-calorie malnutrition, Am. J. Clin. Nutr. **26**:988, 1973.
140. Schroeder, H. A., Nasan, A. P., and Tipton, I. H.: Chronium deficiency as a factor in atherosclerosis, J. Chron. Dis. **23**:123, 1970.

ADDITIONAL READINGS
Water and electrolytes

Almroth, S. G.: Water requirements of breast-fed infants in a hot climate, Am. J. Clin. Nutr. **31**:1154, 1978.

Berenberg, W., Mandell, F., and Fellers, F. X.: Hazards of skimmed milk, unboiled and boiled, Pediatrics **44**:734, 1969.

Bruck, E., Abal, G., and Aceto, T., Jr.: Pathogenesis and pathophysiology of hypertonic dehydration with diarrhea, Am. J. Dis. Child. **115**:122, 1968.

Colle, E., Ayoub, E., and Raile, R.: Hypertonic dehydration (hypernatremia): the role of feedings high in solutes, Pediatrics **22**:5, 1958.

Committee on Nutrition, American Academy of Pediatrics: Water requirement in relation to osmolar load as it applies to infant feeding, Pediatrics **19**:339, 1957.

Coodin, F. J., Gabrielson, I. W., and Addiego, J. E.: Formula fatality, Pediatrics **47**:438, 1971.

Dresher, A. N., Barnett, H. L., and Troupkou, V.: Water balance in infants during water deprivation, Am. J. Dis. Child. **104**:366, 1962.

Winberg, J.: Determination of renal concentration capacity in infants and children without renal disease, Acta Paediatr. Scand. **48**:318, 1959.

Calcium, phosphorus, and magnesium

Avioli, L. V.: Calcium and phosphorus. In Goodhart, R. S., and Shils, M. E., editors: Modern nutrition in health and disease, ed. 6, Philadelphia, 1980, Lea & Febiger, p. 294.

Beal, V. A.: Calcium and phosphorus in infancy, J. Am. Diet. Asoc. **53**:450, 1968.

Cockburn, F., and others: Neonatal convulsions associated with primary disturbances of calcium, phosphorus, and magnesium metabolism, Arch. Dis. Child. **48**:99, 1973.

Fomon, S. J., and others: Calcium and phosphorus balance studies with normal full-term infants fed pooled human milk or various formulas, Am. J. Clin. Nutr. **12**:346, 1963.

Gregor, J. L., and others: Calcium, magnesium, phosphorus, copper, and magnesium balance in adolescent females, Am. J. Clin. Nutr. **31**:117, 1978.

Harvey, D. R., Cooper, L. V., and Stevens, J. F.: Plasma calcium and magnesium in newborn babies, Arch. Dis. Child. **45**:506, 1970.

Keen, J. H.: Significance of hypocalcaemia in neonatal convulsions, Arch. Dis. Child. **44**:356, 1969.

McBean, L. D., and Speckman, E. W.: A recognition of the interrelationships of calcium with various dietary components, Am. J. Clin. Nutr. **27**:603, 1974.

Raisz, L. G.: Physiologic and pharmacologic regulation and bone resorption, N. Engl. J. Med. **282**:909, 1970.

Robertson, N. R. C., and Smith, M. A.: Early neonatal hypocalcaemia, Arch. Dis. Child. **50:**604, 1975.

Stimmler, L., and others: Relations between changes in plasma calcium in first two weeks of life and renal function, Arch. Dis. Child. **50:**786, 1975.

Tsang, R. C., and others: Studies in calcium metabolism in infants with intrauterine growth retardation, J. Pediatr. **86:**936, 1975.

Iron

Beal, V. A., Meyers, A. J., and McCammon, R. W.: Iron intake, hemoglobin, and physical growth during the first two years of life, Pediatrics **30:**518, 1962.

Bowering, J., Sanchez, A. M., and Irwin, M. I.: A conspectus of research on iron requirements of man, J. Nutr. **106:**985, 1976.

Burman, D.: Haemoglobin levels in normal infants aged 3 to 24 months, and the effect of iron, Arch. Dis. Child. **47:**261, 1972.

Committee on Nutrition, American Academy of Pediatrics: Relationship between iron status and incidence of infection in infancy, Pediatrics **62:**246, 1978.

Cook, J. D., and others: Serum ferritin as a measure of iron stores in normal subjects, Am. J. Clin. Nutr. **27:**681, 1974.

Czajka-Narins, D. M., Haddy, T. B., and Kallen, D. J.: Nutritional and social correlates in iron deficiency anemia, Am. J. Clin. Nutr. **31:**955, 1978.

Forth, W., and Rummel, W.: Iron absorption, Physiol. Rev. **53:**724, 1973.

Hallberg, L., and Solvell, L.: Absorption of hemoglobin iron in man, Acta Med. Scand. **181:**335, 1967.

Hoglund, S., and Reizenstein, P.: Studies in iron absorption. V. Effect of gastrointestinal factors on iron absorption, Blood **34:**496, 1969.

Hunter, R. E., and Smith, N. J.: Hemoglobin and hematocrit values in iron deficiency in infancy, J. Pediatr. **81:**710, 1972.

Jacobs, A., Path, F. R. C., and Worwood, M.: Ferritin in serum, clinical and biochemical implications, N. Engl. J. Med. **292:**951, 1975.

Kimber, C., and Weintraub, L. R.: Malabsorption of iron secondary to iron deficiency, N. Engl. J. Med. **279:**453, 1968.

Martínez-Torres, C., Renzi, M., and Layrisse, M.: Iron absorption by humans from hemosiderin and ferritin: further studies, J. Nutr. **106:**128, 1976.

Monsen, E. R., and Cook, J. D.: Food iron absorption in human subjects, IV. The effects of calcium and phosphate salts on the absorption of nonheme iron, Am. J. Clin. Nutr. **29:**1142, 1976.

Underwood, E. J.: Trace elements in human and animal nutrition, ed. 4, New York, 1977, Academic Press, Inc.

Webb, T. E., and Oski, F. A.: Iron deficiency anemia and scholastic achievement in young adolescents, J. Pediatr. **82:**827, 1973.

Wilson, J. F., Lahey, M. E., and Heiner, D. C.: Studies on iron metabolism. I. Further observations on cow's milk–induced gastrointestinal bleeding in infants with iron deficiency anemia, J. Pediatr. **84:**335, 1974.

Woodruff, C. W., and Clark, J. L.: The role of fresh cow's milk in iron deficiency. I. Albumin turnover in infants with iron deficiency anemia, Am. J. Dis. Child. **124:**18, 1972.

Iodine

Food and Nutrition Board: Iodine nurture in the United States, Washington, D.C., 1970, National Academy of Sciences, National Research Council.

Kidd, P. S., and others: Sources of dietary iodine, J. Am. Diet Assoc. **65:**420, 1974.

London, W. T., Vought, R. L., and Brown, F. A.: Bread—a dietary source of large quantities of iodine, N. Engl. J. Med. **273:**381, 1965.

London, W. T., and others: Epidemiologic and metabolic studies of a goiter endemic in eastern Kentucky, J. Clin. Endocrinol. Metab. **25:**1091, 1965.

Malvaux, P., Beckers, C., and De Visscher, M.: Iodine balance studies in non-goitrous children and adolescents on low-iodine intake, J. Clin. Endocrinol. Metab. **29:**79, 1969.

Trotter, W. R.: Diseases of the thyroid, Oxford, 1962, Blackwell Scientific Publications Ltd.

Vought, R. L., London, W. T., and Stebbings, G. E. T.: Endemic goiter in northern Virginia, J. Clin. Endocrinol. Metab. **27:**1381, 1967.

Copper

Josephs, H. W.: The effect of copper on iron metabolism: a clinical study, Johns Hopkins Med. J. **129:**212, 1971.

Oaski, S., Johnson, D. A., and Freiden, E.: The mobilization of iron from the perfused mammalian liver by serum copper enzyme, ferroxidase, J. Biol. Chem. **246:**3018, 1971.

Schubert, W. K., and Lahey, M. E.: Copper and protein depletion complicating hypoferric anemia of infancy, Pediatrics **24:**710, 1959.

Seelig, M. S.: Review: relationships of copper and molybdenum to iron metabolism, Am. J. Clin. Nutr. **25:**1022, 1972.

Sturgeon, P., and Brubaker, C.: Copper deficiency in infants, Am. J. Dis. Child. **92:**254, 1956.

Manganese

McLeod, B. E., and Robinson, M. F.: Dietary intakes of manganese by New Zealand infants during the first six months of life, Br. J. Nutr. **27**:229, 1972.

McLeod, B. E., and Robinson, M. F.: Metabolic balance of manganese in young women, Br. J. Nutr. **27**:221, 1972.

Zinc

Coble, Y. D., Schulert, A. R., and Farid, Z.: Growth and sexual development of male subjects in an Egyptian oasis, Am. J. Clin. Nutr. **18**:421, 1966.

Coble, Y. D., and others: Zinc levels and blood enzyme activities in Egyptian male subjects with retarded growth and sexual development, Am. J. Clin. Nutr. **19**:415, 1966.

Committee on Nutrition, American Academy of Pediatrics: Zinc, Pediatrics **62**:408, 1978.

Evans, G. W., and Johnson, P. E.: Determination of zinc availability in foods by the extrinsic label technique, Am. J. Clin. Nutr. **30**:873, 1977.

Henkin, R. I., and others: Idiopathic hypogeusia with dysgeusia, hyposmia and dysosmia: a new syndrome, J.A.M.A. **217**:434, 1971.

Meiners, C. R., and others: The relationship of zinc to protein utilization in the pre-adolescent child, Am. J. Clin. Nutr. **30**:879, 1977.

Murphy, E. W., Willis, B. W., and Watt, B. K.: Provisional tables on the zinc content of food, J. Am. Diet. Assoc. **66**:345, 1975.

Pecoud, A., Donzel, P., and Schelling, J. L.: Effect of food stuffs on the absorption of zinc sulfate, Clin. Pharmacol. Ther. **17**:469, 1975.

Pories, W. J., and others: Acceleration of healing with zinc sulfate, Ann. Surg. **165**:432, 1967.

Prasad, A. S., and others: Experimental zinc deficiency in humans, Ann. Intern. Med. **89**:483, 1978.

Ronaghy, H. A., and Halsted, J. A.: Zinc deficiency in females: report of two cases, Am. J. Clin. Nutr. **28**:831, 1975.

Ronaghy, H. A., and others: Zinc supplementation of malnourished schoolboys in Iran: increased growth and other effects, Am. J. Clin. Nutr. **27**:112, 1974.

Sandstead, H. H., and others: Human zinc deficiency, endocrine manifestations and response to treatment, Am. J. Clin. Nutr. **20**:422, 1967.

Sandstead, H. H., and others: Zinc deficiency and brain development in the rat, Fed. Proc. **34**:86, 1975.

Chromium and selenium

Burk, R. F.: Selenium in nutrition, World Rev. Nutr. Diet. **30**:88, 1978.

Hoekstra, W. G.: Biochemical function of selenium and its relation to vitamin E, Fed. Proc. **34**:2083, 1975.

Liu, V. J. K., and Morris, J. S.: Relative chromium response as an indicator of chromium status, Am. J. Clin. Nutr. **31**:972, 1978.

McKenzie, R. L., and others: Selenium concentration and glutathione peroxidase activity in blood of New Zealand infants and children, Am. J. Clin. Nutr. **31**:1413, 1978.

Mertz, W.: Chromium: occurrence and function in biological systems, Physiol. Rev. **49**:163, 1969.

Mertz, W., and Raginski, E. E.: Chromium metabolism: the glucose tolerance factor. In Mertz, W., and Carnatzer, W. E., editors: Newer trace elements in nutrition, New York, 1971, Marcel Dekker, Inc.

Mertz, W., and others: Present knowledge of the role of chromium, Fed. Proc. **33**:2275, 1974.

Tappel, A. L.: Selenium-glutathione peroxidase and vitamin E, Am. J. Clin. Nutr. **27**:960, 1974.

Underwood, E. J.: Trace elements in human and animal nutrition, New York, 1977, Academic Press, Inc.

Zabel, N. L., and others: Selenium content of commercial formula diets, Am. J. Clin. Nutr. **31**:850, 1978.

Fluoride

Daily fluoride supplements and dental caries, Nutr. Rev. **36**:329, 1978.

Dirks, O. B.: The relation between the fluoridation of water and dental caries experience, Int. Dent. J. **17**:582, 1967.

Dunning, J. M.: Current status of fluoridation, N. Engl. J. Med. **272**:30, 1965.

Hennon, D. K., Stookey, G. K., and Muhler, J. C.: Prevalence and distribution of dental caries in preschool children, J. Am. Dent. Assoc. **79**:1405, 1969.

Hennon, D. K., Stookey, G. K., and Muhler, J. C.: Prophylaxis of dental caries: relative effectiveness of chewable fluoride preparations with and without added vitamins, J. Pediatr. **80**:1018, 1972.

Waldbott, G. L.: Fluoride in food, Am. J. Clin. Nutr. **12**:455, 1963.

Magnesium

Nichols, B. L., and others: Magnesium supplementation in protein calorie malnutrition, Am. J. Clin. Nutr. **31**:176, 1978.

5

Collecting and assessing food intake information

Peggy L. Pipes, Judith Bumbalo, and Paula Carman[†]

Nutrition screening, evaluation and/or counseling, and education have become integral parts of many health care, public health, and supplemental food programs that provide services to infants and children. In addition, children perceived as having feeding problems, those who must consume therapeutic diets, and those whose parents are concerned about the adequacy of their food intakes are frequently referred for a team management approach. Plans for modifying food intake in childhood should be based on information more comprehensive than that which identifies excesses or deficits in energy and nutrient intakes and cultural food practices. Health care professionals need to work jointly to synthesize information and establish programs that can be carried out by children and/or their parents. Goals for change in food intake should be identified and periodically reassessed. It is imperative, therefore, that health care professionals recognize the necessity of accurate data collection in relation to the nutrient intake from the food consumed, the developmental level of feeding behavior (oral motor screening), and psychosocial issues affecting behavior and mother-child interactions that effect food and nutrient intake.

It is important to recognize that an assessment of food intake is not an assessment of nutritional status. The latter requires anthropometric data and biochemical and clinical evaluations as well as dietary intake data. Adequately collected food intake data can, however, provide information on which judgments of the adequacy of a child's current food intake can be made and plans for resolving concerns of food and nutrient intake can be designed and assessed. It is important for individuals who collect this information to be aware of the variety of methods of collecting food intake information and to develop skills for screening oral motor difficulties of feeding and psychosocial factors that compromise a child's nutrient intake.

TOOLS FOR COLLECTING DIETARY INTAKE DATA

Health care professionals in clinical settings use a variety of tools for collecting dietary data, each tool having limitations and varying degrees of reliability. The choice of tool will depend on the purpose of the interview, the time commitment of the professional, and cooperativeness of the child and/or parents. Information sought will vary with the problem. For example, detailed docu-

[†]Deceased.

mentation of an early feeding history may be important for counseling parents of young children with feeding problems, whereas this would be inappropriate if the patient were an obese adolescent. Only one tool will be used in some instances, whereas a combination of tools is appropriate at other times. It is important to recognize that valid methods for assessing the dietary intake of groups vary with those designed to collect information on which nutrition education and counseling are to be based. The tools most often used in the clinical setting are the 24-hour recall, the dietary history, and 3- and 7-day food records.

The interview is the most important aspect of any of the tools used, the validity of the information obtained being dependent on the client's understanding of the reasons for the interview and the information sought, the client's comfort with the interviewer, and the interviewer's skills at probing for and validating information. Whether the child or parents should be interviewed depends on a number of developmental and psychosocial factors. Beal found that with few exceptions girls under 12 years of age and boys under 13 to 14 years of age were unlikely to give reliable nutrition histories.[1] However, if there is considerable conflict between a preadolescent and the parents about food intake, it may be important to interview the child individually as well as with the parents so that an appropriate counseling relationship can be established.

It must be remembered that assessment data is only as valid as the child's or parents' willingness to share information with the interviewer. It is important that they feel comfortable with the interview and the individual conducting the assessment. A friendly greeting and clear definition of the purpose of the interview and the reasons for the questions asked aid in establishing rapport with the client. Providing an adequate

diet for children is a very important aspect of mothering. Parents may feel threatened when questioned about a child's food intake. In addition, the interviewer must have reasonable expectations for the respondent. The mother of seven children can not be expected to give information as precisely for one child as does a mother who devotes her time to an only child. A number of meals and/or snacks may be consumed outside the home in a day care center or at school and parents may not know what children receive in these settings.

During the interview the interviewer must be careful to avoid suggesting time, meals, food, or amounts consumed. For example, the question "when does your child first have something to eat or to drink?" is appropriate, whereas the question "does he eat breakfast at 8:00 AM?" is inappropriate. The tone of voice is also important. Neither approval or disapproval should be expressed verbally or nonverbally by facial expression. Food preferences of the interviewer should never be indicated. Silences must be accepted with comfort and parents should be permitted time to formulate answers to questions and to present questions of their own.

24-hour recall

The most common method used for collecting dietary data to characterize the nutrient intake of populations is the 24-hour recall, often used in combination with 1-, 3-, or 7-day food records. The 24-hour recall has also been successfully used to screen children at nutritional risk and can give some indication as to compliance with a dietary regimen during clinical follow-up. It can not be substituted for more intensive methods when judgments regarding the adequacy of an individual child's food intake are to be made.

Parents or the child are asked to relate every food in portion sizes that the child

has consumed for the past 24 hours. The
accuracy of the data depends on the memory
and cooperation of the subject. There is no
assurance that the recall of the day selected
is typical of other days. The accuracy with
which portion sizes are reported can be increased by the use of food models and by
skillful probing.

3- and 7-day food records

The 3- or 7-day diet record or a written
diary of all food and beverages consumed is
a tool commonly used to characterize current
intakes of individual children (see Food
Diary for Children, p. 101, and Food Diary
for Infants, p. 102). Parents are instructed to
measure or weigh portions of food offered
and amounts not eaten and record the
amounts consumed. Parents report that measuring and weighing pose no problems but
that they find the rigidity of recording each
time the child eats difficult. Sometimes they
forget foods that are added to other foods;
catsup, butter, jelly, etc., may be uninten-
tionally omitted from the record. Therefore,
careful instruction as to how to record food
intake is important.

Records covering less than 20 consecutive
meals or 7 days may not provide valid information.[2]

Dietary history

The most accurate method to review dietary intake in retrospect over a period of
time is the research dietary history method
developed by Burke[1] and modified and rede-
scribed by Beal.[3]

By interview the investigator obtains an
estimate of the frequency and amounts of
food consumed in a specified time period,
usually 1 to 6 months. The interview is often
cross-checked with a 24-hour recall and/or
3-day record of food consumed.

Several researchers have cautioned against
using this tool as the sole source of data.
Huenemann and Turner compared the re-
search-type dietary history with 10 to 14-day
weighed food records for a group of subjects
6 to 16 years of age and found that no history
agreed within 20% for all constituents; the
greatest deviations were for vitamins A and
D, calories, riboflavin, and thiamin.[4] Other
investigators compared dietary histories to
7-day food records and 24-hour recalls and
found that dietary histories gave distinctly
higher values than 7-day food records and
24-hour recalls for groups.[5] Trulson compared 7-day food records, an average of three
or more 24-hour recalls, and dietary histories
of clinic patients 7 to 12 years of age. She
found no proof that one method was more
reliable than another, but she preferred the
interview method since it might reveal long-
range dietary practices. The 7-day food records and detailed dietary histories gave results showing closest similarity, but findings
were not consistent.[6]

FOOD DIARY FOR CHILDREN

Instructions

1. Record all foods and beverages immediately after they are consumed.
2. Measure the amounts of each food carefully with standard measuring cups and spoons. Record meat portions in ounces or as fractions of pounds, e.g., 8 oz of milk, 1 medium egg, ¼ lb of hamburger, 1 slice of bread, white; ½ small banana.
3. Indicate method of preparation, e.g., medium egg, fried, ½ cup baked beans with a 2-inch slice of salt pork, 4 oz of steak, broiled.
4. Be sure to record any condiments, gravies, salad dressings, butter, margarine, whipped cream, relishes, e.g., ¾ cup of mashed potatoes with 3 tbsp of brown gravy, ¼ cup of cottage cheese salad with 2 olives, ½ cup of cornflakes with 1 tsp of sugar and ⅓ cup of 2% milk.
5. Be sure to record all between-meal foods and drinks, for example coffee with 1 oz of cream, 12 oz of cola, 4 sugar cookies, 1 candy bar (indicate brand name).
6. If you eat away from home, please put an asterisk (*) in the food column beside the food listing.

Day 1

Date _____ Day of week _____ Weight _____

Time	Food	Amount	How prepared

FOOD DIARY FOR INFANTS

Instructions

1. Record *all* formula, milk, and food that the baby consumes immediately *after* each feeding.
2. If your baby is breast fed, record the time of day the baby is fed and how long the baby feeds.
3. If your baby is formula fed, record the time of day the baby eats, the kind of formula the baby is fed, and the amount he/she actually consumes.
   Infant formula preparation:
   Is the formula iron fortified?
   ☐ Yes   ☐ No
   Formula (brand name): _____
   _____ oz liquid *or*
   _____ tbsp powder
   Water
   _____ oz
   Other (describe): _____
   _____ oz
   _____ tbsp
   Total prepared formula
   _____ oz
4. If the baby spits up or vomits, estimate the amount.
5. Measure the amounts of any other foods carefully in terms of ounces of liquid (e.g., 2 oz apple juice), level tbsp (e.g., 2 tbsp dry rice cereal), or portions of commercially prepared foods (e.g., ½ of a 4.7 oz jar of strained peaches).
6. Does the baby take a vitamin supplement?
   ☐ Yes   ☐ No
   If yes, what kind? _____
   _____ ml per day

Day 1
Date _____ Day of week _____
Most recent weight _____ on (date) _____ .

Time	Food or formula	Amount	Time	Food or formula	Amount

ASSESSING DIETARY INTAKE INFORMATION

When the dietary intake information has been collected, an assessment of the adequacy of nutrients in the foods consumed is performed. The decision as to the method of evaluation and which nutrients will be calculated will be based on the precision and reliability of the information collected, the foods that appear in the dietary records, the interviewer's knowledge of foods as sources of nutrients, and the problem presented for evaluation.

In some instances intake data may be compared to food groups; other times knowledge of foods that are present or absent in the dietary history as sources of nutrients may give sufficient indication of the presence or absence of problems of nutrient intake. If precise and complete information has been collected, hand or computer calculations of nutrients in the foods consumed may be compared to a standard.

When parents are unable or unwilling to give information that can be quantitated, such as when they report intake as bites of meat instead of one-fourth of a 2-oz hamburger patty or when cross-checks reveal inconsistencies, the analysis of food groups or foods as sources of nutrients seems appropriate. If, however, the child is underweight or overweight, or if food sources of a particular nutrient appear on the record only occasionally, calculations of nutrient intake are important. Several computer programs are available. Coding foods consumed and calculations by computer can yield information on a greater number of nutrients more efficiently and quickly than can hand calculation (Table 5-1).

When calculations are complete the data must be compared to a standard. All standards formulated are intended to be used to interpret data on groups of people and are not intended to be used for evaluating the adequacy of nutrient intakes of individuals. The National Research Council's recommended daily dietary allowances for children are generally based on studies of adults from which extrapolations were made for children. A margin of safety above the average requirement is applied to each nutrient. This margin is not standard but varies for each nutrient.

Some programs define children at nutritional risk as those who consume less than two-thirds or three-fourths of the recommended daily dietary allowances of any nutrient and include these children and their families in intensive nutrition follow-up. It may also be important for these children to have a more intensive nutrition evaluation, including biochemical evaluation of their nutritional status.

Growth data can give indications of the appropriateness of the child's energy intake. If rates of weight gain are excessive or inadequate, calculations of the child's energy intake provide important data on which plans for adjustments in energy intake can be made.

Table 5-1. Computer printout of a 1-day food record. Nutrient intake of a 2-year-old girl, 82.40 cm, 14.50 kg.

Item	Food description	Amt (gm)	Cal	Prot (gm)	Ca (mg)	Fe (mg)	Thiamin (mg)	Riboff (mg)	Niacin (mg)	Vit C (mg)	Folate (μg)	Vit A (IU)	Vit D (IU)
974	Eggs, Chicken, hard cooked	48.00	77.28	6.14	25.92	1.10	0.04	0.13	0.05	0.00	23.52	249.60	22.08
461	Bread, white, enriched (3%-4% nonfat dry milk)	25.00	67.50	2.18	21.00	0.63	0.06	0.05	0.60	Unknown	8.75	Unknown	Unknown
1320	Cow's milk, whole (3.5% fat)	360.00	234.00	11.74	428.40	0.18	0.11	0.61	0.30	3.60	18.00	504.00	147.60
1872	Rice, white enriched	50.00	54.50	1.00	5.00	0.45	0.06	0.04	0.50	0.00	8.00	0.00	Unknown
1999	Frankfurters, cooked	50.00	153.50	7.00	2.50	0.75	0.08	0.10	1.25	0.00	Unknown	0.00	0.00
1437	Orange juice, frozen concentrate, diluted	240.00	108.00	1.68	21.60	0.24	0.22	0.02	0.72	108.00	132.00	480.00	Unknown
1304	Macaroni and cheese, baked, enriched	125.00	268.75	10.50	226.25	1.13	0.13	0.25	1.13	Unknown	Unknown	537.50	Unknown
186	Beans, green, canned drained solids	45.00	10.80	0.63	20.25	0.68	0.01	0.02	0.14	1.97	18.00	211.50	Unknown
709	Chicken, fryer, drumstick, fried	35.00	82.25	11.41	5.25	0.81	0.02	0.14	2.49	Unknown	Unknown	49.00	Unknown
3291	Tortilla	30.00	63.00	1.50	60.00	0.90	0.04	0.02	0.30	0.00	Unknown	6.00	Unknown
	Totals		1119.58	53.78	816.17	6.85	0.76	1.39	7.47	113.57*	208.27*	2037.60*	169.68*

Prot *4/cal: .19
Cal/cm: 13.59
Cal/kg: 77.21
Prot/cm: .65
Prot/kg: 3.71
Prot 0.16*:   8.60

SCREENING CHILDREN AT NUTRITIONAL RISK

The objective of screening is to identify infants and children who appear to have nutritional problems that require further investigation. The interview is brief and information sought is qualitative. It is often performed by paraprofessionals (e.g., community health workers, nutrition aides), nurses, or other professionals who assume the role of case manager. The 24-hour recall screening questionnaires or questionnaires filled out by parents may be utilized. (See Screening Questionnaire for Infants, pp. 106 to 107, and Screening Questionnaire for Young Children, pp. 108 to 109.

Anthropometric data plotted on growth grids are also utilized in screening. In general, when children's growth patterns plot at less than tenth percentile, when they are underweight or overweight for their lengths (Chapter 1), or when interviews show patterns of intake that indicate a nutrient consumed in short supply, the children are referred for more intensive counseling.

Some programs utilize definitions of children at nutritional risk as shown below.

Children at nutritional risk*

I. Infants or children who have an inappropriate rate of weight gain
   A. Insufficient weight gain: failure of the infant to gain at a rate in weight and/or length less than appropriate for an infant in his or her percentile since the infant's last clinic visit
   B. Very rapid rate of weight gain
   C. Gross discrepancy between length and weight
II. Infants whose parents feed them improperly prepared formulas
   A. Formulas that are prepared to yield more than or less than 20 cal/oz unless

therapeutically prescribed; formulas are concentrated because of the following reasons:
      1. Parents do not understand concentrated versus ready-to-feed formula
      2. Parents do not add sufficient water to concentrated formula
      3. Parents add additional formula powder to the water
   B. Calorically dilute formulas result from the following:
      1. Parents add additional water to formula
      2. Parents feed skim milk
      3. Parents feed sugar water rather than milk because they do not understand the need for milk in infancy
III. Infants or children who consume more than 40 oz or less than 16 oz of milk a day
IV. Infants whose parents lack skills in feeding technique and/or use equipment that makes it difficult for the infants to consume formula
   A. Infants who are fed at intervals of less than 2 hours or more than 5 hours on more than one or two occasions during the day
   B. Infants whose parents prop the bottle
   C. Breast-fed infants who nurse for inappropriately long periods at each feeding
   D. Infants who are not appropriately burped
   E. Young infants who consistently fall asleep before completing an acceptable caloric intake whose parents are using bottles with firm nipples and have not adjusted the holes for the infant
V. Infants less than 60 days old who consume greater than 145 cal/kg or less than 90 cal/kg
VI. Infants of breast-feeding mothers who have the following problems:
   A. They restrict their intake of food or a group of foods that contributes appreciably to the increment for nutrients during lactation

*From Pipes, P.: Assessing food and nutrient intake. In Erickson, M.: Assessment and management of development changes in children, St. Louis, 1976, The C. V. Mosby Co.

SCREENING QUESTIONNAIRE FOR INFANTS

Infants (from birth to age 1 year)   Yes   No

1. Is the baby breast fed?   ☐   ☐
   If yes, does he/she also receive milk or formula?   ☐   ☐
   If yes, what kind? _____
2. Does the baby receive formula?   ☐   ☐
       If yes ☐ Ready-to-feed
              ☐ Concentrated liquid
              ☐ Other: _____
       How is formula prepared (especially dilution)?

       Is the formula iron fortified?   ☐   ☐
3. Does the baby drink milk?   ☐   ☐
       If yes ☐ Whole milk
              ☐ 2% milk
              ☐ Skim milk
              ☐ Other: _____
4. How many times does he/she eat each day, including milk or formula? ____
5. Does the baby usually take a bottle to bed?   ☐   ☐
       If yes, what is usually in the bottle? _____
6. If the baby drinks milk or formula, what is the usual amount in a day?
       ☐ Less than 16 oz
       ☐ 16 to 32 oz
       ☐ More than 32 oz
7. Please indicate which (if any) of these foods the baby eats and how often:

	Never or hardly ever (less than once a week)	Sometimes (not daily but at least once a week)	Every day or nearly every day
Eggs	☐	☐	☐
Dried beans or peas	☐	☐	☐
Meat, fish poultry	☐	☐	☐
Bread, rice, pasta, grits, cereal, tortillas, potatoes	☐	☐	☐
Fruits or fruit juices	☐	☐	☐
Vegetables	☐	☐	☐

8. If the baby eats fruits or drinks fruit juices every day or nearly every day,
   which ones does he/she eat or drink most often (not more than three)? ____

9. If the baby eats vegetables every day or nearly every day, which ones does
   he/she eat most often (not more than three)? _____

From Fomon, S. J.: Nutritional disorders of children: prevention, screening, and follow up, Publication No. 76-5612, Rockville, Md., 1976, Department of Health, Education, and Welfare.

SCREENING QUESTIONNAIRE FOR INFANTS—cont'd

Infants (from birth to age 1 year) — cont'd	Yes	No

10. Does the person who cares for the baby have use of a
    Stove? ☐ ☐
    Refrigerator? ☐ ☐
    Piped water? ☐ ☐
11. Does the baby take vitamin or iron drops? ☐ ☐
    If yes, how often? _____
    What kind? _____
12. Is the baby on a special diet now? ☐ ☐
    If yes, what is the reason?
    Allergy—specify type of diet: _____
    Weight reduction—specify type of diet: _____
    Other—specify type of diet: _____
    Who recommended the diet? _____
13. Does the baby eat clay, paint chips, dirt, or anything else that is not usually   ☐   ☐
    considered food?
    If yes, what? _____
    How often? _____
14. Do you think the child has a feeding problem? ☐ ☐
    If yes, describe: _____

B. They have questions about scheduling and the use of supplementary feedings

C. They have infants who refuse the breast

D. They are concerned about not having sufficient milk for their babies

VII. Infants of parents who *appear* to have a lack of concern about feeding (e.g., they prop the bottle or do not know what to feed)

VIII. Children whose parents are anxious about what and how their children eat

IX. Infants or children who receive megadoses of vitamins

X. Children who consume inappropriate kinds of semisolids and table food because of the following reasons:
   A. Additions of semisolids to milk
   B. Unavailability of sufficient amounts of iron-containing foods at appropriate levels of growth
   C. Excessive use of semisolids, which distorts the milk intake
   D. Use of excessive quantities of high-carbohydrate foods or alcoholic beverages (e.g., beer, wine, carbonated beverages, cookies, crackers, potato chips, french fries)
   E. Additions of excessive quantities of high-calorie semisolids (e.g., meats, egg yolks, cookies)

XI. Children who refuse an entire group of foods

XII. Children of parents who have questions regarding what or how much to feed

XIII. Children whose parents do not use food to support developmental progression
   A. Progression to finger foods (when the infant reaches out for food [at approximately 6 to 7 months of age], finger foods that will not splinter and cause choking should be added)

SCREENING QUESTIONNAIRE FOR YOUNG CHILDREN

Preschool children and young school-age children

	Yes	No
1. Does the child drink milk?	☐	☐

If yes ☐ Whole milk
☐ 2% milk
☐ Skim milk
☐ Other: _____

If yes, how much?
☐ Less than 8 oz
☐ 8 to 32 oz
☐ More than 32 oz

2. Does the child drink anything from a bottle (for children less than 4 years of age)?   ☐ ☐

If yes ☐ Milk
☐ Other: _____

3. Does the child take a bottle to bed?   ☐ ☐

If yes, what is usually in the bottle? _____

4. How many times a day does the child usually eat (including snacks)? _____

5. Please indicate which (if any) of these foods the child eats and how often:

	Never or hardly ever (less than once a week)	Sometimes (not daily but at least once a week)	Every day or nearly every day
Cheese, yogurt, ice cream	☐	☐	☐
Eggs	☐	☐	☐
Dried beans, peas, peanut butter	☐	☐	☐
Meat, fish, poultry	☐	☐	☐
Bread, rice, pasta, grits, cereal, tortillas, potatoes	☐	☐	☐
Fruits or fruit juices	☐	☐	☐
Vegetables	☐	☐	☐

6. If the child eats fruits or drinks fruit juices every day or nearly every day, which does he/she eat or drink most often? (Not more than three) _____

7. If the child eats vegetables every day or nearly every day which one does he/she eat most often (not more than three)? _____

8. Does the child usually eat between meals?   ☐ ☐

If yes, name the 2 or 3 snacks (including bedtime snacks) that the child has most often. _____

From Fomon, S. J.: Nutritional disorders of children: prevention, screening, and follow-up, Publication No. 76-5612, Rockville, Md., 1976, Department of Health, Education, and Welfare.

SCREENING QUESTIONNAIRE FOR YOUNG CHILDREN—cont'd

Preschool children and young school-age children — cont'd   Yes   No

9. Does the person who cares for the child have use of a
   Stove?   ☐   ☐
   Refrigerator?   ☐   ☐
   Piped water?   ☐   ☐
10. Does the child take vitamin or iron drops or tablets?   ☐   ☐
    If yes, how often? _____
    What kind? _____
11. Is the child now getting a special diet?   ☐   ☐
    If yes, what is the reason? _____
    ☐ Allergy; specify type of diet _____
    ☐ Weight reduction—specify type of diet _____
    ☐ Other—specify reason for diet and type of diet _____
    Who recommended the diet? _____
12. Does the child eat clay, paint chips, dirt, or anything else not usually con- ☐   ☐
    sidered food?
    If yes, what? _____
    How often? _____
13. How would you describe the child's appetite?
    ☐ Good
    ☐ Fair
    ☐ Poor
    ☐ Other: _____

B. Appropriate progression in texture and consistency (when finger foods are introduced, the progression to soft mashed table foods can be begun; when strained meats are refused, finely chopped meat from the table can be offered)

C. Progression from bottle to cup (when the infant is developmentally 9 to 12 months of age, experience with a cup should be offered)

XIV. Children whose parents follow food fads or who have questions about food fads or diets
   A. Feed sugar water or herb tea instead of milk
   B. Feed raw cow's milk or goat's milk

XV. Infants or children with physical handicaps that influence the child's ability to in-gest food (e.g., poor suck, cleft lip or palate, tongue thrust)

XVI. Children of parents who lack skill in home management
   A. Time and money management
   B. Housekeeping
   C. Food procurement

XVII. Children of families who do not take advantage of the resources available to them to aid and improve the nutrition of their children (e.g., W.I.C. food program, school lunch)

XVIII. Children who have specific therapeutic dietary problems

DIETARY ASSESSMENT

Parents and children referred for intensive evaluation of nutrient and energy intake will anticipate a more extensive interview. Even so, the dietitian/nutritionist should carefully explain the purpose of the questions to be asked and reasons for the continuing "how much and how often" questions. Decisions regarding which tool will be used may be made after the parents and/or children arrive and express their concern or lack of concern.

The dietary history, in combination with a 7-day food record, is the preferred and most valid tool currently available for dietary assessment in a clinical setting. These procedures require a skilled nutritionist and are costly in time, and not all parents and/or children can respond with validity even though they may wish to do so.

Some programs utilize a food frequency questionnaire and 24-hour recall, a method that requires less time and is less taxing on the client but yields less valid and useful information.

During this interview the nutritionist collects information about family interactions that affect a child's food intake (e.g., family members present at mealtimes, the use of food as rewards), the food budget and money spent for food, the frequency with which families and children eat away from home, and the families' use of community resources that provide food or nutrition education.

If children are overweight, activity patterns are explored. Discussions about the consumption of vending machine food and the effects of television on eating patterns may also provide important information.

It may be necessary to discontinue the detailed probing necessary for dietary history and utilize only a cross-check if parental tolerance for the continued questions is limited. It is also important to recognize that it may not be possible to obtain sufficient information during one interview; several follow-up clinic or home visits may be necessary to obtain a true picture of the child's feeding history and food intake.

Preschool teachers and public health nurses often provide information about a child's food intake at school and family food patterns.

When dietary data has been collected, an assessment is made of:

1. Parental knowledge of nutrition and appropriate foods for children
2. The adequacy of nutrients provided by the food offered to the child
3. The adequacy of the diet consumed by the child
4. Parental knowledge of and use of community resources to improve the nutritional status of the child
5. Delays in feeding skills that affect food and nutrients consumed
6. Real or potential behavior patterns that can or do compromise a child's nutrient intake
7. The motivation of parents and the child to change the patterns of food intake

If this assessment indicates that adjustments need to be made only in the kinds of food or size of portions offered to and/or consumed by the child or if a therapeutic diet is indicated, plans for modifying the child's food intake should be made with the child and/or parents. The counselor should be aware of community resources that help with the provision of food such as the Supplemental Food Program for Women, Infants, and Children, which provides foods such as iron-fortified formula milk or cheese, eggs, iron-fortified cereals, and vitamin C–containing juices to pregnant women and children under 5 years of age that qualify for the program; the food stamp program, which provides funds that can be spent for foods in the grocery store; and school lunch programs. Clients may need help in contacting agencies that administer the programs. Plans for modifying food intake should be communicated to teachers, school lunch personnel, and others in the child's food environment.

If it appears that the child has delays in feeding skills or eating patterns or that parent-child interactions are also operative in problems presented, the investigator may need to screen for these specific problems so that appropriate referrals can be made.

ORAL MOTOR EVALUATIONS

Children who are developmentally delayed and those who have abnormal muscle coordination may have difficulty with the various skills needed for the process of eating. These skills are normally learned or are already present so early in life that they are taken for granted. A knowledgeable therapist should be involved in the evaluation and planning for any person with motor feeding problems. However, infants and children with these problems are often identified during a dietary intake interview and observation of feeding behavior.

Motor coordination problems may be identified by interview with parents and by observation of children as they eat food and drink liquid. It is important to observe the degree of assistance assumed by parents, as well as the child's abilities. The observer may offer food textures with which the child is not familiar in order to determine if oral developmental delays are caused by a lack of encouragement or a lack of opportunities to make the transition. For example, more tongue, jaw, and lip movement will be seen when a piece of cheese is placed between the molars than when pureed spoon food is offered.

When making the transition to solid foods, the child will initially attempt to use oral patterns that are familiar and habitual even though they may not be effective. Loss of food from the mouth may be caused by immature tongue movement and should not be interpreted as dislike for the food. Placement of food at the side of the mouth reduces food rejection caused by immature tongue movement. Choking, with subsequent coughing, is not unusual during the transition period

from pureed spoon foods to soft table foods. Hiding lumps of solid food within pureed or strained food will not help in making the transition; the solid foods must be perceived in order to learn the motor patterns necessary to deal with them. It is most important not to get upset when a child chokes; ordinarily choking can be handled without assistance, but if there is no coughing or breathing, the evaluator can quickly turn the child upside down or bend the child forward at the hips and tap sharply between the shoulder blades. Fortunately few genuine emergencies arise, but it is important to be prepared by knowing how to handle emergencies. These procedures should be discussed with parents when asking them to try new food textures with the assurance that choking is not life threatening if one knows how to deal with it.

The "Screening of Eating Abilities" (pp. 112 to 116) is a form that can serve as a guideline for information to be recorded. When this is complete, the evaluator should be able to determine if there is a coordination problem of the child's body and/or mouth and if further appropriate resources should be called upon. It should be noted that when age guidelines are mentioned, they are intended to be lenient in recognition of the normal range for acquisition of skills.

If the oral motor screen identifies delays in feeding behavior in the absence of abnormal motor patterns, specific foods to support developmental progress may be suggested (Chapter 14). However, if abnormal motor patterns are identified, referral to specialized therapists is important. If the problem seems to be primarily oral, with good control noted in the head, trunk, and extremities, a speech therapist may be the first contact. If a specialized speech pathologist cannot be located, or if the motor impairment affects other parts of the body (which it usually does), an occupational therapist or physical

Text continued on p. 117.

SCREENING OF EATING ABILITIES
By Paula Carman

Client's name: _____ ID#: _____ BD: _____
Medical diagnosis, if known: _____
Name of evaluator: _____
Name of parent or caregiver: _____ Phone: _____
Other agencies involved: _____

I. Questions to ask of parent or caregiver
  A. What are your greatest concerns in regard to feeding?
  B. What are the food likes and dislikes of _____ in relation to texture, temperature, color, and flavor?
  C. Are some foods more difficult for _____ to eat than others?
  D. Are there any foods that _____ cannot eat?
  E. Does _____ take any medication or food supplements?
  F. When does he/she have meals and snacks?
  G. Does _____ eat with the family?
  H. Who assists at mealtimes (home, school, other)?
  I. How much assistance is _____ given?
  J. What textures are usually eaten (thin liquid, thick liquid, soft spoon food, soft chewy food, ground food, chopped food, crunchy food—see list below)?

II. Tactile sensitivity
  Toward the beginning of the evaluation (before offering food but after the client has had some opportunity to adjust to you as a stranger) the stimuli are applied. First, lightly stroke the front and back of each of the client's hands. Then stroke the front aspect of each arm (after getting clothing out of the way).

APPROPRIATE	QUESTIONABLE APPROPRIATENESS
Neutral or positive response to touch	Muscle tension, moving away from stimulus, or vocal protest
☐ Hand, arm	☐ Hand, arm
☐ Face	☐ Face
☐ Gums, outside teeth, when stroked with a moistened Q-tip	☐ Gums, outside teeth, when stroked with a moistened Q-tip, soft bristle toothbrush

Questionable appropriate responses may be caused by situational variables, but if caregiver reports consistent negative responses, a therapy referral is indicated.

III. Food offered
  These foods are listed in sequence according to difficulty and are grouped into three levels of corresponding normal developmental skills. Ask caregiver to first offer foods commonly eaten at home, then to try some of the other textures at more difficult levels. Watch carefully for amount of chewing, movement of food within the mouth, and tendency to choke. Small amounts of food are offered from each category appropriate to the client's developmental level, so that satiation does not occur too quickly. Thin liquid is offered to every client, but soft spoon foods or soft chewy foods should be omitted when

the client has demonstrated higher level skills. Thick liquid is offered only when thin liquids are difficult (evidenced by choking, liquid running out of mouth).

A. Client less than 5 months old developmentally (needs head and trunk support while eating—i.e., needs to be held in adult's arms, infant seat, special support chairs).
- ☐ Thick liquid (optional, offered when thin liquid is taken with difficulty): milkshake, thinned applesauce, thinned yogurt
- ☐ Thin liquid: milk, water, fruit juice
- ☐ Soft spoon food: applesauce, pudding, yogurt
- ☐ Soft chewy food: cheese, fish, vienna sausage

B. Client 5 to 12 months old developmentally (good head control, needs some trunk support while eating, sits upright in chair).
- ☐ Ground solid food: "junior foods," ground table foods (dry consistency)
- ☐ Crunchy food that dissolves readily: cracker, potato stick
- ☐ Oblong finger food (easier to grasp): potato stick, green bean
- ☐ Small finger food (harder to grasp): Cheerio, puffed cereal
- ☐ Hard crunchy food: melba toast, bread stick

C. Client more than 12 months old developmentally (with good head and trunk control and tongue mobility, lateralization).
- ☐ Chopped table foods
- ☐ Bite-sized table foods: raisins
- ☐ Multitexture foods (solid plus liquid): apple, celery
- ☐ Chewy food: chicken, hamburger, small pieces of well-cooked meat
- ☐ Hard foods that break into diffuse pieces: carrots, nuts

IV. Observations of client eating

Caregiver is asked to feed client in the usual way. Ask whether any particular equipment or furniture is used that may not be present for this observation.

Mark NA (not applicable) if client is younger than stated age. Asterisks indicate posture or movement that is always abnormal; other activity of questionable appropriateness may be caused by neurologic immaturity or other factors.

A. Positioning

APPROPRIATE	QUESTIONABLE APPROPRIATENESS
☐ Held by caregiver (if younger than 1 year) within 30° of upright	☐ Held by caregiver (lying back, asymmetrical, or otherwise unusual)
☐ Within 30° of upright, propped, or special seat (hips flexed 90° in usual sitting angle)	☐ Held by caregiver (older than 1 year)
	☐ Lying on flat surface
☐ High chair	☐ Other: _____
☐ Other: _____	

The health professional may wish to discuss alternative means of positioning if the usual method is questionably appropriate. However, if the client has abnormal muscle tone appropriate positioning is much more difficult to achieve; consultation with a physical therapist or occupational therapist should be obtained. Any of the following behaviors under the "questionable" column indicate need for a consultation or a therapy program.

Continued.

SCREENING OF EATING ABILITIES—cont'd

B. Posture and movement

APPROPRIATE

- ☐ Head in alignment with body
- ☐ Head control stable (expected by 4 or 5 months of age)
- ☐ Arms forward, hands midline (frequent by 4 to 6 months of age)
- ☐ Hands, legs, and feet move freely, without stiffness
- ☐ Hips flex easily for sitting, knees spread apart spontaneously for wide sitting base
- ☐ Trunk straight when sitting (expected by 5 to 6 months of age)

QUESTIONABLE APPROPRIATENESS

- ☐ *Head frequently back or to one side, rotated to one side
- ☐ *Lack of head stability, excess motions, floppy, pushes back, falls forward (older than 5 months)
- ☐ *Arms frequently retracted at shoulders, hands do not come together (older than 4 to 5 months)
- ☐ Legs and feet seem stiff, seldom move, or move in stereotyped patterns
- ☐ *Hips resist bending or intermittantly extend; narrow sitting base, knees pull together
- ☐ *Trunk tilted, slumped, rotated, or arched backwards (older than 5 months)

C. Oral-motor coordination

APPROPRIATE

Jaw

- ☐ Jaw opens and closes easily, controlled to receive food
- ☐ Jaw stabilized without moving when drinking
- ☐ Jaw moves up and down or with slight lateral movements when chewing ("rotary")

QUESTIONABLE APPROPRIATENESS

- ☐ Jaw opens too wide or with tension
- ☐ Delayed jaw opening response to receive food
- ☐ Jaw moves up and down while drinking from cup (retained primitive pattern)
- ☐ Jaw clamps down intermittently (older than 2 years)
- ☐ Lack of up and down movement with solid food
- ☐ Jaw often moves forward while chewing (mandibular facet slip)

Tongue

- ☐ Tongue stays within mouth while drinking
- ☐ Tongue stays within mouth with foods
- ☐ Tongue lateralized, food placed midline

- ☐ Tongue protrudes while drinking
- ☐ Tongue protrudes with spoon foods
- ☐ Tongue moves forward and backward when solid foods are placed at side of mouth, no lateral movement (older than 10 months)
- ☐ Tongue moves forward and backward when foods are presented midline, no lateral movement

Lips

☐ Lips retain liquids
☐ Lips retain spoon foods
☐ Lips move actively while chewing

☐ Liquids not retained well by lips with nipple, with cup (older than 24 months)
☐ Spoon foods not retained well by lips (older than 8 months)
☐ Passive lips while chewing

Swallow

☐ Swallows readily
☐ Swallows liquids, no choking
☐ Swallows solids, seldom chokes

☐ *Delayed swallow, slows eating
☐ Chokes two or more times when drinking liquid from a cup
☐ Chokes two or more times when drinking liquids other than from a cup (bottle, etc.)
☐ Chokes two or more times when solids are fed

Gag reflex

☐ Normal gag reflex (readiness to vomit when pressure applied to pharangeal wall, soft palate, posterior tongue)

☐ *Gag reflex hyposensitive (slow or absent)
☐ *Gag reflex hypersensitive (occurs to pressure on middle or front of tongue or at sight of certain food)

Saliva control

☐ Swallows saliva (doesn't drool)

☐ Drools when not eating (older than 24 months) and when not teething

D. Prehension

Grasping of objects starts with a reflexive closing when the palmar surface of the hand is stimulated; the grasp becomes voluntary with maturity and is gradually refined to use of opposed fingertips. Any observations of questionable quality or prolonged primitive skill level should be cause for further evaluation.

APPROPRIATE	QUESTIONABLE APPROPRIATENESS
☐ Reflexive grasp (fading by 4 months of age)	☐ Wrist flexed, hand often in awkward position
☐ Raking grasp, whole hand (by 8 months of age)	☐ *Hand usually fisted (older than 3 months)
☐ Thumb to side of fingers	☐ *Hand usually limp, or weak grasp
☐ Thumb to fingertips of index and/or middle fingers	☐ Grasps food too tightly
	☐ Raking, use of whole hand (older than 12 months)
	☐ Difficulty releasing grasp (older than 12 months)

Continued.

SCREENING OF EATING ABILITIES—cont'd

E. Hand and arm movement

   A child must have head and upper trunk control before the hand can be used for purposeful reaching. At first the hand and arm movements appear to be random, but an increase in the frequency of purposeful movements is first seen as a child brings the hands to the mouth and the hands together at midline. Reaching for toys and bringing them to the mouth precedes finger-feeding. As control of the trunk improves, arm and hand use matures. A child will usually grab the spoon and help bring it to the mouth long before he or she is able to control it independently. The effort of holding a cup is seen initially as the cup is pushed tightly against the mouth to stabilize it; it is difficult at this stage to stop drinking and put a partially full cup back to the table without spilling. Abnormal muscle tone or lack of head and trunk stability interferes with the quality and effectiveness of hand use.

APPROPRIATE	QUESTIONABLE APPROPRIATENESS
☐ Hand to mouth	☐ *Arms tight, limited movement
☐ Hands to midline, hands together	☐ *Hands usually fisted (older than 2 to 3 months)
☐ Hand touches object purposefully	
☐ Toy to mouth	☐ *Hand frequently misses object, overshoots (older than 6 months)
☐ Holds bottle or drinks from cup (hands may be on cup, adult controls)	☐ No attempt to reach for food or spoon, even when hungry and food is within reach (older than 6 months)
☐ Self-feeds finger foods	
☐ Helps with spoon	
☐ Independent with spoon, spills	☐ Uses spoon with much extraneous movement and spilling
☐ Independent with spoon, no spills	
☐ Holds cup with some assistance	☐ Other: _____
☐ Independent with cup	

F. Cooperation

APPROPRIATE	QUESTIONABLE APPROPRIATENESS
☐ Motivated to eat	☐ Does not seem to care about eating
☐ Accepts food passively	☐ Actively resists eating (turns mouth away or slow to open mouth)
☐ Participates to best of ability	
☐ Socially appropriate behavior	☐ Physical skills not used to potential for self-assistance
	☐ Socially disruptive, attention seeking

   Any observations of questionable cooperation would tend to reduce the validity of other observations. A more thorough evaluation of parent-child interaction during mealtime may be indicated and may be the primary need of the child.

therapist with special interest in neurologic disorders should be contacted. The United Cerebral Palsy Association in each state is usually a good resource for names of treatment centers.

When specialized services are not immediately available, initial steps may be attempted to improve the quality of food intake. It is important to use the basic principles of positioning discussed in Chapter 14 and to use a problem-solving approach that includes feedback from client and caretaker. The rationale for suggested changes should be thoroughly explained and expectations for follow-through must be reasonable. It may take more time to feed a child in the desired position, especially at first, so parents could be asked to try the new procedure at the beginning of each meal or at the meal that is least stressful. Consideration of the client's and caretaker's comfort, feelings, and opinions should be clearly communicated.

When the caretaker does not want to make any changes in the feeding procedure, a compromise suggestion may be to allow a therapist to use the new procedures for a while, until the client is more comfortable and successful. Changes in motor control may be slow to achieve, but changes in the feeding environment are not as difficult to achieve and may have great significance in the long-term social, nutritional, and physical development of the individual.

CONSIDERATION OF PSYCHOSOCIAL FACTORS

Whenever and wherever the nutrition of a child is discussed, consideration must also be given to factors that have no direct relationship to the feeding process. Eating behavior serves as a sensitive barometer of the general adjustment of child, parent, and family. For this reason intrapersonal and interpersonal factors that influence food intake should also be taken into consideration when collecting and assessing information.

Since parents are primarily responsible for providing infants and children with both food and the environment in which it is consumed, attention should be given to the parents' psychosocial well-being, adaptation to the parenting role, and general level of parenting skills. Because patterns of food intake, even in young children, can be altered by emotional status, screening should also consider the socioemotional development of the child. When appropriate food is available and there is no evidence of biologic or organic problems in the child, it is not unusual to find that the cause of a disturbance in food intake is within the psychosocial/emotional category. Such problems can manifest themselves in a variety of ways, for instance, parent or child dissatisfaction with the feeding or mealtime situation, parental neglect or overconcern with food or feeding, anorexia or vomiting, and food aversions or food gorging.

Level of stress/family coping

Infants and children are sensitive to the feelings and attitudes of parents, particularly at feeding time or bedtime. Research by Brandon[7] on the epidemiology of childhood eating disturbances found that the parents of the maladjusted group, as compared to the control group, were younger, more dependent on relatives, regarded as unstable or suffering from mental problems, reported unhappy childhoods, experienced marital conflict, or were regarded as showing disturbed relationships with their children. It is reasonable to hypothesize that parents who are anxious or distressed somehow communicate these states to their babies and young children and that this in turn affects feeding behavior. Older children are also quick to identify tension or conflict between adults at the dinner table and to respond accordingly.

SCREENING QUESTIONNAIRE FOR FAMILY STRESS

	Yes	No
1. During the past year have any of the following occurred in your immediate family?		
Family moved?	☐	☐
Death, divorce, separation, loss of family member?	☐	☐
Marriage, reconciliation, pregnancy, new family member?	☐	☐
Serious injury or illness, problem with aging relative?	☐	☐
Loss of work, change of job, retirement?	☐	☐
Frequent or serious arguments or fights?	☐	☐
Money problems?	☐	☐
Drug or drinking problems?	☐	☐
Trouble with the law?	☐	☐
Some other serious problem?	☐	☐
If yes, what? _____		
2. During the past year:		
Has anyone in your family been seriously upset, depressed, or moody?	☐	☐
Have you been generally happy with your family's way of life?	☐	☐
Have you often felt lonely or cut off from other people?	☐	☐
Have you and your mate had serious differences that you feel may be related to differences in religion, race, nationality, family background?	☐	☐
3. Have you and your children been separated for more than 1 day in the past year?	☐	☐
Do you have someone reliable to take care of your children when you need it?	☐	☐
Are your children cared for daily by someone outside the family?	☐	☐
If yes, has it been the same person for the past year?	☐	☐

Adapted from Metz, J. R., and others: A pediatric screening examination for psychosocial problems, Pediatrics **58**:4, 1976. Copyright American Academy of Pediatrics 1976.

Reality stressors like job or financial worries, recent change of domicile, illness or injury of child and parent are additional factors that can disrupt routines and be associated with temporary symptoms related to food or feeding behavior. Personal problems of the adult family members, for instance, marital discord, unresolved grief, depression, drug use, or lack of self-esteem, also may influence the feeding situation involving children. When the feeding problem appears to be nonorganic, it is appropriate to ask parents a few simple questions to ascertain the emotional climate in the home. This can be done selectively in an interview or by using a questionnaire as a routine part of the assessment process (see Screening Questionnaire for Family Stress, above).

Parental feelings of competence and satisfaction

Clinical observations indicate that parental *feelings* of competence and satisfaction or dissatisfaction with the parental role are psycho-logical factors that also have an influence on the food intakes and feeding behaviors of children. When an individual, for whatever reason, experiences minimal feelings of success in carrying out the activities associated with parenting, the opportunity for experiencing satisfaction decreases proportionately and the stage is set for problems in parent-child interaction. If the parent does not feel adequate in handling child care activities outside of the feeding sphere, lack of confidence or feelings of incompetence can eventually be manifested in a dysfunctional feeding situation. The mother who reported the following impressions was trying to deal with a 3-year-old boy whose diet consisted only of olives, avocados, and salmon:

I'll never forget what I felt like when he was 2 weeks old and I had to care for him completely on my own. It wasn't at all what I expected. I was scared to death and sure that every time he cried I must have done something wrong. There were half-filled bottles all over the house because I worried that the milk might spoil if Gary didn't drink it in 10 or 15 minutes. My mother-in-law didn't help. She is still always giving me suggestions for a better way to do something.

In early infancy the close relationship to and dependence upon the mother, in particular, often become linked with the feeding process. For this reason many individuals equate successful mothering with a well-nourished infant or child and a nonproblematic feeding situation. The comments of the mother of a developmentally delayed toddler with congenital heart disease (still on a diet of pureed foods) are illustrative:

I couldn't do anything about his heart, but I did pretty well at feeding him by that nasogastric tube. Nobody else could do it as well as I did. Now when he doesn't eat I fix a special high-calorie pudding for him so that he doesn't lose weight. He really gobbles it down!

Factors like past experience, age, knowledge of child growth and development, and the input of significant family members or professionals are important determinants of parental feelings of competence.[8] The standards of performance or values that parents hold for themselves, along with their more general feelings of self-esteem, are also related to perceptions of competence. But probably the most significant influence on parental feelings of success or satisfaction is the responsiveness of the child; that is, does the child show developmental and social evidence of a positive response to parenting? With these determinants in mind the following questions can serve as guidelines for eliciting data on the adjustment to parenting and its associated emotional responses:

1. "As you were growing up, did you observe or assist with the upbringing of younger children such as brothers or sisters, relatives, friends, or neighbors?"
2. "How would you rate your maternal feelings on a scale of 1 to 5 with 1 being very maternal and 5 being nonmaternal?"
3. "What has been the biggest surprise or thing you least expected about being a parent?"
4. "How satisfied are you with your child's physical growth and development?"
5. "How satisfied do you feel with your child's social adjustment?"
6. "How much influence does your spouse have on your ideas about child rearing? Do you usually agree or disagree on child-rearing concerns?"
7. "Who or what has had the most influence on your ideas about child rearing? Books, magazines, or the media? Religion? Friends, neighbors, or relatives? Professionals? Formal education or parenting classes?"
8. "When you and your child are getting along as you usually do, how does your relationship with your child make you feel as a parent?"
9. "How competent do you feel about how you handle your life in general?"
10. "How competent do you feel as a parent?"
11. "How competent a parent do you think you

are *from the viewpoint of others* who know you well?"
12. "Before you had your own family, how did you feel about children?"

Parent-child interaction

An integral component of assessment and data collection related to food intake is consideration of the interaction between child and parent. In order to have an indication of the effects of food and the feeding situation on the parent-child dyad, such data should be based on observation of both mealtime and nonmealtime situations. It is important to determine if food-related parent-child problems are situation specific or part of a more basic discord. Ideally, the assessment should be done in the home setting during mealtime *and* free-play situations. If this is not possible, every attempt should be made to simulate natural conditions in the clinic, office, or hospital environment.

Several research methodologies and standardized tools have been developed to evaluate parent-child interaction, for instance, Verbal Interaction Record,[9] Mutual Problem-Solving Task,[10] Nursing Child Assessment Feeding Scales,[11] and Nursing Child Assessment Teaching Scales.[12] Some practitioners may want to obtain training in the use of standardized assessment techniques; however, less formalized methods can also be helpful in collecting data. Using the concepts of affectional ties, propensity to interact, and feedback and reciprocity as organizers, it is possible to identify the essential elements of most interaction between parents and children.

I. **Affectional ties** (refers to the emotional attachment and degree of psychologic involvement between parent and child)
   A. Appropriate interview questions
      1. "Do you believe in such a thing as 'unconditional mother love'? Would you ever use such a term to describe your feelings about _____?"

2. "How old was _____ when you really felt that he/she was *your* child?"
3. "How does _____ know that you love and care about him/her?"
4. "How do you know that _____ loves you?"
5. "Who or what is _____ most attached to?
6. Have you ever regretted the decision to become a parent? Occasionally? Frequently?"
   B. Direct observation
      1. Attentiveness of parent to child's distress; physical comforting
      2. Use of expressions of love or special designations to refer to child *or* use of negative terms to refer to child; no reference to child by name
      3. Evidence of parental pleasure when child is complimented or comments are made regarding parent-child physical resemblances
      4. Evidence of strong mutual need for togetherness and a maximum avoidance of separation *or* parent or child tendency/preference for isolated activity
      5. Willingness to "relinquish child" to care of a stranger

II. **Propensity to interact** (refers to the ability and desire of parent or child to give and receive communication)
   A. Appropriate interview questions
      1. "When _____ is not around, do you ever find yourself thinking of something you want to do with him/her or something you want to tell him/her?"
      2. "Have you been (or are you ever) so preoccupied with adult worries or concerns that you don't have any energy left to interact with _____?"
      3. "Can you identify any person, thing, or situation that interferes with your relationship or communication with _____?"
      4. "How would you describe your relationship with _____?"
   B. Direct observation
      1. Evidence of physical intactness (espe-

cially sensory and perceptual) of parent and child

2. Evidence of emotional intactness of parent and child

3. Presence or absence of reality stressors (as per Family Stress Questionnaire)

III. Feedback and reciprocity (refers to chains of response between parent and child; activity of one that occurs as a direct result of stimuli from the other)

A. Appropriate interview questions

1. "How does _____ let you know that he/she needs something or wants your attention? What is your usual response to this?"

2. "Who or what usually initiates the interaction between you and your child?"

3. "What do you do for _____? What does _____ do for you?"

B. Direct observation

1. Efforts on the part of either parent or child to remain "in touch" (physically or verbally) that are successful

2. Conversation, singing, laughing, or smiling that maintains an extended interaction (one partner answers the other, the latter responds in turn, and so on)

3. Presence or absence of eye contact between parent and child

4. Presence or absence of caretaking activity on the part of the parent in response to behavior (e.g., cry, yawn, request)

5. Manner in which infant or young child is held

6. Attention of parent to cues in the feeding situation (e.g., satiation, hunger, pacing)

When data indicate that the cause of a child's feeding or food intake problem is most likely psychosocial, intervention must be planned accordingly. The primary focus of treatment will most likely be on strategies to alleviate stress and support family coping abilities, on increasing parental knowledge and skill regarding child rearing, or on facilitating the parent-child relationship. In some situations these goals may be accomplished within the context of the feeding situation; however, in the majority of instances more specific treatment is indicated. Reality-based family needs demand rapid provision of concrete services to relieve situational demands. For this reason referral to a public or private family service or social welfare agency may be appropriate. Those situations that require supportive counseling or education and anticipatory guidance may be handled in a variety of ways, for instance, with family therapy, enrollment in parenting classes, referral to a parent group, or one-to-one work with a qualified professional.

The variety of concerns presented about infant's and children's food intake clearly indicates that information sought must be based on the problems presented and the health care professional's judgment. In some instances dietary intake data may provide sufficient information to design plans with parents and children to modify energy and nutrient intakes. In many instances if plans are to be effective the behavioral and psychosocial influences on a compromised food intake must be investigated. Parents of children with oral motor and self-feeding delays may need help in identifying specific foods to support developmental progress. Those with abnormal motor patterns will need therapy.

Screening procedures may identify children with "feeding problems" of multiple etiology for whom an interdisciplinary assessment is appropriate. Factors that must be considered are adequacy of nutrient intake, structural abnormalities of the oral cavity, oral tissue health, medical status, speech development, living environment, social environment, and neurologic integrity (including sensation, motor coordination, and reflex integration). The collective data provides a base on which the cause of the problem may be determined, effective treatment plans may be designed, and progress may be assessed.

The team approach facilitates identification of priorities for treatment and use of a logical step-by-step approach. Periodic reevaluations of identified concerns indicate the effectiveness of programs designed.

REFERENCES

1. Beal, V. A.: The nutrition history in longitudinal research, J. Am. Diet. Assoc. 51:426, 1967.
2. McHenry, E. W., Ferguson, H. P., and Gurland, J.: Sources of error in dietary surveys, Can. J. Public Health 36:355, 1945.
3. Burke, B. S.: The dietary history as a tool in research, J. Am. Diet. Assoc. 23:1041, 1947.
4. Huenemann, R. I., and Turner, D.: Methods of dietary investigation, J. Am. Diet. Assoc. 18:562, 1942.
5. Young, C. M., and others: A comparison of dietary study methods. I. Dietary history vs 7 day record, J. Am. Diet. Assoc. 28:124, 1952.
6. Trulson, M. F.: Assessment of dietary study methods. I. Comparison of methods for obtaining data for clinical work, J. Am. Diet. Assoc. 30:991, 1954.
7. Brandon, S.: An epidemiological study of eating disturbances, J. Psychosom. Res. 14:253, 1970.
8. Sutherland, S.: An exploratory study of the factors which contribute to a material sense of competence among mothers of children in preschools, parenting classes and a day care center, Unpublished Masters thesis, University of Washington, 1980.
9. Lambie, D. L., Bond, J. T., and Weikart, D. P.: Verbal interaction record, monograph 2, High Scope Monograph Series, Home teaching with mothers and infants. The Ypsilanti-Carnegie infant education project: an experiment, Ypsilanti, Mich., 1974, High Scope Press.
10. Epstein, A., and Weikart, D. P.: Mutual problem-solving task, monograph 6, High Scope Monograph Series. The Ypsilanti-Carnegie infant education project: longitudinal follow-up, Ypsilanti, Mich., 1980, High Scope Press.
11. Nursing child assessment feeding scales. In Barnard, K. E., and Eyres, S. J., editors: Child health assessment, part 2: the first year of life, U.S. Department of Health, Education, and Welfare publication no. HRA 79-25, June 1979.
12. Nursing child assessment teaching scales. In Barnard, K. E., and Eyres, S. J., editors: Child health assessment, part 2: the first year of life, U.S. Department of Health, Education, and Welfare publication no. HRA 79-25, June 1979.

ADDITIONAL READINGS

Marr, J. W.: Individual dietary surveys: purposes and methods, World Rev. Nutr. Diet. 13:105, 1971.
Matthews, L. I.: Principles of interviewing and patient counseling, J. Am. Diet. Assoc. 50:469, 1967.
Reshef, A., and Epstein, L. M.: Reliability of a dietary questionnaire, Am. J. Clin. Nutr. 25:91, 1972.
Shapiro, L. R.: Streamlining and implementing nutritional assessment—the dietary approach, J. Am. Diet. Assoc. 75:230, 1979.
Smith, M. A., editor: Guide for nutritional assessment of the mentally retarded and the developmentally disabled, Memphis, Tenn., 1976, Child Development Center, University of Tennessee.
Young, C. M.: The interview itself, J. Am. Diet. Assoc. 35:677, 1959.

6

The development of food patterns in young children

Miriam E. Lowenberg

Food patterns in the United States show distinct cultural characteristics changing as life-styles change. Hurried small breakfasts, mid-morning coffee breaks, and light lunches followed by heavy evening dinners show modern adjustments to change. In the home, snacking is known to have increased as television has become an integral part of the day and night activities of the American family. The current enthusiasm for behavioral control of food intake also points to a need to examine the day's program in order to learn when unneeded calories in food are taken.

At what age are food patterns formed? When does this learning begin? Those who have studied large numbers of children believe now that what happens during the first year of life as well as during the preschool years is of paramount importance. During the first 5 or 6 years of life it is undoubtedly easier to learn to like all foods than it will be later.

The young child is presently introduced early to hamburgers and french fries when families eat out; attesting to this is one quick-meal company's yearly sales—the highest in the restaurant industry. Eating out becomes a helpful respite for the young homemaker or working mother, and a pattern is established for the young child. When a mother hopes to etablish a basic food pattern of meals enjoyed at home she must deal with the child's desire to eat out even though he or she only knows about it because other children talk about eating out.

When we examine our life-styles, however, we must admit that in modern America we may have many different meal patterns. There are inner city patterns of poor or rich families, suburban patterns, and rural patterns of nonfarm and farm families.

The rich and the poor have throughout the ages had different food patterns. Careful professional observers of young children eating in a group can often predict the home environment of an individual child.

First, we will delineate our goals for the development of food patterns. They are the following:

1. Children should be able to eat in a matter-of-fact way sufficient quantities of the foods that are given to them, just as they take care of other daily needs. The preschool child who truly enjoys most foods but is able to eat without fuss those he doesn't especially like will be fortunate later.
2. Children should be able to manage the feeding process independently and with dispatch, without either unnecessary dawdling or hurried eating.

123

3. Children should be willing to try new foods in small portions the first time they are served to them and to try them again and again until they like or at least willingly accept them.

Social anthropologists point to various ways in which children learn *cues* to fit into a social group. Anyone who is interested in guiding young parents or prospective parents must become analytical to determine which patterns produce healthy children and adults. We must also believe that it is possible to set up a home environment to foster the development of desirable food patterns in young children. Often an impersonal professionally trained outsider can point out to young parents how they can set up such an environment. It must be understood that food patterns begin to be formed from the day of an infant's birth. This reminds me of a healthy, happy young mother who telephoned from her hospital room to report the birth of a daughter 4 hours before. She said with joy that her baby had already tried to nurse; this mother, although still tired from the birth process, had already enjoyed the process of even feeble breast-feeding.

Those who are concerned about obesity as our chief problem of malnutrition are wisely pointing out that prevention as the preferred cure should begin early in infancy. A mother who gives her infant from birth the privilege of deciding and asserting that he or she has had enough food is well on the way to solving this problem. When an individual forms a pattern of quitting to eat at the first indication of satiety, it is believed that this encourages the food intake regulatory mechanism to continue to function. Of course, food that produces the growth of good body tissues must be provided so that more than calorie satiety is provided. This is an important part of early food patterning of a child. The food patterns established in a home, it must be emphasized, are reinforced by love of mother and father and, therefore,

have far-reaching effects on lifetime patterns.

No one has ever phrased the functions of parents more aptly than did C. Anderson Aldrich and Mary Aldrich[1] 40 years ago when they said:

According to nature's plan then parents are meant to enter the feeding situation for three reasons:
First, to provide the food,
Second, to support a child's progress from simple to mature methods of eating, and
Third, to make it easy for him to establish his own satisfying feeding habits.

Long ago another principle was observed* that we need to emphasize with parents. *It*

---

*For 12 years the author observed 20 nursery school-children eating their noon meals. Later, for 2 years these ideas were used in the daily feeding of 1000 children, mostly ages 18 months to 6 years, in two shipyard World War II nursery schools. The author's commission as chief nutritionist was to be in charge of the feeding and nutritional development. Feeding for the child's 9 hours at nursery school was carefully planned, and mothers and fathers were also advised and helped to feed their children at home.

When studying the eating patterns and food preferences of the college nursery schoolchildren for 12 years, this situation was used to teach college students about feeding young children. All food was measured onto the child's plate before it left the kitchen serving area; second helpings and leftover foods were measured and recorded. For 1 school year, the adult who ate at a table with two or three children was asked to record each child's reaction to each food and to the menu as a whole. They were to record: was a food too dry? too tough? too acid to be easily eaten? Were there other characteristics that made the food unsuitable? Were the combinations of foods acceptable and liked by the children? As these criticisms came in daily, corrections were made in the menus and recipes for the foods. During the following year the corrected menus and specific foods were again studied, and further corrections were made. During this study each day, a chart was made of the amounts of each food to be served to each child. The head teacher confirmed that when the children's appetites were closely studied a child's specific food intake could be accurately judged. Most thoughtful mothers can do this.

The advice in this chapter is based on the ideas gained from this meticulous study as well as on extensive tests of these ideas.

really is easier and quicker to change the food than it is to change the child. For instance, young children often have trouble swallowing dry food, and when extra milk is added to thin their mashed potatoes they seem thankful. Such methods are explained in detail later in this chapter.

How can an adult really know what foods children like? The answer lies in carefully observing young children while they are eating.

The chart on p. 135 gives approximate amounts of foods, learned from the study described on p. 124, that one can expect the average child to eat. *In no way are these amounts to be used to force a certain amount of food on any specific child.* If any child, however, habitually eats less than the amount in the chart, it is advised that the reasons for this be determined. As always, a particular child's food dislikes, his or her health condition, or specific family circumstances at the time need to be considered.

It has been found over the years that it is wise to serve a child less than he or she may eat rather than more. Modern behavioral conditioning theory confirms the belief that to help a child to be successful reinforces the behavior we hope to foster.

CULTURAL PATTERNS

In the United States many ethnic groups make up our population. Each ethnic food pattern, based on foods available and preferred, comes from the home country and is based firmly on tradition and often on long usage. Specific ways of cooking foods are always dependent on such factors as the fuel available, the time and the energy available for food preparation, as well as the primary interests and patience of the cook. We can appreciate the fact that the generous use of rye breads and fish in the Scandinavian countries is a result of the cool and short growing season, the long coastlines, and the Scandinavian people's knowledge of successful fishing. Even after such countries are able to import other foods, the preferred foods are still used as tradition dictates. The cause for the abundant use by Polynesian peoples of the coconut, tropical fruits and vegetables, and fish, abundant in tropical waters, is obvious.

The history of a people is written in their preferred foods. This explains why schoolchildren in North Dakota and in Georgia react radically differently to rice used as a vegetable. For instance, rice, which grew well in the American southern colonies from early colonial times, has become a preferred food in that part of the country. Rice, when first used in lunches in some schools in North Dakota, was rejected as an unfamiliar food. This must also be recognized when we consider the special place of honor that the vegetable okra holds for those in the "deep South" of the United States. This vegetable is said to have been brought by slaves from Africa, and its preference has even withstood the memory of those sad journeys to which those slaves were subjected. Blends in Creole dishes could only occur where Spanish, French, black African, and American Indian influences came together.

During the latter part of the twentieth century most Americans have come to prize their cultural backgrounds, cultural foods, and differences in food patterns. In summary, two points should be emphasized. First, every ethnic diet must be based on nutritional adequacy, at least to some degree, for the group using it to survive. It has been pointed out that the very poor and food-deficient Irish people of the nineteenth century, who had an extremely limited diet, could scarcely have chosen any two foods as nutritionally adequate as buttermilk and potatoes. The nutritional adequacy for a desirable state of health may point, in some ethnic patterns, to a need for supplementation with some other foods. Adding other needed foods to this basic diet is often much easier than changing the *staple* food of a group. This, however, means that it is desirable to maintain the basic pattern with only the needed supplementation. American Indian children who have been taught to like the wild greens that their families eat, for instance, should be encouraged to follow these food patterns.

Second, children, who at an early age learn the cues of ethnic food patterns, should be allowed to make these patterns as permanent as possible in a new environment. A respect for differences in food patterns influences the way an individual views himself or herself as a worthwhile human being.

POSITIVE REINFORCEMENT

Experience with helping young children form desirable feeding patterns shows that the modern ideas of positive reinforcement of desirable behavior are sound. (For further discussion of behavior modification, see Chapter 15.) Some 40 years ago it was found that children developed desirable feeding patterns when they felt successful and when negative behavior was ignored. It is wise to make an effort to find out why a child does not like or does not readily eat a certain food or combination of foods. Often it is easy to change the food or menu.

Many ideas on how to help children eat successfully are discussed. The size of a child's portions is of paramount importance. When children are presented with less food than they normally eat they are allowed to accomplish the goal that the adult has set; they can then ask for second helpings. This allows them to receive adult approbation, which is a reward to them. However, if for some reason children cannot eat all the food that has been given to them, allowing them to set their own limit shows respect to them, and they can still feel successful. However, when a child restricts his or her food intake to much less than expected over a number of

days, this merits investigating. Improving an environmental situation often corrects this low intake of food (see pp. 129 to 130 for specific suggestions).

HUNGER AND APPETITE

Food is taken into the body to satisfy the primal urge of hunger. According to the physiologist Dr. Anton J. Carlson, there are two unpleasant sensations that are involved in what we call hunger.[2] The first is a generalized weakness and restlessness all over the body, which is probably caused by a need for more sugar in the blood. The second is a definite localized sensation of pains of tension in the upper part of the stomach. These pangs of hunger are comparatively brief and are followed by periods when hunger pain is not felt. The infant and the young child are thought to have frequent and severe hunger pains. In the infant these sometimes are severe enough to cause an outcry as they awaken him or her from sleep. Infants' stomachs have been observed to show feeble hunger contractions 1 hour after nursing and strong hunger contractions 2½ to 3 hours after a feeding. The length of time at which the stomach shows in this way that it is ready for food varies with the individual infant. In the young child of 2 to 5 years of age these hunger pains are somewhat less frequent or pronounced than in the young infant, but they are still quite definite. Normally, food taken into the body gives immediate pleasure to a child when it eases the pain of hunger. If nothing else interferes, food is associated with the easing of pain, and pleasure results from eating.

What is appetite and how does it differ from hunger? And what part does each play in food habits? Most authorities agree that although hunger is an unpleasant sensation, appetite is a pleasurable experience. Appetite is usually defined as the pleasant association of a food with past experiences with that food. Appetite, associated with the sight and odor of food, stimulates the flow of digestive juices and is, therefore, a vital part of good digestion, as has often been demonstrated in the clinic and laboratory.

Many people have searched diligently and long for foods that taste like those mother used to cook when they were children. No doubt her foods were good, but they were probably not incomparable. The remembered foods were eaten at times when the child was thoroughly happy, and, as a result, a strong appetite for them was created. As an individual grows older the zest for the same food may be lessened. There is only the memory of or the appetite for the former food. Appeties for certain foods are undoubtedly built up in children not only from the flavor, color, and texture of the food itself, but also from the many associations with the food.

It must be realized that to be hungry is normal for a young child. To be persistently nonhungry is decidedly abnormal. The child who is not hungry should be taken to a physician who will carefully assess his or her physical well-being (looking possibly for a chronic infection) and his or her daily habits. This child may not get enough brisk exercise in the open air or may need more sleep, a more regular diet pattern, sleep and rest, or a less stimulating environment.

If a child is in good health and is hungry, with a stomach calling urgently for food, food will be eaten to satisfy that urge rather than to satisfy whims. As has been so aptly said, hunger should control the child rather than the child, hunger. This fact may be taken advantage of in many ways. New foods in very small portions may be served at the time of the day when the child is hungriest. It should be remembered that for a young child a new food is a step in the dark; children are generally not as adventuresome as adults. If a child eats the new food when hungry, it will probably leave a pleasant sensation, and the next time this food is served it will be recognized as a friend. Children learn to like a food by tasting it time after time, even though the first tastes are but a few tiny bites.

SETTING UP A FOOD ENVIRONMENT

In helping parents to understand why children eat as they do, it is well to direct their attention to the fact that *behavior is caused*. When causes of behavior are understood, a food problem is on the way to being cured. When parents understand why children eat as they do, these parents can usually set up an environment that promotes a healthy appetite. Often an outside professional person can help a parent to discover these causes and to restructure the environment. Preparental education in which specific appetite problems are discussed can help parents prevent them. Part of this education must emphasize the requirements of a good food environment.

How does a parent set limits in helping a child develop desirable food patterns? The following are suggestions:

1. The mother as "gatekeeper" must recognize that the kinds of food available to the preschool child in the home are what she buys and provides. Many mothers need to be shown that, in this, *she is really in command*. In a well-child clinic, a mother complained that her 3-year-old child was eating too many potato chips, yet she admitted that she was the one who bought them. Of course, other family members must cooperate in not having foods of this kind available.
2. Often parents must decide which of their own food patterns they want to pass on to their children. In discussing problems of preparation for parenthood, young people may need to be assured that they can change their own food patterns; sometimes they may even need to be helped to do this.
3. Feeding programs for groups of preschool chil-

dren have proven again and again that the eating habits of young children can be repatterned under skilled guidance. This should give young parents added confidence.

DEVELOPMENTAL PATTERNS AND HOW TO USE THEM

Children develop for the most part in an orderly pattern—physically, emotionally, and psychologically.

Eating is always dependent on the abilities of the eater. For instance, when normal infants are born they are able to root for a nipple and to suck vigorously to ingest milk. When infants are given a chance to satisfy their hunger in this manner, they attain their first success in eating. As the mother discovers the child's hunger patterns and provides foods to satisfy hunger, she sets up the condition for successful eating.

DIFFICULTIES IN THE FORMATION OF GOOD FOOD HABITS AND WAYS OF AVOIDING THEM

When most infants are fed the first semisolid food, they will often spit it out rather violently—not because they do not want the food but because the motion of the tongue that they have used in sucking food into their mouth is the only motion that they know (see Chapter 7). Now they try this motion again, and the semiliquid cereal or food spatters everywhere. They must now learn an entirely new feeding technique. If they fail in the first efforts, a mother may be well spattered and naturally quite upset. Now they have met their first feeding disaster. To laugh at these efforts is also unwise because the infant learns to do this to make mother laugh. The mother should have prepared herself previously so that she could remain undisturbed by the incident.

Another difficulty enters into this situation —all the previous food has been liquid in character. Now, suddenly, here is a food with

a new texture, besides having a flavor that is different from the usual, mildly sweet milk. Difficulties may be avoided by giving the infant minute amounts of the new food, well moistened and thinned by the familiar milk, until the new food is easily accepted. Weaning begins right here. The infant is being weaned away gradually from an exclusively fluid diet.

In this discussion weaning is used to mean a general process involving, as far as food is concerned, any change in food flavor, texture, consistency, temperature, or method of feeding. Many feeding difficulties arise because the changes are expected to take place *too abruptly* or because adults fail to realize how difficult some of these tasks are for the infant and the young child. A child can and will learn these new things, but neither the parent nor child should become upset over failures at first. Nor must the child come to the realization that the honors of the day are attained by spitting food out or by refusing it. The problem can be avoided by demonstrating the technique for spoon feeding.

At approximately 6 months of age, even before the first tooth appears, most infants make chewing movements with their gums. At this time infants should be given foods such as small strips of oven-dried toast, which offer a chance for chewing at the same time as they soften to allow easy swallowing. It has been observed that when an infant is not given a chance to chew at this time, trouble in mastering this skill may occur later.

When the infant begins to gain the muscular ability to pick up small particles using the thumb and forefingers, particles of soft green beans or peas can be fed (see Chapter 7 for a more detailed discussion of this). These efforts, along with the reaching for the bottle and later holding it, are the infant's first efforts to learn to feed independently.

The stage of developing independence at

9 to 16 or 18 months of age can either be exciting or distressing to a parent. If parents understand that exploring everything new is very important to an infant, they can encourage this exploration by providing new textures and flavors in foods; this allows an infant to discover what a food such as oatmeal feels like. At this stage many infants have learned to crawl out from their former sitting position or to walk. It is no longer satisfying to them to just look at something; they now want to examine it. The wise mother takes advantage of this new learning in providing a wide variety of food. She should not be discouraged at first if the child only feels a food before chewing it.

During the first year an infant has tremendous adjustments to make, only one of which is learning new foods and new methods of eating. In helping this infant to form good patterns, we will be most successful if thoughtful and understanding guidance is · furnished in the following ways:

1. Introducing new textures and flavors gradually
2. Enlarging the child's experience with as many individual foods in as many different forms as possible
3. For the most part, feeding individual foods and not mixtures so that the infant may learn to appreciate foods for their own flavors and textures
4. Observing at what time of day the infant takes the new food most easily and giving it then
5. Being patient with the first efforts and allowing the infant to learn to feed himself or herself; offering help when the infant becomes too tired to finish the process easily
6. Being understanding of the infant's efforts in each new feeding process
7. Above all, securing the entire family's cooperation

The high level of nutritive need of the first year of life is superceded by a slower metabolic rate and a slower rate of growth. Therefore, the child does not need as much food per unit of body weight as before. What is eaten and how it is eaten are now more important than how much is eaten. To watch a young child grow increasingly independent in feeding himself can be as thrilling for a parent as watching the taking of the first steps from chair to chair. Perhaps in no other area of development in young children is progress more individual. Each child should be allowed to try new skills over and over with no record of failures unless development is obviously too slow to show any progress.

When parents understand what children are telling them in the way they eat, rebellion against food can be lessened and future food refusals can be materially reduced. For instance, the realization that the 2-year-old child may have a sporadic appetite, which should not be the cause for undue alarm, may prevent the long-lasting influence of battles over food.

All of this may make the reader believe that we think that, in a family, only the meals for young children are important. This, of course, is not true. But in a happy family situation, priorities have to be individually determined. Sometimes children, who for some months have eaten at the family table, may suddenly be happier eating at their own small table with a parent nearby. Some mothers even find it possible to eat a quiet noon meal sitting with the child at a small table.

SPECIFIC SUGGESTIONS FOR SETTING UP AN ENVIRONMENT TO FOSTER DESIRABLE PATTERNS OF EATING
Physical facilities

Perhaps no arrangements for eating are more important than those that afford physical comfort to a child. Children should always feel secure on a sturdy, well-balanced chair with their feet well supported on the floor or otherwise. They should be able to reach their food on the plate easily without straining their arm muscles. This also provides a better opportunity to eat without the danger of spills. Dishes and utensils, as well as table arrangements, can foster success in eating. It is desirable to give the child sturdy and as nearly unbreakable utensils as possible so that spills and breaking utensils will not give a sense of failure. Also, it is important not to laugh at the child, because if parents laugh at a child's mistakes the child may gain an undue feeling of being the center of attention.

At the time when children's chairs are being purchased, these should be "tried on" (to fit the child's body) as clothing is. Some chairs, for instance, are designed to fit a child's torso and are much more comfortable than are perfectly straight chairs. Wise parents also prepare table surfaces and floors for children's spills. It can be observed that family restaurants have abundant patronage where children's spills are quietly and quickly handled by those serving the food.

Colorful table arrangements intrigue young children and are worth the trouble to provide. When children have developed some skill in eating, they will appreciate eating from the family's best china. It has been found that confidence in a child's accomplishment is usually rewarded by care in handling prized possessions when the child is ready. It is easy to notice children who have had help in gaining skill in successful eating as one observes families eating together in restaurants.

Forks and spoons should be chosen for their suitability for young hands. The spoon, which is the first eating implement a child uses, should have a round shallow bowl and a blunt tip that allows the child to shove food from the plate. A handle that is blunt, short, and easily held in the child's palm is desirable. It must be remembered that at this age a child uses the hand as a mass of muscles. Only after the age of 5 or 6 years is con-

trol of the finer muscles of the fingers accomplished. Forks with short, blunt tines are best adapted to the child's palm. Some parents report, however, that their children enjoy sharper tines with which they can spear food. It must be remembered, however, that sharp tines can be dangerous.

Glasses that sit firmly on the table and are small enough for small hands to encircle have been observed to be the best for the hands of 2- to 4-year-old children. Small delicate handles on cups are difficult for small hands to maneuver.

The shape and weight of the dishes is also very important. The young child delights in pouring his or her own milk. Interesting, squat pitchers with broad handles from which the child can easily pour milk are recommended. Parents can be encouraged to experiment with the dishes and utensils for their children and to look for those that satisfy children's needs.

FOODS CHILDREN LIKE

Patient observing and long experience in feeding young children as well as in counseling parents have given me an insight into what children want in their food. When this point of view is combined with the knowledge of nutrients, children can be adequately and happily fed. The results of these observations are discussed on the following pages.

Menus

Simplicity in menus is a *very important consideration.* At the same time there must be variety to allow young children to learn to know many foods. Variety in foods is a good foundation for an adequate diet.

The following outline gives a general meal pattern that should satisfy nutrient needs in a hungry, preschool child.

A. Breakfast
  1. One high-protein food
     a. One egg *or*

b. 2 oz of muscle meat *or*
c. ¾ to 1 oz of cheese *or*
d. ½ cup of cereal, cooked, *or*
e. 1 cup of dry cereal with 4 to 6 oz milk
2. Bread with butter or margarine (1 slice whole grain² or white enriched bread, plus 1 tsp butter)
3. Milk, 6 to 8 oz
4. Fruit—preferably one serving of citrus
a. 4 oz of orange juice *or*
b. ⅓ to ½ medium-sized grapefruit *or*
c. 1 medium-sized orange
B. **Noon meal**
1. One high-protein food (See breakfast for list of high-protein foods)
a. 1 serving of a thick soup or stew *or*
b. 1 serving of a casserole dish of a protein food in a starchy base
2. Vegetables
a. 1 cooked (see chart, p. 135, for amounts)
b. 1 raw (see chart, p. 135, for amounts)
3. Bread (1 slice whole grain² or enriched white bread with 1 tsp butter)
4. Milk, 6 to 8 oz
5. Dessert
a. Simple dessert based on a combination of milk, eggs, and fruit *or*
b. Serving of fruit
C. **Evening meal**
1. One high-protein food
a. 2 oz meat
b. 1 oz cheese
c. 1 egg
d. or combinations of these and vegetables
2. Vegetables
a. 1 or 2 cooked
b. 1 raw
3. Bread and butter (1 slice whole grain² or enriched white bread with 1 tsp butter)
4. Milk, 6 to 8 oz
5. Dessert (see noon meal, dessert)
D. **Snacks between meals or at bedtime**
These should provide some of needed nutrients and be low in sugar and fat so that they do not interfere with the appetite for the following meal—use, for example, any of the following:
1. Fruit juices with a cracker or a piece of bread *or*
2. Small pieces of fruit *or*

3. Small pieces of raw vegetables *or*
4. Small pieces of cheese with a small piece of bread or cracker

Combinations of food

Most children eat most easily those foods with which they are familiar. It is advisable that a very small portion of a new food be introduced with a familiar and a popular food. If a child only looks at the new food or just feels or smells it at first, this is a part of learning to accept it.

Dry foods are especially hard for children to eat, as is discussed later in this chapter. In planning a menu, always carefully balance a dry food with one or two moist foods. For instance, it is wise to put a slice of meat loaf (relatively dry) with mashed potatoes and peas in a little cream sauce.

Combinations of sharp, rather acid-flavored foods with mild-flavored foods are popular with young children.

Ease of manipulation

The ease of eating a food with the unskilled and seemingly clumsy hands of a young child is very important. Many small pieces of foods such as cooked green peas or beans are difficult for a child to spoon up. These can be mixed with mashed potatoes to make for easier eating.

When a 2-year-old child eats a bowl of thin soup, many trials are made before it is finished. Although it is advisable to serve young children soups occasionally, one must realize that the process of spooning it is tiring. Two things may be done to make soup easier for a child to eat. It may be drunk from a cup, or the soup may be made slightly thicker so that it does not spill from the spoon easily. A prominent soup company promoted a two-way soup, after hiring me as a consultant. I suggested to the company that after a canned soup had been thinned, preferably with milk, it should be strained so that a child could spoon up the solid portion and drink the liquid. It is my belief that soup for children should be either spoonable or drinkable. Later, the child may have soup to be eaten with a spoon when he or she is able to manage a spoon without spilling its contents.

Many foods can be prepared so that a child can eat them with the fingers. Hard-cooked eggs may be served in quarters, cooked meat can be cut in small strips, and cooked green beans can be served as finger foods. Children have been observed to like oranges that have been cut in wedges (skin and all) much better than peeled and diced oranges.

Mixed-up salads, when there are layers of food to be eaten, are much more difficult to eat than simple pieces of raw vegetables with no salad dressing. This preference has also been observed in school lunches where very young schoolchildren are being fed. It is also wise to serve cottage cheese or similar foods separate from the lettuce leaf on a child's plate. Creamed foods served on tough toast are difficult for children to manage.

The size of the pieces of food for children must be given serious consideration. The problem of handling silverware and conveying food to the mouth at this early age is a greater task than many adults realize. Pieces of carrots that slide across the plate and are too small to remain on the fork while they are being lifted to the mouth or cubes of beets so large that they must be cut into bite-size pieces before being eaten exhaust the patience of a 2- or 3-year-old child. Most foods for these children should be served to them in bite-sized pieces. When the child is 4 years of age and older, the skills to cut up some foods may have been developed. If, however, much difficulty in managing is noticed, small pieces for the most part should be served, accompanied by occasional encouragement to cut up some foods. Canned pears and other soft fruits are usually easily cut into bite-sized pieces.

Stringy spinach or tomatoes are a trial for anyone to eat. Much can be done with a handy pair of food shears in the kitchen to make these foods easier to eat. Finger foods such as pieces of lettuce or toast, which may be eaten with the fingers, should be used in meals where some of the foods are difficult to handle. Small sandwiches—that is, a large one cut into four squares—are popular with young children.

Texture

I have found it wise to serve one soft food (for easy eating), one crisp food (to allow easy chewing and enjoyment of the sounds in the mouth), and one chewy food (to use emerging chewing skills without having too much to chew) in each meal for young children.

Some children can fall into the habit of rejecting all foods of a certain texture; this limits the kinds of foods the child tries to eat. See p. 136 for suggestions of how to handle this problem.

Pieces of meat seem to be hard for a young child to eat; this explains why children often prefer hamburgers or frankfurters. Most children's meat can be served as ground meat. In fact, it was often found in nursery school feeding that thrice-ground meat was popular. This is true because the teeth of 2- or 3-year-old children do not grind meat as easily as adult teeth do. When parents want steaks, a roast, or a pot roast, the mother can cook a small portion of ground meat from the freezer for the young child. When ground meat is being cooked, it should be cooked only long enough for the color to change to brown. It should not be allowed to become dry with a hard crust, which is hard for a child to eat. Some children may prefer moderately rare meat, which is even more moist.

Flavor

In general, young children reject strong flavors. Many children, however, do seem to like pickles, some spicy sauces, and beer, which may seem to contradict this. In general, it has been found that children like food that is mildly salted, with about one-half as much salt as is used in adult recipes. Because some authorities now believe that all of us would profit by taking less salt, this may be a good health habit to foster (Chapter 13). In general, pepper and other sharp spices and acids such as vinegar on children's food should also be used sparingly.

Strong-flavored vegetables such as those belonging to the cabbage and onion family are more popular with young children when served raw. If these vegetables are cooked it is recommended that they be placed in an excessive amount of cooking water so that some of the strong flavor can be thrown away. Of course, water-soluble nutrients are thrown away by this process, but teaching children to eat these foods is most important at this time in their lives. A mild-flavored cream sauce also helps to make these vegetables more popular. In fact, this popularity was shown when some children in nursery school asked for very mild-flavored creamed onions after they had eaten dessert.

Because sharply tart fruits are often rejected by young children, such fruits should be diluted with those of mild flavor. Tart oranges were found to be popular when mixed with cooked peaches or bananas. The rule of one tart, one mild, and one crisp is a good one to follow. The crisp fruit may be small unpeeled pieces of apples.

In general, in helping children develop desirable food patterns, it is wise to keep the natural flavor of the food. This leads to the use of only small amounts of sugar. The use of a little honey is also recommended because this is sweeter than an equal amount of granulated sugar and less can be used.

Color

Children have a natural interest in color in their foods, and teaching them to appreciate the lovely fresh color of foods is a worthy aim. Young children are delighted when they may choose one of several different colored desserts. Green, orange, yellow, and pink are popular colors in foods. Children in nursery schools rarely failed to comment on the food to which a tiny sprig of parsley

Fig. 6-1. Preschool children enjoy snacks that are colorful and can be fingerfed.

had been added or to notice bits of hidden color such as tomato, carrot, or parsley in sandwiches.

Cakes, cookies, and candies containing molasses, dried fruits, and nuts provide other nutrients in addition to calories. Natural fruit juices have more of the needed nutrients than sweetened, colored, and artificially flavored drinks. Because the water that fruit juices contain is also desirable for children, strong-flavored juices should be diluted, giving additional water to the child.

SPECIFIC FOOD PREPARATION

Children should be considered when the family plans meals. Many parents do, of necessity, vary their life-styles when they are raising their families, so the importance of food-patterning during this period is emphasized. Young children can be taught that as adults wear different clothes than children, so there also are adult-type foods and drinks. Children have been observed to prefer an orange or a serving of fruit to cherry pie that is being served to adults.

Foods can be made soft enough in texture for young children by adding extra milk to a dry, starchy food.

If the parents prefer strong-flavored vegetables, a small portion for the young child can be rinsed under the hot water faucet before it is served.

A young child may prefer food served at room temperature. In fact, preschool children often appear frightened by hot food. They also often stir hard ice cream until it is soupy and less sharply cold.

While the father serves dinner at the table, the mother may prefer to dish the preschool child's food in the kitchen. This can serve two purposes: (1) young children's hunger makes them impatient participants at a meal, so rapid service of food is desirable, and (2) the mother can easily regulate the amount of food served or can make any sudden changes.

I have discovered that fathers sometimes have more difficulty serving small enough portions to a child than mothers do.

Table 6-1 has been devised from my many years of careful observations of how much the average child can eat easily. Some pediatricians who believe that children should not be forced to eat a specific amount of any food object to setting up such expectations in a chart. Yet mothers often need some help in the amount of food the *average* child can eat easily to get the needed nutrients. Such goals may also prevent mothers from expecting their children to eat more than their children want. These average portion sizes may be too large for a new food, for a disliked food, or for a nonhungry child. Of course, the hungry child can have extra servings.

FOOD DISLIKES

It is safe to allow every person to have at least one or two food dislikes. Except for medically restricted diets, no one food has to be eaten. I am, of course, assuming that a family can afford a varied diet.

Some food dislikes, as has been previously discussed, have unusual causes. A woman reports that sugared oranges always have a flavor of castor oil to her, though she enjoys oranges without sugar. When she was young she was given doses of the then strong-flavored castor oil with sugared oranges to cover its flavor. Though she knows that she only imagines the castor oil flavor in the oranges, she says that even now she thinks "What has been on my spoon, castor oil?" The association of sugared oranges and castor oil has survived with her over many years.

Substitutions for liquid milk, which some children may dislike, can temporarily be made. Powdered milk (4 tbsp substituted for 8 oz of fluid milk) can be added to foods, and cottage or cheddar cheese can be used. When children are in control of their appe-

Table 6-1. Food pattern for preschool children*

Food	Portion size	Number of portions advised	
		Ages 2 to 4 years	Ages 4 to 6 years
Milk and dairy products			
Milk†	4 oz	3 to 6	3 to 4
Cheese	½ to ¾ oz	May be substituted for one portion of liquid milk	
Yogurt	¼ to ½ cup	May be substituted for one portion of liquid milk	
Powdered skim milk	2 tbsp	May be substituted for one portion of liquid milk	
Meat and meat equivalents			
Meat‡, fish§, poultry	1 to 2 oz	2	2
Egg	1	1	1
Peanut butter	1 to 2 tbsp		
Legumes—dried peas and beans	¼ to ⅓ cup cooked		
Vegetables and fruits			
Vegetables		4 to 5 to include 1 green leafy or yellow‖	4 to 5 to include 1 green leafy or yellow
Cooked	2 to 4 tbsp		
Raw	Few pieces		
Fruit		1 citrus fruit or other vegetable or fruit rich in vitamin C	1 citrus fruit or other vegetable or fruit rich in vitamin C
Canned	4 to 8 tbsp		
Raw	½ to 1 small		
Fruit juice	3 to 4 oz		
Bread and cereal grains			
Whole grain or enriched white bread	½ to 1 slice	3	3
Cooked cereal	¼ to ½ cup	May be substituted for one serving of bread	
Ready-to-serve dry cereals	½ to 1 cup		
Spaghetti, macaroni, noodles, rice	¼ to ½ cup		
Crackers	2 to 3		
Fat			
Bacon	1 slice	Not to be substituted for meat	
Butter or vitamin A–fortified margarine	1 tsp	3	3 to 4
Desserts	¼ to ½ cup	As demanded by calorie needs	
Sugars	½ to 1 tsp	2	2

*Diets should be monitored for adequacy of iron and vitamin D intake.
†Approximately ⅔ cup can easily be incorporated in a child's food during cooking.
‡Liver once a week can be used as liver sausage or cooked liver.
§Should be served once or twice per week to substitute for meat.
‖If child's preferences are limited, use double portions of preferred vegetables until appetite for other vegetables develops.

tite and hunger, they may refuse all foods. One cold, winter day in a nursery school when we were weary of preparing food for nonhungry children, we decided to give them a shock. On the usual array of dishes, we placed only 1 tbsp of vegetable meat stew in the soup bowl. No other food was in evidence in the entire dining room, no baskets of sandwiches, no pitchers of milk, no trays of dishes of desserts. When the children took one look, they at once exclaimed "Where's our dinner? Is this all of our dinner?" Rather slowly, second servings were brought in from the kitchen. The food records showed that more food was eaten that day than for any day for several weeks before.

Telling a child that we know he or she doesn't like boiled potatoes and can have more green beans often encourages a good appetite. When a child, however, rejects many foods, as for example, all vegetables or all meat, it is well to investigate the reason for this, if possible. Adequate substitutions may need to be made. For instance, in hot summer weather, fruits can replace cooked vegetables in a child's diet if the family budget can tolerate the extra cost. This serving of fruit sometimes stimulates failing appetites.

At times the mother may need to seek professional help from someone who understands children both from closer observation of many children eating as well as from knowing the findings of research in the area.

In summary, the following can be emphasized:

1. Belief that changes can occur in a child's eating patterns is of primary importance. Eating is one of the pleasures of life. Fortunate is the individual who likes foods he or she needs to eat for the adequate nutrition of the body.
2. The goals set by someone when counseling parents about children's eating should be those that are easily accomplished. Success in following the advice of professional people promotes confidence and positively reinforces the child who succeeds in eating what is presented. When a food dislike is firmly established before the parent seeks help, it will probably not disappear suddenly; only gradual correction can be expected. Progress may not be consistent, and temporary failures to reach the goal must be expected. For instance, in helping a child to learn to eat foods coarse in texture, a mother can freeze coarse-textured cooked vegetables (chunks, that is) in ice trays when she is trying to wean a child from eating only pureed vegetables. Increasing amounts of this coarser food can be added gradually to the child's vegetables.
3. When a child exhibits a strong food dislike, this should be accepted as a fact. Substitution for the missed nutrients often is the wisest plan. Often a temporary release of pressure concerning eating a specific food causes the child to try it later. A mother who was looking at her 3-year-old son's noon meal food consumption record in a nursery school said "But he never eats eggs at home and this noon he had seconds!" That is exactly the reason why a mother enrolling a child is not asked about the child's food dislikes, only about the foods that make the child ill. Another mother said to her son as she looked at the records, "But you don't like turnips!" Whereupon her son answered, "Yours are black. They are white at nursery school. I like them white!" This leads to the next point.
4. Children are good judges of well-prepared food. Sometimes classes in food preparation for parents or prospective parents would be the best approach to handling children's food dislikes.
5. Sometimes the "war" over children's eating has become so sharp that withdrawing one of the combatants is the only solution to a battle over food. Someone other than the mother feeding the child temporarily may also be a solution to the problem.
6. Because children are usually rhythmic in all they do, it is advised that the satisfaction of their hunger should also be kept rhythmic. This means that meals served at the same time each day generally promote a good appetite.

Fatigue, the most defeating factor in children's appetites, is thus avoided. I have found again and again that starving a child to eat does not promote good eating.

COMMON PROBLEMS

It should be remembered that healthy, hungry children will eat if they are given a calm atmosphere in which to eat. This is the first and most important consideration.

One of the most common problems, that of fatigue, has just been discussed. Only sympathy should be extended to the child who, eating at a tearoom in a large store after a morning's shopping, just looks at the food and cries when urged to eat. The child probably needs to rest more than he or she needs to eat.

When a child is regularly more hungry at a certain time of day than at other times, acceptance of this fact is wise. Perhaps the greater hunger at the evening meal is caused by having rested while watching a favorite television program before dinner. Sometimes healthy outdoor running, followed by a quiet rest, restores a lagging noontime appetite. It was found that nursery school food costs increased when the children played outdoors in a warm Iowa March after a cold and confining February.

Some of the earliest eating skills learned by a young child are those of chewing and swallowing. Each of these is accomplished to a great extent by trial and error. Some impatient parents worry over this slow progress.

Swallowing seems to be difficult for some children. They tend to swallow only after the food is thoroughly chewed and finely ground. In fact, some children hold food in the cheeks like chipmunks, and some children have been observed to have eaten all their dessert and still have the vegetable in their cheeks. The fact that some children apparently gain more enjoyment from filling their mouths full of food than from taking small mouthfuls makes learning to chew and swallow a bit complicated for them. These children may almost appear hopeless as they sit with packed mouths. Encouraging them to take small bites and to chew and swallow each mouthful has been successful in some cases.

No discussion of children's food problems would be complete without a discussion of the so-called vegetable war. Sometimes this may be created at first by a generally disgruntled parent who really wants to have the child reinforce his or her own belief that all vegetables are horrible.[1] Perhaps a father associates cooked vegetables with his mother with whom there was always a clash. It is fascinating to read in histories of American colonial times of husbands who refused their wives the money to buy seeds for green leafy vegetables because they considered these foods "fodder." This was, of course, in the "previtamin days." This idea of fodder appears too often in the history of food patterns. Yet we also find in these histories stories of gathering wild greens for use during the so-called hunger weeks of spring when the food preserved for winter was either all gone or too spoiled to be used. It is also interesting to observe in tropical countries of Asia and Africa a vast array of what are to us strange-looking green leafy vegetables that are bought eagerly from native markets.

This rejection of some kinds of foods can easily be passed down from parents to their children. Sometimes a dislike for the usually popular milk can be directly accounted for in this way. The labeling of salads as "women's food" may also have caused some boys to reject them.

All of these influences, although subtle, are definitely effective in the development of food prejudices. Being branded as someone who does not like carrots often prevents a child who would like later to try them from doing so. When we begin to understand the basis of a food prejudice, we are on the way to counteracting it.

It can, however, be stated positively that many children do like well-cooked vegetables, and some raw vegetables are definitely well liked. Of course, we are assuming here that strong acrid odors and unpleasant flavors are not present in these cooked vegetables. When a person, coming in from outdoors and the fresh air, smells unpleasant cooking odors in a poorly ventilated kitchen, a prejudice may precede the actual meal. Sometimes better selection at the market of tender young root vegetables is necessary to prevent the unpleasant "woodiness" in root vegetables.

Another specific food problem concerns the child who is exceptionally fond of sweet foods. This often occurs because parents who are very fond of such food have patterned the child to be overfond of them. Sweet foods used as rewards or as special treats also reinforce the child's desire for sweets. The use of cake for a birthday celebration is too well grounded in American tradition to be uprooted, but we should recognize that when we present a child with a wonderful birthday cake, we are reinforcing the value of a sweet food. One child asked whether fruit cake (always served in his home at Christmas time) was Christ's birthday cake.

In no other area are family influences more strong than in food preferences. The association of mother's food and her love last over years and may supersede all outside influences. Studies have shown that of all meal patterns, Sunday dinner meal patterns change most slowly when a family moves to a new country. A father's influence on a child's food preferences was shown in one study where children were found to dislike the foods that the father disliked.[3] The reason was that, because mothers did not

serve the food fathers disliked, these foods were unfamiliar to the children and they refused them when they were served later.

Modern mothers, buffeted by their children's faith in television advertisements for food as well as by the sweets offered in vending machines at school, sometimes lose faith in their role as the "home gate-keeper." They may need professional bolstering to reinforce their faith in themselves so that they actually do control the food in their homes and in their children's lives.

In summary, to assist children to develop desirable food patterns, it is recommended that:

1. All foods should be well prepared and attractive in color, flavor, and texture, so that the child will feel friendly toward them and eat them happily. Children appreciate and enjoy an attractive plate and often comment on foods being "pretty"; they eat with greatest enthusiasm when there is a variety of flavors and textures in the meal.
2. The environment for eating should be suited to the abilities and comfort of the young eater. This includes appropriate tables and chairs as well as suitable dishes and implements for eating.
3. A child should be expected to have a good appetite and to be hungry when in good health physically and emotionally.
4. Appetite will be fostered if the child is happily excited over the fact that it is mealtime.
5. Pleasant associations with the food will be fostered if the meal can be eaten successfully with reasonable effort. A child should not become too tired physically before the meal has been eaten.

REFERENCES

1. Aldrich, C. A., and Aldrich, M. M.: Feeding our old fashioned children, New York, 1946, Macmillan, Inc.
2. Carlson, A. J.: The control of hunger in health and disease, Chicago, Ill., 1916, University of Chicago Press.
3. Bryan, M. S., and Lowenberg, M. E.: The father's influence on young children's food preference, J. Am. Diet. Assoc. 34:30, 1958.

7

Infant feeding and nutrition

At no time in the life cycle will as many changes in relation to food and nutrient intake be observed as during the first year of life. Influenced by a rapid but declining rate of physical growth and maturation of the oral motor, fine motor, and gross motor skills and relationships established with their parents, infants prepared at birth to suck liquids from a nipple are at 1 year of age making attempts to feed themselves table food with culturally defined utensils. The need for nutrients and energy is dependent on the infant's requirement for maintenance, physical growth, and energy expenditure. The foods offered to infants reflect culturally accepted practice. Infants' acceptance of food is influenced by neuromotor maturation and by their interactions with their parents. One will, therefore, find a variety of combinations of foods and milks consumed by well-nourished children at any month during infancy.

MILK IN THE INFANT'S DIET

That human milk from adequately nourished lactating mothers offers nutritional, immunologic, and psychosocial benefits to infants has never been questioned. Even so, the incidence of breast feeding of the newborn infant fell from 38% in 1946 to 18% in 1966. The duration of breast feeding was short for many infants. Weaning to a commercially prepared formula or cow's milk often occurred in the first 3 months. Reasons for the decline in breast feeding were

multiple. Manufacturers' advertising practices, cultural practices and mores, and changes in social and economic conditions all had an effect. In addition, health care professionals who assumed responsibility for prenatal and postnatal education of mothers failed to appreciate and convey to mothers the many advantages of human milk, and many professionals were not prepared to provide continuing support to mothers as they attempted to establish lactation. Attitudes toward breast feeding have changed in the United States. Although regional differences persist, over half of the mothers now establish lactation before leaving the hospital, and an increasing percentage breast feed for 3 to 6 months. Most normal full-term infants who are not breast fed receive a cow's-milk base commercially prepared formula; very few receive fresh cow's milk. Milk-free formulas are fed to approximately 10% of infants in the first 4 months of life.[1]

Colostrum and transitional milk

The first few days after birth the breast-fed infant ingests a yellowish, transparent fluid called colostrum. Human colostrum contains more protein but less fat, carbohydrate, and energy than does mature human milk. Concentrations of sodium, potassium, and chloride are greater in colostrum than in later milk. Between the third and sixth day colostrum changes to a milk that, compared to mature milk, has a high protein content. By

Table 7-1. Nutrient content of human milk and cow's milk

Constituent (per liter)	Human milk	Cow's milk	Constituent (per liter)	Human milk	Cow's milk
Energy (kcal)	690	660	Minerals		
Protein (gm)	9	35	Calcium (mg)	297	1170
Fat (gm)	45	37	Phosphorus (mg)	150	920
Lactose (gm)	68	49	Sodium (mg)	150	506
Vitamins			Potassium (mg)	550	1368
Vitamin A (IU)	1898	1025	Chlorine (mg)	385	1028
Vitamin D (IU)	22	14	Magnesium (mg)	23	120
Vitamin E (IU)	2	0.4	Sulfur (mg)	140	300
Vitamin K (μg)	15	60	Iron (mg)*	0.56-0.3	0.5
Thiamine (μg)	160	440	Iodine (mg)	30	47
Riboflavin (μg)	360	1750	Manganese (μg)†	5.9-4.0	20-40
Niacin (mg)	1.5	0.9	Copper (μg)	0.6-0.25	0.3
Pyridoxine (μg)	100	640	Zinc (mg)‡	4-.5	3-5
Folic acid (μg)	52	55	Selenium (μg)	20	5-50
Cobalamine (μg)	0.3	4	Flouride (mg)	0.05	0.03-0.1
Ascorbic acid (mg)	43	11			

Adapted from Hambreaus, L.: Proprietary milk versus human breast milk in infant feeding, a critical approach from the nutritional point of view. Pediatr. Clin. North Am. **24:**17, 1977; Siimes, M. A., Vuori, E., and Kuitunen, P.: Breast milk iron—a declining concentration during the course of lactation, Acta Paediatr. Scand. **68:**29, 1979; Vuori, E.: A longitudinal study of manganese in human milk, Acta Paediatr. Scand. **68:**571, 1979; and Vuori, E., and Kuitunen, P.: Concentrations of copper and zinc in human milk, Acta Paediatr. Scand. **68:**33, 1978; and Nayman, R., and others: Observations on the composition of milk-substitute products for the treatment of inborn errors of amino acid metabolism: comparisons with human milk, Am. J. Clin. Nutr. **32:**1279, 1979.

*Median values at 2 weeks and 5 months of lactation.

†Median values at 2 weeks and 5 months of lactation, after which time the manganese content of human milk tends to increase.

‡Median values at 2 weeks and 37 weeks of lactation.

the tenth day the breast-fed infant receives mature milk.

Comparison of nutrient compositions of human milk and cow's milk

Nutrients secreted in human milk vary and reflect individual biochemical variability among women, the diet consumed, the stage of lactation, and the length of time the mother has breast fed.[2] Minimum standards for cow's milk vary from state to state, and one may find differences in milk purchased in various localities. Tables of food values list average nutrients contained in pooled human milk and minimum federal standards for homogenized milk. The content of iron, zinc, copper, and manganese is known to decrease from 2 weeks to 5 or 9 months as children's rates of growth and nutrient needs decline. It is likely that the concentration of other nutrients for which there is as yet no data may also decline during the course of lactation.

Human milk and cow's milk provide similar amounts of water and approximately the same quantity of energy. The nutrient sources of the energy are, however, different. Protein supplies approximately 7% of the calories in human milk and 20% of the calories in cow's milk; the carbohydrate lactose supplies approximately 42% of the calories in human milk and 30% of the calories in cow's milk. The percentage of calories supplied by fat is similar in both milks. The protein content of human milk approximates 0.9 gm/dl, compared to 3.5 gm/dl in cow's milk. Nonprotein nitrogen accounts for 25% of total nitrogen in human milk, 5% of total nitrogen in cow's milk.[3]

Casein and whey constitute the protein in both milks. Amounts of whey protein are similar in each. Cow's milk contains six to seven times as much casein as does human milk, and differences in the casein:whey ratios of the two milks are great. The casein:whey ratio of human milk is 40:60, whereas the casein:whey ratio of cow's milk is 82:18. β-Lactoglobulin, the dominant whey protein in cow's milk, is absent in human milk in which α-lactoglobulin and lactoferrin are the predominant whey proteins.

Human milk has a low content of tyrosine and phenylalanine as compared to cow's milk. Taurine and cystine are present in much higher concentrations in human milk than in cow's milk.[3]

During digestion in the stomach the protein of milk mixes with hydrochloric acid. The result of this process is the formation of curds from the casein and calcium and of a liquid that contains the whey. Because of its lower casein content, human milk forms a soft, flocculent, easy-to-digest curd in the infant's stomach. The increased casein content of fresh cow's milk causes it to form a tough, cheesy, hard-to-digest curd. Homogenization, boiling, and dilution of cow's milk modify the curd and prevent the formation of the hard curds in the stomach so that it is easily digested by the infant.

The total fat content of human milk and cow's milk is similar. Saturated fatty acids predominate in cow's milk. The fatty acid pattern of human milk resembles that of the maternal diet. Diurnal variations occur in human milk, the fat content being higher in the early mornings. Four percent of the calories in human milk but only 1% of the calories in cow's milk is provided by linoleic acid. The content of short chain fatty acids is greater in cow's milk. Later human milk has a higher percentage of fat than foremilk. It has been hypothesized that this may be associated with an appetite control mechanism not available to formula-fed infants whose formula has a constant fat content.[4]

Both cow's milk and human milk contain lipoprotein lipase in the cream fraction that is stimulated by serum and inhibited by bile salts. Human milk contains an additional lipase that is stimulated by bile salts and contributes significantly to the hydrolysis of milk triglycerides. These enzymes contribute significantly to a higher percentage absorption of human milk fat as compared to butter fat.

The concentration of lactose is greater in human milk than in cow's milk. This nutrient is incorporated into galactolipids in the brain and spinal cord. Trace amounts of glucose, galactose, glucosamines, and other nitrogen-containing carbohydrates are also present in both milks. Human milk contains L-bifidus factor, a nitrogen-containing carbohydrate, in concentrations 40 times greater than in cow's milk. This carbohydrate is required by the bacteria *Lactobacillus* for growth.[5]

Both human milk and cow's milk provide adequate quantities of vitamin A and the B complex vitamins. Human milk from well-nourished mothers is a reliable source of vitamin C, whereas processed cow's milk contains very little. Human milk provides greater amounts of vitamin E and lesser amounts of vitamin K than does cow's milk. Human milk contains 2 IU of vitamin D/dl and 1.78 ± 0.39 mg of water-soluble vitamin D sulfate.[6] Most dairies fortify homogenized,

2%, and nonfat milk with 400 IU of vitamin D/quart. Evaporated milk reconstituted with equal amounts of water is fortified with 400 IU/quart.

The mineral content of cow's milk is several times greater than that of human milk. Cow's milk contains more than three times as much calcium and six times as much phosphorus as does human milk. The high phosphate load and calcium:phosphate ratio have been implicated as an etiologic factor of late hypocalcemic tetany of the neonate.

Human milk and cow's milk contain 0.5 mg of iron/100 ml. Forty-nine percent of the iron in human milk is absorbed. Less than 1% of the iron in cow's milk is absorbed.[7]

Human milk contains less zinc than does cow's milk. Most of the zinc in human milk is associated with a low molecular weight fraction; in cow's milk it is associated with a high molecular weight fraction. Animal studies suggest that the bioavailability of zinc in human milk is 59%, in cow's milk 43% to 51%.[8]

The high protein and mineral content of cow's milk places a much greater osmolar load on the kidney of the infant and obligates a greater amount of water for excretion. The margin of safety is smaller. Cow's milk may not supply sufficient amounts of water when the environmental temperature is high. Neither milk may provide adequate amounts of water when requirements are increased by fever, vomiting, or diarrhea.

Anti-infective characteristics of human milk

In addition to nutrients, human colostrum and milk contain antibodies, enzymes, and other factors absent or present in only minute amounts in cow's milk—factors that provide infants with protection against enteric infections.[9]

Lactobacillus microorganisms in the gas-trointestinal tract, whose growth is dependent on L-bifidus factor, produce acetic and lactic acids. The resulting acidic environment interferes with the growth of certain pathogenic organisms such as *Escherichia coli* and *Shigella* and provides a medium in which lysozymes are stable. Lysozymes exert their effect by destroying bacterial cell membranes after the organisms have been inactivated by peroxides and ascorbic acid also present in human colostrum and milk.

Immunoglobulins (antibodies) to many different types of organisms including pertussis, staphylococci, *E. coli,* and *Salmonella* have been identified in colostrum and, in smaller amounts, in mature human milk. Since these immunoglobulins are not absorbed, they exert an effect only against microorganisms that enter the body through the gastrointestinal tract. Infants who are breast fed by mothers with high titers of antibodies to poliomyelitis are resistant to infection with orally administered polio vaccine. It is, however, believed that human milk does not completely inhibit the effectiveness of the vaccine. Lactoperoxidase, an enzyme present in human milk and saliva, aids in killing streptococci and may act on other organisms.

Large amounts of lactoferrin and small amounts of transferrin (iron-binding proteins), in human milk, exert a bacterial effect. Lactoferrin is less than 50% saturated with iron. It is bacteriostatic because it deprives bacteria of the iron-containing environment necessary for their normal cell growth.[10]

Because of the presence of these and other anti-infective factors, infants who receive human milk have a lesser incidence of gastrointestinal and other infections than those fed other milks. This is true of those who live in well-sanitized environments as well as those who live under constant risk of environmental contamination.[11]

Anti-allergenic characteristics of human milk

The intestine of the newborn infant is permeable to macromolecules. Secretory IgA in human milk promotes closure of the gut and, therefore, decreases the permeability of allergens. Cow's milk protein β-lactoglobulin and serum bovine albumin are the most common allergens in infancy. Breast feeding is the best prophylaxis for food allergy during infancy.

Modified cow's milk formula for infants

Modified, commercially manufactured formulas prepared from nonfat cow's milk are readily available and are generously used for feeding in early infancy. Cow's milk is modified to reduce the solute load by reduction of the protein and mineral content. The curd tension is reduced by homogenization and heat treatment to produce an easily digested protein.

Two manufacturers (Wyeth, Ross Laboratories) combine demineralized whey with nonfat milk to produce a product with a whey:casein ratio similar to that of human milk. Minerals removed from the whey by electrodialysis are added in concentrations similar to that of human milk, resulting in simulated human milk.

Combinations of vegetable oils, a high percentage of which are absorbed in infancy, are added, and carbohydrate is added to increase the caloric concentration to approximate that of human milk and cow's milk. Vitamins and minerals are added. Formulas are marketed both with and without ferrous sulfate in amounts that provide 12 mg of iron/quart.

Nutrients provided by commonly used formula preparations are shown in Table 7-2.

Soy formulas

The most commonly used products for infants who have conditions that contraindicate the use of cow's milk are the soy milks. The most frequently used formulas are constructed of protein isolated from soy meal fortified with methionine, corn syrup and/or sucrose, and soy or vegetable oils to which vitamins and minerals have been added. The trypsin inhibitor in raw soybean meal is inactivated during heat processing. The goitrogenic effect of soy is diminished by

Table 7-2. Nutrient content of commercially available milk-base formulas

Nutrient (per 100 ml)	Amount	Nutrient (per 100 ml)	Amount
Energy (kcal)	67	Pyridoxine (μg)	40-42
Protein (gm)	1.5-1.6	Vitamin B$_{12}$ (μg)	0.1-0.2
Fat (gm)	3.6-3.7	Folic acid (μg)	5-10
Carbohydrate (gm)	7.0-7.3	Calcium (mg)	44-54
Vitamin A (IU)	165-260	Phosphorus (mg)	33-46
Vitamin D (IU)	40-42	Magnesium (mg)	4.1-5.2
Vitamin E (IU)	0.9-1.5	Iron (mg)*	Trace-1.3
Vitamin C (mg)	5.4-5.7	Zinc (mg)	0.36-0.5
Thiamine (μg)	52-69	Copper (mg)	.041-.062
Riboflavin (μg)	57-100	Iodine (μg)	6.7-10
Niacin (mg)	0.6-1.0		

*Iron-fortified formulas contain 12 mg of iron/32 oz; others contain only a trace.

Table 7-3. Nutrient content of soy formulas (soy isolates, vegetable or soy oil, corn syrup solids and/or sucrose)

Nutrient (per 100 ml)	Amount	Nutrient (per 100 ml)	Amount
Energy (kcal)	67	Pyridoxine (μg)	40-41
Protein (gm)	1.8-2.5	Vitamin B_{12} (μg)	0.21-0.30
Fat (gm)	3.4-3.6	Folic acid (μg)	5.3-10.4
Carbohydrate (gm)	6.4-6.8	Calcium (mg)	70-83
Vitamin A (IU)	167-250	Phosphorus (mg)	50-63
Vitamin D (IU)	40-42	Magnesium (mg)	5-7.81
Vitamin E (IU)	1.0-1.5	Iron (mg)	1.0-1.2
Vitamin C (mg)	5.4-7.3	Zinc (mg)	0.3-0.5
Thiamine (μg)	40-52	Copper (mg)	0.04-0.06
Riboflavin (μg)	62-104	Iodine (μg)	1.5-4.7
Niacin (mg)	0.7-0.9		

heating and the addition of iodine. Ranges of nutrients in the soy isolate formulas are shown in Table 7-3.

Formula preparation

Manufacturers market formulas as liquid concentrates to be prepared for feeding by mixing equal amounts of the liquid and water. Ready-to-feed formulas that require no preparation are available in an assortment of sizes (4 oz, 6 oz, 8 oz, and 32 oz bottles and cans). Powdered formula that is prepared by mixing 1 level tbsp of powder in 2 oz of water is also available. One recommended evaporated milk formula is prepared by mixing 13 oz (one can) of evaporated milk with 2 tbsp of corn syrup and 18 oz of water. All of the formulas, when properly prepared and adequately supplemented, provide the nutrients important for the infant in an appropriate caloric concentration and present a solute load reasonable for the normal full-term infant. Errors in dilution caused by lack of understanding of the proper method of preparation, improper measurements, or the belief of the parents that their child

should have greater amounts of nutritious food can lead to problems.

Result of errors in formula preparation. Failure to gain appropriately in height and weight has been observed as a result of dilution of ready-to-feed formulas in the manner concentrates are prepared. Mothers have been known to add extra water to formula in the belief that more dilute formula might reduce spitting up by their infants.

Feeding undiluted concentrated formula increases calories, protein, and solutes presented to the kidneys for excretion and may predispose the young infant to hypernatremia and tetany as well as obesity. Problems of improper formula preparation have most frequently been reported with the use of powdered formula and occur most often when an increased need for water caused by fever or infection is superimposed on consumption of an already high-solute formula. Infants fed concentrated formula during such illnesses may become thirsty, demand more to drink, or refuse to consume more liquid because of anorexia secondary to illness.[12] When presented with more milk concentrated in the protein and solutes, the osmolality of the blood increases and hypernatremic dehydration may result. Cases of cerebral damage and gangrene of the extremities have been reported to be the result of hypernatremic dehydration and metabolic acidosis.[13,14] The feeding of undiluted evaporated milk for 5 days after an illness during infancy has been reported to be the cause of gangrene resulting in the loss of limbs in a 6½-week-old infant.[15] Infants who have been fed improperly prepared concentrated and ready-to-feed formulas with less dramatic long-term effects have been noted by many who counsel parents of very young infants. Anticipatory guidance of parents of young infants should include information on the variety of formulas available with which to feed their infants and differences in methods of preparation of each product.

Sterilization of formulas. Although terminal sterilization is recommended for infant formulas, many parents do not follow this practice but prepare formulas by the clean technique, one bottle at each feeding time, and immediately feed the infant. Several researchers have found no differences in incidence of illness or infection of infants fed formulas prepared by the clean technique or by terminal sterilization regardless of socioeconomic background or housekeeping practices.[16,17] Formulas prepared by both methods result in milk that produces aerobic bacteria.

If formulas are to be prepared by the clean technique, it is important that the hands of the person preparing the formula are first carefully washed. All equipment to be used during preparation, including the cans that contain the milk, the bottles, and nipples, must be thoroughly washed and rinsed. Once opened, cans of formula must be covered and refrigerated. The formula is prepared immediately before each feeding.

After the formula has been heated and the infant has been fed, any remaining milk should be discarded. Warm milk is an excellent medium for bacterial growth.

Milk consumed by older infants

Although the American Academy of Pediatrics has recommended that infants who are not breast fed receive iron-fortified formulas throughout the first year of life, homogenized cow's milk is offered to many infants by 5 to 6 months of age.[1] Some parents feed their infants 2% milk, and a few parents concerned about weight gain and prevention of atherosclerosis give their infants nonfat milk. Neither low-fat milk is appropriate for infants in the first year of life. Two percent milk and nonfat milk are frequently fortified with nonfat milk solids, which increase the protein and mineral content of the milk and increase the solutes that must be excreted by the kidney. It can be anticipated that infants fed nonfat milk will receive an excessive percentage of their calories from protein and that their intakes of calories may be sufficiently reduced that normal increments in weight gain may not be achieved. Studies of male infants who were fed nonfat milk with added linoleic acid between 4 and 6 months revealed that these infants increased their volume of intake of both milk and infant foods. However, since energy intakes were insufficient to meet requirements for growth, fat reserves were depleted, as demonstrated by reductions in fat-fold thickness.[18]

Enteric blood loss as a result of intakes of more than a quart of homogenized milk per day is felt to be one factor responsible for as great as 50% of the iron deficiency in infancy.[19] Reduction of amount of milk consumed or consumption of evaporated milk decreases blood and protein loss. Amounts of homogenized milk consumed should be limited not only because of the potential for blood loss, but because infants who consume large amounts of milk generally reduce their intakes of semisolid foods at an age when it may be developmentally important for them to receive them; they may thus reduce their consumption of food sources of iron.

One manufacturer (Ross Laboratories) markets a formula for the older infant that consists of nonfat milk, corn oil, and sucrose, the caloric concentration of which is reduced to 16½ kcal/oz as compared with 20 kcal/oz in standard formulas. The formula is fortified with both iron and vitamins. Infants fed this milk and pureed foods have been noted to increase their volume of intake, so that when compared with infants consuming a standard formula supplying 20 kcal/oz energy intakes are similar.[20]

Economics of infant feeding

A number of attempts have been made to compare the economic impact of the provision of energy and nutrients to support human lactation with the use of prepared infant formula. Investigators have reported both economic advantages and disadvantages to breast feeding and to formula feeding.

It must be remembered that the numbers of foods that supply important nutrients for lactation are large. Therefore, the economic impact can range from a minimal increase to a sizeable increase over basic food costs.

Young infants who consume a whole milk or evaporated milk formula prepared with added carbohydrate are hypothesized to be receiving the least expensive feeding. However, many infants malabsorb as much as 34% of butterfat ingested. Any savings may be lost in the feces. The cost of commercially prepared formula varies with packaging. Concentrated formulas are the least expensive; ready-to-feed formulas are the most costly. The nutrient support for breast feeding costs about 50% to 60% as much as the ready-to-feed formula.[21]

Feeding the infant human milk can be less expensive or more expensive than commercially prepared formula, depending on the parents' food purchasing practices and selection of foods. The many advantages of human milk far exceed any small monetary advantage to the use of prepared formula. Money saved can be obligated by additional medical care when the resistance factors are not present in the young infant's diet. Parents may need help in the selection of appropriate low-cost foods, but breast feeding should never be discouraged on an economic basis.

Bonding

Klaus and Kennell have shown that the first few minutes and hours of life are important to maternal-infant bonding. This leads to attachment, the unique relationship between two people that is special and lasts forever. Mothers who have immediate skin contact with their infants shortly after birth have significantly more attachment behaviors. Breast feeding facilitates this attachment.[22]

FOODS IN THE INFANT'S DIET

In spite of the fact that no nutritional advantage can be expected from the early introduction of semisolid foods, many families feed them in the first month of life. Semisolid foods are introduced by parents on the advice of physicians, neighbors, and friends and because parents think that it is time for their infants to eat foods other than milk. Some parents add semisolid foods in the hope that they will encourage their infants to sleep through the night, a commonly held belief that has been proven to be untrue.[23] Other parents feed semisolid foods because they think that their infants are hungry or because they consider the acceptance of these foods a developmental landmark.

Many infants receive table food by the time they can sustain a sitting posture. After infants begin to finger feed, increasing amounts of table food are included in their diets.

Semisolid foods

The age of introduction of semisolid foods to infants in the United States declined from 1920, when these foods were seldom offered before 1 year of age, to 1960 to 1970, when they were frequently offered in the first weeks and months of life. Concern that this early introduction of semisolid foods predisposed infants to obesity and allergic reactions caused many health care professionals in the pediatric community to reexamine the appropriate age for the introduction of these foods. It is currently recommended that the feeding of semisolid foods be delayed until the infant's consumption of food is no longer a reflexive process and the infant has the fine, gross, and oral motor skills to appropriately consume them, i.e., at approximately 4 to 6 months of age. Even so, many parents are

reported to continue to offer semisolid foods in the first month of life. Table 7-4 gives suggested guidelines for the introduction of semisolid foods to normal infants.

It appears to make little difference whether fruits or vegetables are introduced first. New foods should be added singly at intervals of no more than every 3 days. The introduction of nitrate-containing vegetables (e.g., carrots, beets, and spinach) is usually delayed until the infant is at least 4 months of age, because the nitrate can be converted to nitrite in the stomach of the young infant. This can result in methemoglobinemia.

Infant's acceptance of semisolid foods. Parents report both immediate acceptance and rejection of semisolid foods, a fact that may relate to the mother's skill in feeding and her attitudes and feelings about these foods. Some parents who believe that the use of semisolid foods is important add them to the formula, cut a larger hole in the nipple,

Table 7-4. Suggested ages for the introduction of semisolid foods and table foods

Food	Age (months)		
	4 to 6	6 to 8	9 to 12
Iron-fortified cereals for infants	Add		
Vegetables		Add strained	Gradually delete strained foods, introduce table foods
Fruits		Add strained	Gradually delete strained foods, introduce chopped well-cooked or canned foods
Meats		Add strained or finely chopped table meats	Decrease the use of strained meats, increase the varieties of table meats
Finger foods such as arrowroot biscuits, oven-dried toast		Add those that can be secured with a palmar grasp	Increase the use of small-sized finger foods as the pincer grasp develops
Well-cooked mashed or chopped table foods, prepared without added salt or sugar			Add
Juice by cup			Add

and feed the semisolid foods in this manner. This practice increases the energy and nutrient composition of the formula and may deprive the infant of experiences that are important in the development of feeding behavior.

Commercially prepared strained and junior foods are offered to many infants. Some mothers prefer to make their own with a blender or strainer. Ready-to-serve single-grain dry cereals such as rice cereal are commonly the first food offered to infants because rice is considered the least allergenic of the cereal grains and because most cereals are fortified with iron. Parents are reported to mix milk with cereal until it is almost liquid. Fruits are commonly reported as favorites. Vegetables appear to be accepted without problems. Preferences have been suggested for yellow vegetables, green beans, and peas; spinach and beets are often reported to be rejected. Strained meats, especially liver, are frequently rejected by infants. Parents state that the infants reject the sticky, granular texture rather than the taste of meats. Older infants are, as a result, often fed strained and junior vegetable and meat mixtures and high-meat dinners.

Food additives and fortification in semisolid foods. Concern that intakes of sodium in the first year might predispose infants to later hypertension has resulted in the deletion of salt from commercially prepared infant foods. Sugar is added only to desserts. All cereals are fortified with niacin, thiamine, and riboflavin. All dry infant cereals are fortified with electrolytically reduced iron. If fortified with iron, strained jarred cereals with fruit are also fortified with ferrous sulfate. Many fruits and mixed dinners are prepared with rice flour or tapioca to increase shelf life.

Home preparation of semisolid foods. It is both possible and economical for parents to prepare semisolid foods for their infants

with a food grinder, blender, or strainer. The foods should be carefully selected from high-quality fresh, frozen, or canned fruits, vegetables, and meats and should be prepared so that nutrients are retained. The area in which the foods are prepared and the utensils used in preparation should be meticulously cleaned. Salt and sugar should be used sparingly, if at all. When the food has been cooked, pureed, and strained it should be packaged in individual portions and refrigerated or frozen so that a single portion can be heated and fed without compromising the quality and bacterial content of the entire batch.

Home-prepared infant foods have a greater energy content than commercially prepared foods and many have a higher salt content. One study found that home-prepared infant foods had 1005% more salt than commercially prepared foods.[24]

Fruit juice. When a high percentage of infants were fed evaporated milk formulas, vitamin C–containing fruit juices were commonly introduced in the first month of life. The widespread use of vitamin-fortified formula and vitamin supplements made this practice unnecessary. Because a sucrose-containing liquid consumed as infants go to sleep sometimes results in extensive dental caries (see Chapter 13), it is generally recommended that the introduction of fruit juice be delayed until it can be consumed from a cup.

Nutrients in semisolids. Ranges of nutrients found in any group of foods for infants are sizeable (Table 7-5).

Strained and junior fruits contribute one third more calories, only a fraction of the vitamin A, but twice as much vitamin C as do vegetables when fed in equal amounts. Vegetables contribute small but important amounts of iron. Fruit juice is fortified with abundant amounts of vitamin C.

Strained and junior meats contribute sig-

Table 7-5. Ranges of selected nutrients per ounce in commercially prepared infant foods

Food	Energy (kcal)	Protein (gm)	Iron (mg)	Vitamin A (IU)	Vitamin C (mg)
Dry cereal	102-114	2.0-10.2	17.0-21.0	0-20	0-1.4
Strained and junior fruits	11-23	0.0-0.2	0.0-2.0	3-206	0.2-35.3
Strained and junior vegetables	7-18	0.2-1.0	0.1-0.4	9-3348	0.6-3.6
Strained and junior meats	27-42	3.6-4.4	.3-1.5	8-10811	.3-.7
Strained egg yolks	58	2.8	0.8	355	0.4
Strained and junior meat and vegetable dinners	20-33	1.6-2.6	0.0-0.3	22-237	0.1-0.5
Strained and junior vegetables and meat dinners	9-70	0.1-1.5	0.1-0.3	4-1114	0.2-1.2
Strained and junior desserts	17-25	0.0-0.8	0.0-0.1	4-71	0.2-8.9

From Gebhardt, S. E., Cutrufelli, R., and Matthews, R. H.: Composition of food, baby foods, raw, processed, prepared, Agriculture Handbook No. 8-3, Washington, D.C., 1978, U.S. Department of Agriculture.

nificant amounts of protein and iron. High-meat dinners contribute less than half as much protein as pure meat; vegetables and meat contribute less than one-fifth as much protein as pure meat. Strained and junior meats and high-meat dinners contribute similar amounts of iron; strained vegetables and meat contribute much less iron. Strained vegetables and meat provide slightly less than half as many calories as meat; high-meat dinners provide 75% as many calories as pure meat. Strained egg yolks have the highest calorie concentration of the prepared infant foods.

Strained and junior desserts are rich in carbohydrate and calories. A few are fortified with vitamin C. All have a sweet taste, and indiscriminate use of these items should be discouraged.

Table food

Food from the family menu is introduced at an early age in the diets of many infants. The age of introduction and type of food offered will reflect cultural practice. For example, crumbled cornbread mixed with pot liquor (liquid from vegetables) may be fed to infants in the southern states by 3 months of age, "sticky" rice may be fed to Oriental infants in the Pacific Northwest by 6 to 7 months of age, mashed beans are often given to Latin American infants at age 2 to 4 months, and mashed potatoes are offered to many infants by 3 to 4 months of age.

Honey, sometimes used as a sweetener for home-prepared infant foods and formulas and recommended for use on pacifiers to promote sucking in hypotonic infants, has been implicated as the only food source of spores of *Clostridium botulinum* during infancy. These spores are extremely resistant to heat and are not destroyed by present methods of processing honey. Botulism in infancy is caused by ingestion of the spores, which germinate into the toxin in the lumen of the bowel. Honey should not be fed to infants less than 1 year of age.[25]

Stages of development of feeding behavior indicate readiness to progress in textures of food and will be discussed in the section on development of feeding behavior. The energy and nutrient composition of foods offered

Table 7-6. Nutrient content of selected table foods commonly fed to infants

Food	Portion size	Energy (kcal)	Protein (gm)	Iron (mg)	Vitamin A (IU)	Vitamin C (mg)
Cooked cereal (farina)	¼ cup	26	0.8	Dependent on level of fortification		
Mashed potato	¼ cup	34	1.1	0.2	10	5
French fried potato	3, 1″ to 2″	29	0.4	0.2		
Spaghetti	2 tbsp	19	0.6	0.2		
Macaroni and cheese	2 tbsp	54	2.1	0.2	107	
Liverwurst	½ oz	45	2.1	0.8	925	
Hamburger	½ oz	41	3.4	0.5	5	
Eggs	1 medium	72	5.7	1.0	520	
Cottage cheese	1 tbsp	5	1.9		23.7	
Green beans	1 tbsp	3	0.15	0.2	43	1
Cooked carrots	1 tbsp	2.81			952	
Banana	½ small	40	0.5	0.35	90	5
Pudding	¼ cup	70	2.2	Trace	102	
Lollipop	1 oz hard candy	109				
Saltine crackers	1	12	0.2			
Vanilla wafer	¼″ thick, 1¾″ diameter	18	0.2			
Cheese strips	¼ oz	28	1.78		92	

From Adams, C. F.: Nutritive value in American foods in common units, Agriculture Handbook No. 456, Washington, D.C., 1975, U.S. Department of Agriculture.

must also be considered. Examples of table foods often offered and their contribution to an infant's dietary intake are shown in Table 7-6.

INTAKES OF INFANTS

Volume of intake and energy consumption is influenced not only by the infant's requirements for maintenance, growth, and activity but also by the parents' sensitivity to and willingness to accept cues of hunger and satiety, parental eagerness for the infant to feed, and the parents' skill at feeding. The caloric concentration of the formula is also a determinant of the volume of intake, calorie intake, and growth in early infancy.[26,27]

Infants feed differently, and mothers vary in their sensitivity to the child's cues. Thoman found that primiparous mothers spent more time stimulating their infants during feeding than did multiparous mothers, yet their infants spent less time sucking during breast feeding and consumed less from bottles at feeding than did infants of multiparous mothers in the newborn period. Primiparous mothers stimulated their infants during pauses between sucking. The stimulation prolonged the pause and reduced the total consumption of food.[28]

Growth response to feeding

Normal breast-fed infants regulate their intakes of milk to meet their needs for normal growth and development. Formula-fed

Table 7-7. Ranges of volume of intake and energy consumption of normal infants

Age (months)	Denver studies (calories/kg/day)	Boston studies (calories/kg/day)
2-3	89-141	90-159
5-6	75-139	82-163
9-12	74-152	75-152

From Rueda-Williamson, R., and Rose, H. E.: Growth and nutrition of infants: the influence of diet and other factors on growth, Pediatrics 30:639, 1962.

infants have been reported to regain their birth weights more rapidly than do breast-fed infants.[29] Weight gains of formula-fed infants have been found to be equal to or slightly greater than those of breast-fed infants in the first 4 months of life.[29,30] Beal reports that infants in her study who were breast fed longer than 6 months had greater increments in weight gain at 1 year of age and were heavier for length at that time than formula-fed infants.[31]

Energy intakes

Per unit of size, infants consume the greatest number of calories between ages 14 and 28 days, a time known to many pediatricians as the hungry period.[26] Mothers who are breast feeding often find it necessary to provide supplemental bottles at the end of a breast feeding when the breasts are emptied for several days during this hungry period, after which lactation adjusts to increased intakes and breast feeding alone can be resumed. After this time, although total quantity and energy intakes increase, intakes per unit of size decrease. Infants consume greater amounts of food and nutrients as they grow older but less and less per unit of body size.

Wide ranges of volume of intake and energy consumption throughout the first year of life have been noted in formula-fed infants by several researchers.[32-34] Table 7-7 shows

Table 7-8. Fiftieth percentile of male and female infants in Denver study of normal infants

Age (months)	Male (calories/kg/day)	Female (calories/kg/day)
0-1	115	115
1-2	131	131
2-3	116	115
4-5	101	104
9-12	101	97

From Beal, V. A.: Nutritional intake. In McCammon, R. W., editor: Human growth and development, 1970. Courtesy of Charles C Thomas, Publisher, Springfield, Illinois.

ranges reported in Boston and Denver studies.

The fiftieth percentile of intake of male and female infants in the Denver studies is shown in Table 7-8.[35]

Between the fifth and twelfth month of age the fiftieth percentile of intake remained at 100 or 101 kcal/kg/day in males and gradually declined from 104 to 97 kcal/kg/day in females.

Studies by Fomon and associates have shown that the caloric concentration of the formula influences calorie intake during the first 41 days of life. Female infants who were fed formulas calorically concentrated to 100/kcal/100 ml (30 kcal/oz) reduced their volume of intake but consumed greater numbers of calories, while those who were fed formulas calorically diluted to 54 kcal/100 ml (16.5 kcal/oz) increased their volume of intake but consumed fewer calories, as compared to infants who were fed formulas of normal caloric concentration. After this period, adjustments in volume of intake were sufficient so that calorie intakes were similar for the entire 111-day study period. Infants who were fed the calorically concentrated formula were, however, heavier for their lengths at 111 days of age than were infants who had been fed the calorically dilute formulas.[27] Male infants who were fed formulas concentrated to 133 kcal/100 ml (40 kcal/oz) reduced their volume of intake but consumed greater numbers of calories during the first 84 days of life and experienced "supernormal" rates of growth in both length and weight during the first 42 days of life, as compared to infants who were fed formulas providing 67 kcal/100 ml (20 kcal/oz).[26]

FEEDING BEHAVIORS

Defining developmental readiness for changes in textures of food and the acquisition of self-feeding skills is important in establishing realistic goals for normal and handicapped infants and children. Illingworth and Lister have defined a "critical or sensitive" period of development in relation to eating, a time at which a specific stimulus, solid food, must be applied in order for the organism to learn a particular action, that of accepting and eating table food, which is more difficult to masticate.[36] They point out that an infant learns to chew at about 6 or 7 months of age, thus he or she is, at this point, developmentally ready to consume food. If solid foods are withheld until a later age, the child will have considerably more difficulty in accepting them.

In 1937 Gesell and Ilg published observations of their extensive studies of the feeding behavior of infants.[37] Their observations are as valid today as they were then. Cineradiographic techniques developed since then have permitted more detailed descriptions of sucking, suckling, and swallowing.[38,39]

Development of feeding behavior is dependent on the maturation of the central nervous system, which controls the acquisition of fine, gross, and oral motor skills, each of which influences the child's ability to consume food and the manner in which he or she suckles, sucks, chews, and swallows. Normal development proceeds in an orderly and predictable cephalocaudal sequence. Likewise, the sequence of acquisition of feeding skills occurs in a predictable order influenced by the acquisition of function and behavior.

It is important to recognize that even though the normal neonate is well prepared to suck and swallow at birth, the physical and neuromotor maturation during the first year alter both the form of the oral structure and the methods by which the infant extracts liquids from a nipple. Each of the parameters of change influences the infant's eating skills. At birth the tongue is disproportionately large in comparison to the lower jaw and essentially fills the oral cavity. The mandible is retruded relative to the maxilla, the maxilla protruding over the mandible by approximately 2 ml.[40] When the mouth is closed, the jaws do not rest on top of each other, but the tip of the tongue lies between the upper and lower jaw. There is a "fat pad" in each of the cheeks. It is thought that these pads serve as a prop for the buccinator muscle, maintaining rigidity of the cheeks during suckling.[41] The lips of the neonate are also instrumental in sucking and suckling and have characteristics appropriate for their function at this age. A mucosal fold on the free edge of the gums in the region of the eye tooth buds of both jaws is instrumental in sealing off the oral cavity as the lips close around a nipple. The mucosal fold disappears by the third or fourth month, when the lips have developed muscular control to seal the oral cavity.[41]

The sucking, swallowing, and respiratory centers are located in close proximity within the brain stem. The rhythmic functions must be coordinated to allow for the crossing of the alimentary and respiratory pathways in the pharynx.[42] The newborn infant coordinates sucking, breathing, and swallowing.

The newborn infant sucks reflexively, the young infant (beginning at age 2 to 3 weeks) suckles, and as the infant grows older he or she learns mature sucking. Some description of the two processes, therefore, seems important.

Suckling

Cineradiographic studies by Ardran, Kemp, and Lind have shown that the processes of breast suckling and bottle suckling are similar. The nipple of the breast becomes rigid and elongated during breast feeding so that it closely resembles a rubber nipple in shape, and both assume a similar position in the infant's mouth.[38] The infant grasps the nipple in his or her mouth. The oral cavity is sealed off by pressure from the median portions of the lips assisted by the mucosal folds in the jaws. The nipple is held in the infant's mouth with the tip located close to the junction of the hard and soft palates.

During the first stage of suckling, the mandible and tongue are lowered while the mouth is closed, thus creating a negative pressure. The tip of the tongue moves forward. The mandible and tongue are raised, compressing the anterior end of the nipple. The compression is moved anteroposteriorly as the tip of the tongue withdraws, thus stroking or milking the liquid from the nipple. The retruded position of the mandible maximizes the efficiency of the stroking action.[38,39] As the tongue moves back, it comes in contact with the tensed soft palate, thus causing liquid to squirt into the lateral food channels. The location of the larynx is much higher during infancy than it is in adulthood, and the larynx is further elevated by muscular contractions during swallowing. The epiglottis functions as a breakwater during swallowing. As the liquid is squirted back in the mouth, the epiglottis is positioned so that it parts the stream of liquid, thus passing it to the sides of the larynx instead of over it. Thus liquid does not pass over the laryngeal

entrance during early infancy because of the relatively higher position of the larynx and parting of the stream of liquid by the epiglottis.[41]

Sucking

Mature sucking is an acquired feature of the orofacial muscles. It is not a continuous process. Upon accumulation of sufficient fluid in the mouth, sucking and breathing are interrupted by a swallowing movement. The closure of the nasopharyngeal and laryngeal sphincters in response to the presence of food in the pharynx is responsible for the interruption of nasal breathing.[42]

During swallowing the food lies in a swallow preparatory position on the groove of the tongue. The distal portion of the soft palate is raised toward the adenoidal pad in the roof of the epipharynx. The tongue is pressed upward against the nipple so that the bolus of milk follows gravity down the sloping tongue reaching the pharynx. As the bolus moves downward, the posterior wall of the pharynx comes froward to displace the soft palate toward the dorsal surface of the tongue and the larynx is elevated and arched backward. The bolus is expressed from the pharynx by peristaltic movements of the pharyngeal wall toward the back of the tongue and the larynx. The bolus spills over the pharyngoepiglottic folds into the lateral food channels and then into the esophagus.[39]

The tonsils and lymphoid tissue play an important role as infants swallow; they assist in keeping the airway open and in keeping food away from the posterior pharyngeal wall as the infant is fed in a reclining position, thus delaying nasopharyngeal closure until food has reached the lower pharynx.[36]

As the infant grows older the oral cavity enlarges so that the tongue no longer fills the mouth. The tongue grows differentially at the tip and attains motility in the larger oral cavity. The elongated tongue can be protruded to receive and pass solids between the gum pads and erupting teeth for mastication. Mature feeding is characterized by separate movements of the lip, tongue, and gum pads or teeth.[42]

Sequence of development of feeding behavior

Newborn infants can neither focus their eyes nor direct their hands, yet they find nourishment. The "rooting reflex" caused by stroking of the perioral skin including the cheeks and lips causes an infant to turn toward the stimulus, so that the mouth comes in contact with it. Stimulus placed on the lips causes involuntary movements toward it, closure, and pouting in preparation for sucking.[43] These reflexes thus enable the infant to suck and receive nourishment. Both rooting and suckling can be elicited when the infant is hungry but are absent when the infant is satiated.[44] During feeding the neonate assumes a tonic neck position, the head rotated to one side and the arm on that side extended while the other is fisted. The infant seeks the nipple by touch and obtains milk from the nipple with a rhythmic suckle.[37] Semisolid foods, introduced at an early age into the diets of many infants fed by spoon, are secured in the same manner as is the milk, by stroking movements of the tongue with the tongue projecting as the spoon is withdrawn. Frequently, food is expelled from the mouth.

By age 5 weeks the infant can focus the eyes on faces, and by age 12 weeks the gaze can be shifted. At age 10 weeks the infant is able to recognize the breast or bottle as the source of food. By age 16 weeks the more mature sucking pattern has become evident, with the tongue moving back and forth as opposed to the earlier up-and-down motions. Spoon feeding is easier because the infant can draw in the lower lip as the spoon is removed. The tonic neck position has faded,

and infant assumes a more symmetrical position with the head at midline. The hands close on the bottle.[37] By age 20 weeks the infant can grasp on tactile contact with a palmar squeeze. By age 24 weeks he or she can reach for and grasp an object on sight. In almost every instance the object goes into the mouth.

Between 24 and 28 weeks of age the beginning of chewing movements, an up-and-down movement of the jaws, occurs. This, coupled with the ability to grasp and the hand-to-mouth route of grasped objects, as well as sitting posture, indicates a readiness of the infant to finger feed. Infants at this age grasp with a palmar grasp. Therefore, the shape of the food presented for the child to finger feed is important. Cookies, melba toast, crackers, and teething biscuits are frequently introduced at this stage (Fig. 7-1).

Between 28 and 32 weeks of age the infant gains control of the trunk and can sit alone without support. The sitting infant has greater mobility of the shoulders and arms and is freer to reach and grasp. The grasp is more digital than the earlier palmar grasp. The infant is able to transfer items from one hand to another and learns to voluntarily release and resecure objects. The beginning of chewing patterns (up-and-down movements of the jaws) is demonstrated. The tongue shows more maturity in regard to spoon feeding than to drinking. Food is received from the spoon by pressing the lips against the spoon, drawing the head away, and drawing in the lower lip. The infant is aware of a cup and can suck from it. Milk frequently leaks from corners of the mouth as the tongue is projected before swallowing.[37]

The introduction of soft mashed (but not strained) foods is appropriate at this stage of development. In fact, it is at this stage of development that Illingworth believes it is critical to introduce the infant to harder-to-masticate foods.[36]

Fig. 7-1. Six-month-old infant demonstrates readiness to finger feed.

Fig. 7-2. Ten-month-old infant becomes interested in feeding himself.

Between age 6 and 12 months the infant gradually receives greater amounts of food from the family menu and less and less of the pureed and strained items. Foods should be carefully selected and modified so that they are presented in a form that can be manipulated in the mouth without the potential of choking and aspiration, as may occur with small grains of rice or corn. Many parents mash well-cooked vegetables and canned fruits and successfully offer them to their infants. Well-cooked ground meat dishes such as ground meat in gravies or sauces appear to be easily accepted, as are liverwurst, minced chicken livers, and drained tuna fish. Custards, puddings, and ice cream soon become favorites.

By age 28 weeks infants are able to help themselves to their bottle in sitting postures, although they will not be able to tip the bottle adaptively as it empties until about age 32 weeks. By the end of the first year they can completely manage bottle feeding alone.

By 32 weeks of age infants bring their heads forward to receive the spoon as it is presented to them. The tongue shows increased motility and allows for considerably increased manipulation of food in the mouth prior to swallowing. At the end of the first year, infants are able to manipulate food in the mouth with definite chewing movements.

During the fourth quarter of the first year, the child develops an increasingly precise pincer grasp. The bottle can be managed alone and can be resecured if it is lost. Infants at this age are increasingly conscious of what others do and often imitate the models set for them.[37] By age 1 year the patterns of eating have changed from sucking to beginning rotary chewing movements. Children understand the concept of the container and the contained, have voluntary hand-to-mouth movements and a precise pincer grasp, and can voluntarily release and rese-

cure objects. They are thus prepared to learn to feed themselves, a behavior they learn and refine in the second year.

FEEDING THE INFANT

Presented with the breast of an adequately fed lactating mother or the nipple on a bottle of properly prepared formula, the hungry infant receives both biochemical and psychosocial nurturance. Although studies of Holt and associates have indicated that infants accept cold formula, most mothers warm the milk to body temperature.[45] The infant held in a semireclining position who is offered the nipple sucks and receives the major portion of nourishment in 20 minutes. Most physicians recommend a flexible self-demand

Fig. 7-3. Mother feeds her 3-week-old infant in semireclining upright position.

schedule. Newborn infants will initially feed six to eight times a day at intervals of 2 to 4 hours and will consume 2 to 3 oz at a feeding. By age 2 weeks most infants will have increased the amount of milk consumed at a feeding and reduced the number of feedings to six. By age 2 months most infants are fed five times a day and sleep through the night. By age 6 months most consume three meals and four milk feedings a day.

Infants swallow air as well as formula during feeding. Holding the child in an upright position and gently patting the back encourages expulsion of swallowed air and prevents distention and discomfort.

Difficulties in infant feeding

During feeding both the mother and infant receive satisfaction and pleasure. The infant is pleased because hunger is satiated, the mother because she has fulfilled the needs of her newborn infant. Infants learn that they can trust their mothers to feed them and that they please their mothers by eating. Successful feeding provides the basis for the warm, trusting relationship that develops between infants and their mothers.

Difficulties in feeding resulting from a weak suck, improper equipment such as firm nipples with small holes, or other causes are frustrating to both infants and their mothers. Hungry infants cry more frequently, demanding to be fed more often, and may create anxiety in conscientious and concerned mothers.

Since infants have not yet learned to separate themselves from others in the environment, they perceive the feelings of others as their own immediate feelings in any particular situation. Thus they are easily susceptible to parental anxieties and may reflect these by crying and by not eating well. When the infant does not eat well, parental anxieties may increase. Thus the cycle can begin. It is possible that such infants will feed more easily when presented the bottle by a less intense person. However, when the infant is successfully fed by another, the parent's feelings of inadequacy and anxiety may be increased.

In order to achieve successful mother-child feeding experiences, it is important to work directly with the mother. It may be necessary for the professional to determine any problems with equipment used and positioning, then to model a calm, relaxed feeding situation for the mother. Care should be taken not to usurp the mother's role, thus increasing her feelings of inadequacy. An approach that seems to be beneficial to all concerned is to (1) model a feeding, (2) sit beside the mother and talk her through a feeding while showing her how to utilize a relaxed position, (3) reinforce her mothering behaviors, and (4) help her to become aware of cues from the infant that he or she is relaxed.

This method may need to be used for several feedings until the mother and infant can achieve a successful, relaxed experience. Even then, parents may need further support in their continuing efforts to create a relaxed and warm relationship with their infants during feeding.

It is important for parents to recognize that newborn infants demonstrate a pattern of crying in early life and that a crying infant is not a symptom of inadequate mothering. The amount of time an infant cries increases from age 2 weeks to approximately 6 weeks, when it peaks. After this time crying decreases. The major concentration period is from 6 to 11 PM. Other periods of crying occur in the morning from 4 to 7 AM and 9 to 11 AM. By age 10 weeks most infants become more quiet.[46] Seldom is this crying a symptom of allergy and it is no indication for formula change.

Parents of colicky babies—those who are otherwise healthy and well fed but who cry constantly for several hours, draw their legs onto their abdomens and pass large amounts of gas—often request changes in the infants' formulas. This rarely resolves colic, and frequent change in formulas should be discouraged. It has been suggested that colic in some breast-fed infants may be resolved by eliminating milk from the mothers' diets.[47]

Both spitting and/or regurgitation can occur in infants and usually causes concern to parents. During the early months of life some otherwise healthy infants spit a small amount of any milk or food ingested at each feeding. Although the infants do not fail to thrive parents may seek help in resolving this situation. There is no therapy. The problem usually resolves itself by the time the infants can sustain sitting. Regurgitation, the effortless expulsion of gastric contents, is a symptom that demands medical evaluation. The most common cause of persistent regurgitation is gastrointestinal reflux, the result of decreased pressure in the lower esophageal sphincter. Positioning in an infant seat at a 45° to 60° angle may help, but it will not decrease the amount of contact of gastric acid on the esophageal mucosa. Surgery may be indicated.[48]

Some infants are easily distracted by noise or by other influences in the environment. Such infants feed more easily at the night feeding. Presentation of the bottle in a quiet and partially darkened room by a rested mother may promote successful feeding for both the mother and her infant.

Many parents perceive their infants as having feeding problems. Problems in order of frequency have been reported to be refusal of a particular food because of taste or texture, dissatisfaction with amount consumed, spitting up, and developmentally related problems such as refusing the bottle or refusing to be fed and only finger feeding.[49] Such difficulties are usually of short duration and rarely compromise an infant's nutrient intake or physical growth. Parents, however, may need reassurance that their infant's development is normal and that their food-related behaviors are not of nutritional concern.

Recognizing cues of satiation and readiness to progress

Successful infant feeding is generally regarded in our society as a measure of competent parenthood. As such, it is a reinforcing experience to parents. They must learn to recognize and to accept their infant's cues, as the infant uses a variety of cries and vocalizations to express needs. Frequently, parents, for one reason or another, cannot always discriminate their infant's cries. Consequently, they give food to satisfy all types of infant discomforts. The infant, in turn, may not learn to discriminate hunger from other discomforts, and may learn to rely on eating to satisfy a wide variety of needs. Parents must learn to recognize satiation of hunger in infants and be willing to accept their infant's expressions of satisfaction, to set limits on amounts of food offered to eager eaters, and to decline the natural inclination to overfeed infants who please others by accepting more food. Parents who are eager for their infant to empty the bottle encourage excessive intakes of food and can reinforce eating to the extent that obesity may result. Infants may be offered food and formula by many people: parents, baby sitters, aunts, siblings, and others. Mothers who are dissatisfied with the infant's food intake may find that the infant has reduced the intake to compensate for food offered by others.

Additional cues that parents must recognize are those that indicate the infant's readiness for increasingly independent feeding experiences. The infant's ability to put objects to his or her mouth and to chew on them indicates a readiness to utilize increasingly solid foods and to begin finger feeding. Anticipatory guidance to parents during this period about developmental changes is an important factor in their acceptance of and adaptation to their infant's behavior.

Recognizing needs for nutrients and energy in the infant's diet

Most infants consume foods that provide nutrients in excess of recommended amounts, with the exception of iron. Human milk, cow's milk, and formula provide the major source of protein and calcium and important sources of vitamin A and the B vitamins in early life. Breast-fed infants may receive supplements of iron, vitamin D, and fluoride. Iron-fortified formulas contribute appreciable amounts of iron in early infancy. When enriched cereals are introduced into the diet another important source of iron is available.

Because of the great variability in calories and nutrients provided by foods offered to infants, selection of foods and the amounts offered should be based on the infant's rate of gain in height and weight as well as on nutrient needs. The introduction and acceptance of iron-containing foods prior to the time homogenized milk replaces iron-fortified formula or iron supplements are discontinued is important, because the infant must continue to consume foods that provide this nutrient as it is deleted from milk or supplements. Fruit juice offers sources of vitamin C when vitamin-containing formulas are no longer consumed. It seems reasonable to encourage parents of infants whose gains in weight are more rapid than gains in length to feed the lower-calorie infant foods such as vegetables and dinners. Parents of infants whose increments of weight gains are small should be encouraged to feed greater amounts of the higher-calorie strained meats and fruits. Amounts of semisolid foods offered to infants should be adjusted to their appetites and rates of weight gain. Experiences with a variety of flavors and textures are thought to be conducive to acceptance of a variety of foods in later life.

REFERENCES

1. Fomon, S. J.: What are infants fed in the United States? Pediatrics **56**:350, 1975.
2. Macy, I. G., and Kelly, H. J.: Human milk and cow's milk in infant nutrition. In Kon, S. K., and Cowie, A. T.: Milk: the mammary gland and its secretion, vol. II, New York, 1961, Academic Press, Inc.
3. Hambraeus, L.: Proprietary milk versus human breast milk in infant feeding, Pediatr. Clin. North Am. **24**:17, 1977.
4. Hall, B.: Changing composition of human milk and early development of an appetite control, Lancet **1**:779, 1975.
5. György, P.: The uniqueness of human milk, Biochemical Aspects, Am. J. Clin. Nutr. **24**:970, 1971.
6. Lakdawala, D. R., and Widdowson, E. M.: Vitamin D in human milk, Lancet **1**:167, 1977.
7. McMillan, J. A., and others: Iron absorption from human milk, simulated human milk, and proprietary formulas, Pediatrics **60**:896, 1977.
8. Johnson, P. E., and Evans, G. W.: Relative zinc availability in human breast milk, infant formulas, and cows milk, Am. J. Clin. Nutr. **31**:416, 1978.
9. Goldman, A. S., and Smith, C. W.: Host resistant factors in human milk, J. Pediatr. **82**:1082, 1973.
10. Chandra, R. K.: Immunological aspects of human milk, Nutr. Rev. **36**:265, 1978.
11. Larsen, S. A., and Homer, D. R.: Relation of breast versus bottle feeding to hospitalization for gastroenteritis in a middle-class U.S. population, J. Pediatr. **92**:417, 1978.
12. Chambers, T. L., and Steel, A. E.: Concentrated milk feeds and their relation to hypernatraemic dehydration in infants, Arch. Dis. Child. **50**:610, 1975.
13. Macaulay, D., and Watson, M.: Hypernatraemia in infants as a cause of brain damage, Arch. Dis. Child. **42**:485, 1967.
14. Comay, S. C., and Karabus, C. D.: Peripheral gangrene in hypernatraemic dehydration of infancy, Arch. Dis. Child. **50**:616, 1975.
15. Abrams, C. A. L., and others: Hazards of overconcentrated milk formula, J.A.M.A. **232**:1136, 1975.
16. Hargrove, C. B., Temple, A. R., and Chinn, P.: Formula preparation and infant illness, Clin. Pediatr. **13**:1057, 1974.
17. Kendall, N., Vaughn, V. C., and Kusakcroglu, A.: A study of preparation of infant formulas, Am. J. Dis. Child. **122**:215, 1971.

18. Fomon, S. J., and others: Skim milk in infant feeding, Acta Paediatr. Scand. **66:**17, 1977.
19. Woodruff, C. W., Wright, S. W., and Wright, R. P.: The role of fresh cow's milk in iron deficiency. II. Comparison of fresh cow's milk with a prepared formula, Am. J. Dis. Child. **124:**26, 1972.
20. Fomon, S. J., and others: Recommendations for feeding normal infants, Pediatrics **63:**52, 1979.
21. Lamm, E., Delaney, J., and Dwyer, J. T.: Economy in the feeding of infants, Pediatr. Clin. North Am. **24:**71, 1977.
22. Klaus, M. H., and Kennell, J. H.: Maternal-infant bonding: the impact of early separation or loss on family development, St. Louis, 1976, The C. V. Mosby Co.
23. Beal, V. A.: Termination of night feeding in infancy, J. Pediatr. **75:**690, 1969.
24. Kerr, C. M., Reisinger, K. S., and Plankey, F. W.: Sodium concentration of homemade baby food, Pediatrics **62:**331, 1978.
25. Arnon, S. S., and others: Honey and other environmental risk factors for infant botulism, Pediatrics **94:**331, 1979.
26. Fomon, S. J., and others: Relationship between formula concentration and rate of growth of normal infants, J. Nutr. **98:**241, 1969.
27. Fomon, S. J., and others: Influence of formula concentration on caloric intake and growth of normal infants, Acta Paediatr. Scand. **64:**172, 1975.
28. Thoman, E. B.: Development of synchrony in mother-infant interaction in feeding and other situations, Fed. Proc. **34:**1587, 1975.
29. Fomon, S. J., and others: Food consumption and growth of normal infants fed milk-based formulas, Acta Paediatr. Scand. Suppl. 223, 1971.
30. Fomon, S. J., and others: Growth and serum chemical values of normal breast fed infants, Acta Paediatr. Scand. Suppl. 202, 1970.
31. Beal, V. A.: Breast and formula feeding of infants, J. Am. Diet. Assoc. **55:**31, 1969.
32. Beal, V. A.: Nutritional intake of children. I. Calories, carbohydrate, fat and protein, J. Nutr. **50:**223, 1953.
33. Rueda-Williamson, R., and Rose, H. E.: Growth and nutrition of infants: the influence of diet and other factors on growth, Pediatrics **30:**639, 1962.
34. Fomon, S. J., Owen, G. M., and Thomas, L. N.' Milk or formula volume ingested by infants fed ad libitum, Am. J. Dis. Child. **108:**601, 1964.
35. Beal, V. A.: Nutritional intake. In McCammon, R. W., editor: Human growth and development, Springfield, Ill., 1970, Charles C Thomas, Publisher, p. 63.
36. Illingworth, R. S., and Lister, J.: The critical or sensitive period with special reference to certain feeding problems in infants and children, J. Pediatr. **65:**839, 1964.
37. Gesell, A., and Ilg, F. L.: Feeding behavior of infants, Philadelphia, 1937, J. B. Lippincott Co.
38. Ardran, G. M., Kemp, F. H., and Lind, J.: A cineradiographic study of breast feeding, Br. J. Radiol. **31:**156, 1958.
39. Ardran, G. M., Kemp, F. H., and Lind, J.: A cineradiographic study of bottle feeding, Br. J. Radiol. **31:**11, 1958.
40. Subtelny, J. D.: Examination of current philosophies associated with swallowing behavior, Am. J. Orthod. **51:**161, 1965.
41. Peiper, A.: Cerebral function in infancy and childhood, New York, 1963, Consultant's Bureau, p. 396.
42. Gwynne-Evans, E.: Organization of the oro-facial muscles in relation to breathing and feeding, Br. Dent. J. **91:**135, 1952.
43. Bosma, J. F.: Maturation of function of the oral and pharyngeal region, Am. J. Orthod. **49:**94, 1963.
44. Ingram, T. T. S.: Clinical significance of the infantile feeding reflexes, Dev. Med. Child Neurol. **4:**159, 1962.
45. Holt, L. E., and others: A study of premature infants fed cold formula, J. Pediatr. **61:**556, 1962.
46. Brazelton, T. B.: Crying in infancy, Pediatrics **29:**579, 1962.
47. Jakobsson, I., and Lindberg, T.: Cow's milk as a cause of infantile colic in breast-fed infants, Lancet **2:**437, 1978.
48. Cohen, S.: Developmental characteristics of lower esophageal sphincter dysfunction: a possible mechanism for infantile chalasia, Gastroenterology **67:**252, 1974.
49. Harris, L. E., and Chan, J. C. M.: Infant feeding practices, Am. J. Dis. Child. **117:**483, 1969.

ADDITIONAL READINGS

Almrath, S. G.: Water requirements of breast-fed infants, Am. J. Clin. Nutr. **31:**1154, 1978.
Anderson, T. A.: Commercial infant foods: content and composition, Pediatr. Clin. North Am. **24:**37, 1977.
Beal, V. A.: On the acceptance of solid foods, and other food patterns of infants and children, Pediatrics **20:**448, 1957.
Beal, V. A.: Dietary intake of individuals followed through infancy and childhood, Am. J. Public Health **51:**1107, 1961.
Berenberg, W., and others: Hazards of skim milk, unboiled and boiled, Pediatrics **44:**734, 1969.
Breast feeding and avoidance of food antigens in the prevention and management of allergic disease, Nutr. Rev. **36:**181, 1978.

Committee on Nutrition, American Academy of Pediatrics: Commentary on breast feeding and infant formulas, including proposed standards for formulas, Pediatrics 57:278, 1976.

Filer, L. J.: Early nutrition: its long-term role, Hosp. Practice 13:87, 1978.

Fomon, S. J., and others: Influence of fat and carbohydrate content of diet on food intake and growth of male infants, Acta Paediatr. Scand. 65:136, 1976.

Guthrie, H. A.: Effect of early feeding of solid foods on nutritive intake of infants, Pediatrics 38:879, 1966.

Larson, B. L., and Smith, V. R., editors: Lactation, a comprehensive treatise, vol. III, Nutrition and biochemistry of milk/maintenance, New York, 1974, Academic Press, Inc.

Lebenthal, E.: Use of modified food starch in infant nutrition, Am. J. Dis. Child. 132:850, 1978.

Paxson, C. L., Adcock, E. W., and Morris, F. H.: Osmolalities of infant formulas, Am. J. Dis. Child. 131:139, 1977.

Pipes, P.: When should semisolid foods be fed to infants? J. Nutr. Educ. 9:57, 1977.

8

Between infancy and adolescence

Peggy L. Pipes and Jane Rees

Between infancy and adolescence, changes in children's rates of growth, continuing maturation of fine and gross motor skills, and personality development influence not only the amounts of food consumed and the manner in which children consume food, but also those foods that are acceptable to them. Food habits, likes, and dislikes are established, some of which are transient, many of which form the base for a lifetime of food, and thus nutrient, intake. Environmental influences and parental behaviors reinforce or extinguish food-related behaviors.

NUTRITION PROBLEMS OF PRESCHOOL AND SCHOOL-AGE CHILDREN

Although clinical signs of malnutrition are rarely found in children in North America, there is evidence that there are children who are receiving diets that are inadequate in quantity and/or quality. Nutritional status studies have shown that children from low-income families frequently are shorter than those from families with greater economic resources and have indicated that limited intakes of food may be compromising their growth potential. In some poverty-level populations groups of children have been identified that have shown both clinical and biochemical evidence of malnutrition. All preschool children are at risk for iron deficiency anemia, which appears to be a greater prob-

lem in children of low-income families than in children of other groups. Dental caries as a result of excessive intakes of sweet foods, poor dental hygiene, and lack of dental care are common among all groups of children.

There are children who are receiving sufficient amounts of food, others who are consuming excessive amounts of food, and some who are receiving diets that are inadequate both in quality and quantity.

Ethnic and geographic variations in nutrient deficiency concerns have been found in various populations. Spanish-American children from migrant families in the south central and southwestern states have been noted to have a high incidence of biochemical and clinical signs of vitamin A deficiency. Clinical signs of rickets and biochemical evidence of inadequate intakes of protein, folate, iron, and ascorbic acid have been noted in some children of migrant families in Colorado.[1,2] Low intakes of niacin have been noted among Mexican-American children in California and Colorado.[1,3] Navajo Indian children in Montana were found to have low dietary intakes of calcium and vitamins A and C. Biochemical evidence of inadequate intakes of iron, vitamin A, and riboflavin was also noted.[4] White Mountain Apache children in Arizona were noted to have biochemical evidence of inadequate intakes of vitamins A and C.[5] School-age children from low-income families who had biochemical evidence of iron deficiency have been identified in Pennsylvania.[6] Biochemical evidence of riboflavin deficiency has been found in children from poverty groups in New York.[7]

Studies of dietary intakes of children have shown that protein and riboflavin are commonly consumed in excess of recommended amounts. The nutrients least likely to be consumed in recommended amounts are iron and vitamin C. The national nutritional status study of preschool children conducted by Owen and associates showed that nutrient consumption per 1000 calories, with the exception of ascorbic acid, is similar at all economic levels.[8] The children they studied from low-income families consumed less food; therefore, the total intake of nutrients and energy was less. Protein intakes were found to be in excess of requirements at all ages. Black children consumed an average of 1 mg of iron/day more than white preschoolers at all ages. Cereal grains were the major contributors of iron. Vitamin C intakes were unrelated to energy intakes, and children of parents who had more money to spend for food consumed greater amounts of ascorbic acid. Other studies have shown that vitamin A intake is also unrelated to energy intake.[9] A high percentage of preschool children in all studies has been found to be receiving multiple vitamin supplements. A decrease in the use of supplements with age has, however, been noted.[10]

Mothers of 10% of the preschool children in a nutritional status study in the North Central Region of the United States reported that their children had conditions that required modification of the kinds or amounts of food consumed.[9] Compliance with dietary modifications necessary to control chronic diseases such as diabetes, celiac disease, allergies, and others is difficult in childhood. Children want to eat the same food as their peers and family. Teachers and friends are not always sympathetic with the need to restrict or modify intakes of food. Restriction of several groups of foods such as may be necessary for children who have multiple allergies makes adequate energy intakes difficult. Thus children who must modify their intakes of food are at risk for nutritional deficits.

RESPONSIBILITIES OF FAMILIES FOR CHILDREN'S FOOD INTAKES

Children from infancy to adolescence are dependent on their parents for the selection of food they consume at home. As they grow older, have money to spend, attend school, and interact with larger numbers of individuals, the decisions as to their selection of food become increasingly their own. Since the preschool and the preadolescent periods are important in the formation of attitudes toward food, it is important that foods that supply the nutrients be available to children. Parents need also to understand and support children in their food-related behaviors so that food habits are formed that are conducive to an adequate nutrient intake. Children need some experiences in selection of food, yet parents need to set limits so that consumption of foods that provide adequate amounts of nutrients is achieved.

Studies have repeatedly shown that it is usually the mother who is the gatekeeper, the person who decides which foods are to be purchased and how these foods are to be prepared. She makes the decision on the basis of the money available to be spent for food, the time she has to devote to food preparation, the foods that her family enjoys, her skills and interest in food preparation, her knowledge of nutrition, and the value she places on nutrient intake.

The educational level and nutrition knowledge of the mother influence the nutritional quality of the diet. Eppright and associates noted that as the nutrition knowledge of the mother increased, preschool children's intakes of calcium, iron, riboflavin, and ascorbic acid increased.[11] They also found that nutrition knowledge was significantly related to positive attitudes toward meal planning and food preparation. Caliendo and associates found that the more positive mothers felt about meal planning, the importance of good nutrition for their children, and their roles as homemakers, the more likely were the children to receive good quality in meals; the more discontent, nervous, and unhappy the mothers were with their roles as homemakers the lower was the dietary quality of the children's food intakes.[12]

Parents often need both help in interpreting the nutrition information to which they have been exposed and direction to valid sources of information. Sources of nutrition information vary among groups of parents. Low-income families reportedly receive their nutrition information from relatives and friends. Other families rely heavily on lay sources such as magazines, newspapers, books, radio, and television. Some of the information presented in these sources lack validity, and often conflicting information is presented in any two sources. In addition, advertising and merchandising often play on parents' emotional responses to suggestion and imply a false need for certain foods or supplements.

Convenience is another factor many mothers consider when they select food for their families. Working mothers may rely heavily on prepackaged frozen meals and have been known to leave the decision to the child as to which one he or she would like for dinner. Parents may need help in selection of convenience foods and combinations of other foods that, when served with them, provide a balanced nutrient intake. They may also need help in developing food preparation skills.

Mothers select and prepare foods that they believe their families will enjoy. Bryan and Lowenberg found that 89% of mothers eliminated from the family menu or served infrequently those foods that their husbands disliked.[13] In the study conducted by Eppright and associates, 81% of the mothers planned meals on the basis of their husbands' food likes and dislikes, and 72% chose foods on the basis of the food likes and dislikes of other family members. Fifty-eight percent considered food likes and dislikes of children.[14]

In addition, preschool children often accompany their mothers to the grocery store and request specific foods. Sixty-eight percent of mothers have reported that they sometimes buy foods that are requested. Eighteen percent stated they always purchased the items. Sugar-coated cereal is the food most frequently requested.[9]

Peer group pressures also have an influence on the children's request for food and the mother's selection at the supermarket. Mothers who view candy, carbonated beverages, and potato chips as not of the best nutritional or economic value may purchase them simply because other children have them. Mothers may provide them for their children because they observe other parents using these foods as an expression of affection for their children.

FACTORS AFFECTING FOOD INTAKE

Provision of appropriate amounts and kinds of food does not ensure that children will consume foods that support an appropriate nutrient intake. Children imitate the models of food acceptance set for them. They learn to control concerned parents by the food they accept or reject. Emotional factors influence food acceptance and intake.

Parents and siblings provide a model of food acceptance and feeding behavior that children imitate. Thus food likes and dislikes of parents and older siblings are often passed on to younger children. It has been suggested that the older siblings exert an even greater influence by the models they set than do parents.[9] Unresolved conflicts about food intakes and feeding behavior may as a result be passed on to future children.

Food may be offered by parents, aunts, grandmothers, and others to show affection and to reward children for desired behavior; it is also often withheld for punishment. These nonnutritive uses of food lay the framework within which many attitudes about foods are formed and influence those foods that are acceptable to children. Foods withheld or used as rewards become desired foods; those that must be consumed in order to receive the more desired become less acceptable. Since many other reinforcers and punishers are effective with normal children, these uses of food are inappropriate. When food reinforcers are necessary to change behavior, careful consideration should be given both to the food used and the design of the program (see Chapter 15).

Attitudes of parents toward child rearing influence nutrient intake. Eppright found permissiveness of parents in relation to eating to be negatively related to the nutritive value of food consumed by the children, adversely affecting all dietary components except fat. Less permissive mothers regulated to some degree the child's food intakes, and as a result children consumed greater amounts of protein, vitamins, and minerals. Sims and Morris found that children of more affluent, nonauthoritarian mothers had higher intakes of calcium and ascorbic acid, whereas children of parents with authoritarian attitudes toward child rearing had higher intakes of calories, carbohydrates, iron, and thiamine.[15]

Lack of structure to eating patterns, including meals and snacks, gives no opportunity for children to develop hunger. The frequency with which food is offered is therefore important (see Chapter 6). Knowledge that a more desired food such as a Popsicle is available after a meal is consumed may reduce a child's motivation to eat at the table.

The emotional environment at mealtime may influence food and nutrient intake. The dinner table is not the place for family battles or punitive action toward children. For eating to be successful, it should occur at a time and in a setting that is comfortable and free from stress and unreasonable demands. Lund and Burk found that mealtime criticism about nonfood-related activities reduced the levels of food consumption and adversely affected intakes of vitamins A and C in 9- to 11-year-old children.[16]

Parents concerned about children's food intake sometimes nag, urge, or even try to force their children to consume what they consider to be the appropriate kind or amount of food. The children soon learn that they can control many aspects of their parents' behavior by refusing to eat. As a result their food consumption may become so limited that growth is compromised and/or nutrient intakes quite limited. Helping parents identify what occurs in this situation and reassuring them about their children's development can alleviate their overconcern about their children's food intakes. As the pressure on children to eat is relieved, they usually increase their food intakes.

Parents themselves may interfere with children's food intakes when they make demands on them that are incompatible with eating. Parents may make such frequent demands on children related to proper use of utensils, position of the chair, and body posture that children do not have uninterrupted time to eat more than one or two mouthfuls. Such children become discouraged and frequently become engrossed in adjusting utensils and the position of the chair and fidgeting; consequently, they reduce their total

Fig. 8-1. Children consume food successfully in a comfortable setting free of stress.

food intakes. Helping parents ignore this behavior and focus conversation on nonmealtime activities can remedy this situation. Making conversation with the children while they are eating can reinforce them for appropriate eating behavior and increase their food intake.

Influence of television on children

In addition to the many familial, cultural, and psychosocial influences on children's food habits, mass media have an impact on children's request for and attitudes toward food. Of the forms of mass media, television has the greatest impact on children because it reaches many children before they are capable of verbal communication.[17] Children spend more time in front of the television set than they do in any activity other than sleeping. It has been estimated that the preschool child watches television for 26.3 hours/week, and the child 6 to 16 years of age for 25 hours/week.[18]

Advertising and programs present models of behavior children may imitate. Advertisers attempt to use children to influence their parents' purchasing behavior. They present frequent cues for food and drink and often encourage consumption of concentrated carbohydrate.

Both parents and health care professionals have expressed concern about the effects of television programming and advertising on health practices of children. Groups have joined together and influenced regulations. Action for Children's Television, a national group formed in Boston, exerted sufficient pressure that vitamins and medicine are no longer advertised on children's television, appeals to children to ask parents for products are no longer common, and program hosts or characters in stories seldom advertise products. Because of the influence of this group, the National Association of Broadcaster's code authority issued new guidelines for advertising time on children's television. As of January 1976, 9.5 minutes/hour of commercial advertising is permissible. One can, therefore, anticipate that 15% of the hours spent watching television will be spent viewing commercials.[19] It is estimated that the child between the ages of 2 and 11 years will view 50 to 55 commercials per day. In 1979 the Federal Trade Commission began hearings on whether regulations on advertising during children's television programs should be imposed. One may anticipate future changes on commercials on children's television programs.

Kindergarten children often are unable to separate commercials from the program and frequently explain them as part of the program.[20] Younger school-age children (5 to 10 years of age) attend more closely to commercials than do older children (11 to 12 years of age).[21] Older children are conscious of the concept of commercials, the purpose of selling, and the concept of sponsorship and are less likely to accept advertisers' claims without question. Children in second grade have been found to have a concrete distrust of commercials based on experiences with advertised products, and children in sixth grade have been found to have global mistrust of all commercials.[20]

Food manufacturers and fast-food establishments use the greatest percentage of advertising time on children's television. A 1975 study of children's programs on Saturday and Sunday in Boston revealed that 68.5% of the advertisements were for food,[19] of which 25% were for cereal, 25% were for candy and sweets, and 8% were for snacks and other food. Ten percent of the advertisements were for quick meals and eating places. Only a few commercials were broadcast for milk, bread, or fruit. Advertisements for sugared cereals outnumbered those for unsugared cereals by a ratio of three to one.

It has been pointed out that certain attributes of food are promoted as being superior to others. The main characteristics presented positively are "sweetness," "chocolatey," and "richness."[22] Many food manufacturers, in other words, deemphasize the physiologic need for nutrients and encourage selection on the basis of sweet flavor. Exposure to such messages may distort a child's natural curiosity toward other characteristics of food such as the fresh crispness of celery or apples.

Studies of Yankelovich and McNeal indicate that children are influenced by commercials and consequently attempt to influence their parents' buying practices.[23,24] In these studies it was also found that commercials for food have the strongest influence and that mothers are more likely to yield to requests for food than for other products. They have a greater tendency to respond to requests from older children but certainly do not completely ignore those of the younger children.[25] Highly child-centered mothers are less likely to buy children's favorite cereals than are mothers who are not as child centered.[26] Crawford and associates reported that two-thirds of mothers interviewed stated that food choices were influenced by television commercials by age 4 years.[9]

Parents must set limits on their children's requests for advertised food and may need support in their efforts to do so. They may need guidance in principles of behavior modification (Chapter 15) and reassurance that it is to the child's advantage to learn that not all advertised products are a part of every child's meal pattern.

THE PRESCHOOL CHILD

During the preschool years rates of growth decrease and as a result appetites decrease. Children learn to understand language and to talk and ask for food. Development of gross motor skills permits them to learn to walk and seek food for themselves. Development of fine motor skills allows them to learn to feed themselves and to prepare simple foods such as cereal and milk and sandwiches. They learn about food and the way it feels, tastes, and smells. Preschool children learn to eat a wider variety of textures and kinds of food, give up the bottle, and drink from a cup. They demand independence and refuse help in many tasks in which they are not skillful, such as self-feeding. As they grow older they become less interested in food and more interested in their environment. They test and learn limits of behavior that are acceptable.

Self-feeding

Children learn to feed themselves independently during the second year of life. Spilling and messiness are marked during the first half of the year, but by their second birthday most children spill very little. Handedness is not established at 1 year of age. Children may grasp the spoon with either hand and may find when they try to fill the spoon that the bowl is upside down. The 15-month-old child will have difficulty scooping food into his or her spoon and bringing food to the mouth without turning the spoon upside down and spilling its contents because of lack of wrist control. By 16 to 17 months of age a well-defined ulnar deviation of the wrist occurs. As a result, only moderate spilling occurs, and the contents of a spoon may be transferred more steadily to the mouth. By 18 months of age the child lifts the elbow as the spoon is raised and flexes the wrist as the spoon reaches the mouth so that only moderate spilling occurs at this age, in contrast to earlier stages of self-feeding. By 2 years of age spilling seldom occurs.

Children are interested in how food feels and often prefer finger feeding to spoon feeding. Foods that provide opportunities for finger feeding should be provided at every meal. Children not infrequently will place food in the spoon with their fingers and may finger feed foods commonly spoon fed, such as vegetables and pudding.

By 15 months of age children can manage the cup, although not expertly. They have difficulty in lifting and tilting a cup and in lowering it to a tray after drinking. The cup is tilted, using the palm, and often is tilted too rapidly. By age 18 to 24 months the cup will be tilted by manipulation of the fingers.

Rotary chewing movements are refined in the second year and are well established by age 2½ years.

Patterns of food intake

Few children pass through the preschool years without creating concern about their food intakes. Between 9 and 18 months of age a disinterest in food becomes apparent and lasts from a few months to a few years.[27] Food jags are common. Likes and dislikes may change from day to day and week to week. For example, a child may demand only boiled eggs for snacks for a week and completely reject them for the next 6 months. Rituals become a part of food preparation and service. Some children, for example, accept sandwiches only when they are cut in half, and when parents quarter them they may throw tantrums. Others demand that foods have a particular arrangement on the plate or that their dishes be placed only in certain locations on the table.

Appetites are usually erratic and unpredictable during this period. The child may eat hungrily at one meal and completely refuse the next. The evening meal is generally the least well received and is of the most concern to the majority of parents. It is possible that a child who has consumed two meals and several snacks has met his or her need for energy and nutrients prior to dinnertime; in this instance consumption of limited amounts of food may be appropriate. It is also important to recognize that much social interaction occurs during the evening meal. This may be overwhelming for the preschooler who is learning not only to eat and interact at the same time but also to master the use of utensils as well as to eat harder-to-masticate foods.

Beal and Eppright and associates report a high percentage of parental dissatisfaction with children's appetites and interest in food between ages 2 and 4 years.[14,27] Concerns most frequently expressed are selection of a limited variety of foods, dawdling, limited consumption of fruits and vegetables, and consumption of too many sweets and too little meat. It is apparent that such problems are those of the parents' lack of insight into normal child development and, if properly managed, need not compromise a child's nutrient intake. Anticipatory guidance about children's food behavior is important for all parents, and intervention is imperative when battles are waged between parents and children about what is to be eaten.

Frequency of eating. Huenemann has pointed out that we are raising a generation of nibblers. Few children conform to a three-meal-a-day pattern. Preschool children consume food an average of five to seven times per day, although ranges of three to fourteen times per day have been noted.[28] Crawford found that by 6 years of age 50% of children ate five times per day.[10] Eppright noted that the frequency of food intakes was unrelated to nutrient intakes except when children consumed food less than four or greater than six times a day. Children in this study who consumed food less than four times a day consumed fewer calories and less calcium, protein, ascorbic acid, and iron than average intakes of other children their age. Those who consumed food more than six times a day consumed more energy, calcium, and ascorbic acid than average intakes of children their age.[29] Snacks have been noted to provide almost one-fourth of the total calories, over one-third of the total sucrose, and one-fifth of the total calcium and ascorbic acid ingested by school-age children.[30]

Food preferences. Parents report that preschool children enjoy meat, cereal grains, baked products, fruit, and sweets. They frequently ask for dairy products, cereal, and snack items such as cookies, crackers, fruit juice, and dry beverage mixes.[31] Food preferences during the preschool years seem to be for the carbohydrate-rich foods that are easier to masticate. Cereals, breads, and crackers often are selected in preference to meat and other protein-rich foods. The use of dry fortified cereals as a primary source of many nutrients is increasing.[10] Yogurt and cheese appear to be attaining increasing popularity among young children.

A concern of parents of many children between 1 and 3 years of age is that their children don't like and won't eat meat. In the description of their dissatisfaction, it may become apparent that the children do eat and enjoy chicken, frankfurters, and hamburger but refuse the more fibrous and harder-to-chew steaks and roasts. Foods have not yet been classified in relation to the pressure that must be applied in order to chew them well. Empirical observations, however, indicate that fibrous meats require the greatest pressure of any food consumed and may be difficult for the preschooler to eat. It may be important to focus parents' attention on the many softer, easier-to-chew meats and protein-rich foods that their children are consuming.

Food dislikes in childhood consistently include cooked vegetables, mixed dishes, and liver. Children accept raw vegetables more readily than they do cooked ones but often accept only a limited number. Acceptance of new foods appears to be age related. Owen found that only 6% of the youngest but 18% of the oldest preschoolers in his study would flatly refuse a new food.[8] Since familiarity with food is felt to influence its acceptance, new foods should be offered frequently, even though they have been previously refused.

Milk intakes are erratic and change with age. Beal noted that a reduction in milk intake begins at approximately 6 months of age.[27] Milk may be completely refused at times. Intakes of milk between ages 1 and 4 years approximate 1 to 2½ cups per day. After this age, the total volume of milk consumed increases.

Patterns of nutrient intake

Both longitudinal and cross-sectional studies of nutrient and energy intakes of children have shown large differences in intakes between individual children of the same age and sex; some children consume two to three times as much energy as others.[10,32] After a rapid rise in intake of all nutrients during the first 9 months of life, reductions can be expected in the intakes of some nutrients as increases occur in intakes of others.

Sex differences in intakes of energy and nutrients have been noted by several researchers. In all studies males consumed greater quantities of food, thus greater amounts of nutrients and energy.

During the preschool years there is a decrease in intakes of calcium, phosphorus, riboflavin, iron, and vitamin A because of the omission of iron-fortified infant cereals in the diets of children, their reduction in milk intake, and their disinterest in vegetables. During this period children increase their intakes of carbohydrate and fat. Protein intakes may plateau or increase only slightly.[32] Between 3 and 8 years of age there is a slow, steady, and relatively consistent increase in intake of all nutrients. Since intakes of vitamins A and C are unrelated to energy intakes, greater ranges of intakes of these nutrients have been noted. Black preschoolers in California have been noted to have higher intakes of sodium than whites because of their frequent use of undiluted commercially prepared soups. They were found also to have greater energy intakes than whites between 2 and 4 years of age.[10]

Feeding preschool children

In spite of the reduction in appetite and erratic consumption of food, preschool children do enjoy food and gradually increase their average daily energy intakes. If simply prepared foods that provide a balance of nutrients are presented in a relaxed setting, children will consume an appropriate nutrient intake. Understanding and supportive help from parents and others who offer food to children lay the groundwork for the development of nutritionally sound and satisfying eating practices. Meals and snacks should be timed to foster appetite. Intervals necessary between meals and snacks may vary from one child to another; rarely can the clock be depended on to let one know appropriate intervals and times when it may be important for a child to eat.

Appetites may be satiated when energy needs are met, regardless of a child's need for nutrients. It is thus important that a food selection be provided that ensures that the foods consumed provide nutrients as well as calories. The food should be presented without comment and the child permitted to consume amounts that he or she desires without any conversation focused on what or how much is being eaten. Portions served should be scaled to the child's appetite (see Chapter 6). When the meal is over, food should be removed and the child should be permitted to leave the table.

Occasionally anxious or concerned parents need help with food sources of nutrients usually supplied by food refused and/or in establishing limits to preschooler's food intakes and feeding behavior. Of the commonly expressed concerns limited intakes of milk, refusal of vegetables and meat, eating too many sweets, and limited intakes of food appear to cause the most problems. It is important to recognize that 1 oz of milk supplies 36 gm of calcium, and many children receive 6 to 8 oz of milk on dry cereal daily. Although they consume only 1 to 2 oz at a time, their calcium intakes may be acceptable when they consume milk with meals and snacks. When abundant amounts of fruit juice or sweetened beverages are available children may simply prefer to drink them rather than milk. Other dairy products can be offered when milk is rejected. Cheese and yogurt are usually accepted. Powdered milk can be incorporated into recipes for soups, vegetables, and mixed dishes.

Parents' perceptions of children's dislike of meat may need to be clarified. If in fact preschoolers do consistently refuse all food sources of heme iron, their dietary intakes of iron should be carefully monitored. Parents concerned about children's excessive intakes of sweets may need help in setting limits on amounts of sweet foods they make available to their children. It may be important also to help them convey their concern and the need to set limits on the availability of these foods to other family members, day care operators, and teachers.

When vegetables are consistently refused, wars between parents and children should not be permitted to erupt. Small portions (1 to 2 tsp) should continue to be served without comment and should be discarded if the child does not consume them. Preschool behavior modification programs that included token rewards when children consumed vegetables and another that provided education about specific vegetables served at mealtime have been found to increase children's acceptance and intake of them.[33,34]

If children's food intakes are so limited that their intakes of energy and nutrients are compromised, parents may need help in establishing guidelines so that the children develop appetites. They should offer food sufficiently often that children do not get so hungry that they lose their appetite, yet not so often they are always satiated. Intervals of 3 to 4 hours are often successful. Very small portions of food should be offered, and second portions should be permitted when children consume the foods already served. Attention should always be focused on children when they eat, and never when food is refused.

Group feeding

Increasing numbers of children eat some of their meals outside the home. Preschool children of working mothers may be cared for and fed by baby-sitters or day-care workers. Kindergartens and preschools offer snacks and/or meals, and often food experiences are included as part of the learning exercises provided for children. Day-care centers are licensed by state agencies that mandate the meal pattern and types of snacks to be provided for the children and the percentage of the recommended daily allowances that must be included in the menus. The acceptance of foods presented will be influenced by the same factors that influence children's food intakes at home.

Breakfast may need to be provided for children who receive none at home. Snacks should be planned to complement the daily food intakes. Small portions of food should be served, and children should be permitted second servings of those foods they enjoy. Disliked or unfamiliar foods may be offered by the teaspoon, and the child's acceptance or rejection should be accepted without comment. Children who eat slowly will need to be served first and should be permitted to complete their meals without being rushed to other activities. Teachers should eat with the children without imposing their attitudes about food on them.

A new setting provides an opportunity for children to have exposure to many new foods. Day-care centers, kindergartens, and preschools can provide an important educational setting for both children and their parents. Children learn to prepare food, how food grows, how it smells, and what nutrients it contains. Parents learn through participation, observation, and in conversations with the staff. An organized approach to feeding children must include parents, teachers, and others who offer food to young children. Teachers and day-care workers can provide important information to parents about how children successfully consume food, the nutrients children need, and the foods that provide these nutrients. Parents offer important information to the centers about their children's food acceptance and needs. Each needs to be reinforced positively by the other for their efforts as they successfully provide food for children.

A study of 48 day-care and Head Start programs found that all participating children consumed appropriate intakes of nutrients. Total daily energy intakes were similar for all children regardless of whether one meal and one snack or two meals and two snacks were provided. In fact, when children consumed one meal and one snack, 82% of their energy intakes was provided, but when two meals and two snacks were provided, 84% of energy intakes was consumed in this setting.[35]

THE SCHOOL-AGE CHILD

The school-age period is one of more steady growth accompanied by few apparent feeding problems. A natural increase in appetite is responsible for normal increases in food intake. Because they spend their days at school, children adjust to a more ordered routine. They attempt to gain mastery in physical skills and expend energy in organized sports and games. They learn about food and nutrition as part of their curriculum at school.

School-age children are not without food and nutrition concerns. Unresolved conflicts from the preschool years may persist. Children in their early school years often continue to refuse a food that touches another on the plate or to demand a special arrangement of dishes and utensils on the table. Likes and dislikes have been established but are not necessarily permanent; however they may become so if parents so convinced that children will refuse a food do not offer it to them or if a food dislike is discussed so frequently that children become fully patterned into their food idiosyncrasies.

Undernutrition may have serious consequences for the school-age child. Undernourished children easily become fatigued and are unable to sustain prolonged physical and mental effort and to fully participate in learning experiences. The risk of infection is greater. The child with limited nutrient reserves may, therefore, have frequent absences from school. Hopwood and Van Iden examined physical growth and school performance over a 10-year period in school-age children in Ohio.[36] They found that unacceptable patterns of growth were accompanied by scholastic underachievement. In addition, the longer an individual child grew at a less than expected rate, the less able he or she was to achieve success in school.

Breakfast is an important meal and should include a protein-rich food, since no midmorning snacks are provided in most schools. Children will have to rise earlier in order to eat an unhurried and balanced meal and may have to prepare it themselves. Early morning school activities may make preplanning necessary. Some may find a glass of milk and fruit juice important prior to early sports activities. Studies have shown that when breakfast is consumed children have a better attitude and school record as compared to when it is omitted.[37]

It is important also to recognize that symptoms of obesity and anorexia nervosa may appear during the school-age years in a study of dietary habits and attendant psychosocial factors. Intervention at this time is more likely to be effective than later when the disorders are fully developed.

As children explore the environment of school and peers they are likely to become influenced by these experiences. The credibility of parents is often questioned in the face of advice from teachers, peers, or peers' parents. The school-age child has more access to money, to grocery stores, and, therefore, to foods with questionable nutrient value.

Patterns of food intake

School-age children reduce the frequency of food consumption to four to five times per day on school days. They almost always want snacks after school, which they prepare themselves.[31] Although some increase the varieties of food they accept, many continue to reject vegetables, mixed dishes, and liver, and the range of food they voluntarily accept may be small.

A common difficulty for parents is finding a time when children are willing to sit down and eat a meal. They frequently are so involved with other activities that it is difficult to get them to take time to eat. Often they satisfy their initial hunger pangs and rush back to their other activities and television programs, returning later for a snack. They may become so engrossed in television programs that they demand to eat in front of the television set. In fact, some families have yielded to the pressure to not miss a favorite television program and have moved the evening meal from the dining room table to trays in front of the television. It frequently has been observed that children in such families become so engrossed in the shows that they lose interest in their food.

Snacking between meals and while watch-

Fig. 8-2. School-age children may prefer television programs to meals.

ing television is an important factor in the school-age child's nutrient intake and food habits. Parents can take advantage of urges to snack by planning and providing appropriate foods and discouraging children from responding to advertised suggestions that they ingest sweet foods.

Patterns of nutrient intake

Increases in size are accompanied by steady increases in intakes of energy and of all nutrients. By the school-age years most children have established a particular pattern of nutrient intake relative to their peers.[32] Although wide ranges of intake continue to be observed, those who consume the greatest amounts of food, thus energy and nutrients, consistently do so, whereas those consuming smaller amounts of food maintain lesser intakes of food relative to their peers. Differences in intake between males and females increase gradually to age 12 years and then become marked. Boys consume greater quantities of energy and nutrients than do girls.

School meals

School feeding and nutrition education programs, when adequately implemented, provide not only important nutrients for children, but also an opportunity for them to learn to make responsible choices regarding dietary intake. Unfortunately, not all schools have provided well-prepared food or an optimum environment to encourage its acceptance. In some instances excessive food waste has been reported. In many instances schools have housed snack bars and/or vending machines that provide only sweet foods with high-energy and low-nutrient concentration that competed with the foods that would have provided a balance of nutrients. Factors felt to be responsible for food waste include unpalatability of the food, little choice in menus, children's low preference for vege-

tables, and the continuous availability of "junk food" in the school. Menus have been found to often provide insufficient iron and to offer no options for children who need to reduce their energy intakes to control obesity. Food waste has been found to be greater in elementary school programs than in high school programs. Less milk and a higher percentage of vegetables are returned than other foods.[38] Food handling has also influenced waste, on-site preparation, and service, resulting in the least food returns. Frozen preportioned and reheated lunches have been the least well accepted. Other factors that have been believed to compromise children's food intakes include short lunch periods, long cafeteria lines, and a hurried, unsupervised atmosphere.

Successful programs have included students in menu planning and have prepared and served palatable, attractive food. Other programs have offered "fast foods" that comply with the National School Lunch Program (e.g., pizza, hamburger, milkshakes, and fruits).[39] Students have then had the option of selecting from the food available.

The fact that vending machines in schools, often viewed as money makers for athletic and other school activities, have offered no choice but concentrated sources of sucrose has been a concern to many interested in dental health, control of obesity, and the development of sound food habits for all children. Sufficient concern has been created in some school districts that only machines that provide fruit, milk, nuts, and seeds have been made available to students. Sales have been found to initially decrease but ultimately to increase. One school discovered that they made a greater profit on apples than on chocolate bars.[40]

Since its inception in 1946, the school lunch program has been administered by the Department of Agriculture, which provides cash reimbursement and supplemental foods to feeding programs that comply with federal regulations. Federal regulations require that school lunches and breakfasts be sold at reduced prices or be given free to children of families that cannot afford to buy them. The lunch menus must be planned to meet the guidelines established for the National School Lunch Program. Quantities of food suggested in these guidelines are based on the needs of 10- to 12-year-old children and may be increased or decreased to satisfy needs of younger or older children. The menus provide the following:

1. Eight ounces of unflavored fluid low-fat milk, skim milk, or buttermilk (whole milk or flavored milk may be offered as a choice but a low-fat milk must be offered)
2. Two ounces of protein-rich canned or cooked meat, fish, or poultry, 1 egg, ½ cup of cooked dry peas or beans, 4 tbsp of peanut butter, or equivalent combinations of these foods
3. Two or more portions of vegetables and/or fruit to a total of ¾ cup
4. Bread or bread substitute made with enriched flour

Schools are encouraged to keep fat, sugar, and salt at a moderate level. High school students may choose as few as three of five food items. Breakfast must include liquid milk, fruit or vegetable juice, and bread or cereal.

Current regulations require that schools devise a plan of student and parental involvement in the school lunch program. They may be included in such activities as menu planning, enhancing the eating environment, program promotion, and related student community support activities.

Foods sold in competition with school lunch in snack bars or vending machines must provide at least 5% of the recommended dietary allowances for one or more of the following nutrients: protein, vitamin A, ascorbic acid, niacin, riboflavin, thiamine, calcium, and iron. This regulation eliminates the sale of soda water, water ices, chewing gum, and some candies until after the last lunch period. It should also encourage the offering of more fruits, vegetables, and fruit and vegetable juices in places that compete with the school lunch.

Unfortunately, the nutrition education aspect of school feeding programs has been ignored in many schools. Teachers have thought that nutrition is a boring subject that is difficult to integrate into an already crowded curriculum. Many of them have felt unprepared to teach nutrition. Administrators have not always been supportive of nutrition education. However, careful planning between teachers, school lunch managers, and administrators can result in important learning experiences for all children. Food and nutrition education can be incorporated into social studies, math, art, health education, home economics, and other curricula. Children learn varieties of facts about food and nutrients in their classrooms and can experience those facts in the lunchroom. Teachers and school lunch administrators will need to plan together to integrate this important aspect of nutrition education into the school curriculum.

Although elementary schoolchildren are making more decisions regarding food selection, supervision and supportive guidance may be necessary at lunchtime. Children may give priority to activities other than eating, often rushing through their meals. They may prefer to do without meals rather than reveal the fact that they must receive reduced price or free lunches. Some may refuse to eat many foods on the menu. Disposable aluminum foil trays and plastic spoons are not easy implements for children to use.

Children and their parents may need guidance in the selection of food to be consumed. Overweight and obese children may find it necessary to gain willpower to refuse the gravies and sauces and ask for non-fat milk. As handicapped children enter the mainstream of education, careful planning with parents will be necessary to ensure that mealtimes at school provide appropriate foods as well as nutrients for these children.

As children prepare to enter adolescence, attitudes toward food will be well established. Between infancy and adolescence nutrients and energy provide compounds necessary for growth; reserves of some nutrients are accumulated that prepare children for stress and give preparation for the adolescent growth spurt into which they next enter. Knowledge of nutrition and attitudes toward food they acquire during this period provide a basis for the years when the decisions of food selection become theirs alone.

REFERENCES

1. Zee, P., Walters, T., and Mitchell, C.: Nutrition and poverty in preschool children, J.A.M.A. **213**:739, 1970.
2. Larson, L. B., and others: Nutritional status of children of Mexican-American migrant families, J. Am. Diet. Assoc. **64**:29, 1974.
3. Acosta, P. B., and others: Nutritional status of Mexican-American preschool children in a border town, Am. J. Clin. Nutr. **27**:1359, 1974.
4. Van Duzen, J., Carter, J. P., and Vander Zwaag, R.: Protein and calorie malnutrition among preschool Navajo Indian children, Am. J. Clin. Nutr. **29**:657, 1976.
5. Owen, G. M., and others: Nutrition survey of White Mountain Apache preschool children in nutrition, growth, and development of North American Indian children, Publication No. (N.I.H.) 72-26, Washington, D.C., 1972, Department of Health, Education, and Welfare.
6. Karp, R. J., and others: Iron deficiency in families of iron-deficient inner-city school children, Am. J. Dis. Child. **128**:18, 1974.
7. Lopez, R., and others: Riboflavin deficiency in a pediatric population of low socio-economic status in New York City, J. Pediatr. **87**:420, 1975.
8. Owen, G. M., and others: A study of nutritional status of preschool children in the United States, 1968-1970, Pediatrics **53**:597, 1974.
9. Eppright, E. S., and others: Nutrition of infants and preschool children in the North Central Region of the United States of America, World Rev. Nutr. Diet. **14**:269, 1972.
10. Crawford, P. B., Hankin, J. H., and Huenemann, R. L.: Environmental factors associated with preschool obesity, J. Am. Diet. Assoc. **72**:589, 1978.
11. Eppright, E. S., and others: The North Central Regional study of diets of preschool children. II. Nutrition knowledge and attitudes of mothers, J. Home Ec. **62**:327, 1970.
12. Caliendo, M. A., and others: Nutritional status of preschool children, J. Am. Diet. Assoc. **71**:20, 1977.
13. Bryan, M. S., and Lowenberg, M. E.: The father's influence on young children's food preferences, J. Am. Diet. Assoc. **34**:30, 1958.
14. Eppright, E. S., and others: Eating behavior of preschool children, J. Nutr. Educ. **1**:16, 1969.
15. Sims, L. S., and Morris, P. M.: Nutritional status of preschoolers, J. Am. Diet. Assoc. **64**:492, 1974.
16. Lund, L. A., and Burk, M. C.: A multidisciplinary analysis of children's food consumption behavior, Technical Bulletin No. 265, St. Paul, 1969, University of Minnesota, Agricultural Experimental Section.
17. Somers, A. R.: Violence, television, and the health of American youth, N. Engl. J. Med. **294**:811, 1976.
18. Television, 1976, North Brook, Ill., 1976, A. C. Nielson Co.
19. Barcus, F. E.: Weekend commercial children's television—1975, Newtonville, Mass., 1975, Action for Children's Television.
20. Blatt, J., Spencer, L., and Ward, S.: A cognitive developmental study of children's reactions to television advertising. In Rubinstein, E. A., Comstock, G. A., and Murray, J. P., editors: Television and social behavior, vol. 4, Television in day to day life: patterns of use, Washington, D.C., 1972, U.S. Government Printing Office.
21. Ward, S., Levinson, D., and Wackman, D.: Children's attention to television commercials. In Rubinstein, E. A., Comstock, G. A., and Murray, J. P., editors: Television and social behavior, vol. 4, Television in day to day life: patterns of use, Washinton, D.C., 1972, U.S. Government Printing Office.
22. Gussow, J.: Counternutritional messages of TV ads aimed at children, J. Nutr. Educ. **4**:48, 1972.
23. Yankelovich, D.: Mothers' attitudes toward children's programs and commercials, Newtonville, Mass., 1970, Action for Children's Television.
24. McNeal, J. U.: An exploratory study of consumer behavior of children. In McNeal, J. U., editor: Dimensions of commercial behavior, New York, 1969, Appleton-Century-Crofts.
25. Wackman, D. B., and Ward, S.: Children's informa-

tion processing of television commercial messages. Manuscript based on a symposium at the American Psychological Association Convention, Montreal, 1973. Cited in Sheikh, A. A., Prasad, V. K., and Rau, T. R.: Children's TV commercials: a review of research, J. Commun. **24:**126, 1974.

26. Berey, L. A., and Pollay, R. W.: The influencing role of the child in family decision making, J. Marketing Res. **5:**70, 1968.
27. Beal, V. A.: On the acceptance of solid foods and other food patterns of infants and children, Pediatrics **20:**448, 1957.
28. Huenemann, R. L.: Environmental factors associated with preschool obesity. II. Obesity and food practices of children at successive age levels, J. Am. Diet. Assoc. **64:**489, 1974.
29. Eppright, E. S., and others: The North Central Regional study of diets of preschool children. III. Frequency of eating, J. Home Ec. **62:**407, 1970.
30. Frank, G. C., and others: Dietary studies of rural school children in a cardiovascular study, J. Am. Diet. Assoc. **71:**31, 1977.
31. Lamkin, G., Hielscher, M. L., and Janes, H. B.: Food purchasing practices of young families, J. Home Ec. **62:**598, 1970.
32. Beal, V. A.: Dietary intake of individuals followed through infancy and childhood, Am. J. Public Health **51:**1107, 1961.
33. Ireton, C. L. and Guthrie, H. A.: Modification of vegetable-eating behavior in preschool children, J. Nutr. Educ. **4:**100, 1972.
34. Harrill, I., Smith, C., and Gangever, J. A.: Food acceptance and nutrient intake of preschool children, J. Nutr. Educ. **4:**103, 1972.
35. Williams, S., Henneman, A., and Fox, H.: Contribution of food service programs in preschool centers to children's nutritional needs, J. Am. Diet. Assoc. **71:**610, 1977.
36. Hopwood, H. H., and Van Iden, S. S.: Scholastic underachievement as related to sub-par physical growth, J. Sch. Health **35:**337, 1965.
37. Tuttle, W. W., and others: Effect on school boys of omitting breakfast, J. Am. Diet. Assoc. **30:**674, 1974.
38. Jansen, G. R., and Harper, J. M.: Consumption and plate waste of menu items served in the National School Lunch Program, J. Am. Diet. Assoc. **73:**395, 1978.
39. Fast Food Staple for Type A Lunches, School Foodservice Journal **31:**19, 1977.
40. Crawford, L.: Junk food in our schools: a look at student spending in school vending machines and concessions, J. Can. Diet. Assoc. **38:**193, 1977.

ADDITIONAL READINGS

Beal, V. A.: Nutritional intake of children. I. Calories, carbohydrate, fat, and protein, J. Nutr. **50:**233, 1953.

Beal, V. A.: Nutrition in a longitudinal growth study, J. Am. Diet. Assoc. **46:**457, 1965.

Beyer, N. R., and Morris, P. M.: Food attitudes and snacking patterns of young children, J. Nutr. Educ. **6:**131, 1974.

Blakeway, S. F., and Knickrehm, M. E.: Nutrition education in the Little Rock school lunch program, J. Am. Diet. Assoc. **72:**389, 1978.

Breckenridge, M. E.: Food attitudes of 5-12 year old children, J. Am. Diet. Assoc. **35:**704, 1959.

Brown, M. L., and others: Diet and nutriture of preschool children in Honolulu, J. Am. Diet. Assoc. **57:**22, 1970.

Burke, B. S., and others: Calorie and protein intakes of children between 1 and 18 years of age, Pediatrics **24:**922, 1959.

Burke, B. S., and others: Relationships between animal protein, total protein, and total caloric intakes in the diets of children from one to eighteen years of age, Am. J. Clin. Nutr. **9:**729, 1961.

Caliendo, M. A., and Sanjur, D.: The dietary status of preschool children: an ecological approach, J. Nutr. Educ. **10:**69, 1978.

Clancy-Hepburn, K., Hickey, A. A., and Nevill, G.: Children's behavior responses to TV food advertisements, J. Nutr. Educ. **6:**93, 1974.

Crispin, S., and others: Nutritional status of preschool children. II. Anthropometric measurements and interrelationships, Am. J. Clin. Nutr. **21:**1280, 1968.

Driskell, J. A., and Price, C. S.: Nutritional status of preschoolers from low income Alabama families, J. Am. Diet. Assoc. **65:**280, 1974.

Emmons, L., Hayes, M., and Call, D. L.: A study of school feeding programs, J. Am. Diet. Assoc. **61:**262, 1972.

Fryer, B. A., and others: Growth of preschool children in the North Central Region, J. Am. Diet. Assoc. **60:**30, 1972.

Galst, J. P., and White, M. A.: The unhealthy persuader: the reinforcing value of television and children's purchase-influencing attempts at the supermarket, Child. Dev. **47:**1089, 1976.

Juhas, L.: Nutrition education in day care programs, J. Am. Diet. Assoc. **63:**134, 1973.

Kerry, E., and others: Nutritional status of preschool children. I. Dietary and biochemical findings, Am. J. Clin. Nutr. **21:**1274, 1968.

Lewis, C. E., and Lewis, M. A.: The impact of television commercials on health-related beliefs and behaviors of children, Pediatrics **53:**431, 1974.

Myers, M. L., Mabel, J. A., and Stare, F. J.: A nutrition study of school children in a depressed urban district, J. Am. Diet. Assoc. **53:**234, 1968.

Owen, G., and Lippman, G.: Nutritional status of infants and young children: USA, Pediatr. Clin. North Am. **24:**211, 1977.

Patterson, L.: Dietary intake and physical development of Phoenix area children, J. Am. Diet. Assoc. **59:**106, 1971.

Voichick, J.: School lunch in Chicago, J. Nutr. Educ. **9:**102, 1977.

Wait, B., Blair, R., and Roberts, L. J.: Energy intake of well nourished children and adolescents, Am. J. Clin. Nutr. **22:**1383, 1969.

9

Nutrition and the adolescent

Betty Lucas

The adolescent period is a unique stage in the process of growth and development. A rapidly changing time of "growing up," it is characterized by a wide variability in norms of growth, increasingly independent behavior, and the testing of adult roles. Adolescence lasts nearly a decade and has no specific beginning or end. This critical period of human development occurs at the physiologic, psychologic, and social levels. Changes do not occur simultaneously but at varying rates. Thus a teenager may have several ages at the same time—chronologic, physical, psychologic, and social. Although adolescence may be defined as the teenage years between 12 and 20, physical maturation and changes in nutrient requirements actually begin at younger ages and extend into the third decade.

PHYSICAL GROWTH AND PUBERTY

The velocity of physical growth in adolescence is second only to the rate of growth during infancy. Therefore, there is a high demand for calories and nutrients to support optimal growth. After the relatively latent growth period of childhood, adolescent growth is manifested by an increase in both cell number and size as well as in reproductive maturity. The end of adolescent physical growth is usually signaled by slowing of growth, the completion of sexual maturation, and closure of the epiphyses of long bones. This is a general guide, however, and does not apply to other parameters of growth such as psychologic and social development.

Up to approximately 9 years of age, males and females grow in height and weight at the same rate, with males slightly larger and heavier. The prepubescent growth period begins about 2 years earlier in females than in males. At this time females temporarily are taller and have a larger limb muscle mass than do males. As pubertal growth proceeds, the male develops more muscle and the skeleton enlarges, particularly in the shoulder region. In the female there is a smaller increase in muscle, but the pelvis rounds out and enlarges because of the deposition of fat. At the beginning of the prepubertal period, many children normally lay down excess fat. If a child has not been fat during earlier years, however, this fat will probably diminish gradually in 1 to 2 years.

The most rapid phase of adolescent growth is known as the growth spurt, and its highest point is called the peak. Growth velocity decelerates from birth until the pubertal growth spurt, at which time the increased growth velocity of a 14-year-old boy is comparable to that of a 2-year-old child. The average peak velocities of height and weight

Table 9-1. Average peak velocities of height and weight

	Height	Weight
Males		
Peak velocity	10.3 cm/year	9.8 kg/year
Peak velocity age	14.1 years	14.3 years
Females		
Peak velocity	9.0 cm/year	8.8 kg/year
Peak velocity age	12.1 years	12.9 years

Adapted from Tanner, J. M., Whitehouse, R. H., and Takaishi, M.: Standards from birth to maturity for height, weight, height velocity, and weight velocity, British children, 1965, Part I, Arch. Dis. Child. 41:454, 1966.

are shown in Table 9-1. It can be noted that although the peak velocity age occurs later in males, it is more intense and results in more tissue accretion. Findings from the National Health Examination Survey suggest that American adolescents attain their peak height velocity earlier than do English adolescents: three-quarters of a year earlier for boys and one-quarter of a year earlier for girls.[1] The NHES data, however, is based on a cross-sectional study and cannot be interpreted as longitudinal data.

In females the height spurt signals the beginning of puberty, with pubic hair and breast development being the first notable changes. Menarche occurs at the end of the growth spurt, approximately 9 to 12 months after peak height velocity is attained.[2] The earlier the onset of menarche, the greater the peak velocity of growth and the less time that elapses between peak velocity and menarche. Early-maturing females do not necessarily become taller, but they do complete their growth spurts more quickly and at younger ages. Some studies indicate that these females have more subcutaneous fat, even from childhood years, and a greater predisposition to obesity.[3,4] Frisch and co-work-

ers have proposed the theory that a critical body weight and/or fat composition is necessary to achieve menarche.[5] This theory has been supported by epidemiologic data as well as by observations of females with anorexia nervosa and well-trained athletes with minimal fat stores who develop amenorrhea. Others, however, have shown that this hypothesis is limited in its application to all adolescent females, but that it is a significant factor in the onset of menarche.[6]

In males secondary sexual changes (pubic hair, voice changes, penis and testicular growth) indicate the beginning of the growth period. The height spurt occurs toward the end of the growth period. Males actually lose limb fat at the peak height velocity, probably because of testosterone action, whereas females maintain a positive balance of fat without loss of limb fat.

The stage of puberty is usually determined by using the standards of Tanner and co-workers. From a longitudinal examination of normal children, five stages of pubertal maturation were developed for each sex, beginning with stage 1, the prepubertal child, and ending with stage 5, adult sexual development.[7] These standards of assessment are commonly used in clinical practice today.

Even though it is commonly assumed that full stature is attained by 18 to 20 years of age, data indicate that growth in length can continue for another decade. Results of longitudinal growth studies by Garn and associates showed that from 17 to 28 years of age mean height increments were 1.2 cm for females and 2.3 cm for males.[8] Whether this growth is skeletal or vertebral has not been clearly defined.

In relation to skeletal growth, it must be remembered that stature is not an indicative measure of skeletal mass. At 10 years of age approximately 80% of maximum stature has been attained, but only 50% of adult skeletal mass has been gained. Garn and associates report that skeletal mass increases into the fourth decade, about 4% for males and 6% for females after age 18 years.[8] The continued increase in both skeletal length and mass indicates the need for ongoing calcium retention for a longer period than has been commonly accepted.

Development of sophisticated methodology in the last few decades has enabled the prediction of eventual adult height in children and adolescents. The data most frequently used are the Bayley tables[9] combined with the Greulich-Pyle skeletal atlas[10] to predict height based on present age, height, and bone age. More recently, Tanner and associates formulated an equation for adult height that is based on present height, bone age, and age at menarche for females, with allowance for midparent height.[11]

Sex differences in body composition begin in infancy but are most dramatic by adolescence. Percent of lean body mass rises in adolescents, especially in males, who finish growth with 1.5 times the lean body mass of females. Studies of longitudinal growth parameters in males have shown that the peak increment in lean body mass coincides with peaks in height and weight, and suggest that growth trends in height and lean body mass are more constant than trends in body weight.[12] Fat content is higher in the female after approximately the twelfth year, and by the end of the second decade, it is 1.5 to 2 times the male value. Correspondingly, the female has a lower percentage of body water than does the male. Because of these significant sex differences in the body composition of the adolescent, total body weight alone is not a valid measure with which to assess growth or to predict nutrient requirements.

Over the last century or more, growth records throughout the world have indicated secular trends in growth. These observations show that children are growing taller

and weighing more with each generation. In addition, there is earlier sexual maturation. This early maturation, however, is primarily responsible for children being taller and weighing more at one particular age. There is a shorter growth period and earlier cessation of growth. The eventual adult size has not, however, increased as dramatically. A 10-year-old boy in 1875 might have been only 50% of the way through his growth period, while a 10-year-old boy today might be 60% to 65% mature. Greulich has compared growth parameters of American-born Japanese children in 1956 to data 15 years later and found little difference in heights and weights. This evidence suggests that growth trends have reached a plateau in developed countries.[13]

These factors of puberty—rapid physical growth, sexual maturation, changes in appearance and body shape—have a significant impact on the adolescent's self-esteem, body image, and personality. Because of the wide variability of rates of growth and their timing, there are no "norms" for adolescent growth in conjunction with chronologic age. Our culture does dictate some standards, variable although they may be, and adolescents continually compare themselves to these standards or to their peers. No other age group is as concerned and sensitive about their bodies or as devastated by criticism and comparison as are adolescents. This is particularly true of the obese adolescent and the early or late maturer. It is not unusual to find these adolescents with distorted body images making inappropriate food choices and thus compromising optimal growth.

ENERGY AND NUTRIENT REQUIREMENTS

Since no period of growth is less predictable than adolescence, nutrient allowances are only estimates and should not be applied to individuals. Indeed, most of the allowances have been extrapolated from data on young children and adults. Basically, the highest nutrient and energy demands occur at the peak velocity of growth, thus paralleling the growth rate. Requirements, then, should be determined by sex, age, stage of puberty, and current growth parameters.

Energy

Until the recent revision of the recommended dietary allowances, energy allowances were based on the average kilocalories for adolescent age groups (age 11 to 14 years, age 15 to 18 years). It is obvious that those standards could not be appropriately applied to individuals with varying rates of growth. The current recommended dietary allowances use the same age groups, but include a range of kilocalories for each group and sex. Thus, the range of energy intake for 11 to 14-year-old females is 1500 to 3000 kcal; for 15 to 18-year-old males, it is 2100 to 3900 kcal.[14]

One of the earliest studies of energy intakes, reported by Wait and Roberts in 1932, was based on studies of 52 females aged 10 to 16 years.[15] The variation in size and intake at any age is demonstrated by noting that the 12-year-old girls in this study ranged from 56 to 65 inches in height and from 79 to 149 pounds in weight. Their caloric intakes ranged from 1649 to 2925 kcal, an 80% difference between minimum and maximum values. These investigators first attempted to correlate caloric requirements with physiologic age, accounting for maturation and growth rate. The function of physiologic development in determining energy needs for adolescents is still sometimes ignored.

Heald, Remmell, and Mayer compiled, from previous studies, caloric intake data on 2750 females and 2200 males between the ages of 7 and 20 years.[16] For males, average caloric intakes increased steadily to age 16 years, when the intake reached 3470 kcal, paralleling accelerated growth. From 16 to 19 years of age, caloric intake decreased by approximately 500 kcal. In females the rise in caloric intake increased to age 12 years, when total kcal reached 2550, followed by a gradual decline to age 18 years, when intakes averaged 2200 kcal. Although decelerated growth rate was probably the major factor in decreased caloric consumption, physical activity, which was not differentiated, may have been a factor.

In a longitudinal study conducted by Hampton and co-workers, there was great variation in caloric intakes from day to day for each individual, but more consistent intakes from week to week. According to body fat class, the lean females and average males consumed more kilocalories than did the other groups.[17]

Age or weight alone is not a useful predictor of energy needs. Combinations of kcal/kg/age and kcal/kg/cm are more useful tools. Using a single measure, height in adolescents best expresses energy requirements because it usually correlates well with physiologic development. Wait suggested 16 kcal/cm as a rough estimate of energy needs for females, and data from the longitudinal Child Research Council study give estimated intake percentiles of 10 to 19 kcal/cm for females and 13 to 23 kcal/cm for males, all healthy, growing adolescents 11 to 18 years old.[18]

Basically, little is known regarding actual energy requirements for adolescents. Physical activity and other life-style habits are key factors in considering needs. Adolescents may have widely varying and erratic caloric intakes and still continue to show optimal growth. It is possible that an internal mechanism exists for conserving energy in times of low intake or for eliminating excess energy.

Protein

Reports indicate that protein in the adolescent diet ranges from 12% to 16% of total energy intake.[16,17] Males consistently consume more total protein than do females. Although the recommended dietary allowance for 15- to 18-year-old males is 56 gm of protein, it is not unusual for intakes to be well over 100 gm/day. As with energy, total protein intake increases steadily in males up to approximately 16 years of age, whereas females have highest intakes at age 12 years.

Balance studies by Johnston have helped define optimal needs.[19] He found that a positive nitrogen balance was sustained only when the caloric requirement was satisfied and when 15% of total kilocalories was derived from protein. An important consideration is that a restricted caloric intake during the rapid period of growth will compromise lean body mass accretion and nitrogen retention despite a seemingly adequate protein intake. This situation can occur in adolescents such as those dieting to lose weight or athletes attempting to make a specific weight class.

In the United States, reported intakes of protein usually exceed the recommended dietary allowances, a fact that leads some individuals to question whether persons living in the United States receive too much protein. Hegsted has proposed that there is no strong evidence to support a substantial increase in protein requirements for adolescents.[20] Similarly, the FAO/WHO Expert Committee recommends progressively decreasing levels of safe protein intakes from childhood to adulthood.[21] The actual amount of protein intake will increase with growth, but the amount per kilogram decreases with age. However, some adolescents (e.g., those adhering to extreme reducing diets, those from lower socioeconomic classes, and those eliminating all animal products from their diets) are at risk for suboptimal intakes of protein.

Minerals

Calcium. Because calcium is absorbed more efficiently at lower levels of intake than at higher levels of intake, numerical recommendations have limited use. The amount of calcium needed to maintain a positive balance during growth is thought to be reflected by previous intake, explaining the absence of problems in areas of the world where the daily intake is a minimal 200 to 300 mg of calcium.

In the adolescent, calcium needs are dependent on growth velocity, bone structure and size, and absorption rate. Individual growth variability also influences calcium requirements; the unusually tall adolescent and the early maturer or late maturer will vary considerably in their needs. In relating calcium requirements to skeletal weight, the largest gains of dry weight occur in females between ages 10 and 14 years and in males between ages 12 and 16 years. Calcium retained as bone is approximately 100 mg/day in preschool years; however, this doubles for adolescent females and triples for adolescent males during peak periods of retention.[8] For example, a 14-year-old male may require 600 to 1200 mg of calcium/day, depending on absorption rates of 50% or 25%. The recommended dietary allowance of 1200 mg/day is thus designed to meet the needs of the adolescent who is growing at the fastest rate, and levels less than that may be quite adequate for some adolescents. Those adolescents who are at risk for limited calcium for growth are probably males with unusually rapid rates of bone growth, late-maturing females who are concerned with caloric restriction, and adolescents eliminating milk products from their diets. A low calcium:phosphorus ratio as a result of excess dietary phosphorus or a reduced calcium intake may also compromise optimal calcium status, but this is still a controversial issue. The intake of phosphorus-containing additives used in food processing may add 500 to 1000 mg of phosphorus/day above that found naturally in food.[22] Many of the foods that contain this added phosphorus, such as carbonated beverages, are popular with teenagers.

Iron. Iron is significant because it is frequently marginally adequate or deficient in adolescents. Although females are assumed to be most at risk, data from the HANES survey showed that the greatest prevalence of low hemoglobin and hematocrit levels was among boys.[23] The recommended dietary allowance for both sexes, 11 to 18 years of age, is 18 mg, but this intake is rarely attained without supplements in females. In a review of 12 studies with approximately 1300 females and 1000 males, the average iron intakes were 9.6 to 13.5 mg/day for females and 14.0 to 18.7 mg/day for males.[24]

The higher requirement for iron in adolescence is directly related to rapid growth, which is accompanied by increases in blood volume, muscle mass, and respiratory enzymes. Because of their increased need but often limited intake of iron, adolescents are, therefore, particularly susceptible to iron deficiency anemia.

Excretion of iron from physiologic sources is insignificant with the exception of regular menstrual losses in the female. Hallberg and co-workers reported the mean blood loss during a period as 43.4 ml in all women, with a smaller blood loss of 33.8 ml in 15-year-old females.[25] Although iron loss will vary according to blood loss and length of normal menstrual cycle, it has been estimated that the iron loss is approximately 1.2 mg/day and that iron needs can be met if this amount is retained.[26]

There is little sex difference in iron requirements of children until females begin puberty, at which time their requirements are higher. By age 15 years requirements for both males and females rise sharply. For the females this increase is directly related to menstrual losses. In the males the increase in tissue mass plus the rise in hemoglobin levels, which is probably caused by androgen activity, result in higher requirements. It has been suggested that boys growing at the ninety-seventh percentile may have iron needs greater than the recommended dietary allowances during their growth spurts.[27]

As with other requirements, chronologic age is a poor predictor of iron needs. Daniel has shown that differences in hematocrit values of males are more significant when correlated with sex maturity rating than when correlated with age.[28] The same investigator demonstrated that iron intake increases consistently in both males and females as they progress in maturity stages. He found that intake was greater for males than for females at each maturity rating and that white adolescents had slightly greater intakes than did black adolescents. Following the same trend, iron stores, as measured by transferrin saturation, were consistently higher in males than in females but did not correlate with dietary intake of iron.[29]

Zinc. As more information is acquired about the role and availability of zinc, it will become important to assess this nutrient in the diets of adolescents. In both sexes there is an increase in zinc retention that parallels the increase in lean body mass. In males, the requirement for growth apparently exceeds 400 μg per day.[30] The recommended dietary allowance for adolescents is 15 mg of zinc/day. Although there have been no studies on the zinc requirements of adolescents, increasing evidence suggests that this population is one of the groups most at risk for marginal intakes.[31]

Vitamins

Little satisfactory data are available to establish vitamin requirements for the adolescent, and most recommended amounts are extrapolated from other age groups. Although most needs are met by usual foods, mild vitamin deficiencies are not uncommon in this age group, resulting both from a poorly chosen diet and from the increased metabolic requirements during the growth spurt. In addition to identifying food sources of vitamins, the dietary assessment should also consider any supplements taken by the adolescent, especially large doses of the fat-soluble vitamins A and D.

As with other nutrients, vitamin requirements are best correlated not with age but with growth demands. Using folate as an example, Daniel, Gaines, and Bennett have shown that the sex maturity rating rather than age is a more significant factor associated with dietary intakes of folate.[32] They found that males had higher intakes of folate than did females and that these values increased with maturity levels for both sexes. Plasma folate concentrations were, inversely, higher for females than for males, decreasing with maturity in both sexes. This paradox may represent the greater needs for folate during rapid cell growth, especially in males who may double their muscle mass during adolescence.

In summary, the energy and nutrient requirements of adolescents are directly related to the rate and stage of growth, the highest demand being at the peak velocity of growth. Care should be taken in interpreting common recommendations based on age groups and in comparing individuals to those standards.

FACTORS INFLUENCING FOOD INTAKE

The adolescent is not only maturing physically but is also progressing in social and psychologic parameters. He or she is striving to achieve the developmental tasks between childhood and adulthood. The changes and experiences each encounters affect his or her living pattern and, ultimately, his or her food intake and nutritional status.

Newly acquired independence and decision making result in adolescents spending more time outside the home, thus making independent food choices. It is not unusual for these choices to be made on the basis of sociability, enjoyment, and status, rather than on nutrient content. Activities of school, sports, part-time jobs, interest groups, and peer activities may result in the adolescent being away from home from early morning until after the evening meal. Adolescent lifestyles and independence often result in irregular eating patterns such as skipped meals and increased frequency of snacks.

Because of the multiple changes that are occurring simultaneously during this period of growth, adolescents are usually anxious and dissatisfied with their body images. This bodily overconcern is a normal preoccupation; that it may be distorted and unrealistic does not make it any less important to the adolescent. One study demonstrated this paradox well. It revealed that 70% of the females studied wanted to lose weight but that no more than approximately 15% were actually obese. Fifty-nine percent of males, on the other hand, wanted to gain weight, although only 25% were lower than average in fatness.[33]

Studies also indicate that adolescents are dissatisfied with their body dimensions. For males there is the desire for larger biceps, shoulders, chest, and forearms. Females, conversely, desire smaller hips, thighs, and waists.[33,34] Numerous clinical experiences with adolescents further document this phenomenon.

The body image is further influenced by advertising and mass media, which dictate the "in" look, clothing styles, and other elements of being accepted. In attempting to conform to cultural ideals, adolescents may compromise their own well-being, including optimal nutrient intake. They are also susceptible to food advertising that encourages them to eat an item not for nutritional needs but because it is fun, crunchy, chocolatey, and because it gives them "energy."

Perhaps the strongest influences on the adolescent are peer pressure and the desire to fit in. These influences may come from the immediate peer group or may include respected adults and national idols. This desire to be accepted may be manifested in such dietary practices as embarking on a weight reducing scheme, espousing vegetarianism, indulging in alcohol, or altering diet to complement a muscle-building program. Any harmful results will depend on the practice and how it is carried out, but the initial decision to change is often the result of others' influence rather than health reasons.

REPORTED INTAKES AND EATING PATTERNS

Intakes of adolescents tend to be more variable than those of younger children or adults for the various reasons mentioned previously. Over the years studies have indicated that adolescent diets are lowest or deficient in calcium, iron, ascorbic acid, and vitamin A.[17,35-37] Because females often reduce their energy intakes, they are most at risk for suboptimal intakes. On the other hand, it is not uncommon for the same proportion of adolescents, primarily males, to exceed the recommended allowances for these same nutrients.

Teenagers generally have the reputation of being meal skippers, and this is documented by reports as well as by numerous clinical interviews. Breakfast and lunch are the meals usually missed.[38,39] On the other hand, teenagers tend to eat more often than adults, averaging from two to six times per day. Generally, adolescents eating less than three times a day have poorer diets than those eating more frequently.[17] Schorr and co-workers demonstrated that the complexity of an adolescent's diet (determined by the number of different foods eaten in a 3-day period) increased significantly with increases in the parents' occupational levels, the mother's education, and the adolescent's employment and social participation.[37] They also found that a more complex diet resulted in increased intakes of calcium, iron, vitamin A, and ascorbic acid.

The snacking habits of teenagers have long been maligned, with parents and professionals alike being concerned about the "empty-calorie" foods being consumed. Various studies, however, have shown that this between-meal eating contributes significantly to the total nutrient intake.[17,35,40] The most limiting nutrients provided by snacks are usually calcium and iron; low intakes of these two nutrients also occur in the overall adolescent diet. Observation, on the other hand, shows that some teenagers consume large amounts of high-calorie, low-nutrient snack foods. And given the choices available from vending machines, school stores, and neighborhood grocers, it is not unusual for the adolescent to end up with a snack that is high in kilocalories, sucrose, fat, and/or salt but that provides minimal nutrients. This combination of frequent snacks and sucrose consumption is significant in the high incidence of dental caries in adolescence.

Irregular eating patterns seem to be associated, to some degree, with ethnic background and, to a lesser extent, with socioeconomic factors. Surveys have shown that black teenagers have less regular meal patterns than do white teenagers.[39,41] Although there are exceptions, adolescents eating regular meals and snacks tend to have better nutrient intakes than do irregular eaters.

These tendencies, then, make certain groups of adolescents more at risk for suboptimal nutrition than others.

NUTRITIONAL CONCERNS
Obesity

Obesity is probably the most common nutritional and general health problem among adolescents in developed countries. Although the incidence is not known, estimates of obesity range from 10% to 20%. In numbers this represents more than 10 million adolescents in the United States. Realistically, the prognosis for these teenagers is poor: 80% of them will remain obese as adults,[42] and they will be more resistant to treatment. This is an important fact to consider in helping obese adolescents set realistic goals.

As in adults, obesity in teenagers is seldom an isolated problem but is combined with social and psychologic difficulties. It is not a moral issue, nor is it a simple medical problem. Many health care workers have found that it is a mistake to equate obesity solely with overeating and to treat the adolescent with an inspirational lecture accompanied by a diet.

Characteristics. Although there is no typical obese adolescent, certain physical characteristics seem to persist. These include rapid weight gain in the first year of life, earlier maturation, earlier menarche, a highly endomorphic physique, and advanced bone age.[43,44] This is especially true for those who have been obese through the growing years.

Since adolescents are, in general, sensitive about their bodies, obese teenagers are especially affected by the social rejection and derogatory attitudes in our culture. In our society, which admires and merchandises slimness, obese teenagers are under constant pressure to change their bodies to conform with social norms. Monello and Mayer have shown that obese girls have traits in common with other minority groups, such as obsessive concern (with overweight and food), passivity, withdrawal, self-contempt, and actual discrimination.[45] In reality obesity does affect attractiveness, popularity with the opposite sex, ability to obtain a job, college acceptance, and other practical life situations. These teenagers may experience so much humiliating rejection and poor self-esteem that they become socially isolated. In addition, their consistently low level of activity requires fewer calories. This combination of emotional and environmental factors often leads to more severe obesity. A vicious circle ensues whereby food and eating may be the only outlets for frustration and depression (Fig. 9-1).

Food practices and activity patterns. In considering the food practices of obese adolescents, one should remember that they may not be consuming excessive calories. Studies have shown that the caloric intakes of some obese adolescents are equal to or lower than those of nonobese adolescents.[46,47,17] There is a tendency for obese teenagers to eat less frequently and to skip more meals, especially breakfast. Expressions such as "I'm not hungry in the morning" and "Eating breakfast makes me sick" are common. Often an accompanying pattern is the frequent or continuous eating from after school until late in the evening.

Another major factor is the inactivity of obese adolescents as compared to normal weight adolescents. This has been demonstrated by activity records and motion picture sampling.[46-48] Indeed, it is not hard to imagine why body-sensitive overweight teenagers decline to participate in sports and activities that make them feel awkward, embarrassed, and exhausted. In addition, many obese adolescents are eliminated from participation in organized sports because of poor performance. Because they expend few-

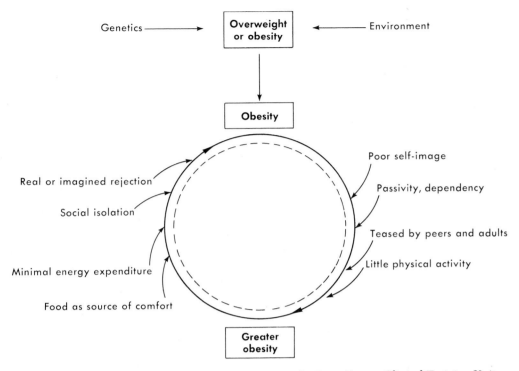

Fig. 9-1. Factors that contribute to obesity. (Diagram by Betty Lucas, Clinical Training Unit, Child Development and Mental Retardation Center, University of Washington, Seattle, Wash.)

er calories, they may eat less than normal weight adolescents and yet still gain weight, or at least maintain their weights. This seeming self-denial without results often causes feelings of frustration and hopelessness in the individual.

Treatment. It has been estimated that the odds against an overweight adolescent becoming an average weight adult are 28 to 1.[49] Despite these discouraging statistics there is a large demand for adolescent weight control programs from parents, teachers, health professionals, and teenagers themselves. Adolescence can certainly be a critical period of influence in the establishment of positive health attitudes and practices. On the other

hand, not recognizing the complex make-up of the obese adolescent or establishing unrealistic treatment plans can subject both the adolescent and the helping professional to feelings of failure and discouragement.

In most cases conventional methods such as rigid diets and/or parental control have produced poor results. Anorectic drugs are usually contraindicated because of their ineffectiveness and because of the potential of abuse. Jejunoileal bypass surgery has not been used to any extent because of its postoperative morbidity and unknown effects on growth. For those adolescents, however, who are morbidly obese (more than 100% above expected weight) and have not been successful in previous reducing attempts, gastric bypass has been shown to be an effective treatment method without the complications of jejunoileal surgery.[50]

Behavior modification techniques are being used increasingly in the treatment of adult obesity. This therapy can be useful in working with teenagers, but success will depend on the motivation, maturity, and family support of the adolescents. A behavioral approach alone seems to have limited application to the situation of the obese adolescent. Programs that have included physical activity and behavioral components as well as diet have demonstrated more success, but few long-term follow-up studies have been done.[51]

Assessment. To determine the best therapeutic approach for the obese adolescent, a myriad of factors must be considered. One clinical assessment tool that addresses the complexity of the problem is shown on p. 190. By assessing these factors, preferably through an interdisciplinary team process, a treatment approach can be planned to meet the needs of the individual.

Those adolescents who have a poor self-esteem, who are significantly depressed, and who are dependent and immature will generally require intensive counseling before they can deal with the weight problem. Those individuals who are more motivated and relatively unencumbered by the severe psychologic aspects will probably have success with a program that includes dietary guidance, physical activity, behavioral components, and supportive counseling. Reports indicate that such a combined approach can be effective, both in clinical and school settings.[52-54]

Clinical management. Successful treatment of the obese adolescent usually involves more than one health professional and requires an understanding of adolescent development as well as skills in counseling.

The ideal program incorporates decision making by the adolescent and is realistic in its time frame.

Goals for treatment need to acknowledge the adolescent's pubertal stage. For those in their growth spurts, weight can be maintained or slowly increased over time, allowing for changes in the ratio of lean body mass and fat. Both teenagers and parents must understand that weight gain is expected in periods of growth. For those who have completed their growth spurts, the plan will probably include actual weight reduction by loss of fat.

From a practical aspect, most obese adolescents will benefit from nutrition education because they have tried various types of diets or have acquired misinformation regarding obesity. Too often they are not aware of the basic concepts of energy balance (calories consumed versus calories expended), or they may have the idea that a calorie is only negative and undesirable. Rather than being talked to or given information to read, these adolescents will respond best if they are included in activities and problem solving. Keeping food records, assessing their activity patterns, trying new recipes, calculating caloric values, analyzing popular fad diets, or checking labels at the supermarket give adolescents a feeling of responsibility and accomplishment. The professional can help them to focus on food behaviors they would like to change as well as to consider alternatives for handling such food-oriented situations as holidays or snacks. They should, in all cases, be encouraged to make their own decisions. Role playing is often an effective tool in this regard.

Physical exercise is often given little credit in the treatment of obesity in general. For the adolescent, activity should be encouraged and reinforced as a permanent aspect of his or her life-style. In many cases it provides an alternative to eating as well as a

CLINICAL ASSESSMENT OF EATING DISORDER

Motivation
  Desire to lose weight
  Goals
  Insight
Family characteristics
  Eating disorders
  Other diseases
  Natural or other parent
Parental attitude toward weight problem
  Role of food in family
  Perceptions of weight problem
  Attempts to intervene
Social relationships
  Friends
  School
  Social life and activities
  Social skills
  Teasing
Growth and adiposity
  Weight history
  Maturation stage
  Body fatness
  Growth velocity
  Age

Mental function
  Psychological testing
  School performance
Emotional/psychologic status
  Depressed
  Locus of control
  Body image
  Self-esteem
  Oral expression
  Coping skills
  Compulsiveness
Eating behavior
  Control over food intake
  Meal pattern
  Bizarre eating habits
  Knowledge of nutrition
  Nutritional adequacy
Medical data
  Clinical findings
  Thyroid status
Physical activity
  Exercise and frequency
  Family activity patterns
  Hobbies and interests
  Personal feeling about activity

Developed by Mahan, K., and Rees, J., Adolescent Clinic and Child Development Mental Retardation Center, University of Washington, Seattle, Wash.

means to increase energy expenditure with or without caloric restriction. Regular exercise yields positive changes in body composition, such as decreases in body weight and relative fat and increases in lean body mass, as well as cardiovascular benefits.[55]

It is vital to encourage activities that the teenager enjoys. The activities should be relatively inexpensive and feasible and should have potential for continuing on into adulthood. Popular activities include bicycling, swimming, skating, walking, running, and tennis. For the significantly obese, care should be taken to assess the teenager's abilities and to program a slow, consistent increase in exercise. Actual fitness testing has been used in a clinical setting to plan realistic exercise programs for obese adolescents and to engage their interest and motivation.[56] This testing includes strength, flexibility, endurance, and cardiorespiratory function. The steps of assessing fitness levels and planning subsequent activity programs are outlined on p. 191.

FITNESS: TESTING AND PLANNING IMPROVEMENT PROGRAMS

1. a. Have client sit quietly and relax for 3 to 5 minutes.
   b. Take pulse for 10 seconds.*
   c. Record *resting heart rate (RHR):* _____
2. a. Find intensity of exercise required to reach *training heart rate (THR)*† immediately after exercise. THR for teens 20 to 22 beats/10 seconds.

   Stop with the exercise that achieves 20 to 22 beats/10 seconds. This is the exercise to use initially in the improvement program.

   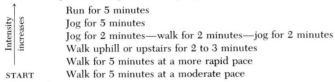

Intensity increases ↑	Run for 5 minutes
	Jog for 5 minutes
	Jog for 2 minutes—walk for 2 minutes—jog for 2 minutes
	Walk uphill or upstairs for 2 to 3 minutes
	Walk for 5 minutes at a more rapid pace
START	Walk for 5 minutes at a moderate pace

   b. Monitor pulse return toward RHR after each exercise level—it should be below 16 beats/10 seconds by 5 minutes.

   _____   _____   _____   _____
   Immediate ⟶ 1 minute ⟶ 2 minutes ⟶ 5 minutes ⟶ . . .

3. *Improvement program:* To maintain THR for 15 minutes 4 to 5 days/week:
   a. Work with client to design an individualized program that is comfortable for him/her.
   b. Plan 5-minute warmup—move at level below the level that maintains THR.
   c. Exercise at intensity that maintains THR.
   d. 5-Minute cool down—back to warmup speed—client should not sit or lie down immediately.
   e. Use a combination of exercise levels and types, if necessary.
   f. If the client is ill, he/she should begin after illness at lower intensity and return slowly to intensity achieved before illness
4. a. Retest every 3 to 4 weeks
   b. Increase intensity of exercise to maintain THR.
   c. Client can increase time spent doing the exercise by 5-minute increments, up to 30 minutes.
   d. When client has reached jogging level and maintained it for 6 to 8 weeks, increase THR to 22 to 25 beats/10 seconds.
   e. Client can use any aerobic activities (e.g., jogging, bicycling, skating, dancing) or combinations that the client prefers.

Developed by Scott, B., and Rees, J., Adolescent Program, University of Washington, Seattle, Wash.
*10-second time segment is easiest to measure and use.
†*Maximum heart rate* (MHR): ≈ 200 beats/minute for persons under 20 years of age (Cumming, G. R., Everatt, D., and Hastman, L.: Bruce treadmill test in children: normal values in a clinic population, Am. J. Cardiol. 41:69, 1978). THR is 60% of MHR for persons with poor initial fitness, 75% of MHR for persons who are fit (i.e., 60% of 200 = 120 beats/minute = 20 beats/10 seconds [20 to 22 beats/10 seconds for normal variation]).
Note: Contraindications for testing and initiating fitness program will be revealed by routine medical history and physical examination.

BE SIZEWISE
Don't Lose
Your Balance.

Feelings

Learn to know and
like yourself

Have realistic goals
for yourself

Don't substitute food for
love and companionship

Build satisfying relationships with your family
and friends

Get help for problems you
can't cope with alone

Activities

Do interesting things—
quiet as well as energetic

Take time to relax
everyday

Don't let eating be
your only recreation

Do some strenuous
activity every day

Share active and quiet
time with friends

Nourishment

Be good to your body—
give it what it needs

Don't starve or
stuff yourself

Know what's in the
food you eat

American Heart Association of Washington
4414 Woodland Park Avenue North
Seattle, Washington 98103

Fig. 9-2. © American Heart Association of Washington.

Fig. 9-3. Adolescent and nutritionist discuss management of weight control.

Group treatment is commonly used for many adolescent difficulties, including obesity. It may range from intensive treatment in a summer camp to weekly sessions in a school or clinical setting. Groups will vary according to their general goals, their leaders, and their members. The specific goals of group sessions may include the acquisition of nutrition information, the use of behavior modification tools, physical activity, social skills improvement, emphasis on a positive image, and the development of peer relationships. Success by group treatment cannot be measured by weight loss alone, but also by evaluating psychosocial parameters. For some adolescents, willing attendance at group sessions, initiating a conversation, or reporting a personal achievement to the group will be a big step. The group leader plays a critical role. He or she should have an understanding of adolescent development in general, an awareness of the varying complexity of the obese teenager, and skills in group process.

The obese adolescent should be individually assessed whether one-to-one therapy or group therapy is used, because although some common characteristics exist, there is no typical overweight teenager. Programs may vary with the individual, but in all cases attention should be given to the adolescent's diet, activity, and feelings. This concept has been developed as a teaching tool in one area (see Fig. 9-2).

The following guidelines can assist the professional in helping the obese adolescent.

1. *Supportive counseling.* This should be provided on a consistent basis (at least once a month) and is often long term.
2. *Setting realistic goals.* These may include specific weight goals (weight maintenance, slow weight gain, or weight loss), activity patterns, food-related behaviors, or others. Goals should be short term and should be developed in sequence.
3. *Positive reinforcement.* This may include changes in food habits and exercise patterns and progress in areas other than weight loss.

The scale is not the only measure of success.
4. *Patience.* Too often the professional is ready to give up and conveys this to the adolescent as failure.

Because of the poor prognosis for many obese teenagers to achieve ideal weight, the professional working with them should avoid setting unrealistic goals or leading them to believe that they can accomplish the impossible. For these individuals obesity should be considered a chronic condition, and treatment goals should include working toward the adolescent's acceptance of the idea of lifelong weight control. Once this concept can be maturely accepted, goals of ongoing modification of eating patterns and activity patterns can be emphasized.

Despite poor prognosis and lack of long-term success of obesity treatments, program efforts for obese adolescents usually yield positive changes, although they may be small and difficult to measure. But for the individual teenager, these effects can be significant by enhancing his or her present situation and/or by providing information and skills that can be used at a later time.

Anorexia nervosa

Anorexia nervosa is an eating disorder with underlying serious developmental and psychologic disturbances. It occurs almost exclusively among females, and the symptoms are usually manifested in the midteens. The initial symptoms include amenorrhea, weight loss, compulsive physical activity, and preoccupation with food. Anorexia nervosa often is physically manifested as a response to real or imagined obesity. In many cases, everyday events or remarks critical of their bodies precipitate the weight loss. Initially, the weight goals may be reasonable, but with success these individuals are reinforced both externally and internally to continue losing weight. When weight goals are reached, new

lower ones may be established. Dieting becomes a primary focus of their lives, described by Bruch as "a relentless pursuit of thinness."[57]

Anorexia is actually a misnomer in this disorder. Patients do not lack hunger, but rigidly deny and control it. As outlined by Bruch, a pattern of denial occurs—denial of thinness, hunger, fatigue, and personal effectiveness.[57]

The disorder may be characterized by progressive and/or significant weight loss, alternating "binge" eating with dieting and avoidance of any "fattening" foods. These young women are usually very clever at concealing their gorging of food, self-induced vomiting, and heavy use of laxatives. There is a dramatic increase in hyperactive behavior and compulsive exercise patterns. The hyperactivity may begin as routine physical exercise but may increase, as the disorder progresses, to compulsive jogging and calisthenics, denying the need for adequate rest, even to the inability to sit down for more than a moment. Of significance is the fact that the physical activity is usually done alone.

These individuals are often preoccupied with food and will prepare high-calorie dishes for their families but limit themselves to a taste or nothing. Aspects of nutrition are also of great interest to them, and in fact most are more knowledgeable of nutrition than their peers. However, this nutrition knowledge may be distorted, and the individual may be unable to practically conceptualize the information. The bizarre eating habits of individuals with anorexia nervosa may be well hidden, so that family and friends often deny any problems and do not seek help until the disorder becomes severe.

Some psychodynamic features of the anorexia nervosa syndrome include a distorted body image, fear of physical maturation and adulthood, and a tremendous, dependence/independence conflict. Even when the disorder has progressed to the point of emaciation, these anorectic women will deny reality, insisting that they are normal or even still overweight. There is a pattern of doing exceptionally well academically but withdrawing from peer relationships in preference for a self-imposed isolation. Their ability to function realistically in a school or work setting, however, may be significantly compromised. Family histories of patients with anorexia nervosa reveal an increase in psychopathology among families, as well as a higher prevalence of obesity and anorexia nervosa. Some evidence also suggests an increased incidence of perinatal complications in these individuals.[58] Classically, the family is very achievement oriented and successful at economic, social, and academic levels, but parents may have a significant marital discord. The parents' need to control and the anorectic's need to please form the basic conflicted relationship that demands resolution for the patient with anorexia nervosa.

It is well to remember that not all individuals with anorexia nervosa exhibit the classical characteristics. Approximately 5% to 10% are male; some cases are not manifested until later adulthood; and other cases do not show dramatic weight loss or common psychologic behaviors. These atypical cases may not be readily diagnosed, but they deserve appropriate treatment.

In recent years, there have been numerous studies on the metabolic and endocrine abnormalities often associated with this disorder, focusing primarily on pituitary and hypothalamic function.[59,60] Some of these abnormalities mimic the results of studies on semistarvation, but it remains unclear whether these alterations are specific for anorexia nervosa or are effects of not eating.

With the continual weight loss and semistarvation, these individuals are in poor nutritional status. Fluid and electrolyte imbalances can result from induced vomiting and

purging. Long-term debilitation results in death in a small percentage of cases.

Treatment and management of anorexia nervosa is varied and controversial. Most programs include nutritional, medical, and psychiatric support. Cases of severe debilitation require hospitalization and refeeding, to which there may be a positive response by the patient. On the other hand, it is not unusual for the patient to sabotage treatment attempts by hiding food, performing surreptitious exercise, or attaching weights to her body before stepping on the scale. Satisfactory weight gain by a patient in an institution cannot be interpreted as success because of the high incidence of later relapse. It is essential that the underlying developmental problems be resolved. But a hospital stay and subsequent weight gain can be the first stage of a comprehensive program.

One of the most comprehensive treatment programs has been developed by Crisp and associates in England. The in-patient program includes an initial psychiatric assessment, a refeeding program with bed rest, and ongoing individual and family psychotherapy.[61] Emphasis is put on the psychologic environment, which should be accepting and supporting of the patient. After attaining normal weight, the patient is allowed more freedom, but the hospital stay continues to provide ongoing counseling.

Behavior modification, in which weight gain is required to earn certain privileges or activities, has been used with some initial success.[62] This method of therapy has been criticized for its lack of long-term evaluation and its focus on only tangible measures.[63] Critics feel that it tends to undermine the patient's individuality, which is essential for success. In a recent study, 81 patients were randomly assigned either to behavior modification therapy or to the standard hospital therapy. No significant difference in weight gain was found between the two groups after

35 days.[64] Some experts, however, believe that behavior modification can be a useful tool in initial phases of treatment.[65]

Long-term psychotherapy has been a component of treatment, preferably with the family involved, if at all possible. More recently, good success has been reported on the use of the family therapy approach developed by Minuchin, which focuses on familial relationships and functioning.[66] This method reports to have a high success rate if patients and families are treated within a year of the onset of the syndrome.

Common features of anorexia nervosa are the strong resistance to treatment and the high incidence of relapse or partial recovery. Some of these patients will manifest varying degrees of the symptoms in adulthood. Despite these prognostic factors, very few follow-up evaluations have been conducted on the long-term outcome of the various treatment modes used for anorexia nervosa. Hsu and co-workers in England recently reported on the outcome of a follow-up study of 100 patients. The time lapses ranged from 4 to 8 years after the initial clinic visit.[67] All but 12 of the patients had been involved in refeeding programs and/or psychotherapy. Using the criteria of near normal weight, regular menstruation, and satisfactory psychosexual and psychosocial adjustments, 48% had a good outcome. Poor outcome was associated with longer duration of illness, lower body weight during illness, older age of onset, the presence of vomiting, compulsive overeating, anxiety when eating with others, poor social adjustment in childhood, and disturbed parental relationships. Although this study did not look at methods of treatment, the low mortality of the severely ill patients supports the use of weight gain and psychotherapy for these patients.

Russell suggests that the disease will run its natural course and that the roles of the professionals are to do their best to support the patient during this time.[68] Health care professionals should watch for symptoms (often well disguised) in suspect individuals and attempt to intervene early. Whether the person with anorexia nervosa is treated as an in-patient or an out-patient, the goals of management should include (1) maintaining a positive nutritional state, (2) achieving physical and developmental maturation, and (3) providing therapy for the patient to work out underlying conflicts and emotional disorders.

Pregnancy in adolescence

Although the overall birth rate in the United States is declining, this is not the case for the adolescent age group. During the last two decades, the rate of pregnancy among 15- to 19-year-old girls has decreased, but since the number of teenage girls has nearly doubled, the number of live babies born has not changed.[69] On the other hand, birth rates among females under 15 years of age continue to rise at an alarming rate. These trends have resulted in an increase in the proportion of teenage births from 17% in 1966 to 19% in 1975.[70] In addition, out-of-wedlock births have increased among adolescents; it is estimated that 85% of births to those 15 years old or younger and 23% of births to 19-year-old girls are illegitimate.[69] Another particular concern is the trend of young teenagers to have more children, have them closer together, and have more unwanted and out-of-wedlock births.[71]

Teenage mothers have more complications during pregnancy and give birth to a higher percentage of stillborn infants and low birth weight infants. Also, their infants have higher rates of neonatal and infant mortality.[72] Some of these adverse effects are believed to be related to socioeconomic status and other environmental factors that are hard to isolate. The American Academy of Pediatrics states that an increase in low birth weight infants and preeclampsia are the two major complications related to the teenage pregnancy itself.[69] The incidence of births of babies weighing less than 2500 gm is significantly higher among all adolescents, but especially among those who give birth before they are 15 years of age. Recent data suggest that gynecologic age, or time interval since menarche, is a better base of comparison for high incidence of births of low birth weight infants than is chronological age.[73] Low gynecologic age is associated with a higher incidence of births of low birth weight infants.

The pregnant teenager characteristically does not receive early prenatal care, thus increasing her risk for a poor outcome. A subsequent pattern of dropping out of school and thus decreasing future employability, having no financial independence, and often having little emotional support all create a poor psychosocial milieu for the adolescent.

Females are particularly at nutritional risk when pregnancy occurs before their own growth is completed, mainly before 17 years of age. In addition their nutrient stores may be minimal at the time of conception because of poor eating habits and dieting attempts. For the young, early-maturing female, pregnancy is an extra demand on a body that is still growing rapidly and that has not reached skeletal maturation.

Studies indicate that many pregnant adolescents receive inadequate amounts of nutrients (primarily iron, calcium, calories, and vitamin A) and that they have lower biochemical values.[74,75] The multiple nutrient demands of adolescent growth and pregnancy, combined with a poor food intake, do not predict an optimal outcome of pregnancy. Generally, the nutrient needs of pregnant adolescents are estimated by adding the recommended dietary allowances for pregnancy to the allowances for 15- to 18-year-old females.[76] These nutrient levels may be an overestimation for some individuals, depending on changes in nutrient absorption, hormonal alterations, or decreased physical activity. But unless the adolescent is obviously mature, the additive allowances of adolescence plus pregnancy are probably the best guides in planning diets for this group. Each individual should be assessed for current intake and life-style. Many pregnant girls decrease their levels of physical activity, and thus may not require all the calories allowed. Iron and folic acid needs are increased substantially during pregnancy; these nutrients are often found marginally in adolescent diets. A prenatal supplement, therefore, is usually standard practice to cover the increased needs.

Pregnant teenagers are just as likely as other teenage girls to have patterns of meal-skipping, poor snacks, overconcern about weight, and limited food choices. Professionals working with pregnant girls to improve nutritional status and the subsequent pregnancy outcome should be cognizant of the patients' life-styles and habits as they affect eating behavior. Establishing rapport is an initial priority, followed by working cooperatively with the adolescents to gradually and progressively improve nutritional intakes. A wide variety of counseling approaches can be successful, depending on the characteristics of patient and professional, but an authoritarian model is not usually beneficial.

The psychosocial factors imposed on the pregnant female can cause her to be in a situation where she is alone, has no emotional support, has little or no money to buy food, and does not seek prenatal care. A team of health care providers with expertise in multiple areas is best suited to meet her needs. In the last decade or more, comprehensive programs have been developed that include prenatal care, nutritional guidance, psychologic counseling, family planning, and continued schooling. This type of program, if available in a community, no doubt is the most appropriate resource to optimize the outcome for both the teenage girl and her baby.

Sports and athletics

Participation in a variety of physical activities is enjoyed by most adolescents. This may range from the organized, competitive sport and daily training to weekend skiing and bicycle trips. Regardless of the type of sport, optimal nutrition is a basic requisite for training and maintaining good physical performance. It is probably not coincidental that Olympic gold medal winners come from those countries with a high level of nutritional status.

As with the nonathlete, the diet of the athlete must supply optimal amounts of energy, protein, water, fat, carbohydrates, vitamins, and minerals. The specifics of nutrient needs and problem areas are dealt with in Chapter 10.

Despite the influence of good nutrition, dietary practices alone cannot be counted on for super powers or to supply the "winning edge." It is not unusual for adolescent athletes to emulate the professional star, including modeling a "winning" diet or accepting an endorsement of a food supplement or vitamins. Coaches and trainers, who work closest with the athlete, may also allow or encourage undesirable dietary practices because of their lack of nutrition expertise or their hope that the practice will improve performance. Many dietary practices relating to foods included or excluded in the athlete's diet are often based on psychologic reasons or superstitions rather than on physiologic and nutritional soundness.

Ideally, more nutrition education should be available to coaches, trainers, and others who greatly influence the young athlete. A study demonstrated that physical education students who had a college nutrition course scored higher than those who received nutri-tion information from parents and coaches.[77] Because adolescents are developing lifelong eating habits, it is desirable that those adults guiding them should reinforce positive dietary practices.

Alcohol

Increased attention has been given recently to the problem of alcohol consumption in adolescence. It has been reported that more than 90% of high school students have had at least some experience with alcohol by age 18 years, and most have their first exposure under parental supervision between ages 12 and 15 years.[78] Currently, alcohol use among females is almost as high as among males.

Alcoholism or "problem drinking" in the adolescent age group has been difficult to define, because most definitions and classifications of alcoholism have been based on adult males. In most cases adolescent drinkers are identified by higher rates of alcohol-related problems such as school difficulties, psychologic problems, and arrests and/or delinquency. Young people tend to drink less regularly than do adults, but they consume larger amounts at a time (i.e., binge drinking).[79]

The degree of nutritional risk for drinking adolescents will depend on the frequency and amount of their alcohol consumption. It is known that alcohol has deleterious effects on nutritional status in more than one way. First, the alcoholic beverage, which has almost no nutritional value, displaces food that provides nutrients for growth. Ethanol provides energy, at 7 kcal/gm, but significantly dilutes the nutrient content of the diet, making the individual at risk for nutritional deficiencies. In addition, continued alcohol consumption has a direct toxic effect on the gastrointestinal mucosa, interfering with digestion and absorption.[80] This adverse effect occurs independently of the malabsorption that can result from alcoholic cirrhosis. The nutrients most likely to be deficient are pyrodoxine, folic acid, thiamin, and vitamin B_{12}. In many cases of chronic alcoholism, the malnutrition that exists is a result of both an inadequate diet and the alcohol's direct action on the gut.

For the pregnant adolescent who consumes alcohol, there is the risk of producing a child with fetal alcohol syndrome.[80] More subtle effects on the offspring may be caused by the alcohol itself or by the combination of alcohol and a marginal diet.

Nutritional status evaluations of adolescents should not neglect the area of alcohol consumption. Some individuals may initially withhold this information, in which case the interviewer should adopt a nonthreatening approach. Those adolescents who have significant alcohol problems obviously need comprehensive programs of counseling and rehabilitation, but it is appropriate that nutritional therapy and education be a component of such treatment.

Acne

Problems of poor complexion, blackheads, and pimples are dreaded by all adolescents of both sexes. Many experience these problems to some degree during puberty, and a small percentage are affected by a full-blown case of the clinical disease, acne vulgaris. Although teenage acne is subject to fads and fallacies regarding cause and treatment, there is nothing mysterious about this phenomenon. Acne is not caused by eating chocolate, french fries, or carbonated beverages, despite popular thought to the contrary. The sebaceous glands of the skin are under hormonal control, chiefly that of androgens; thus the rapid acceleration and increase of hormone production are directly related to the skin changes.

There is no rationale for recommending a specific diet in the treatment of acne, although any food that seems to be aggravating for an individual should be limited. Medical treatment of acne vulgaris involves both topical and systemic medications. Retinoic acid (a vitamin A acid) is sometimes used as a topical agent in difficult cases, but its use requires physician supervision.[81] Large doses of vitamins, however, will not alleviate the symptoms of acne and may lead to toxicity of fat-soluble vitamins. In preventing or lessening the symptoms, a basic diet providing optimal nutrients will help ensure healthy skin, but again, specific foods should not be eliminated unless they are suspect for the adolescent. An optimal diet combined with good skin care will not prevent the superficial signs of acne but will help lessen the severity of the symptoms.

Nontraditional eating patterns

Adolescents are going through a period of development in which they are forming values and testing their newly acquired independence. This may be manifested in unusual eating patterns for a variety of reasons. Reference has already been made to the obese teenager who tries the latest reducing diet with hopes of a quick cure and the young athlete who ingests protein supplements and vitamins to improve his or her performance. Both individuals are subject to nutrition misinformation, the end results of which may vary from being harmless to a situation in which growth is compromised.

More young people are adopting nontraditional eating patterns such as vegetarianism, a yoga diet, or "natural" foods, among others. Motivation for these dietary changes may include asserting independence, a particular philosophy or religion, an ecologic or environmental concern, rebellion against adults, or a genuine interest in health. Any detrimental effects of these dietary practices on the optimal nutritional status of adolescents will depend on the particular diet, the volume and variety of foods it includes, and the length of time it is practiced. Specific nutrients likely to be at risk in vegetarian and other nonmeat diets are discussed in Chapter 11. These same nutritional risks are applicable for the rapidly growing adolescent.

A positive aspect in working with these teenagers is their built-in interest in nutrition, even though their information sources may not be completely reliable. Initial assessment should be made as to whether the practice is beneficial, neutral, or harmful. Reinforcement can certainly be given to the adolescent who has decreased consumption of concentrated carbohydrates and packaged snack items in favor of more fruits, vegetables, and whole grains. The positive aspects of the dietary regimen can be emphasized and stress placed on moderation and variety, with enough calories provided to promote growth.

In the case of unhealthy dietary patterns, concrete supportive data are more likely to be accepted by questioning adolescents than are superficial answers. They want to know specific nutrient information and the scientific reasoning behind a recommendation, not a review of the basic four food groups. Because some of these adolescents do not seek health care through established avenues, successful nutrition counseling and education have been demonstrated by rap sessions and team efforts in free clinics, youth centers, and other places accepted by them.[82,83] An initial appeal to their interest in nutrition and their desire to be healthful persons will help in establishing a good rapport.

IMPLICATIONS FOR NUTRITION EDUCATION

Adolescents in the United States are not experiencing the dire results of malnutrition, despite the fact that some of them do not receive optimal nutrition. This realization is significant when considering methods and approaches to nutrition education for this age group.

A survey of over 1300 high school students revealed that nutrition was a subject of relatively low interest compared to other areas of health, for reasons such as boring subject matter, repetition of material learned earlier, learning "useless" facts, and superficial presentation.[84] Despite reports showing that teenagers are concerned about weight and growth,[34,85] this survey reported the lowest response of knowledge regarding weight loss and gain. In addition, female high school graduates with previous home economics courses incorporating foods and nutrition do not necessarily demonstrate better nutrition knowledge, attitudes, and practices than those without such courses.[86]

This information reveals a definite need for innovative nutrition education approaches to the adolescent. Leverton points out some positive aspects in reaching adolescents: (1) they get hungry, (2) they like to eat, (3) they want energy, vigor, and the means to compete and excel in whatever they do, and (4) they have many good food habits that were established in childhood.[87] Primary assets such as these yield access points to reach the adolescent at his or her own level of interest and readiness. By respecting the adolescent's ideas about food, it is easier for the health professional to emphasize the positive aspects and to build on them.

In addition to their roles in the family, adolescents also have significant roles as students and consumers. At school, a well-designed nutrition curriculum incorporated with relevant subjects can provide a base of knowledge. In a larger sense the school can be a nutrition laboratory, providing practical experience not only in science and health classes, but also in the lunchroom and at the vending machine. As consumers, teenagers are increasing their power in the marketplace but are also the targets of sophisticated advertising. To make rational food choices, they need practical information about food labeling and purchasing, nutrient density of foods, and how to analyze advertisement messages.

Because today's teenagers are generally more sophisticated and knowledgeable than in the past, they will usually respond to nutrition information in terms of growth and development, even in physiologic parameters. With respect to future parenthood, it is obvious that the female should have an understanding of the impact of long-term nutrition on the outcome of pregnancy. However, since research indicates that the father's food preferences are the most influential factor in family food choices, appropriate nutrition education for the male adolescent is just as vital.

Practical experience has shown that visual aids or other media developed specifically for adolescents lead to stimulating discussion and an increased interest in many areas of nutrition. Some novel and successful attempts at getting a nutritional message across to teenagers have included the use of a fantasy comic format and a radio/television media campaign using prizes and contests.[88,89] Many of these efforts have been primarily experimental in nature, however, reaching only a limited audience. One would hope that in the future appropriate program planning would support the use of innovative educational techniques to provide nutrition knowledge and concepts to all adolescents.

It should be remembered that food is only one part of the exciting and rapid journey to adulthood, and that nutrition education can be incorporated along with many aspects of adolescents' life-styles and at various stages of readiness. In completing their own growth and maturity, adolescents are nearing the time when they will influence and make decisions regarding the food habits and nutritional status of the next generation.

REFERENCES

1. Height and weight of youths 12-17 years, Washington, D.C., 1973, Department of Health, Education, and Welfare.
2. Marshall, W. A., and Tanner, J. M.: Variations in pattern of pubertal changes in girls, Arch. Dis. Child. **44:**291, 1969.
3. Hammar, S. L., and others: An interdisciplinary study of adolescent obesity, J. Pediatr. **80:**373, 1972.
4. Garn, S. M., and Haskell, J. A.: Fat thickness and developmental status in childhood and adolescence, Am. J. Dis. Child. **99:**746, 1960.
5. Frisch, R. E.: Critical weight at menarche, initiation of the adolescent growth spurt, and control of puberty. In Grumbach, M., Grave, G., and Mayer, F., editors: Control of the onset of puberty, New York, 1974, John Wiley & Sons, Inc.
6. Crawford, J., and Osler, D.: Body composition at menarche: the Frisch-Revelle hypothesis revisited, Pediatrics **56:**449, 1975.
7. Tanner, J. M.: Growth at adolescence, ed. 2, Oxford, 1962, Blackwell Scientific Publications Ltd.
8. Garn, S. M., and Wagner, B.: The adolescent growth of the skeletal mass and its implications to mineral requirements. In Heald, F., editor: Adolescent nutrition and growth, New York, 1969, Meredith Corp.
9. Bayer, L. M., and Bayley, N.: Growth diagnosis, Chicago, 1959, University of Chicago Press.
10. Greulich, W. W., and Pyle, S. I.: Radiographic atlas of skeletal development of the hand and wrist, ed. 2, Stanford, Calif., 1959, Stanford University Press.
11. Tanner, J. M., and others: Prediction of adult height from height, bone age, and occurrence of menarche at ages 4 to 16 with allowance for mid-parent height, Arch. Dis. Child. **50:**14, 1975.
12. Parizkova, J.: Growth and growth velocity of lean body mass and fat in adolescent boys, Pediatr. Res. **10:**647, 1976.
13. Greulich, W. W.: Some secular changes in the growth of American-born and native Japanese children, Am. J. Phys. Anthropol. **45:**553, 1976.
14. Food and Nutrition Board: Recommended dietary allowances, ed. 9, Washington, D.C., 1980, National Academy of Sciences, National Research Council.
15. Wait, B., and Roberts, L. J.: Studies in the food requirement of adolescent girls. I. The energy intake

of well-nourished girls 10 to 16 years of age, J. Am. Diet. Assoc. **8**:209, 1932.

16. Heald, F. P., Remmell, P. S., and Mayer, J.: Caloric, protein, and fat intakes of children and adolescents. In Heald, F. P., editor: Adolescent nutrition and growth, New York, 1969, Meredith Corp.

17. Hampton, M. C., and others: Caloric and nutrient intake of teenagers, J. Am. Diet. Assoc. **50**:385, 1967.

18. Beal, V. A.: Nutritional intake. In McCammon, R. W., editor: Human growth and development, Springfield, Ill., 1970, Charles C Thomas, Publisher.

19. Johnston, J. A.: Protein requirements of adolescents, Ann. N.Y. Acad. Sci. **69**:881, 1958.

20. Hegsted, D. M.: Current knowledge of energy, fat, protein, and amino acid needs of adolescents. In McKigney, J., and Munro, H., editors: Nutrient requirements in adolescence, Cambridge, Mass., 1976, MIT Press.

21. Report of a Joint FAO/WHO Ad Hoc Expert Committee: Energy and protein requirements, World Health Organization Technical Series No. 522, FAO Nutr. Meet. Ser. No. 52, Geneva, 1973, World Health Organization.

22. Committee on Nutrition, American Academy of Pediatrics: Calcium requirements in infancy and childhood, Pediatrics **62**:826, 1978.

23. Abraham, S., Lowenstein, F. W., and Johnson, C. L.: Preliminary findings of the first health and nutrition examination survey, United States, 1971-1972: Dietary intake and biochemical findings, Washington, D.C., 1974, Department of Health, Education, and Welfare.

24. Bowering, J., Sanchez, A. M., and Irwin, M. I.: A conspectus of research on iron requirements of man, J. Nutr. **106**:985, 1976.

25. Hallberg, L., and others: Menstrual blood loss—a population study, Acta Obstet. Gynecol. Scand. **45**:320, 1966.

26. Frenchman, R., and Johnston,; F. A.: Relation of menstrual losses to iron requirements, J. Am. Diet. Assoc. **25**:217, 1949.

27. Hepner, R.: General discussion of adolescent nutrient requirements and recommended dietary allowances. In McKigney, J., and Munro, H., editors: Nutrient requirements in adolescence, Cambridge, Mass., 1976, MIT Press.

28. Daniel, W. A.: Hematocrit: maturity relationship in adolescence, Pediatrics **52**:388, 1973.

29. Daniel, W. A., Gaines, E. G., and Bennett, D. L.: Iron intake and transferrin saturation in adolescents, J. Pediatr. **86**:288, 1975.

30. Sanstead, H. H.: Zinc nutrition in the United States, Am. J. Clin. Nutr. **26**:1251, 1973.

31. Greenwood, C. T. and Richardson, D. P.: Nutrition during adolescence, World Rev. Nutr. Diet. **33**:1, 1979.

32. Daniel, W. A., Gaines, E. G., and Bennett, D. L.: Dietary intakes and plasma concentrations of folate in healthy adolescents, Am. J. Clin. Nutr. **28**:363, 1975.

33. Huenemann, R. L., and others: A longitudinal study of gross body composition and body conformation and their association with food and activity in a teenage population: views of teen-age subjects on body conformation, food and activity, Am. J. Clin. Nutr. **18**:325, 1966.

34. Dwyer, J., and others: Adolescent attitudes toward weight and appearance, J. Nutr. Educ. **1**(2):14, 1969.

35. Wharton, M. A.: Nutritive intake of adolescents, J. Am. Diet. Assoc. **42**:306, 1963.

36. Lee, C. J.: Nutritional status of selected teenagers in Kentucky, Am. J. Clin. Nutr. **31**:1453, 1978.

37. Schorr, B. C., Sanjur, D., and Erickson, E. C.: Teenage food habits, J. Am. Diet. Assoc. **61**:415, 1972.

38. Hodges, R. E., and Krehl, W. A.: Nutritional status of teenagers in Iowa, Am. J. Clin. Nutr. **17**:200, 1965.

39. Huenemann, R. L., and others: Food and eating practices of teenagers, J. Am. Diet. Assoc. **53**:17, 1968.

40. Thomas, J. A., and Call, D. L.: Eating between meals: a nutrition problem among teenagers? Nutr. Rev. **31**:137, 1973.

41. Daniel, W. A.: Adolescents in health and disease, St. Louis, 1977, The C. V. Mosby Co.

42. Abraham, S., and Nordsieck, M.: Relationship of excess weight in children and adults, Public Health Rep. **75**:263, 1960.

43. Seltzer, C. C., and Mayer, J.: Body build and obesity: who are the obese? J.A.M.A. **189**:677, 1964.

44. Heald, F. P., and Hollander, R. J.: The relationship between obesity in adolescence and early growth, J. Pediatr. **67**:35, 1965.

45. Monello, L. F., and Mayer, J.: Obese adolescent girls: an unrecognized "minority" group? Am. J. Clin. Nutr. **13**:35, 1963.

46. Johnson, M. L., Burke, B. S., and Mayer, J.: Relative importance of inactivity and overeating in the energy balance of obese high school girls, Am. J. Clin. Nutr. **4**:37, 1956.

47. Stefanik, P. A., Heald, F. P., and Mayer, J.: Caloric intake in relation to energy output of obese and

nonobese adolescent boys, Am. J. Clin. Nutr. **7:** 55, 1959.

48. Bullen, B. A., Reed, R. B., and Mayer, J.: Physical activity of obese and nonobese adolescent girls appraised by motion picture sampling, Am. J. Clin. Nutr. **14:**211, 1964.

49. Stunkard, A. J., and Burt, V.: Obesity and the body image. II. Age at onset of disturbances in the body, Am. J. Psychiatry **123:**1443, 1967.

50. Soper, R. T., and others: Gastric bypass for morbid obesity in children and adolescents, J. Pediatr. Surg. **10:**51, 1975.

51. Coates, T. J., and Thoresen, C. E.: Treating obesity in children and adolescents: a review, Am. J. Public Health **68:**143, 1978.

52. Seltzer, C. C., and Mayer, J.: An effective weight control program in a public school system, Am. J. Public Health **60:**679, 1970.

53. Christakis, G., and others: Effect of a combined nutrition education and physical fitness program on the weight status of obese high school boys, Fed. Proc. **25:**15, 1966.

54. Stanley, E. J., and others: Overcoming obesity in adolescents, Clin. Pediatr. **9:**29, 1970.

55. Moody, D. L., and others: The effects of a jogging program on the body composition of normal and obese high school girls, Med. Sci. Sports **4:**210, 1972.

56. Rees, J.: Personal communication, 1980.

57. Bruch, H.: Eating disorders, New York, 1973, Basic Books, Inc., Publishers.

58. Halmi, K. A., and others: Pretreatment evaluation in anorexia nervosa. In Vigersky, R., editor: Anorexia nervosa, New York, 1977, Raven Press.

59. Casper, R. C., Davis, J. M., and Pandey, G. N.: The effect of the nutritional status and weight changes on hypothalamic function tests in anorexia nervosa. In Vigersky, R., editor: Anorexia nervosa, New York, 1977, Raven Press.

60. Vigersky, R. A., and others: Anorexia nervosa: behavioral and hypothalamic aspects, Clin. Endocrinol. Metabol. **5:**517, 1976.

61. Crisp, A. H.: A treatment regime for anorexia nervosa, Br. J. Psychiatry **112:**505, 1965.

62. Stunkard, A.: New therapies for the eating disorders, Arch. Gen. Psychiatry **26:**391, 1972.

63. Bruch, H.: Perils of behavior modification in treatment of anorexia nervosa, J.A.M.A. **230:**1419, 1974.

64. Eckert, E. D., and others: Behavior therapy in anorexia nervosa, Br. J. Psychiatry **134:**55, 1979.

65. Pertschuk, M.: Behavior therapy: extended follow-up. In Vigersky, R., editor: Anorexia nervosa, New York, 1977, Raven Press.

66. Rosman, B., and others: A family approach to anorexia nervosa: study, treatment, and outcome. In Vigersky, R., editor: Anorexia nervosa, New York, 1977, Raven Press.

67. Hsu, L. K. G., Crisp, A. H., and Harding, B.: Outcome of anorexia nervosa, Lancet **1:**61, 1979.

68. Russell, G.: General management of anorexia nervosa and difficulties in assessing the efficacy of treatment. In Vigersky, R., editor: Anorexia nervosa, New York, 1977, Raven Press.

69. Committee on Adolescence, American Academy of Pediatrics: Statement on teenage pregnancy, Pediatrics **63:**795, 1979.

70. Fielding, J. E.: Adolescent pregnancy revisited, N. Engl. J. Med. **299:**893, 1978.

71. Trussell, J., and Menken, J.: Early childbearing and subsequent fertility, Fam. Plann. Perspect. **10:**209, 1978.

72. Committee on Maternal Nutrition, Food and Nutrition Board: Maternal nutrition and the course of pregnancy, Washington, D.C., 1970, National Academy of Sciences, National Research Council.

73. Zlatnik, F. J., and Burmeister, L. F.: Low "gynecologic age": an obstetric risk factor, Am. J. Obstet. Gynecol. **128:**183, 1977.

74. King, J. C., and others: Assessment of nutritional status of teenage pregnant girls. I. Nutrient intake and pregnancy, Am. J. Clin. Nutr. **25:**916, 1972.

75. McGanity, W. J., and others: Pregnancy in the adolescent. I. Preliminary summary of health status, Am. J. Obstet. Gynecol. **103:**773, 1969.

76. Worthington, B. S.: Nutritional needs of the pregnant adolescent. In Worthington, B. S., Vermeersch, J., and Williams, S. R., editors: Nutrition in pregnancy and lactation, St. Louis, 1977, The C. V. Mosby Co.

77. Cho, M., and Fryer, B. A.: Nutritional knowledge of collegiate physical education majors, J. Am. Diet. Assoc. **65:**30, 1974.

78. Morrissey, E. R.: Alcohol-related problems in adolescents and women, Postgrad. Med. **64:**111, 1978.

79. National Institute on Alcoholism and Alcohol Abuse: Technical Support Document to the Third Special Report to the U.S. Congress on Alcohol and Health, Washington, D.C., 1978, Department of Health, Education, and Welfare.

80. Roe, D. A.: Alcohol and the diet, Westport, Conn., 1979, Avi Publishing Co.

81. Esterly, N. B., and Furey, N. L.: Acne: current concepts, Pediatrics **62:**1044, 1978.

82. Frankle, R. T., and others: The door, a center of alternatives: the nutritionist in a free clinic for adolescents, J. Am. Diet. Assoc. **63:**269, 1973.

83. Erhard, D.: Nutrition education for the "now" generation, J. Nutr. Educ. **2:**135, 1971.

84. Dwyer, J. T., Feldman, J. J., and Mayer, J.: Nutritional literacy of high school students, J. Nutr. Educ. **2:**59, 1970.

85. Deisher, R. W., and Mills, C. A.: The adolescent looks at his health and medical care, Am. J. Public Health **53:**1928, 1963.

86. Schwartz, N. E.: Nutritional knowledge, attitudes, and practices of high school graduates, J. Am. Diet. Assoc. **66:**28, 1975.

87. Leverton, R. M.: The paradox of teenage nutrition, J. Am. Diet. Assoc. **53:**13, 1968.

88. Mapes, M. C.: Gulp: an alternate method for reaching teens, J. Nutr. Educ. **9:**12, 1977.

89. Alexson, J. M., and DelCampo, D. S.: Improving teenagers' nutrition knowledge through the mass media, J. Nutr. Educ. **10:**30, 1978.

ADDITIONAL READINGS

Barnes, H. V., editor: Symposium on adolescent medicine, Med. Clin. North Am. **50:**1279-1525, 1975.

Brasel, J.: Factors that affect nutritional requirements in adolescents. In Winick, M., editor: Nutritional disorders of American women: current concepts in nutrition, New York, 1977, John Wiley & Sons, Inc.

Cheek, D. B.: Body composition, hormones, nutrition and adolescent growth. In Grumbach, M. M., Grave, G. D., and Mayer, F. E.: Control of the onset of puberty, New York, 1974, John Wiley & Sons, Inc.

Hammar, S. L.: The role of the nutritionist in an adolescent clinic, Children **13:**217, 1966.

Heald, F. P., editor: Adolescent nutrition and growth, New York, 1969, Meredith Corp.

Heald, F. P., Daugela, M., and Brunschuyler, P.: Physiology of adolescence: nutrition, N. Engl. J. Med. **268:**243, 1963.

Hinton, M. A., and others: Eating behavior and dietary intake of girls 12 to 14 years old, J. Am. Diet. Assoc. **43:**223, 1963.

Huenemann, R. L., and others: Teenage nutrition and physique, Springfield, Ill., 1974, Charles C Thomas, Publisher.

Ikeda, J.: For teenagers only: change your habits to change your shape, Palo Alto, 1978, Bull Publishing Co.

Nutrition for athletes: a handbook for coaches, Washington, D.C., 1971, American Association for Health, Physical Education, and Recreation.

Pipes, T. V., and Vodak, P. A.: The Pipes fitness test and prescription, Los Angeles, 1978, J. P. Tarcher, Inc.

Young, C. M., Sipin, S. S., and Roe, D. A.: Body composition of pre-adolescent and adolescent girls, J. Am. Diet. Assoc. **53:**25, 1968.

10

Nutritional considerations for children in sports

Bonnie Worthington-Roberts

Interest in sports and physical fitness has increased dramatically among children and adolescents. No longer is athletic competition and training restricted to boys in varsity team sports. Much enthusiasm has developed among women, and individual sports have gained in popularity among girls and boys of all ages. In general, this interest in athletic performance is viewed as beneficial to the health of our youth. This is true when the intensity of involvement is not excessive and when sensible health maintenance practices are encouraged.

Health maintenance for growing athletes encompasses many aspects, including attention to diet and nutrition. Primary objectives include the following:

1. Relaxed, supportive, loving home environment
2. Sufficient (but not excessive) training or athletic practice
3. Sufficient sleep
4. Adequate food and fluid
5. Appropriate medical attention for disease prevention and injury management
6. Support and encouragement in the face of error or defeat

This chapter is adapted from Worthington-Roberts, B. S.: Diet and athletic performance. In Contemporary developments in nutrition, St. Louis, 1980, The C. V. Mosby Co.

The area of diet is unfortunately filled with superstition and myth about "optimum practices." Special diets or foods are often advocated and the use of supplements is frequently recommended. Often scientific proof is lacking to support special diets or supplement programs. Instead, however, the enthusiasm of the trainer may be more than adequate to motivate compliance. Very few studies have been undertaken on nutritional needs of *growing* athletes. Most published research has dealt with adolescents who agreed to be studied while training for specific sports. Data on normal, moderately active children may also be considered in determining nutritional recommendations for athletes (see Chapter 9).

CALORIES

Sports activities differ widely in the amount of energy required to support them (Table 10-1). In general, however, a child in sports requires a greater caloric intake than does the sedentary youngster. Whereas the average 10-year-old boy may expend between 2000 and 2800 kcal/day, the majority of boys this age who are running great distances or exerting themselves in other physical activities may expend an additional 300 to 700 kcal/day. The caloric needs of pre-

205

Table 10-1. Approximate energy cost of various exercises and sports

Sport or exercise	Total calories expended/minute of activity
Climbing	10.7-13.2
Cycling	
5.5 mph	4.5
9.4 mph	7.0
13.1 mph	11.1
Dancing	3.3-7.7
Domestic work	
Bed making	3.5
Dusting	2.5
Ironing	1.7
Cleaning floors	3.5
Football	8.9
Golf	5.0
Gymnastics	
Balancing	2.5
Abdominal exercises	3.0
Trunk bending	3.5
Arms swinging, hopping	6.5
Rowing	
51 strokes/minute	4.1
87 strokes/minute	7.0
97 strokes/minute	11.2
Running	
Short distance	13.3-16.6
Cross-country	10.6
Tennis	7.1
Skating, fast	11.5
Skiing	
Moderate speed	10.8-15.9
Uphill, maximum speed	18.6
Squash	10.2
Swimming	
Breaststroke	11.0
Backstroke	11.5
Crawl	14.0
Walking	
2 mph	2.5
3 mph	3.5
5 mph	5.5
Watching television	1.5
Wrestling	14.2

Modified from Nutrition for athletes: a handbook for coaches, Washington, D.C., 1971, American Alliance for Health, Education, and Recreation, p. 26.

adolescent girls are similar to those of boys for moderate and heavy exercise. In adolescence, however, when boys become relatively larger, their total daily needs in all circumstances become greater. The size of the individual, the level of training, and the type of sports activity engaged in are major factors determining total daily caloric needs (Fig. 10-1).[1-5]

Besides being used for basal metabolism and physical activity, calories are required to support normal growth. Growing athletes, therefore, demand somewhat more calories per kilogram of body weight than those athletes who are mature. During adolescence (especially for boys), when growth rate is extremely rapid, the caloric needs may be very great. The consequence of insufficient calorie ingestion may be a lack of sufficient energy to perform optimally in sports events, and in some cases growth may be impaired.

In general, the athlete's greatly increased caloric expenditure automatically increases the appetite, with the result that he or she ingests more food. Although it is unlikely that an athlete in heavy physical training will gain too much weight, caloric intake greater than the daily energy expenditure is not recommended, as it results in unnecessary fat deposition with subsequent increased work load to the heart. The increased caloric requirements are best met by increasing food intake across the board, without significantly altering the proportions of the micronutrients or macronutrients of the diet. There are no known "special" food sources that supply "extra reserves of energy" that are not provided by other foods with the same nutrients.

Energy sources

The immediate source of energy for muscle work is adenosine triphosphate (ATP), which is formed in muscles largely by metabolism of carbohydrates and fats. It can be

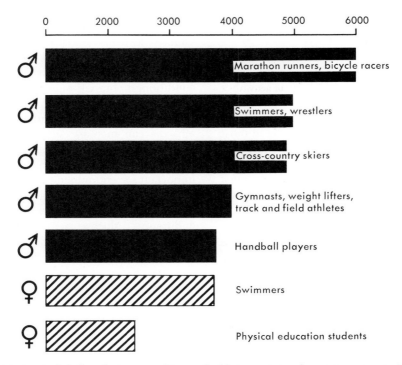

Fig. 10-1. Typical daily calorie expenditure of athletes training for various sports. (Data obtained from Saltin, B.: Fluid electrolyte and energy losses and their replenishment in prolonged exercise; and from Rogozkin, V. A.: Some aspects of athlete's nutrition. In Parizkova, J., and Rogozkin, V. A., editors: Nutrition, physical fitness, and health, Baltimore, 1978, University Park Press.)

metabolized rapidly to meet the needs of sudden episodes of activity in intensive short-term exercise. Since ATP is metabolized without the use of oxygen, the reaction is classified as anaerobic. This type of reaction is important during strenuous exercise, when the heart and lungs cannot deliver oxygen quickly to the muscles. If energy is needed for more than brief spurts, the high-energy compound in muscles, called phosphocreatine (PC), can almost instantaneously provide the energy required to regenerate ATP. Within a matter of minutes of vigorous exercise, however, the small stores of ATP-PC are used up, and then the body must turn to another source of energy in order to regenerate the ATP-PC system.[5-7]

Glycogen is the second energy source for muscles. It is stored in limited amounts in muscle cells and can be metabolized within the muscle cells to restore ATP. This activity is carried out primarily in the absence of oxygen; thus it is also classified as anaerobic. The level of glycogen storage in skeletal muscles is modified to some degree by dietary composition. It is possible to load muscles with unusually high levels of glycogen by adherence to a specially designed nutrition program used in conjunction with proper conditioning. The principles of glycogen loading and the available data on its effectiveness and safety are discussed on pp. 216-218.

As prolonged exercise gradually depletes the stores of ATP-PC and muscle glycogen, the body increasingly resorts to another source of energy. This last type of fuel comes from the aerobic metabolism of carbohydrates (glucose) and fats (Fig. 10-2). In most children, a considerable amount of stored fat is available, but its slow rate of metabolism makes it a less efficient source of quick energy. For reasons that are not presently clear, fat does not seem to be available to maintain performance at very high intensities of muscle work (i.e., 60% to 70% VO₂ maximum*). Neither the supply of free fatty acids

*VO₂ max is a term used to express the percentage of maximum oxygen consumption of a working individual; work physiologists use this term to express the severity of a specific type of work or exercise.

exogenous to active muscle[8] nor the endogenously available muscle triglyceride[9] can fully replace the essential role of carbohydrates. It is true, however, that the highly conditioned competitor works long hours in conditioning activities to improve oxygen-burning capacity. With intensive training, athletes can increase significantly their efficiency in utilizing fatty acids and ketones as energy sources.[10,11] This is particularly important for endurance events in which glycogen usage may be partially spared as fat is burned. In sports activities requiring much endurance, glucose metabolism makes a minor contribution to total energy needs.

Carbohydrate, however, is widely recognized as the most readily available source of energy. The simple sugars from digested carbohydrate are absorbed from the small intestine and are taken via the bloodstream

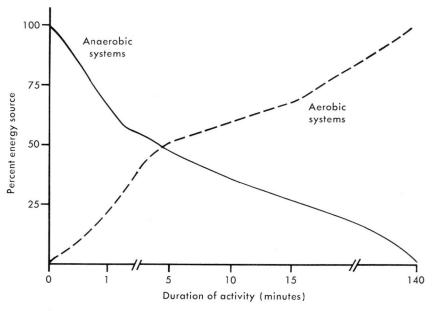

Fig. 10-2. Variation in energy source over time. (Modified from Matthew, D. K., and Fox, E. L.: The physiologic basis of physical education and athletics, Philadelphia, 1971, W. B. Saunders Co.)

to the liver; here fructose and galactose are largely converted to glucose, which reenters the bloodstream for transport to body tissues, particularly brain and skeletal muscle. A fairly small amount of circulating glucose is converted to glycogen for storage in liver and muscle. The importance of glycogen is viewed as substantial when athletic involvement extends over long periods of time. Carbohydrate administration during competitive efforts may prevent the premature depletion of liver glycogen stores and improve endurance performance.[12] With provision of a carbohydrate diet, long-distance cyclists have ridden further,[13] long-distance cross-country skiers have raced faster,[14] long-distance canoeists have paddled faster,[15] and soccer players have scored more goals in the latter parts of games.[16] Availability of carbohydrate is a major limiting factor, and its ingestion during performance or in conjunction with prior exercise recovery plays an important role in the total well-being of the athlete.

PROTEIN

Physical activity, even when vigorous, does not significantly increase the need for dietary protein.[17,18] While views to the contrary prevailed in the distant past, a number of studies have since demonstrated no increase in combustion of protein during heavy exercise as compared with a period of rest. Even after glycogen stores have been depleted, continued exercise does not cause a significant increase in the amount of protein metabolized. It is true, however, that training and competition demand greater amino acid retention when muscles are being developed and blood volume is increasing. Increases in lean body mass, enzymatic protein, myoglobin, and hemoglobin are typical effects of training that may temporarily require greater protein utilization.[18] Athletes who develop proteinuria, hemoglobinuria,

or myoglobinuria as a result of prolonged intense exercise may also require higher levels of protein until these conditions subside. Overall, the increase in protein need is small and is easily accommodated through common food selections.

Sweating does not increase significantly the need for protein in the athlete. Sweating as a result of vigorous physical activity does increase nitrogen loss, and this may amount to 600 mg after 2 hours of strenuous exercise by the mature man.[17] If this activity lasts for 4 hours in 1 day, the nitrogen lost through sweat would be about 1.2 gm; replacing this loss through dietary sources would require an extra 7.5 gm of protein, an amount obtained in three or four bites of meat.

The performing athlete, like everyone else, must replace nitrogen losses incurred each day. The child and adolescent must go one step further and provide sufficient nitrogen (as dietary protein) for physical growth. Precise data are unavailable on protein requirements of either the mature adult who is developing his muscle mass or the growing child or adolescent who is engaged in a muscle development program. Obviously their needs are measurably greater than those of comparable individuals who are not engaged in rigorous physical conditioning.

Table 10-2 provides a liberal estimate of protein requirements for the rapidly growing, tall, adolescent male athlete. To begin with, the 70 kg adult male loses approximately 4 gm of nitrogen/day through the urine, feces, and skin; this level of nigrogen is equivalent to approximately 25 gm of protein.[17] Obviously, there is individual variation that could conceivably (according to available data) increase the protein needs of some adults by about 30%. This estimation increases protein needs from 25 to 32.5 gm/day. Allowing for 4 hours of strenuous exercise with consequent sweat losses of nitrogen, an additional 7.5 gm of protein is re-

Table 10-2. Estimated daily protein need of the large, rapidly growing male athlete with a developing muscle mass

Basis for need	Protein (gm)
Replacement of nitrogen lost through urine, feces, skin, and other sites (for 70-kg male)	24.5
Provision of 30% extra protein for individual variation (for 70-kg male)	7.5
Replacement of nitrogen lost through sweat during 4 hours of strenuous exercise (for 70-kg male)	7.5
Coverage of increased protein need of growing muscle mass (for 70-kg male)	7.5
Coverage for extra protein associated with rapid growth in adolescence (liberal estimate)	10.0
Extra protein allotment for the exceptionally large male (liberal estimate)	10.0
TOTAL	67.0

Data obtained in part from Durnin, J. V. G. A.: Protein requirements and physical activity. In Parizkova, J., and Rogozkin, V. A., editors: Nutrition, physical fitness, and health, Baltimore, 1978, University Park Press.

Table 10-3. Protein content of representative American foods

Food	Portion size	Protein (gm)
Milk	1 cup	8
Hamburger patty, broiled	3 oz	23
Egg	1	7
Yogurt	1 cup	8
Steak	3 oz	20
Cheddar cheese	1 oz cube	7
Chili con carne	1 cup	19
Chicken drumstick	1	12
Tuna	3 oz	24
Peanut butter	1 tbsp	4
Whole wheat bread	1 slice	3
Spaghetti (noodles only)	1 cup	5
Minestrone soup	1 cup	5

quired, or a total of 40 gm of protein/day for the 70-kg male. If muscle mass is being markedly increased, an extra 6 to 7 gm of protein might be added to the requirements, but only during the phase of active muscle building. If one liberally estimates an extra 10 gm of protein/day for the rapidly growing adolescent boy, the total daily protein requirement now should be approximately 55 to 60 gm. For those young males who are exceptionally large, the protein needs may be somewhat greater. Even if the needs were to reach 70 gm/day, this amount is readily obtained through ingestion of ordinary foods (Table 10-3).

The majority of athletes tend to consume far more protein than the estimated requirement. It is known, for example, that most common diets provide 10% to 15% of calories from protein. It follows, then, that with high-calorie diets substantial amounts of protein may be readily obtained (Table 10-4). Athletes emphasizing high-protein foods may consume even higher levels of protein each day.

An obvious question is whether excessive protein consumption improves in any measurable way the short- or long-term performance of athletes. In one investigation, the effect of protein supplements was assessed in 32 male competitors.[19] Sixteen of the men were given a protein supplement as they proceeded through the basic training program in Marine Officer Candidate School. Physical performance was evaluated in all subjects before, during, and after the program. Both the supplemented and nonsupplemented groups significantly improved their physical performance scores from program onset to program termination, but no significant dif-

Table 10-4. Representative levels of protein intake associated with varying levels of calorie intake

Calorie intake	Calories derived from protein		Protein intake (gm)	
	10%	15%	10%	15%
2000	200	300	50	75
2500	250	375	65	94
3000	300	450	75	113
3500	350	525	88	132
4000	400	600	100	150
4500	450	675	113	169
5000	500	750	125	187
6000	600	900	150	225
7000	700	1050	175	263

ference was observed between the groups.

Therefore, most growing athletes consume far more protein than can be effectively utilized for maintenance or growth. Consequently, a portion of each day's protein supply is utilized for energy or is stored as fat with the nitrogen waste being excreted in the urine. Although this high protein intake is generally not hazardous, it is usually expensive and it promotes loss of appetite and diarrhea. Production of excessive nitrogen waste always increases fluid requirements, so that efficient urinary excretion is achieved. For the athlete at risk for dehydration, this latter observation clearly suggests some cause for concern.

VITAMINS

Vitamins are obviously required for health and are essential for optimal physical performance. However, the attitude has unfortunately developed that the more of a good thing one gets, the better. Few controlled studies have been conducted on athletes to assess vitamin needs and effects of supplements. The limited available data support small increases in demand for B vitamins based on their roles in many biochemical reactions that make energy available for muscle work. In general, however, the higher the energy expenditure of the athlete, the higher the calorie and vitamin intake. It is important to recognize that daily B vitamin needs may be met by consumption of a balanced American diet, even when needs are slightly increased by regular high-energy expenditure in physical performance. Whether *excessive* intake of vitamin supplements contributes effectively to improved performance is a matter open to much debate. Controlled investigations do not support their "nutritional" merit, but the placebo effect cannot be ignored.

Several studies have been undertaken to assess the value of vitamin E supplements for athletes.[20,21] Sharman[20] studied two groups of adolescent swimmers who were provided daily with either 400 mg of α-tocopherol acetate or placebos in addition to their normal diets. The swimmers were studied for 6 weeks, and all were involved in daily swimming workouts and supportive exercises. Before and after the supplementation program, a variety of anthropometric measurements were recorded and performance was tested by evaluation of cardiorespiratory efficiency and motor fitness. Although training was found to significantly improve the performance of swimmers in both experimental groups, vitamin E did not produce any obvious benefits.

In a later study by Lawrence and co-workers,[21] two groups of well-trained competitive swimmers were observed. The first group was given 90 IU of α-tocopherol acetate/day for 6 months, whereas the second group was given placebos. A swimming endurance test was given before the start of the supplementation and after 1, 2, 5, and 6 months. No difference in swimming endurance was observed between the two groups during the 6 months. A comparable study on a younger, less trained group of competitive swimmers again revealed that vitamin E supplementation did not effect swimming endurance.

The effect of vitamin C supplementation has also been studied by several investigators. Bailey and colleagues[22] observed 40 young males, 20 of whom were classified as trained and the remainder as untrained. Performance on various treadmill tests was recorded before and after a 5-day ingestion of 2 gm of ascorbic acid/day or placebos. The purpose of the study was to determine if vitamin C had any effect on oxygen uptake and ventilatory adjustment in trained and untrained subjects before, during, and after exercise. The results provided no indication that ascorbic acid supplementation improved performance in any measurable way.

Vitamin supplements are not generally recommended for several basic and important reasons. First, excess water-soluble vitamins cannot be stored in the body effectively and thus are rapidly excreted in the urine when tissue saturation occurs. Second, the fat-soluble vitamins are retained and stored in the body, and daily high-potency supplements of vitamin A and/or vitamin D are known to be toxic and sometimes fatal. Third, a balanced diet containing more than approximately 1800 kcal/day should provide satisfactory levels of all vitamins. Only the person surviving on "junk foods" or existing on a very restricted vegetarian regimen might find the diet inadequate in its vitamin content.

MINERALS

The most significant effect of exercise on mineral nutrition is the loss of electrolytes through sweat. In general, sweat contains approximately 20 to 30 mEq (460 to 690 mg) of sodium/liter, so when sweating is excessive, losses up to 350 mEq (8050 mg) may occur each day in the acclimated adult male. This amount may be greater in the nonacclimated individual, and in either case it is great enough to disturb fluid and electrolyte homeostasis.[2]

Observations of children during strenuous running show that children under age 12 years sweat less but stay cooler.[23] Apparently, younger children have a better ratio of surface area to weight than do older children and adults, and thus they are able to dissipate heat more effectively without as great a fluid loss. Young children, therefore, exhibit less risk of dehydration and electrolyte imbalance than adolescents and adults. This situation does not mean, however, that attention to fluid replacement should be overlooked in this population.

Salt can be replaced on a regular basis by salting foods to a satisfying taste. Use of salt tablets is generally unnecessary, and sometimes they may even cause gastrointestinal disturbances resulting from fluid movement into the gut. If rates of water loss exceed 5 to 10 pounds in a given contest or workout, some consideration might be given to specific salt replacement.[6] Adding salt to the normal diet may adequately cover needs but use of *dilute* salt-containing fluids may also be considered. Commercially available electrolyte drinks are pleasantly flavored and may be diluted since most are more concentrated than they need to be for greatest effectiveness and comfort. Since thirst alone may not prompt sufficient water intakes during intense competition and/or extreme heat, regularly scheduled periods for fluid replacement should be part of any athletic training program.

Attention to potassium replacement may be more important than consideration of sodium needs. The amount of potassium lost through sweat is negligible when environmental tempeature is mild and exercise level is moderate. Under conditions of moderate to extreme heat, however, potassium losses may be considerable if exercise is heavy and prolonged. A recent study by Lane and associates[24] involved assessment of potassium and sodium balance in volunteer runners performing in a hot climate with high humidity. Estimated losses of potassium tended to exceed the daily level of intake recommended for healthy Americans, especially in persons who were poorly acclimated. Consequently, it seems well to emphasize the value of high-potassium foods (Table 10-5) for athletes losing much sweat each day.[25] Electrolyte beverages may also be provided if they are palatable, hypotonic, and balanced in their content of glucose, chloride, sodium, and potassium.

Iron is another mineral of major importance to maintenance of optimal condition in the athlete. Adequacy of iron status is now known to significantly effect endurance and physical performance.[26,27] Iron is presently available in limited amounts in the American diet; this limited supply is a major concern for menstruating girls, premenopausal women (pregnant and nonpregnant), and rapidly growing adolescent boys whose needs are greater than other members of the population.[28]

Research on iron deficiency in animals and humans indicates that inadequate iron intake results in loss of strength and endurance, easy fatigability, shortening of attention span, loss of visual perception, and compromised learning ability.[29,30] The iron-deficient athlete, therefore, should be identified and should be provided with iron supplements and dietary counseling on useful food sources of iron. Female athletes using the intrauterine device are especially good candidates for iron supplements, because excessive menstrual blood loss often occurs when the device is employed.[31] Most sensibly, however, prevention of iron deficiency

Table 10-5. Potassium content of common foods

Food	Portion size	Potassium (mg)
Banana	1 small	370
Orange	1 small	200
Grapefruit	½ medium	135
Potato	1 2¼" diameter	407
Tomato	1 small	244
Carrot	1 large	341
Celery	1 small inner stalk	68
Beef steak	½ lb	325
Chicken breast	3½ oz (uncooked)	350
Salmon	3½ oz (uncooked)	399
Bread, white	1 slice	20
Bread, whole wheat	1 slice	63
Milk, whole	½ cup	176
Cheese, American	1 oz	23

is a better approach than treatment of the problem once established; thus general dietary guidelines to athletes should emphasize iron-rich foods of both animal and vegetable origin. When the self-selected diet appears inadequate to fulfill daily needs for iron, a low-level supplement may then be worthwhile in the maintenance of satisfactory long-term iron status.

A worthwhile note regarding iron is that "conservation" is occasionally noted in the female competitor of menstrual age.[32,33] Menarche reportedly is delayed in young women who are actively involved in physically demanding athletics (Fig. 10-3). Secondary amenorrhea is known to result from excessive weight loss leading to establishment of a low percentage of body fat. Although many young athletes with amenorrhea have low body weights, no obvious association between fatness and menstrual

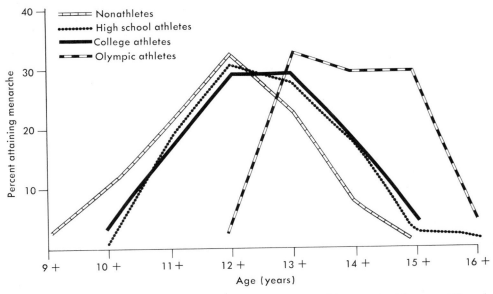

Fig. 10-3. Relative distributions of ages at menarche in nonathletes and athletes at different competitive levels. The athletes attained menarche significantly later than did the nonathletes, and the Olympic athletes attained menarche significantly later than did the high school and college athletes. (From: Malina, R. M., and others: Age at menarche and selected menstrual characteristics in athletes at different competitive levels and in different sports, Med. Sci. Sports **10**:218, 1978.)

regularity has been observed among athletes observed in several studies.[33,34] Theoretically, amenorrhea may ultimately improve the iron status of the competitor. It is uncertain, however, whether ongoing suppression of the normal female menstrual pattern produces any lasting harm to the health and reproductive performance of such women.

WATER

Attention to daily water requirements is of major importance to athletes of all calibers.[1-7] Water is obviously needed as the supporting medium in which all body reactions occur. In addition, it is extremely important in body temperature regulation; excessive heat generated by exercise must be dissipated, and this is done most effectively through the evaporation of sweat. This mechanism fails to function effectively, however, if the water supply is inadequate to meet the needs of the sweat glands.

A well-conditioned athlete who exercises in high temperatures will voluntarily drink more fluid. Some conscientious attention to water needs must be maintained, however, because creation of a water deficit of approximately 3% of total body water is associated with deterioration in performance in both males and females. Individuals in prime physical condition can function effectively until body water equal to 4% to 5% of body weight is lost; at this point, athletic performance clearly deteriorates. The conscientious athlete never allows a deficit of this degree to develop.[12]

Negative fluid balance is commonly noted in competitive wrestlers attempting to "make weight." Aggressive efforts to quickly lose pounds may involve induced sweating and spitting as well. Vaccaro and co-workers[35] observed college wrestlers in an effort to assess dehydration and rehydration before competition. Body weight, hematocrit values, and plasma protein concentration were determined at the normal state, at weight certification, and just prior to competition. Results of analyses confirmed that wrestlers cannot regain in 5 hours all of the fluid lost in the process of "making weight." Thus they enter most wrestling matches in a relative state of dehydration.

FIBER

Fiber in foods is now well recognized as a valuable component of the diet of man. Even though the human gastrointestinal tract is incapable of effective digestion and absorption of this material, it serves beneficial roles in the gut of promoting normal motility and regulating the rate and character of digestive/absorptive processes. Because fiber does remain in the gut along with fluid, which it may retain, it may add to body weight at a time when the athlete would prefer to be at a low, healthy state. In addition, it may be broken down, to some degree, by bacteria in the large bowel. This may involve the production of gas, which may disturb the feeling of optimal readiness for precise athletic competition. On occasion, therefore, it may behoove the competitor to use moderation in consumption of fiber prior to weigh-in or actual competition.

ALCOHOL

Some adolescent athletes have the mistaken notion that moderate alcohol consumption improves their performance.[36] In fact, ethanol cannot be used as an energy source for exercise; it does not influence maximal oxygen consumption during exercise, nor does it affect anaerobic energy expenditure through sources such as ATP and PC. Overall, the effect of alcohol on physical performance appears to be negative on all counts; decreased performance has been reported thus far in tests of dynamic balance, visual tracking, arm steadiness, body sway, and various other psychomotor tasks. It is interesting to note, however, as did one high school alcoholic, that the sensation promoted by alcohol was deceptively positive. One student stated the following in a recent interview:[36]

I would drink before going to school and I'd get to physical education class rarin' to go. But the coordination wasn't there. *I felt* I could perform better but it was all in my head. In reality, I really performed worse.

"HEALTH FOODS" AND THE VEGETARIAN DIET

A wide variety of foods are presently available to consumers in the United States. Most of these foods provide some valuable contributions of nutrients along with the ever-present calories. Some foods are better than others in the amounts of nutrients provided within a given calorie allotment. Ingestion of an array of basic foods may allow for establishment and maintenance of health. No foods carry magical properties that make them especially effective in promotion of optimal physical performance.

It is generally wise to be leery of advertisements that tout the value of a new "health food." Often such products are quite expensive and provide nothing more than can normally be obtained from a balanced American diet. The typical athlete usually consumes a sizable number of calories each day. The majority of such individuals consequently obtain their required nutritional support through food sources in the daily menu. Consequently, supplements are entirely unnecessary, with the exception of the several circumstances referred to in this text.

The vegetarian diet can support good health, providing that basic pitfalls are avoided (see Chapter 11). Satisfactory non-meat sources of iron, calcium, vitamin B_{12}, zinc, protein, and calories must be selected. Combining vegetable proteins so that they complement each other is especially important for the strict vegetarian athlete. Since most vegetables provide calories in a more dilute form than do animal materials, the athlete must attend carefully to meeting calorie needs, so that growth will be maintained along with energy level for athletic competition.

NUTRITIONAL PREPARATION FOR ATHLETIC PERFORMANCE
Short-term events

Prior to a short-term athletic contest, a general well-balanced diet should be consumed. Immediately before the competition, muscular work should be limited, so that muscle sources of energy will be plentiful. Between several scheduled short-term events, time should be allowed to replenish these energy sources (e.g., ATP, PC, and glycogen) and clear the by-products of anaerobic metabolism (e.g., lactic acid). An adequate supply of carbohydrate and water should be available throughout the day. Fruit juices are popular with many athletes, but some prefer complete liquid meals or other easily digested foods. A sensation of lightness may be promoted by restriction of high-fiber foods, such as the following:

1. Whole grains (e.g., cereals, breads, and other derivatives)
2. Dried peas and beans
3. Nuts and seeds
4. Fruits, especially raw with skins

5. Vegetables, especially raw with skins, stems, and seeds
6. Bran

Avoidance of high-fat foods, which demand long-term digestion, will also support a feeling of readiness. The following is a list of representative high-fat foods:

1. Butter and margarine
2. Cream, sour cream, ice cream, mayonnaise, gravy, and salad dressings
3. Meats, especially fried or fatty
4. Creamed dishes
5. Most cheeses and cheese dishes
6. Pastry
7. Bacon and sausage
8. Chocolate

Gas-forming foods should be minimized in the diet if gas formation is disturbing or distracting to the athlete. Gas-forming foods include the following:

1. Melons
2. Sulfur-containing vegetables such as cabbage, cauliflower, radishes, brussels sprouts, turnips, onions, rutabagas, green peppers, dried peas and beans, lentils, apples, corn, and avocados
3. Others (different for each person)

Long-term events

Preparation for lengthy competitive activities involves attention to the same basic nutrition principles encountered in other circumstances. In addition, sensible eating practices on the day of the event should be followed. On the morning of the competition, high-bulk foods and fatty foods should be avoided, and choices should be made from available carbohydrate sources. In preparing for a lengthy afternoon competition, a light lunch that is low in residue and fatty foods should be taken at least 2½ hours before the starting time. Foods that are satisfying to the individual should be selected.

In choosing high-carbohydrate foods for consumption on competition day, effort should be made to avoid those that are too concentrated in form. Such foods include honey, glucose syrups, and high-sugar/high-electrolyte beverages. Such concentrated solutions, when present in the gut, may provoke the movement of water from body tissues into the gut lumen to balance the osmotic condition; this phenomenon may be associated with abdominal discomfort and diarrhea, which may aggravate poor gastric function already present in the nervous athlete. Diluted, sweetened fruit juices or fruit-flavored drinks are tolerated better than are more concentrated products. Caffeine-containing beverages (e.g., cola drinks) are of questionable merit because of their initial ability to act as stimulants followed by a tendency to produce depression in young athletes.

Some athletes in recent years have utilized the glycogen-loading diet to maximize muscle glycogen stores for moderate to long-term activities.[37-39] Since the readily available anaerobic energy sources in muscle cells are exhausted within 5 minutes (or less) of heavy physical activity, a substantial store of glycogen is very useful, since enough oxygen cannot be supplied to muscle to meet energy needs through metabolism alone. Glycogen stores support an increase in anaerobic energy production just when it is needed. An example of the value of extra muscle glycogen is provided in Fig. 10-4: the work times of men on bicycle ergometers were markedly increased as muscle glycogen stores were augmented.

Glycogen stores can be greatly increased by adherence to a high-carbohydrate regimen during the week preceding competition. For some athletes a high-carbohydrate diet has been proven successful for improving performance when moderate to long-term energy support is demanded. The glycogen-loading diet was developed as a follow-up to data originally collected by Swedish physiologists. These workers conducted studies of muscle glycogen content during the course of a week of controlled dietary intake (Fig. 10-5). It was found that on a normal diet, the average concentration of glycogen in muscle tissue was approximately 1.75 gm/100 gm of muscle. After 3 days on a diet limited largely to fat and protein, the glycogen level fell to 0.6 gm/100 gm of muscle. When the diet was reversed to include large amounts of carbohydrate, the level increased to 3.5 gm/100 gm muscle. The same studies demonstrated that if the specific muscle was exercised strenuously to specifically deplete it of glycogen while on a low-carbohydrate diet, the subsequent institution of a high-carbohydrate diet caused the glycogen in the muscle to rise to 4.7 gm/100 gm in the exercised muscle. This Swedish work thus demonstrated that glycogen stores could be practically tripled through diet modification in conjunction with a program to first deplete then replete muscle glycogen content.

The glycogen-loading diet as it traditionally is prescribed involves 6 days of attention to dietary manipulation, as illustrated in Fig. 10-6. If the athletic event is to be held on Saturday, one starts on the preceding Sunday evening or early Monday morning by consuming a diet that is rich in protein and fat, with carbohydrate representing only approximately 10% of the daily calories. After several days of this depletion phase, most athletes find that they tire easily and perform suboptimally during practice sessions. On the third day, the high-protein, high-fat regimen is replaced by a high-carbohydrate diet. Carbohydrate-rich foods are emphasized in this period, but protein and fat may still be consumed at reasonably normal levels. Some athletes have used flavored beverages that are rich in glucose to supply part of the carbohydrate needs; these needs may also be met, however, through consumption of such carbohydrate-rich items

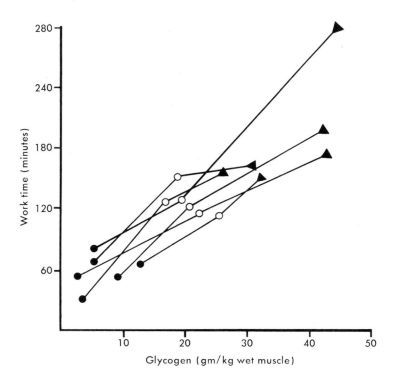

Fig. 10-4. Relationship between initial muscle glycogen content in quadriceps femoris and work time in six subjects on bicycle ergometers with the same relative load three times each with 3-day intervals. Diets before exercise: (1) mixed (open circle), (2) carbohydrate-free (closed circle), and (3) carbohydrate-rich (triangle). (Redrawn from Bergstrom, J., and Hultman, E.: Nutrition for maximal sports performance, J.A.M.A. **221**:999, 1972.)

as lemonade, raisins, noodles, and breads.

Adherence to the glycogen-loading diet requires dedication on the part of the athlete, particularly during the first phase, when carbohydrate intake is rigorously restricted. During this time, the specified diet is significantly different from that usually consumed. The fatigued feeling that often develops during this period may prove frustrating and discouraging to the athlete in training. Consequently, it is wise to use the glycogen-loading regimen with considerable discretion; it probably should not be undertaken for every competition during the season, but

should be reserved for those few occasions when special preparation is clearly in order. It has been shown, in fact, that it is impossible to attain extremely high muscle glycogen storage at more frequent intervals than a few weeks, even if the program is carefully followed. At other times, the athlete may prefer to emphasize the high-carbohydrate aspect of the diet for 3 to 4 days preceding competition. This is obviously much easier to accomplish, because the several days of fatigue associated with the high-fat, high-protein depletion phase may then be avoided.

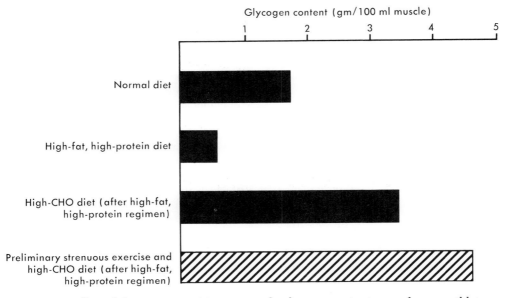

Fig. 10-5. Effect of dietary composition on muscle glycogen content on endurance athletes. CHO = carbohydrate. (From Bergstrom, J., and Hultman, E.: Nutrition for maximal sports performance, J.A.M.A. **221**:999, 1972. Copyright 1972, American Medical Association.)

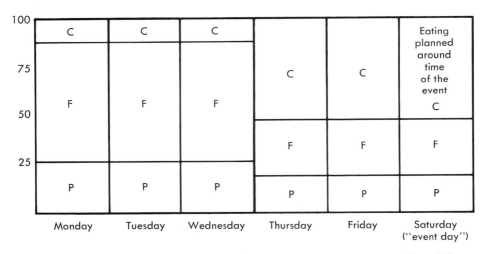

Fig. 10-6. Diagrammatic representation of daily dietary composition of an athlete following the strict glycogen-loading routine. C = Carbohydrate, F = Fat, and P = Protein. (In some cases, Wednesday's routine may be like Thursday's and Friday's if a shorter depletion period is specified.)

Just how safe the glycogen-loading diet is remains to be confirmed through continued observation.[40,41] Glycogen retains water, and both substances may be deposited in muscle to such an extent that a feeling of heaviness and stiffness may be experienced. The weight increase caused by water retention may reduce the ability of the athlete to take up oxygen maximally. Carbohydrate loading has also been reported to produce cardiac pain and electrocardiographic abnormalities in an older marathon runner.[40] The effect of this practice on heart function is distressing enough to caution all athletes against its use without expert advice from competent health care professionals.

A recent finding of considerable interest is that moderate caffeine consumption prior to an endurance event may allow for a moderate delay in the use of muscle glycogen stores.[42-45] This effect appears to be related to the role of caffeine in elevating plasma-free fatty acids. Studies conducted in both rats and humans have revealed delays in development of exhaustion when caffeine is provided in moderate doses prior to physical performance. Although use of this stimulant may be attractive to competitors involved in endurance sports, the potential dangers of excessive caffeine consumption should be carefully considered.

The pregame meal

Many superstitions exist in our society about which foods to consume before competition. In reality, there is no magic formula that is clearly indicated for every person. Since individuals differ with regard to food preferences, psychologic crutches, and digestive response to stress, a variety of food items and eating schedules may support good preparation. Still, a few basic comments about sensible eating in the hours just preceding the scheduled event are appropriate:

1. The diet should include familiar foods that the athlete believes "will make him win."
2. Energy intake should be sufficient to prevent hunger and faintness during the period of competition.
3. The foods chosen should be relatively easy to digest, so that the stomach and upper gut are empty at the time of competition.
4. Fluid intake should be sufficient to maintain an optimal level of hydration throughout the day.
5. Gas-forming foods should be selected with discretion and should be avoided if they pose problems for the athlete.
6. Meals should not be skipped entirely, because the overall performance capacity of the athlete may ultimately suffer.

At times the liquid pregame meal may be chosen as a sound alternative to other available options. Commercial products such as Sustagen, Sustacal, and Ensure provide a palatable high-carbohydrate, high-calorie, high-fluid pregame diet. These products typically provide sufficient amounts of fat and protein to promote satiation and palatability, but the fluid character of the meal allows for its easy passage through the stomach and small intestine. Aside from these characteristics, a liquid diet has no particular advantage that warrants its serious consideration as a diet of choice. If the team or athlete accepts such a preparation and believes that it optimizes status prior to competition, then certainly it may be justifiably selected as a sound, nutritious pregame diet.

WEIGHT MANAGEMENT

Adjustment of body weight is sometimes necessary to prepare an athlete to perform optimally in certain sports. Neither weight loss nor weight gain is easily achieved, and both adjustments require appropriate early planning so that goals may be reached within a *reasonable* period of time.[46] Weight that is lost or gained represents mainly fat and muscle; ideally, weight that is lost should consist mostly of fat, whereas weight that is gained should consist predominantly of muscle and its associated fluid. Major changes of this sort do not occur overnight, especially in the absence of physical activity. Planning well in advance of the scheduled competition is an absolute must; any sound program in weight management must emphasize rigorous physical training, not just diet. Only when this philosophy is practiced will one satisfactorily meet and maintain weight gain or weight loss goals. Last-minute attention to weight modification may compromise both the health and performance of the athlete.

Three components are vital to the success of any organized weight management program. First, sufficient time should be allowed; in most cases, a maximum rate of gain of 0.5 to 1 kg of muscle mass/week should be anticipated. Weight loss at a rate of 1 kg/week is usually the desired rate; never should this rate exceed 2 kg/week. Second, all special diets or food plans for weight management should fulfill all nutritional needs, including those for protein, vitamins, and minerals. Vitamin, mineral, and protein supplements are thus not required, although occasionally iron supplements may be justifiably recommended for women of reproductive age. Third, weight management programs are ideally supervised by individuals other than the head coach. This duty is best delegated to a team nutritionist, physicain, trainer, or assistant coach.

During the season of scheduled competitions, some sports (e.g., wrestling) require that preevent body weight be recorded. Weight at this time can be minimized without harm to the athlete by avoidance of salty foods, which promote excessive water retention, and by reduction in intake of dietary fiber, which may linger in the gut lumen and provide unneeded weight. Water intake should not be compromised during this period, and efforts to promote dehydration

as a means of "making weight" (e.g., vomiting, spitting, exercising in plastic suits, sauna bathing, and using diuretics and cathartics) should never be undertaken.

Recent studies provoking much concern report that some young athletes go to incredible extremes to lose body weight or maintain it at an acceptably low level.[47] This is especially evident in the individual whose basal metabolic rate is low to moderate, and whose typical level of body fat is well above 10% of total body weight. To maintain a body composition of 5% fat requires considerable training and dietary self-control for the majority of athletes, male or female. Since females normally support a much higher body fat content, however, the effort required in training and diet is often tremendous. Unfortunately, some athletes place so much emphasis on achievement of minimum body fatness that starvation diets and demanding training schedules are undertaken. Such practices may ultimately adversely affect endurance, physical growth, and psychologic stability.

Attempts to increase body weight are also undertaken by athletes desirous of improving performance. This practice is most commonly encountered in the United States among young men playing football. A variety of diets have been employed in this effort, but essentially what is needed is sufficient calories and protein to support tissue deposition. Somewhat larger portions of basic foods may provide what is needed. Alternatively, nutritious high-calorie snacks may be added to the diet. Diets that are rich in saturated fats and cholesterol should be avoided. Vitamin and protein supplements serve no useful purpose in the overall plan.

Increases in body weight ideally result from creation of lean body mass instead of fat. Increasing muscle mass can only result from muscle work. An intake of approximately 2500 extra calories is needed to acquire 0.5 kg of muscle tissue. The addition of 750 to 1000 kcal/day to a regular diet will provide the energy needs for gaining 0.5 to 1 kg/week as well as for the increased energy output of the muscle-training program. Specific details of a muscle development program should be geared to the age and condition of the athlete. Progress should be assessed at regular intervals by measuring fatfold thickness and body weight, reviewing dietary practices and problems, and judging psychologic and emotional status. Excessive deposition of body fat may indicate that the muscle-training program requires modification.

SUMMARY

Common sense clearly should prevail in assessing the nutritional needs of the growing athlete. Sufficient calories must be consumed to support growth and activity. Fluid and electrolytes lost during practice or competition must be replaced to avoid the consequences of dehydration and electrolyte imbalance. Protein, vitamin, or mineral supplements are generally unnecessary, but occasionally an iron supplement may serve to correct iron deficiency or maintain iron balance in adolescent boys and girls. Weight management efforts should be approached sensibly, without focus on achieving minimal weight through promotion of fluid loss. Eating prior to competition should be scheduled to avoid retention of undigested food material in the gut at the time of the event. Foods that are easy to digest should be selected with avoidance of unnecessary fat, fiber, and gas-forming fruits and vegetables. No special diet is recognized as clearly the ticket to success. However, if ingestion of a certain food provides a psychologic edge, selection of it must be considered potentially advantageous.

REFERENCES

1. Astrand, P., and Rodahl, K.: Textbook of work physiology, New York, 1970, McGraw-Hill Book Co.
2. Saltin, B.: Fluid, electrolyte and energy losses and their replenishment in prolonged exercise. In Parizkova, J., and Rogozkin, V. A., editors: Nutrition, physical fitness, and health, Baltimore, 1978, University Park Press.
3. Rogozkin, V. A.: Some aspects of athlete's nutrition. In Parizkova, J., and Rogozkin, V. A., editors: Nutrition, physical fitness, and health, Baltimore, 1978, University Park Press.
4. American Alliance for Health, Physical Education and Recreation: Nutrition for athletes: a handbook for coaches, Washington, D.C., 1971.
5. Bobb, A., Pringle, D., and Ryan, A. J.: A brief study of the diet of athletes, J. Sports Med. Phys. Fitness 9:255, 1969.
6. Matthews, D. K., and Fox, D. K.: The physiologic basis of physical education and athletics, Philadelphia, 1971, W. B. Saunders Co.
7. Smith, N. J.: Food for sport, Palo Alto, Calif., 1976, Bull Publishing Co.
8. Ziegler, K. L., and others: Muscle metabolism during exercise in man, Trans. Assoc. Am. Physicians 81:266, 1968.
9. Carlson, L. A., Ekelund, L., and Froberg, S. O.: Concentrations of triglycerides, phospholipids, and glycogen in skeletal muscle and of free fatty acids and beta-hydroxybutyric acid in blood in man: response to exercise, Eur. J. Clin. Invest. 1:248, 1977.
10. Hendriksson, J.: Human skeletal muscle adaptation to physical activity, Unpublished data, Karolinska Institute, Stockholm.
11. Saltin, B., and others: The nature of training response: peripheral and central adaptations to one-legged exercise, Acta Physiol. Scand. 96:289, 1976.
12. Ryan, A.: Round table—balancing heat stress, fluids and electrolytes, Phys. Sports Med. 3:43, 1975.
13. Brooke, J. D., Davies, G. J., and Green, L. F.: The effects of normal and glucose syrup work diets on the performance of racing cyclists, J. Sports Med. Phys. Fitness 15:257, 1975.
14. Karlsson, J., and Saltin, B.: Diet, muscle glycogen and endurance performance, J. Appl. Physiol. 31:203, 1971.
15. Green, L. F., and Bagley, R.: Ingestion of glucose syrup drink during long distance canoeing, Br. J. Sports Med. 6:125, 1972.
16. Muckle, D. S.: Glucose syrup ingestion and team performance in soccer, Br. J. Sports Med. 7:340, 1973.

17. Durnin, J. V. G. A.: Protein requirements and physical activity. In Parizkova, J., and Rogozkin, V. A., editors: Nutrition, physical fitness, and health, Baltimore, 1978, University Park Press.

18. Consolazio, C. F., and others: Protein metabolism of intensive physical training in the young adult, Am. J. Clin. Nutr. 28:29, 1975.

19. Rasch, P., and others: Protein dietary supplementation and physical performance, Med. Sci. Sports 1:195, 1969.

20. Sharman, I.: The effects of vitamin E and training on physiological function and athletic performance in adolescent swimmers, Br. J. Nutr. 26:265, 1971.

21. Lawrence, J. D., and others: Effects of tocopherol acetate on the swimming endurance of trained swimmers, Am. J. Clin. Nutr. 28:205, 1975.

22. Bailey, D. A., and others: Effect of vitamin C supplementation upon the physiological response to exercise in trained and untrained subjects, Int. J. Vitam. Nutr. Res. 40:435, 1970.

23. Barnes, L.: Preadolescent training: how young is too young? Phys. Sports Med. 7:114, 1979.

24. Lane, H. W., and others: Effect of physical activity on human potassium metabolism in a hot and humid climate, Am. J. Clin. Nutr. 31:838, 1978.

25. Lane, H. W., and Cerda, J. J.: Potassium requirements and exercise, J. Am. Diet. Assoc. 73:64, 1978.

26. Finch, C. A., and others: Iron deficiency in the rat: physiological and biochemical studies of muscle dysfunction, J. Clin. Invest. 58:447, 1976.

27. Sproule, B. J., Mitchell, J. H., and Miller, W. F.: Cardiopulmonary physiological responses to heavy exercise in patients with anemia, J. Clin. Invest. 39:378, 1960.

28. Committee on Nutrition of the Mother and Preschool Child: Iron nutriture in adolescence, Washington, D.C., 1976, Department of Health, Education, and Welfare.

29. Leibel, R. L.: Behavioral and biochemical correlates of iron deficiency, J. Am. Diet. Assoc. 71:398, 1977.

30. Worthington-Roberts, B. S.: Suboptimal nutrition and behavior in children. In Contemporary developments in nutrition, St. Louis, 1980, The C. V. Mosby Co.

31. Worthington, B. S., and Doan, R.: Nutrition and family planning. In Worthington, B. S., Vermeersch, J., and Williams, S. R.: Nutrition in pregnancy and lactation, St. Louis, 1977, The C. V. Mosby Co.

32. Malina, R. M., and others: Age at menarche and selected menstrual characteristics in athletes at different competitive levels and in different sports, Med. Sci. Sports 10:218, 1978.

33. Feicht, C. B., and others: Secondary amenorrhea in athletes, Lancet 2:1145, 1978.

34. Peterson, M.: Personal communication, 1978.

35. Vaccaro, P., Zauner, C. W., and Cade, J. R.: Changes in body weight, hematocrit and plasma protein concentration due to dehydration and rehydration in wrestlers, J. Sports Med. 16:45, 1976.

36. Alcohol and athletes, Phys. Sports Med. 7:39, 1979.

37. Astrand, P.: Diet and athletic performance, Fed. Proc. 26:1772, 1967.

38. Astrand, P.: Nutrition and physical performance, World Rev. Nutr. Diet. 16:59, 1973.

39. Bergstrom, J., and Hultman, E.: Nutrition for maximal sports performance, J.A.M.A. 221:999, 1972.

40. Mirkin, G.: Carbohydrate loading: a dangerous practice, J.A.M.A. 223:1511, 1973.

41. Nelson, R. A., and Gastineau, C. F.: Nutrition for athletes. In Craig, T. T., editor: The medical aspect of sports, Chicago, 1974, American Medical Association, pp. 19-21.

42. Costill, D. L., and others: Effects of elevated plasma free fatty acids and insulin on muscle glycogen usage during exercise, J. Appl. Physiol. 43:695, 1977.

43. Hickson, R. C., and others: Effects of increasing plasma free fatty acids on endurance, Fed. Proc. 36:450, 1977.

44. Rennie, M. J., Winder, W. W., and Holloszy, J. O.: A sparing effect of increased plasma fatty acids on muscle and liver glycogen content in exercising rat, Biochem. J. 156:647, 1976.

45. Costill, D. L., Dalsky, G. P., and Fink, W. J.: Effects of caffeine ingestion on metabolism and exercise performance, Med. Sci. Sports 10:155, 1978.

46. Smith, N. J.: Gaining and losing weight in athletes, J.A.M.A. 236:149, 1976.

47. Croyle, P. H., Place, R. A., and Hilgenberg, A. D.: Massive pulmonary embolism in a high school wrestler, J.A.M.A. 241:827, 1979.

11

Vegetarian diets for children

Cristine M. Trahms

Using plant foods as the primary source of nutrients in the diet is not a new concept, but it is a fairly recent phenomenon in the United States.

In the past many religious groups have strongly advocated the importance of a meat-free diet, and this practice continues today. Traditionally, religious groups chose to be vegetarian for reasons of moral purity and/or food sanitation. The general populations of many countries have also long been vegetarian or near vegetarian, not necessarily by choice but because of limited food availability. The availability of food choices and the adequacy of the total food supply are often not considered as effect modifiers when the adequacy of a vegetarian diet is discussed. The practice of eating meat does not inherently ensure good health, just as the practice of not eating meat does not ensure poor health. The nutrition/health/social mores/ food choice interrelationships are very complex. The exclusion of one food source or food group does not necessarily swing the pendulum of health or nutritional adequacy in either the positive or the negative direction. Therefore, when discussing vegetarianism—the concept of non–meat eating—one must consider other factors carefully.

Generally, a "vegetarian" is considered an individual who chooses to not eat meat, poul-

try, or fish, and a "vegan" (pure vegetarian) is an individual who chooses to not eat any animal products at all. However, people do not base their food choices or life-styles on tidy categories. Therefore, many people who call themselves vegetarians, may in fact eat meat as often as once per week or twice per month. On the other hand, people may choose extremely rigid diets that forbid them yeast and honey or they may eschew the use of wool, leather, or cotton because they are considered animal products. In this chapter, a vegetarian will be considered a person who has chosen to omit meat, poultry, and fish from his or her food intake pattern, and a vegan will be considered a person who has chosen to eat only plant foods (i.e., no animal products).

HEALTH ADVANTAGES AND DISADVANTAGES

Recent work with population subgroups has indicated that there are health advantages to the vegetarian food pattern. Much of this work has centered on adults in industrialized countries and specialized subgroups of the population that have made additional life-style changes in addition to omitting meat from their food patterns. It was found that some of the advantages of vegetarianism include lower total body weight,[1] decreased

224

incidence of cancer of the colon,[2] lower blood lipid levels,[3] and decreased incidence of osteoporosis.[4]

In general, factors such as abstinence from smoking and alcohol, great interest in exercise, and/or seclusion from the rest of society must be considered as potential intervening or modifying variables for religious subgroups.

Much of the work that points out the disadvantages of a vegetarian diet has been conducted in third world countries, where the total amount of food and the food choices available are very limited. Thus, many of these people would probably not choose to be vegetarians, but they have no alternative. Energy deficit and lack of food to provide specific nutrients must be considered when interpreting these reports. In this country the negative impact of a vegetarian diet has also been reported. Often young adults become overzealous in following specific teachings or omitting specific foodstuffs from their food patterns. One classic example of overzealousness is the Zen macrobiotic followers, who felt that tea and brown rice were the way to ultimate purity of body and soul. Even the leaders of the group warned against this extreme practice and encouraged a more moderate food intake pattern that included grains, legumes, fruits, and vegetables. The health disadvantages of the vegetarian diet have been documented primarily among those people who have chosen the vegan (pure vegetarian) diet. In general, the more restricted the pattern of food choices is, the more likely that individual is to be at high nutritional risk. (The same can be said for popular weight-reduction formats.) Young children and pregnant women, who are generally considered to be at high nutritional risk, are thought to be particularly vulnerable to food intake patterns that limit the quantity or the kinds of food for consumption.

INDIVIDUALS WITH SPECIAL NEEDS

In the few sketchy reports on the outcome of the pregnancies of women who were vegans or vegetarians, there appear to be no detrimental effects to the mother or the offspring if the mother chooses a food pattern that provides the required nutrients in appropriate quantities to support the pregnancy. Hardinge and co-workers[1] included several pregnant vegetarian women in one of their early nutritional status reports. The food intake patterns and calculated nutrient intakes were grouped with those of other adults, but they appeared adequate. The infants were reported to be of normal birth weight. Thomas and associates[5] reported on the health of vegans during pregnancy, comparing 14 vegans (28 pregnancies) and 18 controls (41 pregnancies). There were no differences in rates of stillbirths, toxemia, or anemia between the groups. There were also no differences in the birth weights of the infants. Few (3%) of the women who were vegan took iron supplements during pregnancy. They also breast fed their infants more frequently and for longer periods than did the control mothers. No data on weight gain during pregnancy were reported. Another report found no differences in birth weights between the vegetarian children (both extensive and limited food group avoidances) and the control children.[6]

It has been well documented that young children can indeed grow normally on diets comprised entirely of cereal proteins if the diets are carefully formulated. Knapp and associates[7] rehabilitated 102 malnourished male infants aged 5 to 14 months and then offered nine different formulations that were isocaloric (100 kcal/kg) and contained 2 gm of protein/kg. The children fed soybean, rice, cottonseed, cottonseed and rice, cottonseed and peanut, rice and soybean, soybean and peanut, or cow's milk formulas all demonstrated equivalent nitrogen retention. In crossover studies, the children fed wheat plus lysine, rice and cottonseed, and peanut and rice formulas grew at rates equivalent to the cow's milk–fed children. The children fed only peanut formulas did not retain as much nitrogen as did the cow's milk–fed children, and the children fed only rice formulas did not grow as well as did the cow's milk–fed children. It should also be noted that although the growth curves were equivalent, the children fed cow's milk diets demonstrated smoother growth curves. Recent reports have indicated that deficits in height and weight may occur among young children on vegan diets in the United States.

Young vegan children were significantly shorter (p <0.001) and lighter (p <0.005) than were age- and sex-matched vegetarian children and control children.[8] Dwyer suggested an environmental influence on the size of young children.[9] When adjusted for midparental height, 61% of 119 preschool vegetarian children were less than the tenth percentile for height. In another report, 72 white children less than 5 years of age living at home were longitudinally measured using standardized technique.[6] Thirty-four children had parents who consumed macrobiotic diets, 12 were members of yoga groups, 12 were Seventh-Day Adventists, and 14 had no group affiliation. Almost all (96%) of the children had been or were still being breast fed. The vegetarian children younger than 2 years showed mean weight and length velocities that were lower than the Harvard norms, whereas those of the older vegetarian children were comparable to the Harvard norms.

Young children consuming diets consisting only of plant foods seem to be at greater risk for nutritional deficiencies related to intakes of protein, calcium, total energy, essential fatty acids, riboflavin, and possibly vitamins B_{12} and D. This is in part related to family food choice patterns and in part to the individual preferences of the child who may or may not eat the foods that are offered.

An example of nutritional risk caused by limited food choices is the young child who was offered a grain beverage called kokoh consisting of rice, sesame seeds, and oats in a reasonable protein complement. However, the quantities offered to the child or that the child was willing to take did not provide adequate nutrients to support normal growth. The young infant being exclusively breast fed by a mother who is marginally or definitely vitamin B_{12} deficient may have an increased risk of deficiency. Older children who consume diets severely restricted in animal foods may also be at risk if the choices of foods available to them are severely restricted and exclude all animal foods.

Young children in developing countries who are breast fed but whose diets are not supplemented with additional foods may suffer adverse nutritional effects after 4 to 6 months, especially if they are weaned to a cereal gruel or other form of predominantly vegetarian diet. However, in these cases it must be remembered that other factors (e.g., poor sanitation and poor health care) may be important variables.

Reports of cases in the United States describe the severe malnutrition of one young child fed no animal products and no cereals,[10] a striking case of kwashiorkor of a young child on a vegan diet,[11] and poor weight attainment in children fed cereal-based formulas.[12] In another series of case reports,[13] four infants who were fed "cult" diets presented as severely malnourished to health care workers. Apparently the infants were fed restricted quantities of kokoh (a grain and cereal beverage) and limited quantities of other foods. Although the nutritional data presented in the report are sketchy, it would appear that the nutrient limitation was quantity of food rather than quality of food. All of the children were rehabilitated (e.g., growth increased) on vegetarian or near vegetarian diets within a few months. Unfortunately, legal intervention was necessary to change family food management patterns for the benefit of the children. In all of these reports, the number of children evaluated was very small and long-term observations on growth or nutrient intake were not made, but the questions these reports raise are disturbing.

Calculation of nutrient intakes of preschool children has shown that children whose diets excluded all animal products consumed significantly less total protein, fat, calcium, and riboflavin (p <0.01) than did vegetarian children and control children.[14] Intakes of iron and calcium were also calculated at lower than acceptable levels. Ten children on Zen macrobiotic diets were described as being at the fortieth percentile for height and weight.[15] Nutrient intakes were calculated as less than optimal, that is, less than 60% of the recommended dietary allowance for most nutrients except calcium and riboflavin, which were even lower.

Recent reports indicate that preschool children may also be at risk for vitamin D deficiency if they are consuming diets restricted in animal products. Eight-eight percent of 52 children on macrobiotic diets had vitamin D intakes of less than 100 IU/day[16] as compared to vegetarian children, of whom only 18% had vitamin D intakes this low. Although five children had pathologic findings related to bone mineralization, roentgenograms did not indicate rickets. Clinically, only three children demonstrated signs (bowed legs) that could possibly be attributed to vitamin D deficiency. The serum calcium and serum phosphorous levels of both the children on macrobiotic diets and the vegetarian children were within normal limits. Eight of the children on macrobiotic diets and two of the vegetarian children had elevated serum alkaline phosphatase levels.

Young breast-fed infants whose mothers are vegan may be at risk for vitamin B_{12} deficiency. Case reports cite growth failure and other clinical signs of vitamin B_{12} deficiency in infants who were breast fed by vegan women.[17,18] Apparently, these infants required more vitamin B_{12} than could be supplied by the breast milk of women with marginal vitamin B_{12} stores.

FACTORS INFLUENCING THE INTAKES OF YOUNG CHILDREN

The young child is dependent on caretakers to provide adequate foods as sources of nutrients. Food preferences are demonstrated early in life and this may also affect adequacy of intake. The older infant and toddler with rigid food preferences despite adequate food availability may be at risk for deficits of specific nutrients.

The young child on a food intake pattern comprised totally or primarily of plant proteins may have problems obtaining an adequate intake of energy if the volume of food required to meet energy needs is large. Often a legume milk (commercially prepared or home prepared with a sufficient energy concentration) will provide an easily ingested volume of protein, energy, and other nutrients for the young child.

In addition to volume, texture may also influence the adequacy of the intake of the young child on a vegetarian diet. Many foods that contain adequate quantities of protein must be texture modified for the young child, for instance, beans (legumes) must be well cooked and mashed or pureed. Even rice must be mixed with liquid and mashed for the infant. Whole grain breads may not be well chewed by the young child, and consequently the nutrients may not be well absorbed. The same is true for nuts and seeds, dried fruits, and some vegetables.

PROTEIN NEEDS OF YOUNG CHILDREN

Protein utilization is affected by a variety of factors, including quality and quantity of ingested protein, percent of calories as fat, total energy intake, biologic variation of the individual, and growth and maintenance needs (e.g., age and nutritional state). Calculating protein utilization, and consequently protein needs, is a complex undertaking because many of the relationships are not clearly defined and/or are extremely difficult to measure.

Much work is being done to document protein utilization among young children and the ability of vegetable protein diets to maintain growth and nitrogen balance for young children or to rehabilitate them from malnutrition or illness. The infectious process is a confounding variable that is difficult to quantitate, and it affects the utilization of nutrients.

Many combinations of grain and legume proteins have been evaluated in terms of maintenance of nutritional health or the rehabilitation of malnourished children in developing countries. Evaluation of a macaroni product containing 60% corn (maize), 30% defatted soy flour, and 10% wheat germ indicated nutritional recuperation in both the experimental and control groups of children.[19] The protein quality of most common grains and legumes consumed by young children in Mexico was evaluated.[20] Combinations of corn and soy in ratios of 80:20 and 90:10 had highest protein quality. Combinations of corn and beans (50:50) and wheat and beans (50:50) were better than single sources of corn, wheat, or beans but were not significantly different from each other.

A CSM (68% corn, 28% defatted soy flour, 5% nonfat dry milk) infant food demonstrated that a small percentage of protein from animal foods enhances the value of a food product as a sole source of nutrients for young infants. This formulation promoted nitrogen retention similar to that of casein.[21]

A soybean protein textured food (soy protein isolate) with added egg albumin and wheat gluten has a protein quality of about 80% of that of milk. Children required 138 mg of nitrogen from the soy food as compared to 97 mg of nitrogen from milk to maintain nitrogen equilibrium.[22] This food was readily accepted by the children.

The question of lysine fortification of wheat products and long-term improvements in the growth of children dependent on this cereal for almost all of their protein intake remains an elusive question. For very young infants, it may be that wheat protein is inadequate to maintain normal growth and development.[23]

Fat absorption in young children is dependent on levels of dietary protein intake.[24] Very low protein intakes with adequate energy intakes are detrimental to maximum fat absorption and may ultimately increase total energy requirements. Children on diets containing 5% or more of energy as protein (FAO/WHO recommendation) showed improvement of apparent fat absorption as protein intakes increased.

All of this information on relative biologic value or utilization of protein is interesting, but in this country few if any children must exist on a single food that, in turn, must supply all or the majority of nutrients. The young formula-fed infant is the exception. Formulations of infant food must be done very carefully to meet the rigorous nutrient requirements to support normal growth and development.

Choosing protein foods for young children

It is important that the protein sources offered to young children be appropriately combined so that the pattern of amino acid intake will be adequate to support normal growth and development. Careful attention to combining plant proteins in the best proportion for optimal utilization is a must. Appetites of young children fluctuate widely on a day-to-day basis, making it important that all foods eaten provide nutrients rather than calories only.

In combining plant proteins, not only must

foods that supplement the most limiting amino acids of each other be combined, but they should be combined in specific proportion for the most efficient utilization of protein. The ratio is specific for each combination. Examples of satisfactory combinations include the following: (1) ¾ cup of dry rice with ¼ cup of dry beans; (2) ¾ cup of dry rice with 1 cup milk or ¼ cup of milk powder; and (3) 3¼ cup of wheat flour with ¼ cup of soy grits and ½ cup of sesame seeds. Complementation of proteins is also a useful and practical way to enhance the value of foods readily accepted by young children. One can easily accomplish this by adding a small amount of soy grits while oatmeal is being cooked or by adding wheat germ, soy flour, or dry milk to muffins pancakes, cookies, and breads. The simple method called the Cornell Triple Rich Flour Formula developed at Cornell University complements the proteins of baked products. According to this formula, before any flour is put into the measuring cup the following should be measured into the bottom of the cup: 1 tbsp of soy flour, 1 tbsp of dry milk, and 1 tsp of wheat germ. The cup is then filled with flour.

Preschool children are in the process of developing their individual food patterns and are not amenable to eating foods because they are good protein sources. The difficulty of encouraging young children to eat a sufficient volume of legumes, grains, seeds, and nuts in forms that they can easily digest and encouraging them to eat foods in a precise proportional relationship is very great. For young children without dairy foods or eggs in their diets it is difficult to provide sufficient quality and quantity of proteins and an adequate amount of calories to support adequate growth.[14]

ENERGY NEEDS OF YOUNG VEGETARIAN CHILDREN

It is possible that the volume of food required to meet the energy needs of young children may interfere with adequate intakes. This is especially true for those children who are offered foods without modification of texture. In most studies, the foods offered to children were texture modified into beverages with constant energy per unit of volume so that the children could easily ingest the required volume to meet energy needs. This theoretical or research strategy may not be appropriate for the practical application of foods as sources of nutrients for this age group.

Energy intake should be adequate to promote growth in channel on acceptable growth charts. As for any child, parental size should be considered when evaluating the growth of children.

MEETING THE NUTRIENT NEEDS OF YOUNG VEGETARIAN CHILDREN

Protein and energy needs of young children must be stated as a dyad to provide guidelines for the relative adequacy of these dietary components. This dyad should include some factors for individual variation in energy, for the possibility that these needs may to some degree be independent of protein needs, and for the degree of adaptation of expenditure to suit intake or vice versa. Examples of recorded food intakes of vegan, vegetarian, and nonvegetarian children that show the variety of foods and general quantities needed to provide reasonable intakes of nutrients are given in Table 11-1.

A model proposed by Payne[25] suggests that an adequate, safe protein:energy ratio in young children is close to 5%. Since most cereal grains seem to provide protein levels close to this, energy deficit rather than protein deficit may be the cause of protein/energy malnutrition in children in developing countries.

Many nutrient needs can be met by careful planning and by including foods that are equivalent sources of specific nutrients. Table 11-2 defines foods as sources of nutri-

Table 11-1. Recorded 1-day intakes of young children

Food	Portion size	Food	Portion size
Child no. 1 (aged 12 months) — inadequate vegan intake		**Child no. 3 (aged 13 months) — vegetarian intake**	
Oatmeal, cooked	½ cup	Milk, whole	9 oz
Raisins	1 tsp	Cereal	
Yellow squash, cooked	½ cup	Cornmeal, dry	¼ cup
Apple	1 medium	Wheat germ	3 tbsp
Oatmeal, cooked	1 cup	Milk	¼ cup
Yams, cooked	½ cup	Apple	1 tbsp
Pudding		Soybeans, cooked	1 cup
Apple cider	1 cup	Apricot, dried	2 halves
Arrowroot flour	1 tsp	Apple	½ medium
No supplements		Potato, baked	½ small
TOTAL ENERGY INTAKE	610 kcal	Tomato	1 small
TOTAL PROTEIN INTAKE	12 gm	Cheddar cheese, grated	¼ cup
Child no. 2 (aged 14 months) — better vegan intake		Soy oil	2 tsp
Kokoh	1¼ cup	Milk	9 oz
Rice	½ cup	Milk	9 oz
Sweet rice	¼ cup	No supplements	
Whole oats	⅛ cup	TOTAL ENERGY INTAKE	1280 kcal
Sesame seeds	⅛ cup	TOTAL PROTEIN INTAKE	66 gm
Wakame	½ tsp	**Child no. 4 (aged 12 months) — nonvegetarian intake**	
Squash	⅓ cup	Peach, canned	½
Whole wheat noodles	½ cup	Link sausage	2
Miso soup		Toast, white	½ slice
Miso	1 tsp	margarine	½ tsp
Scallions	1 tsp	Egg yolk	1
Onion	1 tsp	2% Milk	8 oz
Kokoh	1¼ cup	2% Milk	8 oz
Nori	1 piece	Veal	50 gm
Cauliflower	¼ cup	Cracker	1
Aduki beans, cooked	⅓ cup	Rice, cooked	½ cup
Watercress	1 sprig	Tomato	¼ medium
Brown rice Kayu (1:5)	1¼ cup	2% Milk	8 oz
Squash, cooked	¼ cup	2% Milk	8 oz
Apple, baked	2 tbsp	Supplement: Poly-vi-sol	6 ml/day
Raisins	1 tsp	TOTAL ENERGY INTAKE	1020 kcal
No supplements		TOTAL PROTEIN INTAKE	58 gm
TOTAL ENERGY INTAKE	1140 kcal		
TOTAL PROTEIN INTAKE	35 gm		

Table 11-2. Key nutrients to consider when choosing food patterns

If these foods are excluded	Then these nutrients are limited	Replace with these foods
Meat, fish, poultry	Protein, iron, energy, zinc, folate, vitamin B_{12}, thiamine, essential fatty acids	Milk, dairy products, grains, legumes
Milk, dairy products	Protein, energy, calcium, vitamin B_{12}, vitamin D, and riboflavin	Legumes, soy milk (fortified), dark green vegetables
Grains	Protein, iron, niacin, riboflavin, zinc, fiber	Legumes, dairy products
Legumes	Protein, iron, zinc, calcium, fiber	Grains, dairy products
Fruits	Vitamin A, vitamin C, fiber, folate	Vegetables
Vegetables	Vitamin A, vitamin C, fiber, folate	Fruits

ents and the foods that can be exchanged to provide the equivalent nutrients. This scheme may be employed not only by vegetarians but also by those who have specific food likes and dislikes or by those who for some other reason feel the need to restrict the variety of choices in their food intake patterns.

COUNSELING THE VEGETARIAN FAMILY

The word "vegetarian" has a specific nuance or value system attached to it for each person who has chosen to apply that label to him or herself. The health care professional in the counseling role should carefully examine his or her own biases and, whether they are negative or positive, try to approach the family or household as open-mindedly as possible.

It seems reasonable that one should first ask the family to describe the foods regularly included and excluded in the family's diet and the individual's diet (Chapter 5). A recent survey of women in Seattle indicated the importance of this approach.[26] Less than 50% of the persons who described themselves as vegetarians never ate meat, 30% ate meat once or twice per month, and nearly 10% ate meat as often as once per week.

Every food pattern that a person chooses

has some positive aspects, which should be defined and reinforced. Clinical experience would indicate that a counseling/supportive role is much more effective than a directive (e.g., argumentative) approach. People can, in fact, adequately meet their nutrient needs in a wide variety of ways, and the individual variability or standard deviation of needs is quite wide.

For the infant and young child linear growth and rate of weight gain can be used as indices of appropriate energy intake. The mother of an exclusively breast-fed infant should be questioned about the adequacy of her own intake and should be advised of all the usual guidelines regarding adequate fluid, protein, calcium, and energy to maintain health and support lactation.

Some provisions should be made to ensure that the breast-fed infant receives adequate supplies of iron, vitamin B_{12}, and vitamin D. Recent evidence[27] indicates that iron in breast milk is well absorbed by the infant, so if the mother's diet provides adequate amounts of iron the needs of the infant should be met. Vitamin B_{12} may be a concern, especially if the mother's levels are low or if she has chosen a vegan diet. A supplement or additional food choices may be necessary to provide adequate quantities of this nutrient. There is, however, some evidence[28] that fermented soy products (e.g., tempeh and miso) may be "contaminated" during the fermentation process, thus providing a reasonable source of vitamin B_{12} for those persons who regularly consume the products. Vitamin D may also be a concern for those infants who receive minimal exposure to the sun. Again, options such as foods containing vitamin D or supplements (either synthetic or natural—e.g., cod liver oil) can be presented to the family. Usually, if the need for the particular nutrient can be clearly documented the parents are willing to reexamine their philosophic basis for making food choices and a reasonable decision and/or compromise can be reached for the ultimate nutritional welfare of the child.

When breast feeding is not feasible, the infant needs to receive adequate quantities of a properly prepared formula. This can be a commercial soy formula or a cow's milk formula, but it must provide adequate quantities of critical nutrients such as protein, calcium, iron, energy, and vitamins B_{12}, A, and D. It has been demonstrated[29] that fortified soy formulas can promote normal growth and development in infants. Less work has been done on evaluation of the nutrient properties of grain milks. Reports[11-13] indicating poor growth in young children consuming grain milks were complicated by the inappropriate dilution and volume of milk offered to the children. Grain and legume blends formulated into milks and appropriately supplemented certainly have the potential of meeting the needs of young children, but none are currently available in the United States.

Home-prepared infant formulas with a cow's milk or goat's milk base and supplemented with calcium, yeast, lactose, and other vitamin and mineral preparations are not advised. These types of formula are susceptible to errors in measurement and dilution; thus they put the infant at risk for excess of specific nutrients and potential renal solute problems.

Home-prepared soy milk supplemented with vitamin B_{12} can provide an appropriate base for the child who also consumes a wide variety of other foods. One family in our clinical experience prepared soy milk for the children. The soy milk was supplemented with crystalline vitamin B_{12} and the hulls and pulp of the soy remaining after milk preparation were carefully used in mixed dishes and baked goods. Tofu (soy cheese) was used frequently in mixed dishes. The children enjoyed all of these foods and drank adequate quantities of the milk with enthusiasm, particularly if it was flavored with vanilla and served ice-cold.

Many adolescents and young adults who choose vegetarian or semivegetarian food patterns are concerned with their own health and the nutrition that is basic to it. Often their food choices are based, at least in part, on political and philosophic convictions. These people need information and supportive counseling to make sound health decisions as well as the political or philosophic statement of their choice.

Young adolescents who are not yet emancipated from the nuclear family may use food selection as a means of establishing independence. In this situation parents need to remain flexible, tolerant, and interested in the adolescent's convictions regarding food choices. When there is little understanding the food pattern can quickly become another point of intense family conflict. It must be remembered that an unusual food pattern is not necessarily a harmful food pattern. The parents and the adolescent need guidance to discern the difference. Any direct criticism of food choices may be considered personal criticism, so counseling must be supportive. It should reinforce the positive aspects of the chosen food pattern and consider the energy and nutrient needs required for growth, development, and physical activity. Nonjudgemental discussion of alternatives and a mutual decision-making process be-

Table 11-3. Combinations of food for vegetarian diets

Food	Ingredients
Oatmeal, cooked	¾ cup of cooked oatmeal with 2 tsp of soy grits, ⅓ cup of milk
Scalloped potatoes	½ cup of potatoes, ½ cup of milk
Macaroni and cheese	½ cup of cooked macaroni, 3 tbsp of grated cheese
Rice pudding	½ cup of cooked rice, ¼ cup of milk
Peanut butter sandwich on whole wheat bread	½ tbsp of peanut butter, 1 slice of bread
Tortillas with beans	2 tortillas, ¼ cup of cooked beans
Whole wheat and soy muffin	2 tbsp of whole wheat flour, 1 tsp of soy flour, 1 tbsp of milk
Sesame and oatmeal cookies	1 tbsp of oatmeal, 1 tbsp of whole wheat flour, 1½ tsp of sesame, ½ tbsp of milk

Table 11-4. Vegetarian food guide

Food group	Portion size	Number of portions Pregnant	2 to 3 years	4 to 6 years
Breads, cereals, pasta	1 slice of bread ⅓ cup of granola ¾ cup of cooked cereal 1 biscuit, muffin 1 tbsp of wheat germ ¾ cup of cooked rice	6	3	3
Protein foods				
Legumes, meat analogues	1 cup of cooked beans ¼ cup of peanut butter 6 oz of tofu	¾	⅛	¼
Nuts and seeds	3 tbsp	1	⅛	¼
Dairy products				
Milk	1 cup of milk, yogurt 1 oz of cheese 4 tbsp of cottage cheese	4	2-3	2-3
Eggs		1½	1	1
Fruits and vegetables	1 cup, raw ½ cup, cooked ½ cup of juice	5-6	2	3
Extra foods	No requirement (recommendation)			

Modified from Smith, E. B.: A guide to good eating the vegetarian way, J. Nutr. Educ. 7:109-111, 1975.

tween health care worker, adolescent, and parent can guide adolescents in making healthful and responsible food choices (see Table 11-3).

In addition to the food guide (Table 11-4), the following point should be kept in mind when counseling a family that has chosen to become vegetarian: the goal of the health care professional is the same as when counseling a nonvegetarian family—that is, to promote good health through reasonable food choices. Responsibilities would include the following:

1. To support the individual and the family in every positive aspect of the chosen food pattern
   a. By being nonjudgmental about the stated reasons for specific food choices
   b. By recognizing the wide variety of food choices that are appropriate to maintain good health
   c. By understanding the food taboos and food preferences and the reasons for them
2. To evaluate the food intake of a specific family member, identifying those nutrients might be at risk for deficient intake because of food choices or food preparation methods
   a. By helping the family recognize the differing needs of infants, young children, adolescents, adults, pregnant women, and sedentary individuals
   b. By working with the individuals to identify food as sources of nutrients
3. To encourage the family members to purchase foods that provide the most nutrients for the money
   a. By encouraging the evaluation of foods for their nutrient content, packaging, and processing
   b. By encouraging the use of simple foods, whole grains, fresh fruits, and vegetables
   c. By encouraging the use of cooking methods that conserve nutrients

SUMMARY

The more restrictive food choices become, the more difficult it is to plan a nutritionally adequate diet. Vegetarian diets that include prudently chosen plant foods and a reasonable amount of dairy foods are adequate to support normal growth and development for people of all ages, including young children, pregnant women, and lactating women. Robertson and associates[30] have compiled a helpful manual entitled *Laurel's Kitchen*, which includes recipes for those who choose nonmeat food patterns.

REFERENCES

1. Hardinge, M. G., and Stare, F. J.: Nutritional studies of vegetarians. I. Nutritional, physical, and laboratory studies, J. Clin. Nutr. **2:**73-82, 1954.
2. Burkitt, D. P.: Epidemiology of cancer of the colon and rectum, Cancer **28:**3-13, 1971.
3. Sacks, F. M., and others: Plasma lipids and lipoproteins in vegetarians and controls, N. Engl. J. Med. **292:**1148-1151, 1975.
4. Ellis, F. R., Scura, H., and Ellis, J. W.: Incidence of osteoporosis in vegetarians and omnivores, Am. J. Clin. Nutr. **25:**555-558, 1972.
5. Thomas, J., Ellis, F. R., and Diggory, P. L. C.: The health of vegans during pregnancy, Proc. Nutr. Soc. **36:**46A, 1976.
6. Shull, M. W., and others: Velocities of growth in vegetarian preschool children, Pediatrics **60:**410-417, 1977.
7. Knapp, J., and others: Growth and nitrogen balance in infants fed cereal proteins, Am. J. Clin. Nutr. **26:**586-590, 1973.
8. Trahms, C. M., and others: Restriction of growth and elevated protoporphyrin in children deprived of animal protein, Clin. Res. **25:**179, 1977.
9. Dwyer, J. T., and others: Preschoolers on alternate lifestyle diets, J. Am. Diet. Assoc. **72:**264-270, 1978.
10. Erhard, D.: The new vegetarians, Nutr. Today **8:**4-12, 1973.
11. Berkelhamer, J. E., and others: Kwashiorkor in Chicago, Am. J. Dis. Child. **129:**1240, 1975.
12. Robson, J. R. K., and others: Zen macrobiotic dietary problems in infancy, Pediatrics **53:**326-329, 1974.
13. Roberts, I. F., and others: Malnutrition in infants receiving cult diets: a form of child abuse, Br. Med. J. **1:**296-298, 1979.
14. Trahms, C. M., and Feeney, M. C.: Evaluation of diet and growth of vegans, vegetarian, and non-vegetarian preschool children, Fed. Proc. **34:**675, 1975.
15. Brown, P. T., and Bergan, J. G.: The dietary status of "new" vegetarian, J. Am. Diet. Assoc. **67:**455-460, 1975.
16. Dwyer, J. T., and others: Risk of nutritional rickets among vegetarian children, Am. J. Dis. Child. **133:**134-140, 1979.
17. Higginbottom, M. C., and others: A syndrome of methylmalonic aciduria, homocystinuria, megaloblastic anemia and neurologic abnormalities in a vitamin B_{12} deficient breast fed infant of a strict vegetarian, N. Engl. J. Med. **299:**317-323, 1978.
18. Lampkin, B. C., and Saunders, E. F.: Nutritional

vitamin B$_{12}$ deficiency in an infant, J. Pediatr. **75:**1053-1055, 1969.

19. Beghin, I., and others: Assessment of biological value of a new corn-soy-wheat noodle through recuperation of Brazilian malnourished children, Am. J. Clin. Nutr. **26:**246-258, 1973.

20. Valencia, M. E., and others: Protein quality evaluation of corn tortillas, wheat flour tortillas, pinto beans, soybeans, and their combinations, Nutr. Rep. Int. **19:**195-201, 1979.

21. Graham, G. G., and others: Dietary protein quality in infants and children. IX. Instant sweetened corn-soy-milk blend, Am. J. Clin. Nutr. **26:**491-496, 1973.

22. Bressani, R., and others: Protein quality of a soybean protein textured food in experimental animals and children, J. Nutr. **93:**349-359, 1967.

23. Vaghefi, S. B., and others: Lysine supplementation of wheat proteins: a review, Am. J. Clin. Nutr. **27:**1231-1245, 1974.

24. MacLean, W. C., and others: Effect of the level of dietary protein intake on fat absorption in children, Pediatr. Res. **11:**774-778, 1977.

25. Payne, P. R.: Safe protein-calorie ratios in diets: the relative importance of protein and energy intake as causal factors in malnutrition, Am. J. Clin. Nutr. **28:**281-291, 1975.

26. Johnston, P. K.: Infant feeding among Seventh-Day Adventists, unpublished master's thesis, University of Washington, Seattle, Wash., 1979.

27. Saarinen, U. M., and Siimes, M. A.: Iron absorption from breast milk, cow's milk, and iron supplemented formula, Pediatr. Res. **13:**143-147, 1979.

28. Liem, I. T. H., and others: Production of vitamin B$_{12}$ in tempeh, a fermented soybean food, Appl. Environ. Microbiol. **34:**773-776, 1977.

29. Fomon, S. J., and others: Requirements for protein and essential amino acids in early infancy: studies with soy-isolate formula, Acta Paediatr. Scand. **62:**33-38, 1973.

30. Robertson, L., Flinders, C., and Godfrey, B.: Laurel's kitchen: a handbook for vegetarian cookery and nutrition, Berkeley, 1976, Nilgiri Press.

12

Diet and hyperactivity

Betty Lucas

Over the last two decades, the terms "hyperactivity," "hyperkinesis," and "learning disability" have become commonly used in American homes, in classrooms, and in the mass media and printed media. Although the disorder is ill defined and poorly understood, it has been identified as one of the most common problems among school-age children in this country. An estimated 5% to 10% of schoolchildren are believed to be affected by hyperactivity. Males are affected more often than females; reported ratios vary from 3:1 to 9:1.[1,2]

A multitude of diagnostic terms have been used to describe the behavior and learning problems seen in these children—hyperkinetic syndrome, minimal brain dysfunction (MBD), learning disability, and others. This difficulty with labels indicates the current uncertainty regarding etiology and the tendency to emphasize symptoms rather than the overall problem. It may be that the hyperactive child syndrome is really a group of varying disorders with different etiologies.

The hyperactive child is usually diagnosed by the presence of specific characteristics, which include the following:

1. Motor restlessness
2. Short attention span
3. Low tolerance for frustration and failure
4. Emotional lability
5. Average or above average intelligence
6. Poor impulse control
7. Learning difficulties
8. Incoordination and clumsiness
9. Easily distracted
10. Aggressiveness

A diagnosis is made on the basis of finding in a child several symptoms that have been present for at least 1 year, and in many instances since infancy. Although a true diagnosis of hyperactivity is a result of assessment by medical and/or educational specialists, many children are often labeled hyperactive by less formal measures of behavior in the school or home. Irregardless of the looseness of the diagnosis, the main focus of those involved with the child becomes treatment and management.

ETIOLOGY OF HYPERACTIVITY

A variety of causes of the hyperactive child syndrome have been proposed over the years, yet the etiology remains relatively unknown. It is quite possible that there may be various etiologies, with hyperactivity and its associated behaviors being the common expression.

Perinatal complications such as anoxia, toxemia, prematurity, and infection have long been suggested as causes, as have insults during the early years, including head injuries, seizures, or infections. There is some suggestion of a genetic component, with an increased family history of hyperactivity and learning disabilities in the identified children.[3,4]

Dietary factors have also been implicated as causes of hyperactivity. One of the most well-known theories is that proposed by Feingold, who identifies salicylate compounds and food additives as causes.[5] Some experts also suggest that food allergy is highly correlated to the incidence of the syndrome, with basic foods such as milk, wheat, and egg being common culprits.[6] Of any foodstuff, sugar is most often pinpointed currently as a cause of hyperactivity and behavior disturbances, primarily in the popular media.

Other environmental factors that have been suggested in the etiology include exposure to fluorescent lights and heavy metals such as lead. An unstable home environment or poor emotional relationships can also cause a child to exhibit some of the symptoms of hyperactivity.

More recent evidence suggests a biochemical basis for the hyperactive child syndrome. Although a disorder in serotonin metabolism has been implicated in this disorder, subsequent research has not supported the association. However, studies of cerebrospinal fluid in children have provided evidence that the metabolism of the catecholamine dopamine may be involved in the mechanism.[7]

In general, the etiology of hyperactivity continues to be a puzzle. Some of the proposed causes are mere associations without supportive data. Further investigations are needed to increase our understanding of the etiology of hyperactivity.

TREATMENT

The most widely used and accepted forms of therapy for hyperactivity are medication, behavioral management, and special educa-

tion. Stimulant medication has been used for more than 40 years and its effectiveness is well documented.[8] The most commonly used drugs are dextroamphetamine (Dexedrine) and methylphenidate (Ritalin). Although the exact mechanism by which these drugs work is not fully understood, hyperactive children respond to the medication with reduction in such undesirable behaviors as motor restlessness, short attention span, and irritability. When the child is calmed down and is paying more attention, the assumption has been made that academic performance will improve. Recent evidence, however, suggests that stimulant drugs do not necessarily improve school learning and that long-term outcomes are no different from those of children who have no medication.[2,9] Some specialists believe that long-term treatment of hyperactivity should emphasize behavior modification, parental counseling, and special school programs. Yet, stimulant medication continues to be the most common therapy.

Dietary treatments of the hyperactivity syndrome have become more popular in the last decade. Included in this group are diets that eliminate certain constituents (e.g., food additives, salicylate compounds, and sugar) and megavitamin therapy. These diets and megavitamin therapy are discussed on pp. 240 to 245.

STIMULANT MEDICATION AND ITS EFFECT ON GROWTH

One of the appeals of stimulant medication is its immediate dramatic effect with few toxic side effects. Anorexia is often noted as a side effect, but most authorities believe that this disappears or at least diminishes after a few weeks. Some weight loss is also initially reported, but generally it is believed to be transient. These assumptions have been supported by evidence that tolerance to stimulant drugs develops in the treatment of obesity.

Safer, Allen, and Barr first reported on the negative effects of stimulant medication on physical growth.[10] They found that hyperactive children receiving dextroamphetamine and methylphenidate had suppressed weight gain and height increase as compared to established norms. A later study of 63 hyperactive children of the same group showed that long-term use of dextroamphetamine resulted in a highly significant suppression of growth in weight and height. Methylphenidate caused a less striking growth suppression, and only when the dosage was 20 mg/day or more. Safer and Barr reported that tolerance developed to the weight-suppressant effects of dextroamphetamine after 3 years, but a tolerance to its inhibition of height growth did not develop.[11]

In a subsequent report Safer, Allen, and Barr presented data demonstrating a growth rebound in children who discontinued medication during the summer.[12] The growth rates were 15% to 68% above the expected increment for the age groups. These findings suggested that, in general, the degree of growth rebound is proportional to the degree of original drug suppression. Depending on the drug and dosage, however, a child may not be able to completely compensate in the summer for the growth suppression incurred during the school year.

Other reports have documented no growth-suppressing effects of stimulant drugs; in fact, Gross reported growths in weight and height greater than expected after the children were receiving medication for more than 3 years.[13,14] Although most investigations have dealt mainly with dextroamphetamine and methylphenidate, pemoline (Cylert) seems to have the same growth-suppressing effect.[15]

A recent review of this subject concludes that there is considerable evidence that stimulant drugs moderately suppress growth in weight and also result in minor suppression of stature increase.[14] There appears to be a dosage effect with higher doses causing more suppression. Any diminished growth in the prepubertal child is apparently not evident in adulthood. However, the effects of treatment during puberty and adolescence is not known. Weiss suggests discontinuing the use of stimulants for adolescents a year or two before closure of the epiphyses.[16]

The mechanism by which stimulant medication inhibits growth is unclear. Theories that have been postulated include (1) decreased energy intake resulting from the anorexia, (2) inhibition of growth hormone secretion, (3) decreased production of somatomedin, (4) a direct effect on bone and cartilage development, and (5) depressed blood prolactin levels.[14,15] For many of these proposed mechanisms the data are conflicting and sketchy.

Two clinical case studies have documented the effect of stimulant drugs on nutrient and energy intakes.[17] In both boys, who were followed for 12 months, energy intakes were reduced when receiving medication, significantly so at higher levels. Methylphenidate appeared to have a less severe effect on energy intake than did dextroamphetamine. Increasing the drug dosage resulted in decreased kilocalorie levels (Fig. 12-1). This suggests that actual reduced food consumption and subsequent low energy intakes may explain the growth retardation in these children. However, it is quite possible that a combination of reduced energy intake and drug-induced endocrine abnormalities may be involved.

Numerous clinical observations indicate that hyperactive children receiving stimulant medication tend to present a variety of feeding problems. Families and school personnel often report pickiness, dawdling at mealtime, school lunches refused or returned home, and disinterest in food. Some children have been observed to consume large amounts of

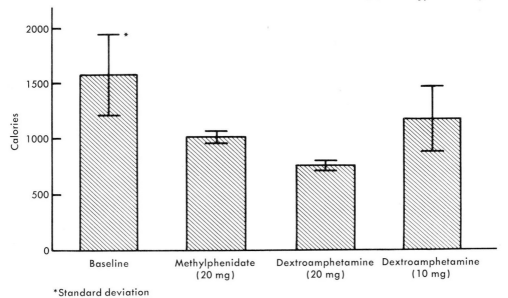

Fig. 12-1. Calorie intake of one subject during baseline and drug therapy periods. (From Lucas, B., and Sells, C. J.: Nutrient intake and stimulant drugs in hyperactive children, J. Am. Diet. Assoc. **70**:373, 1977.)

concentrated carbohydrates and other low-nutrient foods because parents are concerned that the child eat something. Because of their children's poor appetites and slow growth, families frequently resort to bribery, indulgence, and threats to induce them to eat. It is easy to understand how a preoccupation with food and eating can lead to frustration for parents and children, resulting in inappropriate behaviors and interactions at meal-times. When the children discontinue medication during vacations dramatic increases in appetite and food consumption are often noted by parents.

Since it has been estimated that approximately 300,000 children in the United States are receiving stimulant medication,[18] it is reasonable to assume that a significant number of them may be at risk for suppression of optimal physical growth. For health professionals and educators working with these children, the efficacy of the medication should be assessed periodically using standard double-blind procedures. Frequent monitoring of height and weight is essential to follow longitudinal changes in growth.

As for practical dietary management, it is important to know the type of drug, dosage, and time of administration. Since the drug effect takes approximately 30 minutes to be clinically manifested, meals should be offered with or before the medication dose in order to take advantage of optimal appetite. The drug effect is usually minimal or absent after 4 to 6 hours, and energy-producing foods of high-nutrient density should be offered at that time. Each child should be evaluated individually with regard to drug administration, meal and snack routine, and appetite response. Coordinating the child's daily schedule is essential to provide optimal nutritional status and physical growth. Some families may benefit from counseling regarding specific feeding problems.

FOOD ADDITIVES

In recent years the idea that chemicals added to food can cause children to exhibit a variety of behavior patterns such as restlessness, irritability, and short attention span has become popular. One of the most well-known proponents of this idea is Benjamin Feingold, an allergist and the author of a popular book on the subject of diet and hyperactivity.[5] He proposes that the cause of hyperactivity is related to the intake of artificial colors and flavors. He correlates the increased incidence of hyperactivity and learning disabilities with increased use of these substances in our food supply over the past few decades.

As an allergist, Feingold developed this theory as an outcome of clinical work with allergy patients. Many patients were sensitive to aspirin, which contains salicylate. This then led to the elimination of natural foods containing salicylate. In addition, since many individuals were also allergic to tartrazine (a yellow dye), all artificial flavors and colors became suspect and were also eliminated.

It is worth noting that these artificial colors and flavors are widespread in our food supply. Of some 2800 intentional additives used in foods, approximately 2100 are flavorings and 31 are colors, most of which are synthetic.[19] Most concerns regarding additives center on safety issues and potential carcinogenicity. Two specific substances, however, apparently cause adverse physical reactions in susceptible individuals. These are monosodium glutamate, which precipitates the "Chinese restaurant syndrome," and tartrazine, which causes an allergic response in persons who are also sensitive to aspirin.[20,21]

The Feingold diet

Feingold's thesis is that some individuals are genetically predisposed to react to these salicylate compounds and low molecular weight chemicals, but that the response is not an allergic reaction. An "innate releasing mechanism" is believed to be involved in the disturbance.[5]

The Feingold diet is based on eliminating all foods containing natural salicylates (Table 12-1), all artificial colors and flavors, and more recently the preservatives butylated hydroxyanisole (BHA) and butylated hydroxytoluene (BHT).[22] Besides foods, items also excluded are aspirin, toothpaste, cough syrup, vitamins, and most medications for children. The entire family is encouraged to follow the diet, rather than isolating the child. In most cases, more time and energy are required for menu planning, shopping, and food preparation. Reading labels is essential, and most mixed and prepared foods must be made from scratch. For many families this new emphasis on food constitutes a major change in their life-styles.

After a child responds positively to the

Table 12-1. Food containing natural salicylates

Almonds	Mint leaves
Apples	Nectarines
Cider and cider vinegars	Oranges
Apricots	Peaches
Blackberries	Prunes and plums
Cherries	Raspberries
Cloves	Strawberries
Cucumbers and pickles	Tea, all kinds
Currants	Tomatoes
Gooseberries	Oil of wintergreen
Grapes and raisins	
Wine and wine vinegars	

From Feingold, B. F.: Hyperkinesis and learning disabilities linked to artificial food flavors and colors. Copyright 1975, American Journal of Nursing Company. Reproduced with permission from the American Journal of Nursing, May 1975, vol. 75, no. 5.

Feingold diet for approximately 4 to 6 weeks the natural fruits and vegetables are gradually reintroduced to the child's diet as tolerated. This is commonly referred to as the modified Feingold diet. Interestingly, most of the data on natural sources of salicylates are old and are based on less sophisticated techniques than are available today. More recently, food technologists have analyzed some of the foods prohibited in the Feingold diet and have found no measurable levels of salicylate in grapefruit, lemons, oranges, tangelos, strawberries, and almonds.[23]

A response rate of approximately 48% has been reported by Feingold.[5] He believed that most of the failure to respond to the diet was caused by poor compliance with the program. Feingold was criticized because of the lack of control studies, primarily subjective data, and failure to report findings in reputed journals. Despite these criticisms, the diet became popular with the general public.

The National Advisory Committee on Hyperkinesis and Food Additives was formed to deal with the issue. Their report was critical of the lack of double-blind controlled experiments on Feingold's theory.[24] Questions were raised as to how adoption of the diet affected family dynamics and interaction, whether suggestibility and expected improvement were factors, and whether ratings that were global and subjective rather than specific and objective were valid. Subsequently, the committee established guidelines for experimental studies to test the Feingold hypothesis.

Experiments on the Feingold diet. Some initial reports showed marked improvement in children who were maintained on the Feingold diet.[25-27] In most instances, however, no control group or standardized objective ratings were used. In addition, the families knew they were trying the Feingold regimen.

One of the first double-blind controlled studies on the Feingold diet was conducted by Conners and co-workers with 15 children and two diets (the Feingold diet and a control diet).[28] Some improvement in behavior was noted while the children were on the Feingold diet, but only teachers' ratings were significant. There was difficulty in disguising the different diets from the families, and there were inconsistencies in the findings when the diet order was changed.

The same investigators later reported on 16 hyperactive children who showed a minimum 25% improvement in behavior while on the Feingold diet. The children completed an 8-week double-blind challenge period in which they continued on the diet but were given specially prepared chocolate cookies with or without artificial color additives. The results showed no difference in behavioral parameters between challenge and placebo periods. Interesting findings, however, included indications that younger children were more susceptible to the challenge, and that a greater number of performance deficits were noted when measured 1 to 2 hours after ingestion of the cookies with the additives. A subsequent phase of the experiment showed some deterioration in behavior when parents rated younger children within 3 hours of the challenge, suggesting a transient pharmacologic effect of the additives.[29]

A group of Australian investigators also considered the issue of possible time-limited effects. Using tartrazine as a challenge substance, they found no difference between challenge and placebo periods for the entire sample of 22 children. However, when they selected a subgroup of those children less than 8 years of age who showed a 25% improvement in behavior, there was a significant increase in symptoms immediately following the challenge.[30] Further replications of these findings are needed.

Harley and co-workers conducted a study with 36 school-age boys and 10 preschool boys by using the Feingold diet with a control diet.[31] An ambitious study design included supplying all the food for the families weekly, as well as providing food for school snacks and parties. When evaluated by neurologic, psychologic, and behavioral parameters, the results showed no significant improvement in the school-age boys. Ratings of the preschoolers showed a positive response to the diet, but the sample size was small and only parents reported. In a subsequent phase of the study, nine of the original children who had shown some positive response to the diet were put through a challenge regime for 9 weeks. This consisted of maintaining the Feingold diet and adding cookies or candy bars with or without the food color additives. No significant differences were noted between challenge and placebo, but one child did appear to respond with alterations in behaviors.[32]

In another study, comparison was made between the effect of the Feingold diet and use of stimulant medication.[33] Four different treatments were used for a week at a time: medication or placebo plus the diet with or without the additives. The ratings indicated some improvement with the Feingold diet, but stimulant medication was more effective than diet in decreasing hyperactive behaviors. On the other hand, teacher ratings suggested that the behavior was worse when the children were receiving placebo medication and the additives.

Weiss and co-workers studied 22 children aged 2½ to 7 years whose parents thought they were "super responders" to the Feingold regime but who had not been diagnosed as hyperactive. In a double-blind trial, the children continued on the diet for 11 weeks but were challenged eight times with a carbonated beverage containing food color additives, receiving a placebo beverage the other days. Two children responded adversely to the additives when rated by parents and observers, one dramatically.[34]

One of the criticisms of the controlled challenge study design is that the dose of additives has not been large enough to produce a response. Most of the studies have used 27 to 35 mg/day of mixed artificial colors in their challenge material—an amount that is supposed to represent an average intake for American children. Canadian researchers have recently suggested that the reaction to the additives may be related to dosage. Using a hospital clinical research unit, they challenged 40 children with 100 to 150 mg of the artificial colors and then measured response by a laboratory learning test rather than ratings.[35] The children's performance was significantly worse after receiving the challenge than after receiving the placebo, supporting the dose/response relationship. On the other hand, this information does not support Feingold's contention that even a single minor infraction of the diet causes a dramatic change in behavior. This study also suggests that laboratory learning tests may be a more sensitive measure of additive response than the behavior rating scales.

The nutritional adequacy of the Feingold diet was first assessed by Conners and co-workers.[28] They found that the diet produced poorer nutrient intakes than the control diet but that it still met the recommended dietary allowances. Intakes of ascorbic acid were particularly low because of the exclusion of the natural salicylate-containing foods, many of which are excellent sources of this vitamin. In a later report, the modified Feingold diet (eliminating only artificial colors and flavors) was analyzed for nutrient adequacy.[36] Food records for 54 children were collected and calculated during baseline and diet periods. Mean intakes compared favorably to the recommended dietary allowances, and nutrient intakes did not change significantly while the subjects were on the Feingold regimen. The assumption might be made that the overall nutrient quality of the modified Feingold diet might be better than a control diet, since many foods containing the artificial flavors and colors are low nutrient–density items. A market survey in this study, however, showed that in each category of foods there were foods free of the additives that were of comparable nutritional quality to those foods excluded.

Overall, the controlled double-blind studies have not supported the Feingold diet as an effective therapy for hyperactivity. The positive response that has been reported in uncontrolled studies and open trials is believed to be a placebo effect and/or the result of a significant change in the socioemotional environment of the child. It is certainly understandable that a family with a hyperactive child might expect a positive outcome from a diet that is relatively simple and without side effects. In addition, the focus on the dietary regimen may change the family setting—i.e., by bringing them together on a mutual project, giving positive attention to the hyperactive child, and lessening blame, changes that could result in a decrease in behaviors.

On the other hand, evidence does exist that a small subgroup of hyperactive children benefit significantly from the diet. The research data suggest that the Feingold diet is effective for approximately 1 out of every 50 hyperactive children.[37] Although this calculated incidence of 2% is far from the 50% success rate reported by Feingold, it remains that some hyperactive children, perhaps 5% to 10%, will be dramatically improved on the regimen.

A lot of unknowns remain regarding food additives and behavior in children. Future investigations will hopefully shed more light on the issue. Areas deserving more research include the suggestion that preschool children are more susceptible, the question of whether there is an immediate pharmaco-logic-related response, and the possibility of an additive dose/behavior relationship.

The Feingold diet has been tried, or is being currently used, by thousands of children in the United States. The nonprofit National Feingold Association exists with approximately 100 local associations, whose primary purpose is to assist families in adapting to the program. From a clinical management standpoint, care should be taken to do a comprehensive assessment of the hyperactivity in the individual child and to discuss the various management options with the parents. For those parents who wish to use the dietary approach and who believe that it works, the reality of improvement cannot and should not be denied irregardless of the source(s) of that improvement. In addition, the modified Feingold diet, as long as it includes a wide variety of foods, can be quite adequate nutritionally. Positive effects may include improved nutrition for the entire family and more interest in the topic. Health professionals should take care, however, to counsel the family not to disregard the potential help provided by special education, behavioral management, and other therapy modalities that can combine appropriately with the diet.

MEGAVITAMIN THERAPY

The use of large doses of certain vitamins to treat hyperactivity and MBD has become increasingly popular in recent years. Originating primarily from the popular press, lay groups, and some professionals, megavitamin therapy is loosely defined and varies a great deal in practice from individual to individual. It is also a component of "ortho-molecular psychiatry," which is defined by Pauling as "the achievement and preservation of mental health by varying the concentrations in the human body of substances that are normally present, such as the vitamins."[38] The basis of megavitamin therapy is that hyperactive children have biochemical imbalances and that these disturbances can be eliminated by the consumption of large amounts of certain vitamins.

Megavitamin therapy was first used to treat schizophrenia, using nicotinic acid.[39] Currently, proponents of this treatment recommend its use for a variety of disorders including hyperactivity, MBD, autism, mental retardation, and degenerative diseases. Suspecting vitamin deficiency as a cause of mental and behavioral problems is a result of existing nutritional knowledge on deficiency states. Classic examples are the neurologic and mental changes noted in persons with niacin deficiency (pellagra) and thiamine deficiency (beriberi).

Most commonly, megavitamin therapy includes niacin, ascorbic acid, pyridoxine, and calcium pantothenate. On the other hand, personal clinical experience has indicated that children receiving megavitamin therapy may be taking a wide assortment of vitamin and/or mineral supplements with or without expert guidance.

Generally, established medical professionals have not supported the megavitamin theory of treatment. A task force report of the American Psychiatric Association concluded that the claims of megavitamin advocates have not been confirmed by well-controlled studies and that most of the data are anecdotal.[39] Similarly, a statement by the American Academy of Pediatrics reported that "megavitamin therapy as a treatment for learning disabilities and psychoses in children, including autism, is not justified on the basis of documented clinical trials."[40]

Two recent studies have tested megavitamin therapy using double-blind controlled studies. Arnold and co-workers reported on 31 children with MBD who received either placebos or megavitamins during a two-week trial.[41] The megavitamin regimen was that advocated by Cott—1 gm of niacin, 1 gm of

ascorbic acid, 100 mg of pyridoxine, 200 mg of pantothenate calcium, and 500 mg of glutamic acid, all twice daily. Parent and teacher behavior ratings taken before and after the trial showed no significant difference in the two groups. Only two children responded so well that stimulant medication was not considered necessary; they were both in the placebo group.

In an investigation by Kershner and Hawke, 20 children with learning disabilities were put on a low-carbohydrate, high-protein diet and then given either megavitamins or placebos for 6 months.[42] They were evaluated before and after this period with a combination of intellectual, school achievement, perceptual, and behavioral measures. Results showed no difference between the two groups and thus failed to support the claim that megavitamins are helpful to children with learning disabilities. Most of the children, regardless of their group, showed behavioral progress; this may be a result of the diet alone or it may be a placebo effect. Both of these studies were unable to support the theories advocated by the proponents of megavitamin therapy.

Potential dangers do exist from consuming large doses of vitamins, although the literature is not extensive and reports on children are relatively few. Toxicity from excess fat-soluble vitamins (A and D) has been documented.[43] Although these vitamins are not included in the standard megavitamin treatment, clinical experience reveals that some practitioners commonly recommend vitamins A and D or that families may, on their own initiative, include them in their regimen. Other biochemical complications that have been reported are the destruction of vitamin B_{12} by large amounts of ascorbic acid, hyperbilirubinemia and liver damage by large doses of nicotinic acid, and liver damage by vitamin B_6.[44,45] A case of severe vitamin A intoxication has been reported for a 4-year old child who was receiving megavitamins for MBD.[46] In another case, an 11-year old boy who had been taking megavitamins for 4 years developed cholelithiasis, hepatitis, and thyroid dysfunction; he became well after a cholecystectomy and discontinuation of megavitamins.[47]

It is easy to understand why a family with a troubled child would respond to the appeal of megavitamin therapy. But too often it plays on the false hopes and guilt of the parents or provides a subject for blame. Some families can spend considerable money on vitamins and yet not deal with the basic problem related to the child's behavior.

There is no sound data to support the use of megavitamins with hyperactive children, yet the concept that some individuals may have increased needs for certain nutrients cannot be ignored. From a practical standpoint, the nutritional status of each child should be assessed and appropriate dietary intervention should be planned. In working with parents who choose to use megavitamins for their child, one needs to help them to recognize the practice as helpful, neutral, or harmful and to provide accurate information. At times counseling may be indicated to help families recognize and consider other treatment options.

SUGAR

Sugar (sucrose) has been implicated, mainly in popular books and anecdotal reports, as a causative factor in a multitude of diseases and disorders. Included in this group of disorders are diabetes, obesity, heart disease, and hypoglycemia, as well as mental and behavioral disorders such as hyperactivity, depression, and psychoses. One practitioner believes that sugar is the most common food substance causing adverse behavior reactions in children.[48] In addition, parents, teachers, and school nurses report dramatic negative changes in some children after receiving a load of sugar. Anecdotal stories describe children "climbing the walls" the day after Halloween.

All of these reports, however, are subjective and are not based on controlled studies. The only direct cause/effect relationship between sugar and disease is the role of sugar in dental caries; no such relationship exists with other diseases. Well-designed investigations of the correlation between sugar intake and behavior are needed.

As a people, Americans consume large amounts of sugar, more than 100 lb per capita/year. It has been estimated that sugar represents approximately 24% of the average energy intake.[49] Many foodstuffs that are high in sugar are low in nutrients, and thus they dilute the nutrient quality of the diet. Indeed, reducing or eliminating sugar in the diet serves to improve the overall nutritional and dental health of both child and family. These positive changes in families' diets have been observed in personal clinical experience. The professional can reinforce the dietary changes while stressing the lack of data supporting a sugar/behavior association.

ALLERGY

Food allergies are known to produce respiratory, gastrointestinal, and/or skin manifestations in the susceptible individual. Some experts also believe that they cause behaviors commonly found in hyperactive children— excessive activity, lack of attention, and irritability.[6] True allergies are a result of the production of antibodies against specific proteins in the foods that the child eats. The most common food allergens are the proteins of milk, egg white, and wheat.

There have been reports indicating that hyperactive children have a higher incidence of food allergies and that they respond positively to an elimination diet, thus supporting a causal relationship between food allergies and hyperactivity.[6,50,51] Some of these reports are subjective, however, and controversy exists regarding the validity and interpretation of the allergy tests used.

In cases in which food allergy is suspected it is appropriate to obtain a thorough diagnosis by an expert clinician, including a double-blind food challenge.[52] However, there is no guarantee that behavioral symptoms will improve. Currently, no strong evidence is available to support a direct relationship between food allergy and hyperactivity; but the possibility that some children have adverse behavior reactions to food, whether they be immunologic reactions or not, cannot be ruled out.

SUMMARY

The role of diet in hyperactivity seems to produce more questions than answers. Although no sound data have definitively implicated dietary factors as causes or shown dramatic improvement as a result of diet treatment, not all the evidence is clear-cut. Studies of free-living populations have their design and control limitations; other investigations remain to be done.

The various proposed dietary treatments for hyperactivity have not been supported by documentation. It appears that a small percentage of children, however, may be susceptible to certain substances in foods (i.e., color and flavor additives), and it cannot be ruled out that some children might react to large amounts of commonly consumed foods. On the other hand, it remains difficult to ascertain the environmental and emotional aspects that may affect a child's behavior.

For the professionals working with these children and their families, it is important that an objective and comprehensive assessment and diagnosis be done initially. Children using stimulant medication should have their physical growth monitored frequently, and nutritional counseling should be available as needed.

When working with families who are using some of the dietary approaches (e.g., Feingold diet, megavitamins, sugar-free diet), remaining open-minded and objective is critical. In that way rapport can be maintained, and thus the professional continues to be a resource. For the individual child, the actual dietary practices should be assessed as to adequacy and rationale. Obviously, positive changes in the diet should be reinforced, such as decreasing sugar consumption or using more nutrient-dense foods. For practices that are undesirable or potentially harmful (such as some megavitamin doses) one can discuss these with the family on a factual level and incorporate them in any decisions to change. Lecturing or emotional appeals are usually not productive.

Hyperactive children tend to be very difficult to manage and hard to live with. Their families deserve a lot of credit for doing as well as they do in handling the symptoms and subsequent problems. It is certainly a relief to them, then, when a dietary treatment decreases the negative behaviors and makes their child more enjoyable and less stress-producing for the family. Despite whatever components were involved in the change, their success is real and should not be denied.

The years to come will no doubt bring more information and definitive answers to the questions posed by this topic.

REFERENCES

1. Safer, D. J., and Allen, R. P.: Hyperactive children: diagnosis and management, Baltimore, 1976, University Park Press.
2. Weiss, G., and Hechtman, L.: The hyperactive child syndrome, Science **205:**1348, 1979.
3. Millichap, J. G.: The hyperactive child with minimal brain dysfunction, Chicago, 1975, Year Book Medical Publishers, Inc.
4. Wender, P. H.: Minimal brain dysfunction in children, New York, 1971, John Wiley & Sons, Inc.
5. Feingold, B. F.: Why your child is hyperactive, New York, 1974, Random House, Inc.
6. Crook, W. G.: Food allergy—the great masquerader, Pediatr. Clin. North Am. **22:**227, 1975.

7. Shaywitz, S. E., Cohen, D. J., and Shaywitz, B. A.: The biochemical basis of minimal brain dysfunction, J. Pediatr. **92**:179, 1978.
8. Eisenberg, L.: The clinical use of stimulant drugs in children, Pediatrics **49**:709, 1972.
9. Kolata, G. B.: Childhood hyperactivity: a new look at treatment and causes, Science **199**:515, 1978.
10. Safer, D. J., Allen, R. P., and Barr, E.: Depression of growth in hyperactive children on stimulant drugs, N. Engl. J. Med. **287**:217, 1972.
11. Safer, D. J., and Allen, R. P.: Factors influencing the suppressant effects of two stimulant drugs on the growth of hyperactive children, Pediatrics **51**:660, 1973.
12. Safer, D. J., Allen, R. P., and Barr, E.: Growth rebound after termination of stimulant drugs, J. Pediatr. **86**:113, 1975.
13. Gross, M. D.: Growth of hyperkinetic children taking methylphenidate, dextroamphetamine, or imipramine/desipramine, Pediatrics **58**:423, 1976.
14. Roche, A. E., and others: The effects of stimulant medication on the growth of hyperkinetic children, Pediatrics **63**:847, 1979.
15. Dickinson, L. C., and others: Impaired growth in hyperkinetic children receiving pemoline, J. Pediatr. **94**:538, 1979.
16. Weiss, G., and others: Effect of long-term treatment of hyperactive children with methylphenidate, Can. Med. Assoc. J. **112**:159, 1975.
17. Lucas, B., and Sells, C. J.: Nutrient intake and stimulant drugs in hyperactive children, J. Am. Diet. Assoc. **70**:373, 1977.
18. Krager, J. M., and Safer, D. J.: Type and prevalence of medication used in the treatment of hyperactive children, N. Engl. J. Med. **291**:1118, 1974.
19. Lehman, P.: More than you ever thought you would know about food additives, FDA Consumer, Department of Health, Education, and Welfare Publication No. (FDA) 79-2115, Washington, D.C., 1979, U.S. Government Printing Office.
20. Nagy, M.: Monosodium glutamate and the "Chinese restaurant syndrome," J.A.M.A. **225**:1665, 1973.
21. Zlotlow, M. J., and Settipane, G. A.: Allergic potential of food additives: a report of a case of tartrazine sensitivity without aspirin intolerance, Am. J. Clin. Nutr. **30**:1023, 1977.
22. Feingold, B. F.: Public lecture, Seattle, Wash., June 1, 1979.
23. Aschoor, S., and Chu, F. S.: Analysis of salicylic acid and methyl salicylate in fruits and almonds, Personal communication, 1978.
24. The National Advisory Committee on Hyperkinesis and Food Additives: Report to the Nutrition Foundation, New York, 1975, The Nutrition Foundation, Inc.
25. Cook, P. S., and Woodhill, J. M.: The Feingold dietary treatment of the hyperkinetic syndrome, Med. J. Aust. **2**:85, 1976.
26. Brenner, A.: A study of the efficacy of the Feingold diet on hyperactive children, Clin. Pediatr. **16**:652, 1977.
27. Salzman, L. K.: Allergy testing, psychological assessment and dietary treatment of the hyperactive child syndrome, Med. J. Aust. **2**:248, 1976.
28. Conners, C. K., and others: Food additives and hyperkinesis: a controlled double-blind experiment, Pediatrics **58**:154, 1976.
29. Goyette, C. H., and others: Effects of artificial colors on hyperactive children: a double-blind challenge study, Psychopharmacol. Bull. **14**(2):39, 1978.
30. Levy, F., and others: Hyperkinesis and diet: a double-blind crossover trial with a tartrazine challenge, Med. J. Aust. **1**:61, 1978.
31. Harley, J. P., and others: Hyperkinesis and food additives: testing the Feingold hypothesis, Pediatrics **61**:818, 1978.
32. Harley, J. P., Matthews, C. G., and Eichman, P.: Synthetic food colors and hyperactivity in children: a double-blind challenge experiment, Pediatrics **62**:975, 1978.
33. Williams, J. I., and others: Relative effects of drugs and diet on hyperactive behaviors: an experimental study, Pediatrics **61**:811, 1978.
34. Weiss, B., and others: Behavioral responses to artificial food colors, Science **207**:1487, 1980.
35. Swanson, J. M., and Kinsbourne, M.: Food dyes impair performance of hyperactive children on a laboratory learning test, Science **207**:1485, 1980.
36. Harper, P. H., Goyette, C. H., and Conners, C. K.: Nutrient intakes of children on the hyperkinesis diet, J. Am. Diet. Assoc. **73**:515, 1978.
37. Wender, E.: Food additives and hyperkinesis, Am. J. Dis. Child. **131**:1204, 1977.
38. Pauling, L.: On the orthomolecular environment of the mind: orthomolecular therapy, Am. J. Psychiatry **131**:1251, 1974.
39. American Psychiatric Association task force on vitamin therapy: Megavitamins and orthomolecular therapy in psychiatry, Nutr. Rev. Suppl. **1**:44, 1974.
40. Committee on Nutrition, American Academy of Pediatrics: Megavitamin therapy for childhood psychoses and learning disabilities, Pediatrics **58**:910, 1976.
41. Arnold, L. E., and others: Megavitamins for minimal brain dysfunction: a placebo-controlled study, J.A.M.A. **240**:2642, 1978.
42. Kershner, J., and Hawke, W.: Megavitamins and learning disorders: a controlled double-blind experiment, J. Nutr **109**:819, 1979.
43. Committee on Safety, Toxicity, and Misuse of Vita-

mins and Trace Minerals, National Nutrition Consortium: Vitamin-mineral safety, toxicity, and misuse, Chicago, 1978, American Dietetic Association.

44. White, P. L.: Megavitamin this and megavitamin that, J.A.M.A. **233:**538, 1975.
45. Winter, S. L., and Boyer, J. L.: Hepatic toxicity from large doses of vitamin B_3 (nicotinamide), N. Engl. J. Med **289:**1180, 1973.
46. Shaywitz, B. A.: Megavitamins for minimal brain dysfunction: a potentially dangerous therapy, J.A.M.A. **238:**1749, 1977.
47. Wright, K.: Personal communication, 1978.
48. Crook, W. G.: Personal communication, 1979.
49. Select Committee on Nutrition and Human Needs, U.S. Senate: Dietary goals for the United States, ed. 2, Washington, D.C., 1977, U.S. Government Printing Office.
50. Tryphonas, H., and Trites, R.: Food allergy in children with hyperactivity, learning disabilities and/or minimal brain dysfunction, Ann. Allergy **42:**22, 1979.
51. Rapp, D. J.: Does diet affect hyperactivity? J. Learning Disabilities **11:**56, 1978.
52. May, C. D.: Diagnosis of hypersensitivity to food. In Committee on Nutrition, American Academy of Pediatrics: Pediatric nutrition handbook, Evanston, Ill., 1979, American Academy of Pediatrics.

13

Special concerns of dietary intake during infancy and childhood

Common concerns related to food and nutrient intake during infancy and childhood include excessive energy intakes, food allergies, dental caries, and lactose malabsorption. Diets of children who modify their food intakes to control these conditions often need to be monitored for adequacy of nutrient intakes. In addition, parents and professionals frequently have questions about the long-term effects of nutrient intakes during childhood. These special concerns will be discussed in this chapter.

ENERGY BALANCE

Obesity is a frequent concern in clinics that serve adolescents. Lack of success in achieving sustained weight reduction of obese adolescents has focused attention on identifying children at risk and motivating families to alter life-styles and environmental and psychosocial factors that contribute to the development of this condition.

Obesity in childhood

Obesity is a major health hazard predisposing the affected adult to a greater risk of hypertension, cardiovascular disease, diabetes, gallbladder disease, and degenerative joint disorders than persons of normal weight. Obese adolescents face discrimination at college entrance, and obese adults are discriminated against in job placement and ad-

vancement.[1] Obese adolescents have been observed to exhibit psychosocial difficulties. They frequently have distorted body images and low self-esteem and may become socially isolated. They have been described as leading a "Cinderella-like" existence.[2]

Many obese children become obese adolescents and adults. Abraham and Nordsieck found that 80% of females and 86% of males who were overweight at ages 10 to 13 years were overweight 20 years later.[3] Retrospective investigations have shown that approximately 30% of the obese adults had a history of juvenile obesity.[4] Early-onset obesity is more severe and resistant to treatment than is obesity acquired later in life.[5]

Definition. Obesity is defined as an excessive deposition of adipose tissue. It differs from overweight, which implies only weight in excess of average for height. Overweight can result from increased lean body mass, adipose tissue, or both. Forbes has suggested that there may be two types of obesity in childhood and adolescence: one type characterized by increased lean body mass in addition to fat, a tendency for tallness, advanced bone age, and a history of overweight since infancy; and another type with no increase in lean body mass, normal bone age and height, and weight gain in the midchildhood or late childhood years.[6]

Weight greater than 20% of normal for

249

height is one criterion that has been used to define obesity. Such standards, although they show trends for populations, are not applicable to individual children. The use of weight standards tends to underestimate fatness in children less than 6 or 7 years of age and frequently overestimates adiposity in adolescents.[7] Diagnosis of grossly obese children is easily made by visual inspection. Recognition of less severely obese children versus those who are overweight because of increased muscle mass requires measurements that give indications of body composition. Identification of children who are overfat and are settled into patterns of growth indicative of future obesity requires that measurements of body composition be included in health examinations, just as other measurements of growth are obtained. As described in Chapter 1, standards for tricep fat-fold measurements with calipers have been published for all age groups. Use of these measurements to define greater than normal increases in adipose tissue of infants and children as they grow older will aid in identifying children for whom preventive measures should be applied.

Etiologic factors in obesity. Studies of rats and other animals have definitively shown that, in animals, genes carrying obese traits are transmitted to offspring. Mayer has described many genetic obesities including a hereditary hypoglycemia syndrome and a genetically controlled spontaneous degeneration of the hypothalamus.[8]

Definition of human genetic obesities has been more difficult because of the mixed racial heritage of most individuals and the many environmental factors known to contribute to obesity that cannot be controlled in studies. The high incidence of obesity among parents of obese children and the fact that early-onset obesity appears to be almost intractable lead one to believe that hereditary factors are important. Studies have shown

that 60% to 70% of obese adolescents have one or both obese parents,[9,10] and 40% of obese adolescents have obese siblings. Other studies have found that less than 10% of children of average-weight parents are obese.[11]

Seltzer and Mayer studied weight patterns of different body types. Using Sheldon's somatotypes they described obese adolescent females as more endomorphic and less ectomorphic than nonobese adolescent females.[12] Inherited body type may predispose children to obesity.

Inactivity is another factor known to be operative in the etiology of obesity. Obese adolescents and school-age children are less active than are those of normal weight. Most become obese by ingesting calorie intakes equivalent to or less than their peers. Activity patterns are acquired in childhood. Children learn to enjoy those activities in which their families and peers engage. Parents who enjoy hiking, swimming, and sports often teach their children to engage in and enjoy these physical activities. Parents who spend their hours at home urging their children to be still so that they can watch television or read reinforce inactivity and sedentary living.

As discussed in Chapter 1, there are indications that excessive weight gains during critical periods of development may result in deposition of excessive numbers of adipose cells with which individuals will live for their entire lives. Later reductions in weight result in reduction of the size of the adipose cells, not the number.[13] Questions have been raised as to the validity of this hypothesis.[14,15] It is, however, an interesting speculation that could provide an explanation for the difficulties encountered in efforts to effect weight reductions in those with juvenile-onset obesity.

Several researchers have reported increased birth weights of obese children compared to children of normal weight.[16,17] Others have found no differences in birth weights of the two groups of children. [18,19] Fisch, Bilek, and Ulstrom found that infants who were extremely obese at birth tended toward normal weight at ages 4 and 7 years but that an unusually high percentage retained their stocky physiques. Children who were very obese at ages 4 and 7 years tended to have had stocky physiques at birth. By age 7 years, however, they were joined in their obese and overweight status by a number of children who had normal physiques at birth. [20]

Infant feeding practices have been implicated as a factor in the etiology of obesity during childhood. Many authorities have suggested that bottle-fed infants are more likely to be overfed than are breast-fed infants, since parents have visual recognition of milk intakes and may encourage infants to empty their bottles. Infants fed nonfat milk or 2% milk consume appreciably more milk. It has been hypothesized that this may establish a pattern that will lead to excessive intakes of food in later life. [21] It has also been suggested that the addition of semisolid foods in the early weeks and months of life may result in excessive intakes of energy. Because ingestion of food is primarily reflexive prior to 4 months of age, infants fed semisolid foods with energy concentrations greater than milk (e.g., cereal mixed with formula, strained fruit, and meat) may have increased intakes of energy as compared to infants fed only milk; excessive weight gain may occur.

There has been concern that overfed and/or overweight infants will become programmed to excessive food intakes and obesity. This has not been proven true. Sveger found that only 4 of 23 obese and none of 26 overweight infants remained so at age 4 years. [22] Poskitt and Cole noted an incidence of 2.5% obesity and 11% overweight in a study of 203 4- to 5-year-old children.

Three of five obese children were obese as infants; however, only one in nine obese infants became obese preschoolers. [23] A study in a Swedish urban community found that only 10% of obesity in 7-year-old children could have been predicted from observations of weight gain during infancy. [24]

Interestingly, retrospective studies of obese adolescents have shown that a large percentage of them had feeding problems in infancy, and some had even been hospitalized for failure to gain weight. Seven of ten mothers of obese adolescents studied by Hammar and associates reported seeking advice about feeding their children during infancy at least six times. [2] Seven of the ten obese adolescents had had allergic reactions to food in late infancy and early childhood. Massengale found that 28% to 30% of 92 obese adolescents had histories of feeding problems in the first year of life. [25] Two children had had pyloric stenosis and eight had been hospitalized for poor weight gain or dehydration.

Psychosocial factors and parent-child interactions are important factors that may contribute to obesity in childhood. Children of unwanted pregnancies are often overfed to relieve parental feelings of guilt and ambivalence. [26] Anxious and insecure parents frequently overfeed children as expressions of their concern and love. They usually measure their success as parents by the amount of food their children eat and by how much weight they gain. As previously discussed, children who are reinforced for eating learn that eating pleases their parents; as a result food habits may be established that are conducive to obesity.

Food may be used to reward a desired behavior, to comfort an unhappy or frustrated child, or to compensate for a handicap or problem. These nonnutritive uses of food teach children to rely on food to compensate for emotional and social difficulties, a pattern that may continue throughout a lifetime.

Psychologic trauma has been observed to be another factor associated with the onset of obesity. Bruch noted that fear of hospitalization was associated with the onset of obesity in some children.[26] Kahn found a history of separation from their mothers in 32% of 72 obese children under 12 years of age. Fourteen of the children had experienced rapid weight gains that began shortly after the separations.[27]

Differences have been noted in the incidence of obesity among children from the lower and higher socioeconomic groups. Stunkard and associates, in studies in three Eastern cities, found that at age 6 years 29% of lower socioeconomic white girls were obese. Three percent of girls in the more affluent groups were obese. Differences in the prevalence of obesity fell to a minimum at age 12 years but continued through age 18 years. Obesity in males showed similar though less striking trends by age 6 years. The trend in males did not continue through childhood but was reversed by age 12 years, when the more affluent groups of white males had a greater incidence of obesity than did members of the lower socioeconomic group. By age 18 years the lower socioeconomic groups again showed a greater prevalence of obesity. Socioeconomic differences were not considered important in the genesis of obesity, but rather cultural pressures that encourage weight control were thought to be more operative in the more affluent group.[28]

Garn reported, from analysis of data compiled during the Ten State Nutrition Survey of 1968-1970 and the Preschool Nutrition Survey conducted by Owens and associates, that after the first few years of life and into adolescence the children of the poorest group were leaner and the children of the affluent group were fatter. The higher the socioeconomic status was the greater was the amount of adipose tissue. Females were fatter than males at all ages at comparable income levels. White children had more adiposity than blacks. In adults the relationship between fatness continued in males but reversed for females. Low-income female adults were fatter than those who had greater economic resources.[29]

The two studies obviously present conflicting results. The ten-state survey focused on a low-income population and included rural as well as urban individuals rather than a representative sample of the population. Stunkard and associates studied white schoolchildren in urban areas in the East.[28] Whether the populations studied are different or differences exist in the incidence of obesity in rural and urban children remains unknown.

Prevention of obesity. Regardless of its cause, obesity results when energy intakes exceed energy needs for growth, maintenance, and activity. Its manifestation is usually the result of small excesses of calorie intakes over expenditure for a period of weeks, months, or years. By monitoring rates of growth and deposition of adipose tissue, children can be identified who are accumulating more fat than would be anticipated, and measures to increase activity and/or decrease caloric intakes can be effected.

Adolescents make their own decisions about what and when they eat. Counseling must be directed to the teenagers themselves. Parents control the food available to younger children, create the environment that influences their acceptance of food, and can influence energy expenditure by the opportunities they create for physical activity for their children. It may be important to explore first with parents their reason for encouraging children to consume amounts of food that result in rapid weight gain. Some parents may not recognize that their expectations for the quantity of food they encourage their children to consume are excessive and that the "chubby" child is not necessarily the healthy child. Others may need to resolve their feelings of ambivalence and the need for their children to depend on them.

The activity pattern of both the child and the family should be explored; it may be important to help parents find ways of increasing their child's level of activity. Parents who live in apartments often reinforce sedentary activities to reduce the noise level and complaints from neighbors. Those who live in one-family dwellings may have limited space for activities for children. City park departments, preschools, and schools frequently have programs that offer opportunities for increases in children's activities.

It is important to remember that the range of appropriate energy intakes at any given age is large. Overweight children and children with familial trends to obesity may need fewer calories than their peers. Griffith and Payne found that normal weight 4- to 5-year-old children of obese parents expended 1174 kcal/day as compared to 1508 kcal/day expended by children of the same size and age of normal weight parents. It was interesting that children of normal weight parents expended twice as much energy in physical activity as did those of obese parents.[30] Families of children with a familial tendency to obesity may need help in identifying the kinds and amounts of food that provide an energy intake that will support normal growth and weight gain.

Nutrition counseling should be family oriented and based on normal nutrition, emphasizing foods that provide a balance of nutrients as well as appropriate calorie intakes. Families will need to realize that efforts are directed at reduction in rates of weight gain and are not intended to effect weight loss. They must recognize that the food available and the models set for their child will determine the child's response to

efforts to control weight gain. Family meals may need to be modified to include fewer fried foods, less gravy, and fewer rich desserts. Parents and siblings may have to modify their own eating practices to set appropriate examples. Teachers, baby-sitters, and day-care workers should be alerted to and included in programs designed to control weight. Food experiences at school may need to be modified to exclude corn dripping with butter and chocolate cupcakes so frequently provided for special occasions. Low-calorie snacks such as raw fruits and vegetables can be provided instead of cookies, candy, and hot dogs. The use of food as reinforcers can be modified. Comparative energy values of snack foods are shown in Table 13-1.

Parents and their children need continuing support as they implement programs to prevent obesity and face incredible responses from other members of society. Well-meaning merchants and bankers who provide sweets for children should be encouraged to honor parent's requests to provide nonfood items as alternates. Neighbors, relatives, and other children's parents should support weight-control programs.

Children as they grow older must learn to exercise willpower in refusing amounts of food that result in a positive energy balance. The children themselves should receive positive reinforcement for control of weight gain. They need continuing support, education, and understanding as they grow older. An 8-year-old boy who has been on a weight control program since obesity was reversed at age 27 months expressed the difficulties encountered on such a program. He stated during a recent clinic visit, "It's really hard to control my weight. I'm often hungry. I can't eat as much as the other boys and my food is different from that of the other children in my class. I don't want to get fat, but I don't like being different." He, however, understands his program and knows he will receive

Table 13-1. Approximate energy value of common snack foods offered young children

Food	Portion size	kcal	Food	Portion size	kcal
Cheese cubes	¼ oz	25	Homogenized milk	3 oz	60
Hard-boiled egg	½ medium	36	Chocolate milk	3 oz	80
Frankfurter, 5″ by ¾″	1	133	Cauliflower buds	2 small	2
Pretzel, 3″ by ½″	1	20	Green pepper strips	2	2
Potato chips	10	114	Cucumber slices	3 large	2
Popcorn with oil and salt	1 cup	41	Cherry tomato	each	3
Bread stick, 4½″	1	38	Raw turnip slices	2	5
Saltines	1	12	Dill pickle, large	⅓	5
Graham cracker	2 squares	55	Apple wedges	¼ medium apple	20
Animal cracker	1	11	Banana	½ small	40
Brownie, 3″ by 1″ by ⅞″	1	97	Orange wedges	¼ medium orange	18
Chocolate cupcake	1	51	Orange juice	3 oz	35
Vanilla wafer	1	18	Grape juice	3 oz	60
Yogurt, plain	¼ cup	40	Lemonade	3 oz	40

From Adams, C. F.: Nutritive value of American foods in common units, Agriculture Handbook No. 456, Washington D.C., 1975, U.S. Department of Agriculture.

the guidance and support he desires from his family as he assumes control of his own food selection and management of weight control.

FOOD ALLERGIES IN INFANCY AND CHILDHOOD

The most common chronic condition affecting children is allergies. There is no agreement as to the prevalence of food allergies in children. Various investigators have reported incidences that range from 0.3% to 55%, the incidence reported varying with the criteria used for diagnosis and the population studied.[31] It is known that the incidence of food allergies is greatest during infancy. Children whose parents have allergic reactions to food are at a greater risk of having food allergies than are others.

Allergic responses to food

Manifestations of allergy result from antigen antibody reactions. Any tissue in the body can be the site of an immune reaction.

Reactions may occur in several sites in the same individual in response to a single allergen. Allergic responses to food result in a variety of symptoms that include rhinitis, diarrhea, vomiting, malabsorption, abdominal pain, urticaria, eczema, irritability, and hyperactivity. Symptoms are not specific for any food or for allergies alone. They mimic those of other clinical conditions.

Reactions may occur immediately after a food is eaten (within 4 hours) or may be delayed, occurring within 4 to 72 hours. Both types of responses may be observed in the same child but to different foods. The type of reaction experienced by different children may vary when the same food is ingested. The immediate reaction is thought to be caused by antigenic properties of intact protein, the delayed reaction by antigenic properties of compounds formed during digestion.

The frequency and severity of symptoms may be influenced by psychologic and physiologic stress, the quantity of food consumed at one time, and the frequency with which a food is ingested. Anxiety and worry are known to cause symptoms after ingestion of a food that can be consumed with no problem in the absence of psychologic stress. Allergic reactions to nonfood items such as pollens during hay fever season may cause allergic symptoms to foods that are normally non-allergenic. Reactions may be cumulative in nature. A food consumed spasmodically without any effect may cause symptoms when eaten regularly. Overindulgence in a food that can be consumed in small amounts without problem may cause allergic reactions.

Any food is potentially allergenic. Investigators do not agree on the most important food allergens. However, milk, wheat, eggs, and corn are consistently listed as the most allergenic foods. Other foods to which children are often allergic include chocolate, oranges, soy, legumes, rice, fish, beef, pork, and chicken.[32] Food additives such as flavorings and colors are other items that often cause allergic reactions. Diagnosed allergy to one food item often implies allergy to all food in its botanical group. For example, a child allergic to apples is often also allergic to pears.

The allergenicity of food may be reduced by cooking or processing. For example, some individuals allergic to fresh cow's milk tolerate evaporated milk. Others allergic to a raw fruit or vegetable may eat it without reaction when it is cooked.

Diets used in diagnosis. The variability of symptoms makes diagnosis of allergy a challenge for physicians. Skin tests may identify some food allergens but are generally considered unreliable. Diagnoses are made from dietary histories coupled with parents' perception of symptomatic responses to food, food diaries in combination with records of careful observations of symptoms, and elimination diets.

Detailed dietary histories give the physician indications of the foods and amounts commonly consumed. During the interview parents are questioned as to whether they suspect any food of causing symptoms. Parents appear to report immediate reactions well but often are unaware of foods that cause delayed reactions.

Food diaries are often requested. The parents are asked to record every food (including condiments) the child consumes for a week and to note every symptom the child manifests each day during that time. Careful scrutiny of such records gives the physician clues as to which foods to suspect.

If dietary histories and/or diaries indicate specific foods that appear to be allergenic to the child, these foods are restricted from the diet for a week or more. If improvement occurs, suspect foods are reintroduced and the child is observed for symptoms to confirm the diagnosis. If no improvement is noted, more severe restricted elimination diets are prescribed.

If an adverse reaction to specific foods is suspected, a double-blind challenge with the suspect foods is often used to confirm the diagnosis. Foods believed to cause allergic reactions are eliminated from the diet throughout the period of observation. When the individual is free of symptoms, capsules are filled with a dry form of the food to be tested. Wet foods are freeze-dried and powdered. Older children can generally be persuaded to swallow the capsule. For children under 6 years of age the wet or dry food is masked in other foods consumed. Capsules are given by someone unaware of their contents and the child remains under continuous surveillance in a hospital or office setting so that definitive observations can be made.

If no reaction is noted, repeated challenges using increasingly larger doses of the dry food are conducted until the child consumes 8 gm of the dry food. If no symptoms occur, a placebo control is not necessary. In case of doubt, capsules of glucose are administered and observations for symptoms continue.[33]

Elimination diets. Elimination diets restrict all but a very few foods. The foods included are those that have been proven to produce no reaction in most children. The Rowe cereal-free elimination diet, for example, permits ingestion of only the following foods: tapioca, white potatoes, sweet potatoes and yams, soy milk, lamb, bacon, lamb liver, chicken, apricots, grapefruit, lemon, peaches, pineapple, prunes, pears, cane or beet sugar, salt, sesame oil, soy bean oil, oleomargarine without milk, and unflavored gelatin. Baked products made with soy, potato, and lima bean flour prepared by specific recipes are permitted.[34] The diets are obviously very restrictive but must be carefully followed if food allergens are to be identified. Recipes are provided so that there can be some variability in the child's menu. The diets are followed for periods of 1 week to several months. If there is remission of symptoms, new foods are added at intervals of 5 to 7 days and the child is observed for reactions. If no change in symptoms is noted, a new elimination diet is designed.

A chemically defined product made from crystalline amino acids, glucose oligosaccharides, safflower oil, and recommended vitamins and minerals has been used as an elimination diet. Use of such a regimen until symptoms disappear may be difficult if children spend much of their time away from home and are exposed to food often.[35]

Dietary management of children with food allergies

When foods to which a child is allergic have been identified, they are eliminated from the diet. This may cause no difficulty if the child is allergic to only one food, particularly if it is not often mixed with others.

When food allergies are multiple and/or include foods basic to culturally accepted diets such as milk, wheat, and eggs, however, parents may need help in identifying hidden sources of the food, finding acceptable substitutes, including where these may be purchased, methods of preparation, and menu planning. They must learn to read ingredient statements on labels to avoid hidden sources of allergens and may need direction to cookbooks prepared for individuals with allergies.[36,37]

Parents should have instructions about the foods their children can consume as well as those that must be avoided. The child allergic to cow's milk is often offered a soy milk. Some children, however, are allergic to soy and/or the corn syrup that many manufacturers add to these products. Commercially manufactured or homemade meat-base formulas prepared according to a recipe devised by Rowe[34] may offer acceptable substitutes for infants. A formula constructed of pure amino acids (Nutramigen) may be required for some young infants. This formula is rarely acceptable to older infants and children.

Corn is extremely difficult to avoid. Corn starch is present in salad dressing, most sauces, many puddings and baking mixes, and a large number of other commercially prepared foods. Corn syrup is an ingredient that many manufacturers use in candy, sugar-coated cereals, and formula products.

If wheat is eliminated from the diet, alternate grains for baking must be found. Soy, rice, rye, and potato flours are often acceptable but require special recipes and a sizeable investment of the mother's time in food preparation. Commercially prepared pure rye and rice bread are available but cannot be found in many communities.

If eggs must be omitted, products containing eggs, including noodles, mayonnaise, and many ice creams, puddings, and baked products, are also eliminated. Recipes for baking without eggs are needed as well as commercial sources of ice cream and bread not glazed with egg.

Monitoring nutrient intake

Children with food allergies present potential areas of nutritional concern. Allergic reactions of the immediate type may make eating an aversive experience and cause children to reduce the number and quantity of foods they voluntarily consume. Malabsorption secondary to food allergies may increase nutritional deficits. In addition, parents anxious about the adequacy of an allergic child's food intake or response to a specific food convey that concern to the child who may use acceptance or rejection of food to control his or her parent's behavior. The monotony of the very restrictive diets may discourage children from consuming appropriate amounts of food. Energy and nutrient intakes of children with multiple food allergies should be carefully monitored. Diets of children who are allergic to milk should be monitored for calcium and vitamin D; diets of those allergic to citrus fruits should be monitored for vitamin C. The adequacy of intakes of the B vitamins should be checked when one or more cereal grains are limited.[38]

Children often spontaneously recover from food allergies by age 5 years. Foods to which a child is allergic should be singly introduced and the child observed for symptoms as he or she grows older. If allergic reactions to food continue, both parents and children need continuing support as they exercise willpower in refusing allergenic foods and select a combination of foods to support appropriate nutrient intakes.

CARBOHYDRATE

Dietary intakes of carbohydrate influence the development or control of dental caries. Children who have low lactase levels may find it necessary to limit their intakes of the carbohydrate lactose.

Dental caries

Dental caries, one of the most common nutritional diseases, affects children at all ages and income levels. As with other tissues, nutrition plays an important role during development in the acquisition of sound teeth and the surrounding structures that hold them and in the later susceptibility of the teeth to caries.[39] Once the tooth has erupted, the composition of the diet, the presence of acid-producing bacteria, and the buffering capacity of the saliva interact and result in the control or development of dental caries. Calcified dental tissues, unlike the long bones, which are subject to constant remodeling and repair, do not have the ability to repair themselves. Tooth destruction by decay is permanent.

Etiology. Dental plaque, a prerequisite for dental caries, has been described as a sticky, gelatinous mixture that contains water, salivary protein, desquamated cells, and bacteria.[40] The plaque bacteria, using energy derived from the catabolism of dietary carbohydrate, synthesize a number of toxic substances including enzymes that have the potential to degrade the enamel and dentin and are precursors of acidic fermentation products. These acids and enzymes cause demineralization of the hydroxyapatite of the enamel followed by proteolytic degradation and demineralization of the enamel and dentin. Cariogenic bacteria then invade the tooth, and caries result. The saliva, the pH of which is 6.5 to 7.0, acts as a buffer and provides mechanical cleansing of the teeth.

Sugar. It has been well documented from animal studies and studies of humans in institutions and of outpatients when intakes of sugar could be controlled that sucrose is the most cariogenic carbohydrate and that the incidence of caries can be reduced when the intakes of sucrose are reduced.[41-45] The role of the other sugars and carbohydrates, although known to be contributory, has been less well defined. Animal studies have produced different results, depending on the strain of animal used, the microbial flora, and the diet used. Glucose is thought to be the next most cariogenic sugar, and maltose, lactose, and fructose have been found to have equal effect.[46] Starch has been found to be the least cariogenic of the carbohydrates.

It appears that the cariogenicity of sucrose is related to the high energy of hydrolysis of the covalent bond between the molecules of glucose and fructose. This energy is utilized by cariogenic bacteria to synthesize, among other compounds, extracellular polysaccharides, which are considered important factors in the etiology of dental caries. The polysaccharides may be absorbed on the crystal surface in the enamel and promote growth of cariogenic and other bacteria, act as inflammatory agents, and provide material for the formation of simple cariogenic monosaccharides and bacteria.[46]

The presence of sucrose, or even the total amount of sucrose in the diet, is not the determining factor in the incidence of dental caries. An often-quoted study in an institution for the mentally handicapped in Sweden showed that the more important factors were the frequency with which the sugar is consumed and the adhesiveness of the food to the teeth.[47] The researchers who conducted this 5-year study showed that the consumption of sticky candy between meals produced a high increase in the incidence of dental caries, whereas the increase in incidence of dental caries from the addition of sugar-sweetened water at mealtime was small. When sucrose was fed in chocolate or bread, an intermediate increase in the incidence of caries was noted. It is clear from this and other studies that the length of time the food remains in the mouth and in contact with the tooth is important, as is the number of times a day sucrose is present in the mouth. Snacking at bedtime is especially effective in increasing dental caries. Reduction of the flow of saliva, which occurs during sleep, reduces the natural cleansing mechanism and permits greater fermentation of cariogenic material.[48] It has been proposed that the ingestion of foods that alter the buffering capacity of the saliva (e.g., milk and fats, which form a protective oily film on the tooth surface) may offer some protection for the teeth.[49,50]

Nursing bottle syndrome. A characteristic pattern of decay in infants and young children of all the upper and sometimes the lower posterior teeth, known as nursing bottle syndrome, is often observed in children who are given sweetened liquid by bottle at bedtime.[51,52] As children suck the tongue protrudes slightly from the mouth, covering the lower front teeth. Liquids are spread over the upper and lower posterior teeth. Sucking stimulates the flow of saliva, which washes the debris from the teeth and promotes the secretion of compounds that buffer the acids in the plaque. When children are awake they swallow the liquid quickly. However, if they fall asleep sucking stops, and the salivary flow and buffering are reduced. The sweetened liquid pools around the teeth not protected by the extended tongue and the bacterial plaque have contact with the carbohydrates during the hours of sleep.

Infant formulas, fruit juice, human milk, and cow's milk consumed when infants are falling asleep may cause this decay. To prevent this dental destruction it has been suggested that infants be held when feeding and burped and put to bed as soon as they fall asleep.[53]

Population difference in the incidence of dental caries. Some children appear to be more susceptible to dental caries than others. A study of Japanese, Hawaiian, and white children living in Hawaii showed that Hawaiian children were more affected by dental caries than were Japanese or white children and that the impact of sweet snacks between meals was greater on Hawaiian than on Japanese or white children.[54] In Detroit, Michigan, white children were found to have a much higher caries prevalence than blacks, while no difference was noted in caries prevalence in Columbia, South Carolina, between the races.[55]

Control. The less frequently sucrose-containing foods are consumed and the less ability the foods have to adhere to the teeth, the more positive will be the outlook for control of dental caries. Few children consume food in a three-meal-a-day pattern. In fact, it may be important for them to eat more frequently to consume sufficient calories and essential nutrients. To provide guidance in the selection of snack foods, researchers have defined the cariogenic potential of foods. They have studied the relationship of certain foods on the incidence of caries and the effect that specific foods have in lowering the pH of the dental plaque. The frequency of eating breads, rolls, and cereals has not been associated with an increase in dental caries, whereas the frequency of the consumption of candy and gum has been shown to increase the number and incidence of dental caries.[54] Cookies, cakes, pies, and candies have been shown to give profound falls in pH of the plaque and should be avoided for snacks. It is interesting that the researchers found the more acid-carbonated beverages to depress the pH less than apple and orange juice.[56]

A study of 147 junior high school students' snacking patterns in relation to caries production showed chocolate candy to be the most carious snack food selected. Children who consumed fruit drinks, cookies, or apples at bedtime and between meals had a significant caries increment during the year studied. No carious lesions developed in 47 children who had higher intakes of fruit juice and oranges and lesser use of sugar-sweetened chewing gum than the other children. As the amount of spending money a child had increased, the frequency of snacking increased.[7]

Children should be taught to select foods that provide the essential nutrients and to limit their consumption of cariogenic foods. The important between-meal snacks can be carefully planned to contribute nutrients without creating an oral environment conducive to tooth decay. Sweet foods as dessert items should be consumed as infrequently as is possible within the framework of acceptability to the child and family.

Lactose malabsorption and milk intolerance

Low levels of activity of intestinal lactase, the enzyme that hydrolyzes lactose, the carbohydrate in milk to glucose and galactose, have been reported in 60% to 100% of nonwhites and 0% to 35% of whites in the world's postweaning population. The response of individuals with lactase deficiency to the ingestion of milk varies. Some manifest no symptoms. Others experience symptoms of flatulence, bloating, and cramping and may have diarrhea a few hours after milk is ingested. The amount of milk that must be consumed at one time to produce symptoms ranges from less than 240 ml to 1000 ml. Many persons who are lactase deficient are not intolerant to lactose or to milk. Adults and older children with low lactase levels have usually consumed milk in infancy and early childhood without symptoms. The etiology of the low lactase activity is unknown. It has been hypothesized that it may be caused by a genetic factor with delayed expression. Others believe that the ability to hydrolyze lactose may be related to ecologic changes in populations exposed to dairying for the past thousands of years.[58]

It has been estimated that 70% of black

American adults and 10% to 15% of white Americans have a limited ability to hydrolyze lactose.[59] There is evidence that the onset of diminished levels of lactase occurs in childhood and adolescence. Paige, Bayless, and Graham found that 20% of black elementary schoolchildren refused at least half of the milk in their type A lunch. Seventy-seven percent of those who were classified as non-milk drinkers had evidence of low lactase levels when a lactose tolerance test was performed.[60]

Malabsorption. Unaffected individuals hydrolyze and absorb ingested lactose in the small intestine. If lactase activity is low, only a portion of the sugar will be hydrolyzed. Undigested lactose remains in the lumen of the intestine and has a hyperosmolar effect, drawing large amounts of fluid into the gut. As the sugar is transported to the ileocecal region and first part of the colon, it is attacked by the bacterial flora. Bacterial fermentation of lactose causes the production of carbon dioxide, hydrogen, and low molecular weight acids that interfere with the reabsorption of fluids and electrolytes. The increased fluid load and products of bacterial fermentation cause the symptoms of bloating, flatulence, and abdominal cramping. Diarrhea may also result.

Tests for disaccharide malabsorption. The most accurate way to confirm deficiency of a disaccharidase is measurement of the enzyme activity in the mucosa by a biopsy of the small intestine. Low lactase activity is diagnosed when there is less than 2 units of lactase activity/gm of wet mucosa.[61] Ratios of sucrase to lactase activity are also used to identify low lactase activity. Ratios of sucrase to lactase greater than 4:1 are indicative of diminished lactase activity.[62]

A more commonly used but less satisfactory test for disaccharide malabsorption is a carbohydrate tolerance test. The individual in a fasting state is given 2 gm of carbohydrate/kg of body weight dissolved in water. Blood glucose determinations are obtained while fasting and at half-hour intervals for 2 hours. Normal response to a lactose tolerance test is a rise of 25 mg/100 ml or more from a fasting state.[63] False-positive results indicative of lactose malabsorption may be found in as many as 25% of normal subjects because of delayed gastric emptying.[64] Lactase deficiency is confirmed when symptoms of incomplete digestion of carbohydrate occur.

Calloway, Murphy, and Bauer have shown that lactose-intolerant individuals have elevated concentrations of hydrogen in their breath after consuming lactose and have suggested that measurements of breath hydrogen are ideally suited for mass screening.[65]

Arvanitakis and associates have shown measurements of $^{14}CO_2$ expired 2 hours after the ingestion of isotopically labeled lactose to be a sensitive test for lactase deficiency in adults. The use of an isotope, however, prohibits its use with children.[66]

Lactose intolerance. Three types of lactose intolerance have been identified. Cases of congenital deficiencies of lactase in infancy have been described in which diarrhea continued as long as lactose was consumed but subsided when the carbohydrate was excluded from dietary intake.[67] Some of these affected infants develop normal lactase activities within months, suggesting temporary intestinal injury or delayed development of the enzyme.[68] Others have been described as having a rare inborn error of metabolism. Lactase is missing from birth throughout life even though the histology of the mucosa is normal.[69]

Deficiencies of all disaccharidases may occur secondary to diseases that damage the mucosal wall of the intestine, such as occurs in untreated celiac disease and may occur following a viral or bacterial gastrointestinal infection when diarrhea is prolonged.[70,71]

Lactase deficiency is commonly more severe than deficiencies of the other disaccharidases. Lactase is the last enzyme to return to normal activity after recovery. Protein malnutrition may result in a temporary deficiency of sugar-splitting enzymes.[71] Children with kwashiorkor often have severe diarrhea that improves when lactose is deleted from dietary intake. There have been reports of lactose intolerance in patients treated with antibiotics for long periods of time.[72] Secondary lactase deficiencies are usually temporary, and normal levels of lactase activity return in most persons when the disease is controlled. Offending sugars, however, should be omitted until treatment has effected a solution to the basic problem.

The other form of lactose intolerance found in many healthy populations is commonly acquired with age, being found infrequently in children under age 3 years. The prevalence of lactose malabsorption and intolerance increases with age and varies among ethnic groups. It was found that 29% of 116 black children 13 to 59 months of age had lactose malabsorption but only 18% had symptoms when lactose was ingested.[73] Other studies have shown 11% of 4- to 5-year-old, 50% of 6- to 7-year-old, and 72% of 8- to 9-year-old black children to be lactose intolerant.[74]

Reports also indicate that Mexican-American and Indian populations have a high incidence of lactase deficiency. In a study of 282 Mexican-American children Wateki, Weser, and Young documented that 18% of 2- to 5-year-old and 56% of 10- to 14-year-old children were lactose intolerant.[75] Studies of American Indian children have shown an increase in the incidence of lactose malabsorption from 20% in 3- to 5-year-old children to 70% of 13- to 19-year-old children.[76]

Lactose malabsorption is almost nonexistent in white preschoolers. An incidence of 30% in adolescence has been suggested.[77] Lebenthal, Antonowicz, and Schwachman,

after reviewing 172 intestinal biopsies of New England whites 6 weeks to 50 years of age, found no case of low lactase activity below 5 years. After 5 years of age, two groups were identified: 24.6% had low lactase levels, and the remainder had lactase levels equal to those in the first 3 years of life.[78]

Effect on nutrient bioavailability. When lactose remains unsplit and is not absorbed, there is obviously a loss of calories from this nutrient. The percentage of intake lost is unknown and probably unimportant unless milk provides the major portion of the child's food intake. No differences have been found in nitrogen balance among lactose-tolerant and lactose-intolerant adults who consumed milk or lactose-free milk when energy intakes were considered.[79]

Effect on milk intake. Bowie found nitrogen absorption depressed but retention similar in children with lactose-induced diarrhea who were fed milk in contrast to a disaccharide-free diet. Fat absorption was similar on both regimens. Calcium, magnesium, and phosphorus absorption have been reported to be unaffected by lactose intake in lactose-intolerant persons as compared to lactose-tolerant persons.[80] Lactose intolerance does not indicate intolerance to milk. Affected individuals often consume small amounts of milk without exhibiting symptoms. Some who experience bloating, cramping, and flatulence do not associate the symptoms with milk consumption. The production of symptoms depends on the amount of lactose consumed at one time. Reddy and Pershad have shown that if given in small quantities, lactase-deficient individuals may consume as much as 1 quart of milk/day without symptoms. Stephenson and Latham found that many lactose-intolerant individuals could consume 15 to 30 gm of lactose (1¼ to 2½ cups of milk) at a time with only mild symptoms of abdominal discomfort.[82] Ice-cold milk and milk consumed without food seem to cause greater discomfort than milk consumed with food and milk consumed at room temperature.[83]

Intakes of milk have been shown to be similar in a number of lactase-sufficient and lactase-deficient schoolchildren. No differences were found in milk intakes of lactose-tolerant and lactose-intolerant black children at ages 13 to 59 months, 6 to 7 years, and 8 to 9 years.[73,74] Likewise, no differences were noted in the amounts of milk consumed by lactose-tolerant and lactose-intolerant Mexican-American children.[75] Stephenson, Latham, and Jones found in a study of children in grades 1 to 6 from two schools that racial groups exhibited no differences in milk consumption. Students consumed an average of 6 oz of milk at school and reported drinking an average of 3 glasses of milk/day.[84]

Paige, Bayless, and Dellinger have shown that lactose-intolerant elementary schoolchildren who refused more than half of the milk provided by the school lunch had a maximum blood sugar rise of 12.3 mg/100 ml, whereas the lactose-intolerant children who drank over half of the milk provided had a maximum blood sugar rise of 18.4 mg/100 ml. When given a lactose tolerance test, it appeared that some lactose-intolerant children had sufficient levels to hydrolyze moderate amounts of milk sugar.[83] The blood sugar rise of lactose-intolerant individuals after a lactose challenge may define children who can consume moderate amounts of milk without problems.

Milk is an important source of protein, calcium, riboflavin, and vitamin A, and fortified milk is also a source of vitamin D in the diets of many children. Membership in a racial group known to have a high incidence of lactose intolerance in older children and adults is no indication for limitation of milk in children who do not manifest symptoms. Children who manifest symptoms should be encouraged to consume dairy products in which lactose has been fermented (e.g., yogurt, buttermilk, and cheese). Small amounts of milk may be well tolerated when consumed with meals. Lactose-free milks or milks treated with lactase are commercially available for children in whom symptoms are severe. Some children, however, have reported symptoms when whole, lactose-free, or lactose-hydrolyzed milk was consumed.[85] Lactose is added to many prepared foods. Parents of children with lactose intolerance should be directed to read labels carefully so that additional loads of lactose can be avoided. Diets of all children who limit their intakes of milk should be carefully monitored for vitamin D, and supplements should be prescribed if appropriate.

DIETARY FATS

Intakes of cholesterol and saturated fatty acids and food habits established in childhood are believed by some to be important factors in the development of coronary artery disease. In 1970 a subcommittee of the Inter-Society Commission for Heart Disease Resources recommended changes in the dietary patterns of all age groups.[86] This commission recommended that calorie intakes be adjusted to achieve and maintain normal weight and that cholesterol intakes not exceed 300 mg/day. The group urges that dietary fat contribute less than 35% of the total calories and that fat calories be equally divided among saturated, monounsaturated, and polyunsaturated sources. Other groups and researchers have not considered dietary modification during infancy and childhood appropriate.[87-90] Many investigators have stressed the experimental nature of dietary intervention, the lack of knowledge about the effects of long-term ingestion of diets rich in polyunsaturated fats, and the expense of such changes in dietary patterns. Others have hypothesized that cholesterol may be an essential nutrient in infancy.[91]

Hyperlipidemia

Both cholesterol and triglycerides in the plasma are derived from two sources, dietary intake and endogenous synthesis in the liver and intestines. Dietary cholesterol is absorbed in proportion to the amount consumed. Increases in intakes reduce only partially endogenous synthesis. Endogenous triglycerides are synthesized from carbohydrate, fatty acids, and a variety of two-carbon fragments.

All plasma lipids, cholesterol, triglycerides, and phospholipids are transported in the blood bound to protein, which solubilizes them. Four macromolecule families of plasma lipoproteins are found in the blood. *Chylomicrons* transport the major portion of dietary triglyceride. *Very low-density lipoproteins* (pre-β-lipoproteins) transport endogenous triglyceride. *Low-density lipoproteins* (β-lipoproteins) transport one-half to two-thirds of the total plasma cholesterol. *High-density lipoproteins* transport cholesterol and phospholipids. Low-density lipoprotein cholesterol is transported primarily to peripheral tissue including the smooth muscle of the arterial intima. High-density lipoprotein cholesterol travels through the capillary bed of peripheral tissue and acquires redundant-free cholesterol. It is ultimately carried to the liver, whence it is released and excreted.[92]

A series of genetically determined lipoprotein disorders have been identified. Frederickson, Levy, and Lees have described five hyperlipoproteinemias, each of which requires a different dietary modification.[93,94] Types I and II can be identified and treated during infancy and childhood. Types III, IV, and V are uncommon in childhood.

Type I is a rare disorder characterized by a deficiency of the enzyme lipoprotein lipase, which hydrolyzes chylomicron triglycerides. The disorder, inherited in an autosomal recessive pattern, can be identified in infancy.

There is a massive increase in chylomicrons circulating in the blood. Diets of children so affected must be reduced in total fat to as low a level as possible. Medium-chain triglycerides may be used to increase calorie intakes.

Type II, the most common of the genetic disorders, is characterized by increases in low-density lipoproteins with (type II-B) or without (type II-A) increases in very low-density lipoproteins. The defect is transmitted as an autosomal dominant trait. Homozygotes have cholesterol levels almost twice those of heterozygotes. Screening by determinations of cord blood lipoprotein cholesterol and extensive family studies have been reported to identify children at birth with this disorder. Children with familial type II hyperlipidemia respond to reductions in dietary cholesterol and maintain normal plasma cholesterol levels when they receive diets low in cholesterol and rich in polyunsaturated fats.[95]

Cholesterol concentrations, which are lower in cord blood than in maternal blood, rise after infants are fed. Infants fed human or cow's milk have higher serum cholesterol concentrations than those fed formulas containing corn and coconut oils or soy oil.[91] Several researchers have found that infants fed similarly after weaning from formula or breast milk have similar cholesterol concentrations in the preschool years.[96-98] They have concluded that earlier hypotheses based on studies with rats and pigs, which indicated that a cholesterol challenge in early infancy might be important in establishing a mechanism for low cholesterol levels in adults, are not applicable to humans.

Mean serum cholesterol concentrations rise by 3 to 4 years of age. This increase in total cholesterol is associated with an increase in high-density lipoproteins, not an increase in low-density lipoproteins.[99] Between 6 and 11 years of age no consistent changes in serum lipid or lipoprotein levels occur. There is a trend for total serum cholesterol to decrease and triglycerides to increase between 12 and 17 years of age; this is because low-density lipoprotein levels remain unchanged, whereas high-density lipoprotein levels decrease.[100] After 24 years there is a progressive rise in total cholesterol for the next 30 years.

Studies have suggested that 5% of children in the United States have serum cholesterol levels greater than 200 to 220 mg/dl. It appears that these individuals will maintain their elevated ranks throughout childhood and into adulthood, and they are considered at risk of developing coronary artery disease.[101,102] As they grow older they will be joined by others who enter the ranks of the at risk population.

Etiologic factors in atherosclerosis

Cardiovascular heart disease, considered epidemic in the western world, is responsible for more deaths in the United States than all other causes together. Atherosclerosis is responsible for more than 50% of the deaths resulting from cardiovascular heart disease.

Atherosclerosis is a major specific type of arteriosclerosis, involving primarily the large elastic and medium-sized arteries. Lipids similar to those circulating in the blood accumulate on the intima of the arteries, to which an accumulation of connective tissue and various blood products are added, and plaques result. A number of complications such as hemorrhage, thrombosis, or ulceration can occur in the atherosclerotic lesion and transform plaques into rough, complicated lesions. The plaques narrow the lumen of the arteries and may produce a deficiency of blood flow to some degree. They set the stage for complete occlusion.[103]

Fatty flecks and streaks are present by 3 to 5 months of age in the aortas of all children of all populations. As children age, the number and size of the streaks increase.[104] Studies of animals have suggested that dietary intakes of cholesterol and fatty acids determine whether the fatty deposits are reabsorbed, remain, or develop into atherosclerotic plaques.[105,106]

The average extent of intimal involvement is small in the first 10 years of life. After the first decade the extent of the intimal surface involved by fatty streaks increases rapidly. The lipid in the juvenile fatty streak is predominantly intracellular. There is minimal connective tissue. Black children have more extensive fatty streaks than do children of other ethnic groups. Females have more extensive streaking than do males. This is true in all populations studied, regardless of the incidence of atherosclerosis. After 25 to 29 years of age differences appear. Fatty streaks progress through continued lipid accumulation and lead to plaque formation. These fatty streaks contain much of their lipid in the form of extracellular accumulations in areas where intact cells are scanty. An increase in extracellular components of connective tissue also becomes apparent. Fibrous plaques then appear in a significant number of cases.

Autopsies of soldiers who died in the wars in Korea and Vietnam revealed a striking incidence of atherosclerotic plaques in males in their early twenties. Seventy-seven percent of 300 males killed in Korea were found to have evidence of atherosclerosis, ranging from minimal thickening to complete occlusion of one or more of the main artery branches.[107] Studies of Japanese natives undertaken at the same time revealed no cases in which plaque caused over 50% luminal narrowing. The amount of lipid in the plaques was less in the Japanese than in soldiers from the United States. The researchers concluded that diet was the primary source of the lipid.[108]

Autopsies of soldiers killed in Vietnam revealed a lesser but significant incidence of atherosclerosis. Of the casualties autopsied during this war 45% were found to have atherosclerosis, but only 5% had gross evidence of coronary artery involvement.[109]

A group of pathologists cooperating in the International Atherosclerosis Project examined 25,000 aortas and coronary arteries collected at autopsy in 14 countries. They found more extensive involvement in white men than in white women. Sex differences were not present in black populations.[110] Although the group found that the severity of atherosclerosis was associated with total energy intake derived from fat and the serum cholesterol concentrations in populations, they found no conclusive data that showed a relationship between atherosclerotic lesions and serum lipids and diets of individuals within populations. Their studies showed that the amount of lipid in the intima of the coronary artery of young adults predicted the extent of advanced lesions that occurred in later life in the same population.[110]

Risk factors associated with atherosclerosis. The major risk factors include elevated serum levels of low-density lipoprotein cholesterol, cigarette smoking, hypertension, obesity, sedentary life-style, and a family history of heart disease. All risk factors have been found to be independent and continuous variables. There is no arbitrary serum cholesterol level at which the risk of developing cardiovascular heart disease is increased. As the serum cholesterol level is increased, the risk for atherosclerosis increases. Also, the risk of developing atherosclerosis increases as the number of risk factors increases. Two or three risk factors increase the risk for atherosclerosis in an exponential manner.[111] For example, the obese individual with a moderately elevated serum cholesterol level who has hypertension and smokes cigarettes has a higher risk of developing atherosclerosis than the person who

has a more elevated serum cholesterol level but is lean, active, and does not smoke.

That elevated serum, low-density lipoprotein cholesterol and low serum high-density lipoprotein cholesterol concentrations are risk factors in the etiology of coronary artery disease is well documented. Populations that consume diets rich in cholesterol and saturated fats have higher serum cholesterol concentrations and higher incidences of and mortality rates from premature coronary heart disease than populations that consume diets low in cholesterol and saturated fat. The risk of developing premature atherosclerotic heart disease increases in any population group as the serum cholesterol concentration rises.[111] The Framingham study showed that the risk of myocardial infarction for men 30 to 49 years of age increased five times if cholesterol levels were greater than 260 mg/100 ml as compared to less than 220 mg/100 ml.[112]

Effect of dietary intervention. It has been proven that dietary alterations can reduce serum lipids. Reduction in intakes of dietary cholesterol reduce serum lipids 5% to 8%. Reductions in intakes of saturated fats accompanied by increases in intakes of polyunsaturated fats and reductions in cholesterol can reduce the serum cholesterol by 24%.[89] It has not been possible, however, to establish relationships in individuals between dietary consumption of fat and cholesterol and serum cholesterol levels.

Friedman and Goldberg found that 3-year-old children who had followed low-cholesterol, low–saturated fat diets from birth had serum cholesterol levels of 145 ± 4 mg/dl as compared to 154 ± 1/dl in children who had consumed the standard western diet.[96] Witschi and associates effected a 10% reduction in serum cholesterol levels in 3 weeks in free-living adolescents who followed dietary instructions.[113] Stein and associates reduced serum cholesterol levels 14% in 229 adolescent males who lived in a boarding school in South Africa with dietary intervention.[114]

Anderson, Lifschitz, and Friis-Hansen found a direct correlation between intakes of saturated fat and an inverse relation between the ratio of polyunsaturated to saturated fatty acids of the diet with serum cholesterol levels during infancy. However, they found no relationship between intakes of fat and serum lipid levels in 3- to 4-year-old children.[99]

It has been hypothesized that diet has little to do with the magnitude of risk factors.[115] Others have suggested that diets of all those studied contained excessive amounts of fat, cholesterol, and calories.[116] Still others believe that genetic control predominates in determining the magnitude of the risk factors, including intakes of cholesterol and saturated fats.[111]

Potential difficulties of dietary intervention. Several potential problems have been suggested from the consumption of diets low in cholesterol and rich in polyunsaturated fatty acids. Fomon has hypothesized that such diets in infancy may interfere with myelination of the brain because they do not contain preformed cholesterol.[91] Schubert has pointed out that increases in intakes of polyunsaturated fatty acids increase the requirement of vitamin E.[90] Other suggested consequences of the use of diets high in polyunsaturated fatty acids are increased incidences of gallstones and cancer of the colon.[117,118]

Many questions remain unanswered. Although there is a proven relationship between serum cholesterol and dietary intakes of fat in populations, no association has been found between dietary habits and serum lipid levels or coronary lesions in individuals within populations. It remains to be proven if reductions in serum lipid concentrations can delay the onset of atherosclerosis. The variability in response of individuals to dietary fat is as yet unexplained, although there is a large body of data that suggest genetic control. There are those who believe that serum lipid disorders originate in childhood and think that food habits developed during that time should be patterned to acceptance and selection of diets low in cholesterol and saturated fats and rich in polyunsaturated fats.[119] Others believe that efforts directed toward prevention of atherosclerosis should be focused on the adolescent and young adult.[104] Still others think that dietary intervention should be directed only to susceptible individuals.[88]

There is no difference of opinion that dietary intervention is appropriate for individuals in whom hyperlipoproteinemia has been identified or who have proven coronary artery disease. All agree that obesity and overweight should be discouraged at all ages. The Committee on Nutrition of the American Academy of Pediatrics has recommended that the effect of dietary intervention be tested in children with familial type II hyperlipoproteinemia before it is recommended for all those in the population.[87] It is apparent that until many questions are answered, recommendations for modification of dietary intakes of fat and cholesterol should be individualized to the needs of each child and family.

SALT INTAKE

Essential hypertension, another risk factor in cardiovascular heart disease, is also a major health problem affecting 20% of adults over 40 years of age. Epidemiologic studies have suggested that as with hyperlipidemia, genetic and environmental factors interact to determine an individual's susceptibility to the disorder. Salt has been implicated as one factor that may play a role in the etiology of hypertension.

Success in reducing blood pressure in hypertensive patients with the low-sodium rice diet designed by Kempner caused some researchers to hypothesize that excessive salt intakes could cause hypertension. Dahl became so convinced that salt intakes were important in the development of hypertension that he devoted his life to this research. He studied the effect of salt intakes on thousands of rats, the effect of reduced sodium intake on hypertensive patients, and the relationship of sodium intakes to the incidence of hypertension in populations.[120]

Evidence from animal studies

Meneely and associates induced hypertension in rats by mixing salt with their food and allowing them to consume as much water and food as they wished.[121] They studied six groups of rats, each of which was fed an increasing amount of salt, and found that as sodium chloride intakes increased, elevations in blood pressures increased. Hypertension developed early in those animals who consumed the highest salt intakes. Although increases in blood pressure of groups of animals were related to the level of salt intakes, individual variations within groups were noted. They later fed diets that included extra amounts of salt to three groups of older animals who had been maintained on the basic chow throughout their lives. Elevation in blood pressure did occur, but increases were always less than those of the young animals who ate the same rations.[122]

Dahl and associates found that in unselected rats, blood pressure increases in response to high salt intakes ranged from none to gradually increasing blood pressures, including the malignant phase. Some rats died from hypertension within a few months. There was no increase in blood pressure in one-fourth of the animals in response to increased salt ingestion. The other animals developed increases in blood pressure that were associated with increasing morbidity and mortality.[123]

In successive generations rats were inbred and a strain of rats genetically susceptible to salt was developed. It was found that increased salt intakes of these animals during the first 12 to 13 months after weaning produced hypertension that was sustained regardless of later reductions in sodium intakes. Control rats fed low-sodium mixtures developed no hypertension.[124] Dahl concluded that salt intakes in infancy and early childhood may be more critical than those in later life to persons genetically determined to be responsive to salt intakes. In 1963 he fed those rats bred to be genetically sensitive to salt commercially prepared salted infant foods. Five of seven rats developed hypertension, whereas none of the seven controls who were fed low-sodium diets developed the disorder.[125] At that time he suggested that there may be groups of human infants with similar genetic potentials who are at risk for induced hypertension from salt intakes in early life. He advocated reductions in salt intakes in infancy.

Studies of populations

Dahl studied five population groups whose lifetime salt intakes varied from 4 to 26 gm/day and found that as average salt intakes increased the incidence of hypertension increased.[120]

Gleibermann reviewed studies of 27 populations. Sodium intakes had been estimated by urinary excretion of sodium for 24 hours in some and by estimated salt intakes in others. Her statistical analysis of these studies suggested a direct relationship between salt intakes and blood pressure across population lines.[126]

Oliver, Cohen, and Neel found that blood pressure in Yanomamo Indians who add no salt to their diets failed to increase with age but remained low throughout life.[127]

The relationship of salt intakes of individuals to blood pressure has not been established. Dahl found fewer hypertensive adults among those who salted foods lightly than among those who salted foods heavily.[128] Researchers in the Framingham study were unable to find a correlation between salt intake and blood pressure.[129] Prior and associates and Miall found no relationship between salt intakes and blood pressure of individuals in a Welsh community and a Polynesian group.[130,131]

It appears that some individuals are very sensitive to intakes of salt, whereas others experience no effect.

Salt and infants and children

During the first year of life intakes of sodium increase as infants consume more milk; the increase is more rapid as they begin to consume semisolid foods. In response to concern about the quantity of salt added to commercially prepared infant foods, in 1971 a subcommittee of the Food Protection Committee of the Food and Nutrition Board reviewed the studies and concluded that although the level of salt added to infant foods was not harmful, neither was it beneficial. The subcommittee recommended that the level of salt added to infant foods be reduced and that the upper limit of salt added be 0.25%.[132] However, concern continued until the addition of salt to commercially prepared infant foods was discontinued by all manufacturers.

Many parents make their own infant foods from a variety of foods prepared and seasoned for the family. Studies of semisolid infant foods prepared by 36 mothers showed that they contain 1005% more salt than commercially prepared infant foods.[133]

As the transition is made to table food, salt intakes will reflect family food habits and cultural patterns. The Committee on Nutrition of the American Academy of Pediatrics has pointed out that increasing use of convenience foods has given the food industry a major role in determining salt intakes.[134]

It appears that salting habits are unrelated to a taste threshold or an inborn taste for sodium chloride. Lauer and associates studied three groups of children 11 to 16 years of age whose blood pressures were average, less than the fifth percentile, or equal to or greater than the ninety-fifth percentile. They found no difference in salt threshold or preference in the three groups.[135]

Fomon, Thomas, and Filer studied the acceptance of salted and unsalted foods by 4- to 7-month-old infants. They found that infants accept equivalent amounts of salted and unsalted foods. It appears that a taste for salt is acquired, not inborn.[136]

Humans adapt to a wide range of sodium intakes by varying excretion in relation to intake and nonrenal losses. The Committee on Nutrition of the American Academy of Pediatrics has stated that safe limits for normal children appear to be between 8 and 100 mEq/day.[134] They have recommended that efforts be directed toward reducing or avoiding increases in current levels of salt intakes. Dietary therapy should be individualized to children with identified hypertension and those with family histories of hypertension who may or may not derive benefits from reductions in sodium intakes. It is important to remember that iodized salt is a major source of iodine in the United States. Intakes of children who consume low-sodium diets should be carefully monitored for iodine. A palpable goiter has been noted in two adolescent females whose family had adopted a low-sodium dietary intake because of diagnosed hypertension in the father.

REFERENCES
Obesity

1. Mayer, J.: Overweight causes, cost, and control, New Jersey, 1968, Prentice-Hall, Inc.
2. Hammar, S. L., and others: An interdisciplinary study of adolescent obesity, J. Pediatr. **80:**373, 1972.
3. Abraham, S., and Nordsieck, M.: Relationship of

excess weight in children and adults, Public Health Rep. **75:**263, 1960.

4. Mullins, A. G.: The prognosis in juvenile obesity, Arch. Dis. Child. **33:**307, 1958.

5. Lloyd, J. K., Wolff, O. H., and Whelen, W. S.: Childhood obesity, a long term study of height and weight, Br. Med. J. **2:**145, 1961.

6. Forbes, G. B.: Lean body mass and fat in obese children, Pediatrics **34:**308, 1964.

7. Weil, W. B.: Current controversies in childhood obesity, J. Pediatr. **91:**175, 1977.

8. Mayer, J.: Some aspects of the problem of regulation of food intakes and obesity, N. Engl. J. Med. **274:**610, 1966.

9. Angel, J. L.: Constitution in female obesity, Am. J. Phys. Anthropol. **7:**433, 1949.

10. Rony, H.: Obesity and leanness, Philadelphia, 1940, Lea & Febiger.

11. Gurney, R.: The hereditary factor in obesity, Arch. Intern. Med. **57:**557, 1936.

12. Seltzer, C. C., and Mayer, J.: Body build and obesity—who are the obese? J.A.M.A. **189:**677, 1964.

13. Knittle, J. L.: Obesity in childhood: a problem of adipose tissue development, J. Pediatr. **81:**1048, 1972.

14. Widdowson, E., and Shaw, W. T.: Letters to the editor: full and empty fat cells, Lancet **2:**905, 1973.

15. Ashwell, M., and Garrow, J. S.: Letters to the editor: full and empty fat cells, Lancet **2:**1036, 1973.

16. Shukla, A., and others: Infantile overnutrition in the first year of life: a field study of Dudley, Worcestershire, Br. Med. J. **4:**507, 1972.

17. Sveger, T., and others: Nutrition, overnutrition, and obesity in the first year of life in Malmö, Sweden, Acta Paediatr. Scand. **64:**635, 1975.

18. Wolff, O. H.: Obesity in childhood: a study of the birth weight, the height, and the onset of puberty, Q. J. Med. **24:**109, 1955.

19. Heald, F. P., and Hollander, R. J.: The relationship between obesity in adolescence and early growth, J. Pediatr. **67:**35, 1965.

20. Fisch, R. O., Bilek, M. K., and Ulstrom, R.: Obesity and leanness at birth and their relationship to body habitus in later childhood, Pediatrics **56:**521, 1975.

21. Fomon, S. J., and others: Influence of formula concentration on calorie intake and growth of normal infants, Acta Paediatr. Scand. **64:**172, 1975.

22. Sveger, T.: Does overnutrition or obesity during the first year affect weight at age four?, Acta Paediatr. Scand. **67:**465, 1978.

23. Poskitt, E. M. E., and Cole, T. J.: Do fat babies stay fat? Br. Med. J. **1:**7, 1977.

24. Mellbin, T., and Vuille, J. C.: Physical development at 7 years of age in relation to velocity of weight gain in infancy with special reference to incidence of overweight, Br. J. Prev. Soc. Med. **27:**225, 1973.

25. Massengale, O. N.: The obese adolescent observations on etiology management prevention, Clin. Pediatr. **4:**649, 1965.

26. Bruch, H.: Obesity in childhood. III. Physiologic and psychologic aspects of food intake of obese children, Am. J. Dis. Child. **59:**739, 1940.

27. Kahn, E. J.: Obesity in children: identification of a group at risk in a New York ghetto, J. Pediatr. **77:**771, 1970.

28. Stunkard, A., and others: Influence of social class on obesity and thinness in children, J.A.M.A. **221:**579, 1972.

29. Garn, S. M., with Clark, D. C., and Guire, K. E.: Growth, body composition and development of obese and lean children. In Winick, M., editor: Childhood obesity, New York, 1975, John Wiley & Sons, Inc.

30. Griffith, M., and Payne, P. R.: Energy expenditure in small children of obese and non-obese parents, Nature **260:**698, 1976.

Food allergies

31. Fontana, V. J.: Practical management of the allergic child, New York, 1969, Appleton-Century-Crofts.

32. Speer, F.: Management of food allergy. In Speer, F., and Dockhorn, R. J.: Allergy and immunology in children, Springfield, Ill., 1973, Charles C Thomas, Publisher.

33. May, C. D., and Bock, S. A.: A modern clinical approach to food hypersensitivity, Allergy **33:**166, 1978.

34. Rowe, A. H., and Rowe, A.: Food allergy, its manifestations and control and the elimination diets: a compendium, Springfield, Ill., 1972, Charles C Thomas, Publisher.

35. Hughes, E. C.: Use of a chemically defined diet in the diagnosis of food sensitivities and the determination of offending foods, Ann. Allergy **40:**393, 1978.

36. Conrad, M. L.: Allergy cooking, New York, 1955, Thomas Y. Crowell Co., Inc.

37. Little, B.: Recipes for allergies, New York, 1968, Vantage Press, Inc.

38. Feeney, M. C.: Nutritional and dietary management of food allergies in children, Am. J. Clin. Nutr. **22:**103, 1969.

Carbohydrate and dental caries

39. Shaw, J. H., and Sweeney, E. A.: Nutrition in relation to dental medicine. In Goodhart, R. S., and

Shils, M. E., editors: Modern nutrition in health and disease, ed. 6, Philadelphia, 1980, Lea & Febiger, p. 733.

40. Nizel, A. E.: Nutrition in preventive dentistry: science and practice, Philadelphia, 1972, W. B. Saunders Co.

41. Guggenheim, B., and others: The cariogenicity of different dietary carbohydrates tested on rats in relative gnotobiosis with a streptococcus producing extracellular polysaccharide, Helv. Odontol. Acta **10**:101, 1966.

42. Frostell, G., Keyes, P. H., and Larson, R. H.: Effect of various sugars and sugar substitutes on dental caries in hamsters and rats, J. Nutr. **93**:65, 1967.

43. Harris, R.: Biology of the children of Hopewood House, Bowral Australia, observations on dental caries experience extending five years (1957-1961), J. Dent. Res. **42**:1387, 1963.

44. Templeman, A. J.: The dietary control of dental caries, Aust. Dent. J. **9**:163, 1964.

45. Jay, P.: The role of sugar in the etiology of caries, J. Am. Dent. Assoc. **27**:293, 1940.

46. Makinen, K. K.: The role of sucrose and other sugars in the development of dental caries: a review, Int. Dent. J. **22**:363, 1972.

47. Gustafson, B. E., and others: The Vipeholm dental caries study: the effect of different levels of carbohydrate intake on dental caries in 436 individuals observed for five years, Acta Odontol. Scand. **11**:232, 1954.

48. Palmer, J. D.: Dietary habits at bedtime in relation to dental caries in children, Br. Dent. J. **130**:288, 1971.

49. Weiss, M. E., and Bibby, B. G.: Effects of milk on enamel solubility, Arch. Oral Biol. **11**:49, 1966.

50. Williams, W. L., Broquist, H. P., and Snell, E. E.: Oleic acid and related compounds on growth factors for lactic acid bacteria, J. Biol. Chem. **170**:619, 1947.

51. Fass, E. N.: Is bottle feeding of milk a factor in dental caries? J. Dent. Child. **29**:245, 1962.

52. Finn, S. B.: Dental caries in infants, Curr. Dent. Concepts **1**:35, 1969.

53. Gardner, D. E., Norwood, J. R., and Eisenson, J. E.: At-will breastfeeding and dental caries, J. Dent. Child. **13**:186, 1977.

54. Hankin, J. H., Chung, C. S., and Kau, M. C. W.: Genetic and epidemiologic studies of oral characteristics in Hawaii's schoolchildren: dietary patterns and caries prevalence, J. Dent. Res. **52**:1079, 1973.

55. Bagramian, R. A., and Russell, A. L.: Epidemiologic study of dental caries experience and between meal eating patterns, J. Dent. Res. **52**:342, 1973.

56. Edgar, W. M., and others: Acid production in plaque after eating snacks: modifying factors in food, J. Am. Dent. Assoc. **90**:418, 1975.

57. Clancy, K. L., and others: Snack food intakes of adolescents and caries development, J. Dent. Res. **56**:568, 1977.

Lactose malabsorption and milk intolerance

58. Simoons, F. J.: The geographic hypothesis and lactose malabsorption, a weighing of the evidence, Dig. Dis. **23**:963, 1978.

59. Rosenweig, N. S.: Diet and intestinal enzyme adaptation: implications for gastrointestinal disorders, Am. J. Clin. Nutr. **28**:648, 1975.

60. Paige, D. M., Bayless, T. M., and Graham, G. G.: Milk programs: helpful or harmful to Negro children? Am. J. Public Health **62**:1486, 1972.

61. Protein Advisory Group of the United Nations: Low lactase activity and milk intake, N.Y. P.A.G. Bull., vol. II, no. 2, Spring 1972.

62. Johnson, J. D., Kretchmer, N., and Simons, F. J.: Lactose malabsorption: its biology and history, Adv. Pediatr. **21**:197, 1974.

63. Ament, M. E.: Malabsorption syndromes in infancy and childhood, J. Pediatr. **81**:685, 867, 1972.

64. Newcomer, A. D., and McGill, D. B.: Lactose tolerance test in adults with normal lactase activity, Gastroenterology **50**:340, 1966.

65. Calloway, D. H., Murphy, E. L., and Bauer, D.: Determination of lactose intolerance by breath analysis, Am. J. Dig. Dis. **14**:811, 1969.

66. Arvanitakis, C., and others: Lactase deficiency—a comparative study of diagnostic methods, Am. J. Clin. Nutr. **30**:1597, 1977.

67. Levin, B., and others: Congenital lactose malabsorption, Arch. Dis. Child. **45**:173, 1970.

68. Burke, V., Kerry, K. R., and Anderson, C. M.: The relationship of dietary lactose to refractory diarrhea in infancy, Aust. Paediatr. J. **1**:147, 1965.

69. Holzel, A.: Sugar malabsorption due to deficiency of disaccharidase activity and of monosaccharide transport, Arch. Dis. Child. **42**:341, 1967.

70. Plotkin, G. R., and Isselbacher, K. J.: Secondary disaccharidase deficiency in adult celiac disease (non tropical sprue) and other malabsorption states, N. Engl. J. Med. **271**:1033, 1964.

71. Chandrasekaran, R., and others: Carbohydrate intolerance in infants with acute diarrhea and its complication, Acta Paediatr. Scand. **64**:483, 1975.

72. Bowie, M. D., Brinkman, G. L., and Hansen, J. D. L.: Acquired disaccharide intolerance in malnutrition, J. Pediatr. **66**:1083, 1965.

73. Paige, D. M., and others: Lactose malabsorption in preschool black children, Am. J. Clin. Nutr. **30**:1018, 1977.

74. Garza, C., and Scrimshaw, N. S.: Relationship of lactose intolerance to milk intolerance in young children, Am. J. Clin. Nutr. **29:**192, 1976.
75. Wateki, C. E., Weser, E., and Young, E. A.: Lactose malabsorption in Mexican children, Am. J. Clin. Nutr. **29:**19, 1976.
76. Caskey, D. A., and others: Effects of age on lactose malabsorption in Oklahoma native Americans as determined by breath H$_2$ analysis, Am. J. Dig. Dis. **22:**113, 1977.
77. Committee on Nutrition, American Academy of Pediatrics: The practical significance of lactose intolerance in children, Pediatrics **62:**240, 1978.
78. Lebenthal, E., Antonowicz, I., and Schwachman, H.: Correlation of lactase activity, lactose tolerance and milk consumption in different age groups, Am. J. Clin. Nutr. **28:**595, 1975.
79. Calloway, D. H., and Chenoweth, W. L.: Utilization of nutrients in milk and wheat-based diets by men with adequate and reduced abilities to absorb lactose. I. Energy and nitrogen, Am. J. Clin. Nutr. **26:**939, 1973.
80. Bowie, M. D.: Effect of lactose-induced diarrhea on absorption of nitrogen and fat, Arch. Dis. Child. **50:**363, 1975.
81. Reddy, V., and Pershad, J.: Lactase deficiency in Indians, Am. J. Clin. Nutr. **25:**114, 1972.
82. Stephenson, B. S., and Latham, M. C.: Lactose intolerance and milk consumption: the relationship of tolerance to symptoms, Am. J. Clin. Nutr. **27:**296, 1974.
83. Paige, D. M., Bayless, T. M., and Dellinger, W. S.: Relationship of milk consumption to blood glucose rise in lactose intolerant individuals, Am. J. Clin. Nutr. **28:**677, 1975.
84. Stevenson, L. S., Lathem, M. C., and Jones, D. V.: Milk consumption by black and by white pupils in two primary schools, J. Am. Diet. Assoc. **71:**258, 1977.
85. Paige, D. M., and others: Lactose hydrolyzed milk, Am. J. Clin. Nutr. **28:**818, 1975.

Fats

86. Atherosclerosis Study Group and Epidemiology Study Group of the Inter-Society Commission for Heart Disease Resources: Primary prevention of the atherosclerotic diseases, Circulation **42:**A-55, 1970.
87. Committee on Nutrition, American Academy of Pediatrics: Childhood diet and coronary heart disease, Pediatrics **49:**305, 1972.
88. Mitchell, S., and others: The pediatrician and atherosclerosis, Pediatrics **49:**165, 1972.
89. North, A. F.: Should pediatricians be concerned about children's cholesterol levels? Clin. Pediatr. **14:**439, 1975.
90. Schubert, W. K.: Fat nutrition and diets in childhood, Am. J. Cardiol. **31:**581, 1973.
91. Fomon, S. J.: A pediatrician looks at early nutrition, Bull. N.Y. Acad. Med. **47:**569, 1971.
92. Lewis, B.: Normal and abnormal lipid metabolism in children, Postgrad. Med. J. **54:**181, 1978.
93. Frederickson, D. S., Levy, R. I., and Lees, R. S.: Fat transport in lipoproteins—an integrated approach to mechanisms and disorders, N. Engl. J. Med. **276:**34, 94, 148, 215, 273, 1967.
94. Levy, R. I., and Rifkind, B. M.: Diagnosis and managements of hyperlipoproteinemia in infants and children, Am. J. Cardiol. **31:**547, 1973.
95. Tsang, R. C., Fallat, R. W., and Glueck, C. J.: Cholesterol at birth and age 1: comparison of normal and hypercholesterolemic neonates, Pediatrics **53:**458, 1974.
96. Friedman, G., and Goldberg, S. J.: Concurrent and subsequent serum cholesterols of breast and formula-fed infants, Am. J. Clin. Nutr. **28:**42, 1975.
97. Glueck, C. J., and others: Plasma and dietary cholesterol in infancy: effects of early low or moderate dietary cholesterol intake on subsequent response to increased dietary cholesterol, Metabolism **21:**1181, 1972.
98. Hodgson, P. A., and others: Comparison of serum cholesterol in children fed high, moderate, or low cholesterol milk during neonatal period, Metabolism **25:**739, 1976.
99. Anderson, G. E., Lifschitz, C., and Friis-Hansen, B. F.: Dietary habits and serum lipids during the first 4 years of life, Acta Paediatr. Scand. **68:**165, 1979.
100. Morrison, J. A., and others: Lipids and lipoproteins in 927 schoolchildren, ages 6 to 17 years, Pediatrics **62:**990, 1978.
101. deGroot, I., and others: Lipids in school children, aged 6-17: upper normal limits, Pediatrics **60:**437, 1977.
102. Berenson, G., and others: Serum high density lipoprotein and its relation to cardiovascular disease risk factor variables in children—the Bogalusa Heart Study, Lipids **14:**91, 1979.
103. Strong, J. P., and others: Pathology and epidemiology of atherosclerosis, J. Am. Diet. Assoc. **62:**262, 1973.
104. McMillan, G. C.: Development of arteriosclerosis, Am. J. Cardiol. **31:**542, 1973.
105. Armstrong, M. L., Warner, E. D., and Connor, W. E.: Regression of coronary atheromatosis in rhesus monkeys, Circ. Res. **27:**59, 1970.
106. Wissler, R. W., and others: Atherogenesis in the cebus monkey, Arch. Pathol. **74:**312, 1962.

107. Enos, W. F., Holmes, R. H., and Beyer, J. C.: Coronary disease among United States soldiers killed in action in Korea, J.A.M.A. **152**:1090, 1952.

108. Enos, W. F., Beyer, J. C., and Holmes, R. H.: Pathogenesis of coronary disease in American soldiers killed in Korea, J.A.M.A. **158**:912, 1955.

109. McNamara, J. J., and others: Coronary artery disease in combat casualties in Vietnam, J.A.M.A. **216**:1185, 1971.

110. Geer, J. C., and others: Histologic characteristics of coronary artery fatty streaks, Lab. Invest. **18**:565, 1968.

111. Hatch, F. T.: Interactions between nutrition and heredity in coronary heart disease, Am. J. Clin. Nutr. **27**:80, 1974.

112. Dawber, T. R., and others: The epidemiology of coronary heart diseases: the Framingham inquiry, Proc. R. Soc. Med. **55**:265, 1962.

113. Witschi, J. C., and others: Family cooperation and effectiveness in a cholesterol lowering diet, J. Am. Diet. Assoc. **72**:384, 1978.

114. Stein, E. A., and others: Lowering of plasma cholesterol levels in free-living adolescent males: use of natural and synthetic polyunsaturated foods to provide balanced fat diets, Am. J. Clin. Nutr. **28**:1204, 1975.

115. Connor, W. E., and Connor, S. L.: The key role of nutritional factors in the prevention of coronary heart disease, Prev. Med. **1**:49, 1972.

116. Gotto, A. M., and Scott, L.: Dietary aspects of hyperlipidemia, J. Am. Diet. Assoc. **62**:617, 1973.

117. Sturdevant, R. A. L., Pearce, M. L., and Dayton, S.: Increased prevalence of cholelithiasis in men ingesting a serum cholesterol–lowering diet, N. Engl. J. Med. **288**:24, 1973.

118. Rose, G., and others: Colon cancer and blood cholesterol, Lancet **1**:181, 1974.

119. Breslow, J. L.: Pediatric aspects of hyperlipedemia, Pediatrics **62**:510, 1978.

Salt and hypertension

120. Dahl, L. K.: Salt and hypertension, Am. J. Clin. Nutr. **25**:231, 1972.

121. Meneely, G. R., and others: Chronic sodium chloride toxicity in the albino rat. II. Occurrence of hypertension and a syndrome of edema and renal failure, J. Exp. Med. **98**:71, 1953.

122. Meneely, G. R., and Ball, C. O. T.: Experimental epidemiology of chronic sodium chloride toxicity and the protective effect of potassium chloride, Am. J. Med. **25**:713, 1958.

123. Dahl, L. K., and others: Effects of chronic excess salt ingestion: modifications of experimental hypertension in the rat by variations in the diet, Circ. Res. **22**:11, 1968.

124. Dahl, L. K.: Effects of chronic excess salt feeding induction of self-sustaining hypertension in rats, J. Exp. Med. **114**:231, 1961.

125. Dahl, L. K., Heine, M., and Tassinari, L.: High salt content of Western infants' diet: possible relationship to hypertension in the adult, Nature **198**:1204, 1963.

126. Gleibermann, L.: Blood pressure and dietary salt in human populations, Ecology Food Nutr. **2**:143, 1973.

127. Oliver, W. J., Cohen, E. L., and Neel, J. V.: Blood pressure, sodium values, and sodium related hormones in the Yanomamo Indians: a "no-salt" culture, Circulation **52**:146, 1975.

128. Dahl, L. K., and Love, R. A.: Etiologic role of sodium chloride intake in essential hypertension in humans, J.A.M.A. **164**:397, 1957.

129. Dawber, T. R., and others: Environmental factors in hypertension. In Stamler, J., Stamler, R., and Pullman, T. N.: The epidemiology of hypertension, New York, 1967, Grune & Stratton, Inc., p. 255.

130. Prior, I. A. M., and others: Sodium intake and blood pressure in two Polynesian populations, N. Engl. J. Med. **279**:515, 1968.

131. Miall, W. E.: Follow up study of arterial pressure in the population of a Welsh mining valley, Br. Med. J. **2**:1204, 1959.

132. Filer, L. J.: Salt in infant foods, Nutr. Rev. **29**:27, 1971.

133. Kerr, C. M. Reisinger, K. S., and Plankey, F. W.: Sodium concentration of homemade baby foods, Pediatrics **62**:331, 1978.

134. Committee on Nutrition, American Academy of Pediatrics: Salt intake and eating patterns of infants and children in relation to blood pressure, Pediatrics **53**:115, 1974.

135. Lauer, R. M., and others: Blood pressure, salt preference and relative weight, Am. J. Dis. Child. **130**:493, 1976.

136. Fomon, S. J., Thomas, L. N., and Filer, L. J.: Acceptance of unsalted strained foods by normal infants, J. Pediatr. **76**:242, 1970.

ADDITIONAL READINGS
Obesity

Asher, P.: Fat babies and fat children: the prognosis of obesity in the very young, Arch. Dis. Child. **41**:672, 1966.

Bruch, H.: Eating disorders: obesity, anorexia nervosa and the person within, New York, 1973, Basic Books, Inc., Publishers.

Committee on Nutrition, American Academy of Pediatrics: Obesity in childhood, Pediatrics **40**:455, 1967.

Corbin, C. B., and Fletcher, P.: Diet and physical activity of obese and non-obese elementary school children, Res. Q. Am. Assoc. Health Phys. Educ. **39**:922, 1968.

Crawford, P. B., and others: An obesity index for six month old children, Am. J. Clin. Nutr. **27**:706, 1974.

Huenemann, R. L.: Environmental factors associated with preschool obesity. I. Obesity in six month old children, J. Am. Diet. Assoc. **64**:480, 1974.

Huenemann, R. L.: Environmental factors associated with preschool obesity. II. Obesity and food practices of children at successive age levels, J. Am. Diet. Assoc. **64**:488, 1974.

Lloyd, J. K., and Wolff, O. H.: Childhood obesity, a long term study of height and weight, Br. Med. J. **2**:145, 1961.

Mack, R. W., and Kleinhenz, M. E.: Growth, calorie intake, and activity levels in early infancy: a preliminary report, Hum. Biol. **46**:345, 1974.

Shenker, I. R., Fisichelli, V., and Lang, J.: Weight differences between foster infants of overweight and non-overweight foster mothers. J. Pediatr. **84**:715, 1974.

Winick, M., editor: Childhood obesity, New York, 1975, John Wiley & Sons, Inc.

Whitelaw, A.: Infant feeding and subcutaneous fat at birth and at one year, Lancet **2**:1098, 1977.

Allergy

Bahna, S. L.: Control of milk allergy: a challenge for physicians, mothers, and industry, Ann. Allergy **41**:1, 1978.

Crook, W. G.: Food allergy—the great masquerader, Pediatr. Clin. North Am. **22**:227, 1975.

Dannaeus, A., Johansson, S. G. O., and Foucard, T.: Clinical and immunological aspects of food allergy in children. II. Development of allergic symptoms and humoral immune responses to foods in infants of atopic mothers during the first 24 months of life, Acta Paediatr. Scand. **67**:497, 1978.

Freedman, B. J.: A dietary free from additives in the management of allergic disease, Clin. Allergy **7**:417, 1977.

Fries, J. H.: Chocolate: a review of published reports of allergic and other deleterious effects, real or presumed, Ann. Allergy **41**:195, 1978.

Gerrard, J. W., and others: Cow's milk allergy: prevalence and manifestations in an unselected series of newborns, Acta Paediatr. Scand. Suppl. 234, 1973.

Goldstein, G. B., and Heiner, D. C.: Clinical and immunological perspectives in food sensitivity, a review, J. Allergy **46**:270, 1970.

Kuitunen, P., and others: Malabsorption syndrome with cow's milk intolerance, Arch. Dis. Child. **50**·351, 1975.

Miller, J. B.: Hidden food ingredients, chemical food additives, and incomplete food labels, Ann. Allergy **41**:93, 1978.

Pratt, E. L.: Food allergy and food intolerance in relation to the development of good eating habits, Pediatrics **21**:642, 1958.

Speer, F.: Multiple food allergy, Ann. Allergy **34**:71, 1975.

Speer, F.: Food allergy, the 10 common offenders, Am. Fam. Physician **13**:106, 1976.

Carbohydrate and dental caries

Abbey, L. M.: Is breast feeding a likely cause of dental caries in young children? J. Am. Dent. Assoc. **98**:21, 1979.

Brown, A. T.: The role of dietary carbohydrate in plaque formation and oral disease, Nutr. Rev. **33**:353, 1975.

Enwonwu, C. O.: Role of biochemistry and nutrition in preventive dentistry, J. Am. Soc. Prev. Dent. **4**:6, 1974.

Evaluation of the caries-producing ability of human foods, Nutr. Rev. **36**:249, 1978.

McBean, L. D., and Speckmann, E. W.: A review: the importance of nutrition in oral health, J. Am. Dent. Assoc. **89**:109, 1974.

Newbrum, E.: The role of food manufacturers in the dietary control of varies, J. Am. Soc. Prev. Dent. **4**:33, 1974.

Lactose malabsorption and milk intolerance

Dahlqvist, A., and Lindquist, B.: Lactose intolerance and protein malnutrition, Acta Paediatr. Scand. **60**: 488, 1971.

Food and Nutrition Board: Background information on lactose and milk intolerance, a statement of the Food and Nutrition Board Division of Biology and Agriculture, National Academy of Sciences, National Research Council, May 1972.

Gallagher, C. R., Molleson, A. L., and Caldwell, J. H.: Lactose intolerance and fermented dairy products, J. Am. Diet. Assoc. **65**:418, 1974.

Maclean, W. C., and Graham, G. G.: Evaluation of a low-lactose nutritional supplement in malnourished children, J. Am. Diet. Assoc. **67**:558, 1975.

McGill, D. B., and Newcomer, A. D.: Primary and secondary disaccharidase deficiencies, Prog. Gastroenterol. **2**:392, 1970.

Simoons, T. J.: Perspectives on milk drinking and malabsorption of lactose, Pediatrics **59**:98, 1977.

Fat and cardiovascular disease

Lauer, R. M., and others: Coronary heart disease risk factors in schoolchildren: the Muscatine Study, J. Pediatr. **86**:697, 1975.

Morrison, J. A., and others: Lipids and lipoproteins in

927 schoolchildren, ages 6 to 17 years, Pediatrics **62:**990, 1978.

McBean, L. D., and Speckman, E. W.: An interpretative review: diet in early life and the prevention of atherosclerosis, Pediatr. Res. **8:**837, 1974.

Turner, R. W. D.: Perspectives in coronary prevention, Postgrad. Med. J. **54:**141, 1978.

Woolf, N.: The origins of atherosclerosis, Postgrad. Med. J. **54:**156, 1978.

Salt and hypertension

Weinsier, R. L.: Overview: salt and the development of essential hypertension, Prev. Med. **5:**7, 1976.

14

Nutrition and feeding of children with developmental delays and related problems

Peggy L. Pipes and Paula Carman

Approximately 3% of the population of infants and children are developmentally delayed. A very small percentage of those so affected can be expected to be institutionalized; the remainder will function in the free-living population in their natural homes, in foster homes, or in group homes. It is thus important that health care professionals be alerted to potential problems of nutrient intake and that efforts be made to prevent or alleviate problems amenable to therapy.

DEFINITION OF DEVELOPMENTAL DELAYS

The term "developmentally delayed" includes a wide range of ability from persons so handicapped that there is no head control to those who function in the mildly retarded range who can learn and, as adults, operate in a self-sufficient and productive manner. The etiologies of developmental delays are multiple and include genetic and biologic anomalies and psychosocial and environmental factors that interact to determine the level of function. Activity patterns range from immobility to hyperactivity, motor skills from absence of suck and head control to well-coordinated children, and behavior

from apathy to disruptive behavior. Therefore, no generalizations can be made about developmentally delayed children and their problems of feeding and nutrient intake. However, among populations of developmentally delayed individuals, reasons for concern about feeding and nutrient intake frequently are found.

NUTRITIONAL NEEDS OF THE DEVELOPMENTALLY DELAYED CHILD

Developmentally delayed children require the same nutrients as any individual. There are, however, no dietary standards applicable to groups of developmentally delayed children. Many of these children, although not all, are growth retarded because of a genetic or biologic defect.[1] Syndromes with which growth retardation is associated include Down's syndrome, Prader-Willi syndrome, trisomy 13 and 18, de Lange's syndrome, Hurler's syndrome, Turner's syndrome, Silver's syndrome, Williams' syndrome, and others.[2] Body composition may differ from that of the normal child. Isakkson found reduced body cell mass in children with both spasticity and athetosis caused by atrophy of skeletal muscles resulting from disease and low levels of physical activity.[3] Reduced cell mass may reduce requirements for essential nutrients as well as calories. On the other hand, a reduced cell mass may result from a lifetime of limited nutrient and calorie intakes.

Commonly reported parental and professional concerns relating to handicapped children's food and nutrient intakes include the following:

1. Slow growth in length and lack of appropriate weight gain
2. Excessive weight gain in relation to gains in length
3. Obesity
4. Iron deficiency anemia
5. Refusal of the child to consume specific foods and/or groups of foods
6. Refusal of the child to progress in feeding behavior when developmentally ready
7. Pica
8. Bizarre feeding patterns
9. Lack of appetite
10. Excessive appetite
11. Gagging, vomiting, or rumination
12. Food allergies
13. Limited fluid intake
14. Constipation
15. Abnormal motor patterns that affect the child's ability to consume food
16. Inability or unwillingness of the child to finger feed and/or to self-feed
17. Limited attention span at mealtime
18. Disruptive behavior at mealtime

There have been few studies of nutrient intake or feeding problems of delayed children. Data collected in diagnostic and evaluation centers give indications of common problems. Studies in institutions have given criteria on which estimates of appropriate energy intake may be made. Investigations of children with abnormal motor patterns have suggested problems in achieving appropriate nutrient intakes of children with cerebral palsy. The effects of anticonvulsants on the need for vitamin D and folate have been researched. There have been isolated reports of efforts to control obesity, behavior modification in relation to acceptance of specific textures of food, and the acquisition of self-feeding skills. One diagnostic and evaluation center reported that the most frequent inadequacies of nutrient intake were of ascorbic acid, iron, fluoride, and high-quality protein. Another center found an incidence of 21.3% overweight, 15% underweight, 7.7% bizarre feeding habits, 13.0% inadequate nutrient intake, and 30.6% feeding problems in 500 patients.[4]

Difficulties in weight control are often clustered in specific syndromes. Obesity is commonly a problem in children with Down's syndrome, Prader-Willi syndrome, Carpenter's syndrome, Cohen's syndrome, and Laurence-Moone-Biedl syndrome. Underweight is frequently noted in children with athetoid cerebral palsy, hyperactivity, and behavior problems.

Underweight children with limited energy intakes also commonly have limited intakes of several nutrients because of the limited volume of food they consume. Inadequate intakes of vitamins A, C, and D and folate have been noted to be the most frequent problems.[4]

Nutritional studies

Children with cerebral palsy generally grow in both height and weight at rates less than normal. Weight, however, may be greater than that of normal children of the same height. Leamy found calorie intakes of institutionalized children with cerebral palsy to be considerably below the recommended amounts and suggested that a cyclic phenomenon occurred. The disease restricts growth, and the calorie intake then further limits increases in size.[5] Ruby and Matheny found mouth area involvement closely associated with poor food intake and believed that the extent of mouth involvement and poor growth were generally parallel.[6]

Bone age delays have been reported, indicating less than optimal intakes of nutrients. Hammond, Lewis, and Johnson reported a range of 19 to 35 months delay, Leamy, a range of 1.4 to 47.4 months delay, and Matheny and Krogman, an average of 19.3 months delay in bone age.[5-7]

Studies of free-living populations of children with cerebral palsy have shown acceptable intakes of nutrients other than iron.[8] Dietary intakes of less severely retarded children have been found to be markedly higher in all nutrients except vitamins A and C than intakes of the more severely delayed children. The energy value of the diets are influenced by the children's ability to self-feed. Children with motor involvements and mental retardation severe enough to interfere with their ability to feed themselves tend to consume fever calories than do those who are able to self-feed.[7]

Energy requirements

Culley and Middleton have reported that institutionalized retarded children who are ambulatory have energy requirements similar to those of normal children if height is used as a standard for estimating calorie needs. Because many of the children in their study had short stature, their calorie requirements were less than those of other children the same age. They found that only when motor dysfunction becomes severe enough to cause children to be nonambulatory does it reduce the calorie requirement per centimeter of height significantly.[9,10] Pipes and Holm have reported that children with Prader-Willi syndrome have reduced energy requirements per centimeter of height as compared to energy requirements of normal children.[11] Mertz and associates, on the other hand, reported that a group of emaciated children in an institution for the men-

tally handicapped had energy requirements in excess of those of normal children. Even though such children consumed calorie intakes recommended for their ages they remained emaciated.[12]

Children with spasticity (hypertonia) frequently become overweight for their heights, consuming low-calorie intakes for their ages. Eddy, Nicholson, and Wheeler studied one female with spasticity, an obese 16-year-old quadriplegic, and found her to have a basal energy expenditure of that of a person half her body weight. The girl was confined to a wheel chair; her total energy expenditure was estimated to be 1270 to 1370 kcal/day.[13]

Children with athetosis (mixed pattern of too much and too little tone) consume greater numbers of calories than do those with spasticity and are less likely to become obese because they are able to engage in greater amounts of activity. Some children with athetosis expend energy constantly in involuntary movements. Researchers have found that basal energy expenditures of children with athetosis are similar to those of normal children and that the energy cost of activity depends on the child's capacity for muscular work. As levels of activity reach limits, activity becomes costly and uneconomic.[13]

The activity patterns of developmentally delayed children are often less than those of their peers because of low muscle tone, immobility, or general disinterest in their environments. This inactivity limits their energy expenditures and therefore energy requirements. Grogan and Ekvall found levels of 7 kcal/cm of height necessary to produce weight reduction in children with myelomeningocele.[4] Children with cerebral palsy who have decreased levels of activity have been noted to need 10 kcal/cm of height, whereas those with normal or increased levels of activity need 15 kcal/cm of height.

Recommendations for energy intakes of developmentally delayed children must be individualized. Because physical growth of handicapped children frequently deviates from the norm, kcal/cm of height may prove to be a more useful reference on which to base estimated needs than kcal/kg of body weight.

Drug/nutrient interrelationships

Anticonvulsant drugs prescribed to control seizures increase a child's need for vitamin D and alter folate metabolism. Evidence of vitamin D deficiency has been found in both institutionalized patients and outpatients treated with anticonvulsant drugs for longer than 6 months for control of seizures. It was found that serum calcium levels were normal or low, serum phosphate levels were low, and serum alkaline phosphatase levels were elevated.[14] Plasma 25-OHD levels have been found to be low but levels of 1,25-OHD normal.[15] Cases of rickets and osteomalacia confirmed by roentgenograms have been reported.[16-19] All drugs commonly used to control seizures have been implicated. The incidence of abnormalities increases with duration of therapy. Multiple drug regimens cause the most problems. The drugs do not affect intestinal absorption of vitamin D. It appears that they increase the catabolism and excretion of vitamin D and its biologically active products. They also have a direct inhibitory effect on calcium transport and bone metabolism.[20]

Lifshitz and Maclaren reported an incidence of rickets of 7% in residents younger than 15 years in an institution for the mentally handicapped who had received long-term anticonvulsant therapy. All residents of the institution had received diets providing adequate amounts of calories, protein, fat, calcium phosphate, and supplemental vitamins. Their intakes of vitamin D_2 approximated 800 to 1200 IU/day. Rickets was diagnosed in nonambulatory children with spasticity who had lived indoors most of their lives and who had had infrequent exposure to sunlight, had had frequent chronic infections, and had received combinations of anticonvulsant medications. Rickets healed rapidly, usually with doses of 6000 IU of vitamin D_2 or with 50 units of 25-OHD$_3$ given orally.[16]

Lifshitz and Maclaren also found that residents who received phenobarbital alone had decreased serum calcium levels but no alterations in serum phosphorus levels as compared to children who received no medication. Those who received phenytoin alone had no detectable alterations in serum calcium and phosphorus levels but had increased alkaline phosphatase activity as compared to the controls. Combinations of anticonvulsant medications, however, had highly significant effects on concentrations of serum calcium, phosphorus, and alkaline phosphatase, producing marked drops in serum calcium and phosphorus levels.[16]

Silver and associates found that institutionalized adolescents who received anticonvulsants, who had frequent exposure to sunlight, and whose intakes of vitamin D averaged 85 IU/day had serum calcium levels that were not significantly different from those not receiving anticonvulsants; however, serum phosphorus levels were lower and serum alkaline phosphatase levels were elevated as compared to controls. Three thousand IU of vitamin D_3/week caused rises in phosphate levels and led to radiologic evidence of healing in those children with diagnosed rickets. They found no case of rickets resistant to treatment with vitamin D.[17]

Although many children consume anticonvulsants without biochemical or clinical evidence of rickets or osteomalacia, most of those who take the drugs have significant derangement of mineral metabolism. Serum 25-OHD levels have been found to be 40% to 70% lower than normal values, bone mass 10% to 30% lower than normal values.[20]

Amounts of vitamin D necessary to prevent deficiency and rickets in children receiving anticonvulsant therapy appear to vary depending on the number of anticonvulsant drugs, the dosage the child receives, and the duration of therapy in addition to the pattern of mobility and exposure to sunlight.[18] Hahn suggests an intake of 10,000 IU of vitamin D/week in patients who have been on therapy for 6 months or longer adjusted on the basis of individual response.[20] Silver and associates believe that an intake of 3000 IU/week for children who are exposed to sunlight would be preventive.[17] Rickets recurred in a 14-year-old girl receiving phenobarbital who had recovered from rickets and maintained an intake of 600 IU of vitamin D_2/day when phenytoin was added to the phenobarbital she was receiving daily. An intake of 1200 IU of vitamin D_2/day prevented recurrence.[21] It is obvious that children who receive anticonvulsants should be given larger doses of vitamin D than those who receive no anticonvulsants. It has been suggested that such children be monitored biochemically on a regular basis.[16]

Drug-induced disturbances of folate metabolism have been found in a significant number of patients receiving anticonvulsants. Low serum folate levels accompanied by a fall in red cell folate and cerebrospinal folate levels have been reported in 33% to 90% of patients studied.[22] Megaloblastic anemia is reported to occur in 0.5% to 0.75% of epileptic patients. The symptoms are usually associated with phenytoin therapy but can occur with phenobarbital or primidone therapy.[23] There appear to be two effects of the drugs on folate metabolism. The anticonvulsants interfere with incorporation of thymidine into D.N.A. and can therefore increase folate requirements. Also they may increase the activities of enzymes that catabolize folate or may increase activities or metabolic pathways in which folate is essential.[24] Administration of folate has been reported to precipitate seizures or increase seizure frequency in some patients treated with anticonvulsants. In most patients no effect has been noted.[25]

Yeast tablets given as a natural source of folate to epileptic, mentally retarded patients showed that folate deficiency caused by anticonvulsants could be corrected within 3 months without effect on seizures.[26] Chien and associates have suggested that there may be some folate-sensitive patients and some folate-insensitive patients and that folate should be administered with caution. They describe the effect of an intravenous infusion of folate on an 18-year-old girl treated with phenytoin and phenobarbital who showed electroencephalographic evidence of seizures followed by tonic and clonic seizures after the intravenous administration of 14.4 mg of folate. In the same study there were no reactions to the infusion of 75 mg of folic acid in seven other patients.[27] Although the amounts infused seem large, one might encounter such levels of intake in individuals who are receiving megadoses of vitamins.

Long-term anticonvulsant therapy may be associated with other vitamin deficiency states. Clinical evidence of cardiac beriberi and subclinical ascorbic acid deficiency has been noted in a 28-month-old black girl who allegedly was receiving a full diet in a nursing home and was receiving phenobarbital, phenytoin sodium (Dilantin), and primidone (Mysoline).[28]

FEEDING THE DEVELOPMENTALLY DELAYED CHILD

Planning for feeding developmentally delayed children implies that recommendations for intakes of energy, nutrients, and textures of food as well as expectations for the acquisition of self-feeding skills must be individualized to each child. Some children may be considered children whose oral, fine, and gross motor, language, and personal/social development is proceeding at a less than normal rate. Others may also have physical anomalies that imply the need for special equipment to sustain sitting posture to eat and adaptation of utensils to self-feed.

It is important to recognize that many of the problems of nutrient intake in developmentally delayed children are preventable. Guidance and support for parents as they select foods for their children that provide the nutrients they need and create an environment in which the child learns to consume foods in a manner appropriate for his or her developmental level are important. Guidance may need to be provided as to the appropriate stages at which to change the textures of food, to expect the child to feed himself, and the degree of messiness to expect when a child is self-feeding.

Factors that influence food intake

Because of the many factors that interact to determine the food available to and accepted by the developmentally delayed children, concerns about food and nutrient intake and feeding rarely result from a single cause; many factors must be considered. An understanding of those factors that contribute to problems of food intake is important in planning for feeding of such children.

Developmentally delayed children experience the same responses to parental anxiety about their food intake as any child and in a like manner can control their parents by their acceptance or rejection of food. Most normal preschoolers reduce their intakes of milk and vegetables, go on food jags, and have brittle and unpredictable appetites. It is not unreasonable to expect that developmentally delayed children will present the same food-related behaviors. There may be, in addition, difficulties in feeding developmentally delayed children that are not encountered with normal children.

Developmental level. Delays in motor development may result directly or indirectly in an inappropriate nutrient intake. The development and sequence of acquisition of feeding behaviors of delayed children proceed in the same orderly predictable sequence as that of normal children. The chronologic age at which the developmental stages will occur, however, is not predictable, and wide ranges will be seen both in the timing at which stages occur and the ultimate developmental level of function of delayed children. Abnormal motor and behavioral patterns may interfere with the sequence of development and acquisition of feeding skills.

Failure to recognize developmental readiness may result in failure of parents to provide children with appropriate stimuli. Parents unaware of their children's potential often do not encourage them to progress in the oral motor skills of eating and gross and fine motor skills of self-feeding. Children may be offered strained foods when they are capable of masticating food with a more mature texture; parents may feed the children when they have the ability to learn to feed themselves.

Readiness to accept solids is demonstrated blatantly in normal children and is difficult to ignore. They reach for food and bring it to their mouths. Clues as to readiness for this step in handicapped children may be very subtle, and, as a result, the stage is often ignored. Parents also may not realize the importance of the introduction of solids at the proper time. When parents decide it is time for children to learn to eat table food, conflicts may occur between children and their parents that may be sufficient to appreciably reduce the children's nutrient and calorie intakes. Such children may refuse to eat at all or may skillfully spit out lumps while sucking and swallowing the soft, strained foods.[27]

Parents have reported restraining their

children and forcing them to accept foods with texture. For example, one mother stated that it took four adults to hold her 10-year-old child who was developmentally 4 years of age when she attempted to make the transition from strained to table food. The child eventually accepted the foods but later accepted only small amounts of very soft food and lost weight.

It is important to recognize that some children are hypersensitive in the oral area. It may be important for an occupational, physical, or speech therapist to institute a program to normalize sensation prior to plans for presenting more textured foods to the child.

Children so delayed that they are unable to feed themselves are dependent on other people. Feeding the infant is a culturally defined maternal role, but feeding a handicapped child over a period of many years may become a tedious process that interferes with other activities several times a day. Some parents may become so overwhelmed with such a schedule that they con-

tinue feeding soft foods that do not support developmental progress; others may cease their efforts at feeding their children before the children consume sufficient food. Achieving self-feeding skills may appreciably increase nutrient intake, self-confidence, and self-image. Scales describes an experience in teaching a 13-year-old severely retarded male to feed himself. With this learning the boy gained 9 lb in 6 weeks. A marked improvement in social behavior was noted.[30]

Children whose delays in motor development are such that they lack the ability to learn to walk must be moved by their caretakers. The more weight the children gain, the more difficult they become to lift, move, and care for. Parents and caretakers of such children have expressed concern about the difficulties that may be created for them when children grow and gain and have been known to limit inappropriately the amounts of food they feed. Obesity must be prevented, but children should have the advantage of nutrient and energy intakes that support the best possible growth and develop-

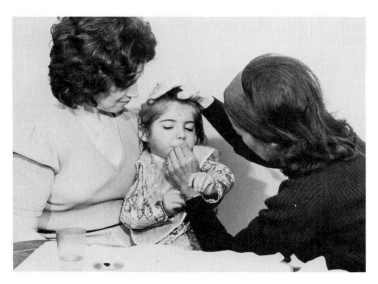

Fig. 14-1. Occupational therapist works for head and lip control with a handicapped child.

ment for them. Parents may need information and counseling in methods of moving and caring for their children and in accepting their need for increased amounts of nutrients and energy.

Abnormal motor patterns and muscle tone. Problems of sucking, swallowing, and coordination of sucking and breathing can be life threatening and may require that the child initially be gavage or tube fed. The retention of primitive reflexes can make the acquisition of mature feeding skills impossible. For example, a child who sucks reflexively when food is placed in the mouth cannot learn to chew until the reflexive sucking is extinguished. Lack of head control makes feeding difficult and self-feeding impossible. Rigidity in the extremities may result in abnormal feeding patterns. Tongue thrusting is sometimes the result of hyperextension and rigidity in the legs. The child cannot learn to bite if he or she cannot grade the movements of the jaws.

Primitive reflexes. The suck and swallow reflexes are normally well established in a term newborn. Bosma cites research showing that the human fetus can develop a functional swallow by 12.5 weeks of gestation and sucking behavior by 14 weeks of gestation.[31] However, premature babies often have a weak suck, which may occur singly or in a few successive sucks, although the pharynx and larynx function competently for swallowing. Competence in sucking and labial closure improves with maturity and experience. Burpee, a physical therapist, reports on a study in progress that measures the effects of early intervention on feeding behavior in premature infants. The hypothesis of this study is that tactile and proprioceptive facilitation of rooting, sucking, and swallowing patterns will improve these responses with resultant increases in weight gains.[32]

Gavage may be necessary for some infants to ensure adequate nutritional intake. Prob-

lems encountered with this approach include difficulty with breathing and increased tactile sensitivity in the oral area. Oral intervention techniques, which are commonly used by physical or occupational therapists, should be continued during this period, as should oral feeding during intervals when the tube is not in place. Termination of prolonged tube feeding is often followed by a difficult adjustment period because of the increased oral sensitivity and abnormal tongue movements that may have developed; however, oral intervention previous to or during that period should reduce these problems.

Protective reflexes. The gag and cough reflexes serve to open the air passage when it is blocked or is in danger of being blocked. A cough reflex is a violent expiratory effort preceded by a preliminary inspiration; the accessory muscles of expiration are brought into action as air is noisily expelled. When related to food, the stimulation is the presence of food or liquid in the laryngeal vestibule that must be expelled so that it does not enter the lungs.

The gag reflex is a vomit response or involuntary attempt to vomit that results from irritation of the fauces (the passage from the oral cavity into the pharynx). When the soft palate is stroked, the response is an arching of the palate (palatal gag response). Pressure on the pharyngeal aspect of the posterior tongue results in intense gagging or may induce a vomit response (pharyngeal gag reflex).[33] In normal development this reflex is sometimes elicited when a baby puts a toy far into the mouth. Soon the child learns to explore with the front aspect of the mouth to avoid triggering the gag reflex and learns from experience how to break down food with chewing so that it can be easily swallowed.

The gag reflex can be inhibited or sensitized (increased) by physiologic and psychologic factors. For instance, a fear of choking resulting from a previous incident may cause a gag response to the sight of a particular food. This behavior usually receives attention from adults, who do not persist in offering the undesirable food. The gag response is not intentional, but it can be reinforced by environmental factors. A physiologic sensitization may occur when a person is not feeling well, is dizzy, or is emotionally upset. The normal reaction to these feelings is to avoid eating. If food were to be offered or forced the reaction might well be a gag response or the more extreme vomit response.

Another factor that influences the sensitivity of the gag reflex is sensory experience. Normally babies put toys and fingers into their mouths and explore the sensations, thus increasing discriminative ability. Children who are unable to get their hands to their mouths often have defensive or avoidance reactions to stimulation on the face and inside the mouth. A gag reflex may be triggered by pressure on the front or middle of the tongue. The treatment for hypersensitivity to tactile stimulation is a gradual, careful program of increasing the sensory experiences. Overstimulation could cause negative emotional and behavioral reactions that would interfere with feeding to a greater extent than the original problem. Therapeutic techniques for normalizing facial and oral sensation are used by occupational, physical, and speech therapists, who vary the intervention according to individual reactions and needs.

If it is suspected that a child does not have a normally responsive gag or cough response, or if a child coughs frequently because of poor oral coordination, it becomes extremely important to position the child appropriately so that the possibility of food or liquid getting into the lungs is minimized. Proper positioning considers the head position in relation to the body as well as the body position. The head should not be tilted back; it should be upright or slightly flexed (5° to 10°). Too much flexion or extension interferes with swallowing. During the swallow, the epiglottis normally folds down, covering most of the opening to the laryngeal vestibule. If the head is tipped back the movement of the epiglottis is restricted and food or liquid can move more easily into the wrong area.

The body position also affects food intake. The closer the axis of the body is to horizontal, the more difficult it is (even for the normal adult) to control food and liquid because of the effect of gravity. The child should be positioned upright or, when support is needed for head and trunk, within 30° of vertical.

Young babies are normally able to drink in the supine position because of a difference in the laryngeal structure.[29] The position of the larynx changes in the first year of life to the more mature structure that works best when the person is upright. When young babies choke frequently or struggle to breathe and suck, a nearly upright position is usually helpful.

Positioning of children. Children with abnormal muscle tone are often difficult to position. It is essential that a pediatric occupational therapist or physical therapist assess each child and design therapy for appropriate positioning. A consistent effort should then be made to follow through with these plans. When formulating therapy plans the therapist considers the following aspects of positioning during feeding.

A child who pushes the head back while eating is probably not doing so voluntarily. The action either reflects the influence of an abnormal reflex or it is a compensatory behavior that reflects a lack of ability to stabilize the head in an upright position. Often the abnormal head position has become a habit and persists after better head control is possible. Although it is difficult to swallow with the head tilted back, it is possible to let the food slide down without swallowing, and many children do use this technique. However, without swallowing the opening to the trachea is not closed, and the chances of choking or aspirating food into the lungs is greatly increased. Food in the lungs may lead to pneumonia. Pressure at the back of the head may trigger more involuntary pushing backward; this pressure may be reduced by changing the shape of the support (e.g., to a doughnut-shaped support) or the firmness of the foam. Any food or other stimulus brought toward a client's face should be brought from a low position with encouragement to visually attend to the stimulus (to reduce startle or withdrawal reaction and to encourage slight head flexion). Withdrawal of the spoon can also influence head position: if the spoon is lifted up and scraped against the upper front teeth the head will tend to tilt backwards.

The position of the arms is also very important for head and trunk control. When the arms are pulled back at the shoulders, the head tends to tilt backwards. A forward position of the arms can be achieved with pillows or rolled towels or by having something to grasp or stabilize against in the forward position. Some children who are unable to use their arms to assist in feeding learn to stabilize them by sitting on their hands or by holding them between their legs. Others learn to grasp the far edge of the wheelchair tray. Some children may be able to actively participate in feeding when the elbows are stabilized.

Trunk position affects head and arm position. If a child is unable to sit upright independently, support should be provided in the form of a backrest. A tendency to fall to one or both sides should be eliminated with supportive pillows. Falling forward is usually caused by inadequate upright trunk control. Chest straps may be somewhat helpful, but they may also cause more slumping. It is preferable to find a chair with a slight back-

ward tilt. However, mealtime should not be the time to make the child work on better head and trunk control.

Leg position affects trunk control and thus affects arm and head control. Many children who have tightness in the leg muscles are quite unstable in sitting. When the legs pull together tightly, the sitting base is narrowed and postural adjustments for balance are impaired. In addition, the hips tend to extend, causing the child's hips to slip forward in the chair. If a wedge pillow is made to fit into the child's chair, it is important to securely fasten and stabilize it so that the large section is always under the child's knees. Another adaptation commonly used to promote a wider base of support is a pummel placed between the child's legs. Stability is improved by also providing foot support at a level that allows the feet to be flat and flexed at the ankle.

Abnormal oral motor patterns resulting from a lack of control of the tongue, lips, and/or cheeks can make eating a difficult and prolonged event requiring patience on the part of the child and the feeder. The amount of food lost from the mouth may be appreciable and may cause an inadequate intake of nutrients. Children so affected require skills of the speech, occupational, and/or physical therapist to achieve motor patterns necessary for feeding.

Screening children to determine the primary concerns and the criteria for referral has been discussed in Chapter 5. The foregoing information should prove useful in improving the quality of food intake when therapy services are not immediately available. It is important to use a problem-solving approach that includes ideas and feedback from client and caretaker. The rationale for any suggestions should be thoroughly explained; expectations for follow-through procedures must also be reasonable. It may take more time to feed a child in the desired position, especially at first, so it may be suggested that the new procedure be used toward the beginning of the meal for a short time. Consideration of the client's and caretaker's comfort, feelings, and opinions is likely to yield good results. Changes in motor control may be slow to develop, but the quality of the daily feeding experience has great impact on the ultimate skills that will develop.

A few children who have abnormal oral motor patterns have difficulty ingesting fluids. As a result, their intakes of liquids are very limited and they remain at risk for dehydration. Fluid intakes of such children should be carefully monitored. Heavily salted foods such as bouillon and commercially prepared soups should be avoided, as should high intakes of other nutrients that obligate water.

Another complaint of many who offer food to children with abnormal motor patterns is that milk increases mucous secretions. Independent reports from numerous parents and professionals lead one to believe that the observations are valid. The difficulty seems to occur only when fluid milk is consumed. Yogurt, cheese, and milk in prepared foods seem to cause no problems. Diets of children who have this problem should be carefully monitored for calcium and vitamin D. Excessive intakes of carbonated beverages that contain much phosphate should be avoided.

Appetite. Lack of appetite as a result of central nervous system damage in some children has been reported. These children never express hunger, and some mothers of such children have stated that setting alarm clocks is an aid in reminding them to feed. Children so affected are rarely pleased by any food and limit the volume of food they consume. The children's unresponsiveness to parental efforts at feeding results in a lack of reinforcement for parents. This lack of positive interplay between parent and child may result in lack of satisfaction in each and may adversely affect the parents' motivation to continue helping the child consume food and the child's motivation to consume appropriate energy and nutrient intakes.

Damage to or developmental defects of the hypothalamus can result in insatiable appetites in children. Children so affected may sometimes gorge, steal food, or eat animal food. Extreme measures such as locking refrigerators and kitchen cupboards have been necessary to control obesity in such children. Food-related behaviors of such children cannot be altered by behavior modification methods.

Behaviors. Children may have inappropriate nutrient intakes and food habits because of learned behavior. Children learn from the model set for them by their parents, peers, and relatives. If examples of poor food habits are set, the children will imitate them. It is very difficult to retrain developmentally delayed children who have learned to reject many foods or groups of foods as a result of parental example.

The behavior pattern and attention span of children affect their calorie and nutrient needs and consumption. Hypoactivity reduces energy expenditure and needs. Lack of planned activity and stimulation for such children often results in boredom and in children spending their days seeking and consuming excessive amounts of food.

Hyperactive children never appear to be quiet and expend much energy in their numerous activities. The attention span of hyperactive children may be limited at the dinner table as in other activities, resulting in very small intakes of food at one time. It may be important to offer hyperactive children frequent small feedings of high nutrient content.

Disruptive and inappropriate behaviors of children make mealtime an unpleasant experience both for the children and the family and can result in inappropriate food intakes. Children quickly learn that behaviors such as throwing food or utensils, stuffing the mouth, spitting out food, and whining generally attract parental attention. In an effort to deal with disruptive behavior many parents try different kinds of tactics. For one meal they may cajole the child into stopping the undesirable behavior, for another they may spank, and for another they may laugh at the child's activity. Since these responses usually occur on an intermittent basis depending on the mood of the parents at the time the disruptive behavior occurs, the effect for the child is one of intermittent positive reinforcement (Chapter 15). Many parents find it effective to remove the child from the table as soon as disruptive behavior occurs. The child should go to his or her room or to another room in the house where he or she does not receive adult attention until the meal is over. The child then does not receive food (except water) until the next meal is served.

While disruptive behaviors are being discouraged it is important to positively reinforce a child's appropriate mealtime behaviors. In this way the child learns the alternative behaviors that parents consider desirable.

Constipation. Constipation is not an unusual problem in children with developmental delays, especially in those who are hypertonic or hypotonic. The infrequent passage of feces or the passage of unduly hard dry fecal matter can result from a variety of causes, such as lack of muscle tone in the intestine or duodenal wall, excessive fatigue, anxiety, inappropriate dietary intake, or failure to establish a routine bowel pattern. When children are constipated, there will usually be complaints of stomachache, distention, swelling of the abdomen, or frank discomfort and pain.

It is possible that increasing the amount of fluid and roughage in the diet may be useful for treating children who are constipated. Parents should also observe for individual food stimuli. In some instances it may be important to limit milk intake to 1 pint/day. Prunes and prune juice are also frequently helpful.

Management of feeding

The diversity of concerns about the food and nutrient intake of handicapped children and the many factors that affect children's level of function and food acceptance imply that the skills of several disciplines may be necessary to effect solutions to concerns about food and nutrient intake and in setting priorities for therapy for individual children. The occupational, physical, and/or speech therapist will be called on to provide therapy for children with abnormal motor tone. The dentist will correct dental caries and malocclusions. A professional who is proficient in behavior modification techniques may be required to change behavior. It is possible that correction of these problems may lead to solutions of concerns about nutrient intake. Parents may, however, need help in planning appropriate foods for their children.

Parents of handicapped children are especially vulnerable to those who sell vitamin supplements and who often promise a cure or improvement. Attempts to coerce children to swallow 75 to 80 vitamin and mineral pills per day have been reported by parents. Careful evaluation of the children's nutrient intakes may alleviate parental concern that dietary insufficiencies are causing the problem.

Parents need to have realistic expectations about the child's potential for physical growth. It is not possible to increase a child's length beyond his or her genetic potential; it is possible to increase a child's weight for length. Parental concern about a child's slow rate of growth may create anxiety about the volume of food the child is consuming. Counseling about expectations and growth response to food intake is important.

Overindulgences are common among

Table 14-1. Developmental stages of readiness to progress in feeding behaviors

Developmental landmarks	Change indicated	Examples of appropriate foods
Tongue laterally transfers food in the mouth Voluntary and independent movements of the tongue and lips Sitting posture can be sustained Beginning of chewing movements (up and down movements of the jaw)	Introduction of soft, mashed table food	Tuna fish; mashed potatoes; well-cooked mashed vegetables; ground meats in gravy and sauces; soft diced fruit such as bananas, peaches, pears, etc.; liverwurst; flavored yogurt
Reaches for and grasps objects with scissor grasp Brings hand to mouth	Finger feeding (large pieces of food)	Oven-dried toast, teething biscuits, cheese sticks, peeled Vienna sausage (food should be soluble in the mouth to prevent choking)
Voluntary release (refined digital grasp)	Finger feeding (small pieces of food)	Bits of cottage cheese, dry cereal, peas, etc., small pieces of meat
Rotary chewing pattern	Introduction of more textured food from family menu	Well-cooked chopped meats and casseroles, cooked vegetables and canned fruit (not mashed), toast, potatoes, macaroni, spaghetti, peeled ripe fruit
Approximates lips to rim of the cup Understands relationship of container and contained	Introduction of cup Beginning self-feeding (messiness should be expected)	Food that when scooped will adhere to the spoon, such as applesauce, cooked cereal, mashed potatoes, cottage cheese
Increased rotary movements of the jaw Ulnar deviation of wrist develops	More skilled at cup and spoon feeding	Chopped fibrous meats such as roast and steak Raw vegetables and fruit (introduce gradually)
Walks alone	May seek food and get food independently	Food of high nutrient value should be available
Names food, expresses preferences; prefers unmixed foods Goes on food jags Appetite appears to decrease		Balanced food intake should be offered (child should be permitted to develop food preferences without parents being concerned that they will last forever)

those who are responsible for the care of the handicapped, and such children frequently receive large amounts of preferred high-carbohydrate, sweet foods. As with anyone, it is difficult to design a food intake pattern that will provide necessary amounts of essential nutrients and maintain weight gain in growth channel if many of the foods consumed supply only carbohydrate and fat and few other nutrients. It may be important to help parents find ways of expressing affection other than in feeding and to make them aware of why they offer the foods they do.

Identifying readiness to progress. Assessing children's developmental levels of function and their readiness to progress in eating and self-feeding is necessary to define reasonable expectations for parents and caretakers. Parents often need help in accepting their children's handicaps and in recognizing their potential to progress.

It is important that changes in food and feeding behavior be effected when the children are developmentally 6 to 7 months old, when they demonstrate readiness to self-feed and to use a cup. Table 14-1 defines important developmental landmarks and suggested food appropriate for changes in feeding behavior.

Assessment of problems and suggested solutions. Efforts at prevention of problems of nutrient intake are not always successful. Frequently expressed concerns about food and nutrient intake of delayed children, factors that need to be assessed, and suggestions for solution are provided in Table 14-2.

Developmentally delayed children frequently experience failure in their many efforts. It is therefore important that any plan to modify a child's food intake pattern be designed so that success is obtainable and so that the child and the parents are reinforced for each gain, however small. Adequate nutrition is important for every child to achieve his or her physical, mental, and emotional potential. Delayed and physically handicapped children should have the advantage of a nutrient intake that can support well-being, optimal growth, and development. Solutions to difficulties in attaining such goals may be complex and may require a multi-disciplined approach.

Table 14-2. Assessment of concerns about foods and nutrients

Symptom	Assessment	Action and/or counseling suggestions
Lack of appetite	What is child's total food and nutrient intake? Is some essential nutrient consumed in insufficient amounts? Is child receiving adequate amounts of food at other meals without having to eat large amounts? Is the food properly prepared? Is child's rate of growth normal in spite of his or her apparent lack of appetite?	Counsel with parents about child's needs and help them obtain needed food Provide only between-meal snacks of high nutrient content at intervals that will not interfere with appetite at mealtime Serve very small portions Provide child with a quiet period before mealtime to prevent weariness Reinforce child's acceptance of food with social reinforcement

Table 14-2. Assessment of concerns about foods and nutrients—cont'd

Symptom	Assessment	Action and/or counseling suggestions
Lack of appetite—cont'd	Is child reinforced? 　While he or she is eating? (appropriate) 　When he or she is not eating? (inappropriate) Is child receiving too many snacks? (inappropriate) Is child too weary to eat at mealtime? Is child attending to eating or is his or her attention diverted at mealtime? Is child psychologically deprived?	Do not reinforce with food Eat with child to provide a model Refer the emotionally deprived child to the nurse or social worker
Refuses specific groups of foods	Is food properly prepared? Has child had previous experiences with the foods? Does child have a model (parents, teacher, peers, etc.) who eats these foods?	Continue offering very small portions of foods refused Reinforce foods accepted with foods child likes Provide a model for child by eating the foods Provide guidance in food preparation for children
Inappropriate feeding behavior: Throwing Gorging Stuffing food in the mouth Will not sit at the table	What started the behavior? What follows the behavior? 　Is child reinforced? 　Is child punished? 　Is child ignored?	All inappropriate behaviors should be ignored even if it is necessary to remove child from feeding situation All attempts at appropriate eating should be encouraged through social reinforcement and food the child likes
Refuses to eat table food; insists on strained food	Has child had experience with table food? 　Has it been offered and refused? 　Has child eaten table food previously but refuses it currently? How is child positioned for feeding? Can he or she sit upright? Has a critical stage of development been ignored? Is child delayed so that strained foods are appropriate for his or her stage of motor development? Can child bite or chew? Is child hypersensitive in and/or around the mouth? Does child have a hypersensitive gag reflex?	Consult with occupational, physical, or speech therapist regarding positioning, development, and hypersensitivity Seat child in upright sitting position (using props if necessary) If child demonstrates readiness: 　Choose a food the child enjoys and place it between back molars (watch your fingers) 　Offer crunchy foods such as arrowroot biscuits, melba toast, crackers (be careful of foods that splinter, such as graham crackers)

Continued.

Table 14-2. Assessment of concerns about foods and nutrients—cont'd

Symptom	Assessment	Action and/or counseling suggestions
Will not bite	Does child have dental caries or malocclusion? Can child close the mouth? Has child been offered foods that require biting? Can child breathe through the nose?	Offer easy-to-bite foods such as arrowroot biscuits and melba toast Manually assist child in closing the jaw Provide social reinforcement when child takes a bite
Does not chew with a rotary motion	Is child delayed so that only munching or sucking is appropriate? Can child lateralize the tongue? Has child been offered foods that require chewing? Is child hypersensitive or hyposensitive? Are foods offered that are too tough to chew?	Consult an occupational, physical, or speech therapist regarding lateralization of the tongue and sensitivity Model for child by demonstrating chewing Manually move the jaw in chewing motions Encourage chewing with social reinforcement and with foods child likes
Refuses harder-to-chew foods	Is hypertonia or hypotonia preventing development of oral motor skills? Does child have dental caries? Is child sufficiently delayed that hard-to-chew foods are inappropriate for him or her? Is there too much in child's mouth at one time for him or her to chew anything adequately? Has child had experience with harder-to-chew foods?	Consult with occupational, physical, or speech therapist about oral motor skills; stimulate area around the lips and mouth before feeding as directed Consult about dental caries Give small bites; reinforce with social reinforcement and foods child likes
Lack of self-feeding	What cues of readiness to self-feed does child demonstrate? Can child bring hand to mouth? Can child hold the spoon? Is child so delayed that self-feeding is inappropriate? Can child sit either unsupported or propped in an upright position? Do adults interrupt when child begins to make efforts to self-feed? Does child have behavior incompatible with self-feeding? Physiologically, does child have any spasticity?	If ready: Behavior modification (i.e., putting the child through the motions of feeding, phasing out assistance) Reinforce child's attempts to: Hold spoon Put spoon in dish Bring spoon to the mouth Close the lips around the spoon Return spoon to dish

Table 14-2. Assessment of concerns about foods and nutrients—cont'd

Symptom	Assessment	Action and/or counseling suggestions
Lack of self-feeding —cont'd	Behaviorally, does child throw food, utensils, etc? Is child receiving attention by not feeding himself or herself? Is child controlling parents by not feeding himself or herself? Is child offered foods that will stick to the spoon? Is child attending to eating or is he or she distracted by others in the environment?	
Lean for height Weight loss Failure to gain adequate weight	Is child receiving sufficient amounts of food? Is child receiving sufficient calories? Is some essential nutrient consumed in inappropriate amounts? How frequently is child given food? At school? At home? Does child eat on a regular schedule? What is the family body type? Does child have an illness or disease contributing to the lack of weight gain? Vomiting or diarrhea? Other chronic illness? What is child's history of weight gain? Has child always been lean? Has child recently lost weight? Is there sufficient food available to child? Is food presented to child in a manner appropriate for his or her level of function and self-help skills? What is child's activity pattern?	Family should keep a food record if there is concern about amounts of food and frequency of eating Feed more frequently; small feedings Provide high-calorie snacks of high nutrient value, such as milkshakes, peanut butter or fruit on crackers or bread Counsel with parents regarding appropriate feedings for the child Reinforce with activities, not with food
Overweight	What foods does child have available at home? How has child's pattern of overweight been achieved?	Offer nonfat milk instead of whole milk, unsweetened fruit instead of desserts Limit fried foods, gravies, and sauces

Continued.

Table 14-2. Assessment of concerns about foods and nutrients—cont'd

Symptom	Assessment	Action and/or counseling suggestions
Overweight—cont'd	Has child gained weight recently? Is child currently gaining weight in the same channel and is overweight a result of earlier feeding experiences? How does the family feel about child's weight? Is child reinforced for eating? What is child's activity level? What is child's snacking pattern?	Provide low-calorie snacks Feed child on a schedule; discourage indiscrimate snacking Limit the number of desserts, cookies, candy, and other sweets offered Increase portion size of vegetables, meat, and fresh fruits; decrease portion size and number of servings of breads, potatoes, cereals, and fatty foods Reinforce with activities, not with food Help the family find ways of increasing child's level of activity Direct efforts at a reduction in the rate of weight gain, not a weight loss
Obesity	Assess as above	Weight reduction diet planned to effect weight loss of no more than 2 lb/month Counsel with all who offer food to child in the weight reduction program Plan physical activities daily in any manner compatible with the child's level of function Provide continuing support for parents and children as the program progresses

REFERENCES

1. Garn, S. M., and Weir, H. F.: Assessing the nutritional status of the mentally retarded, Am. J. Clin. Nutr. **24:**853, 1971.
2. Smith, K. W.: Growth and its disorders, Philadelphia, 1977, W. B. Saunders Co.
3. Isaksson, B.: The nutritional needs of disabled children. In Blix, G., editor: Nutrition in preschool and school age, Symposium of the Swedish Nutrition Foundation, VII, Stockholm, 1969, Almqvist & Wiksell Förlag AB, p. 137.
4. Palmer, S., and Ekvall, S.: Pediatric nutrition in developmental disorders, Springfield, Ill., 1978, Charles C Thomas, Publisher.
5. Leamy, C. M.: A study of the food intake of a group of children with cerebral palsy in the Lakeville Sanatorium, Am. J. Public Health **43:**1310, 1953.
6. Ruby, D. O., and Matheny, W. D.: Comments on growth of cerebral-palsied children, J. Am. Diet. Assoc. **40:**525, 1962.
7. Hammond, M. I., Lewis, M. N., and Johnson, E. W.: A nutritional study of cerebral palsied children, J. Am. Diet. Assoc. **49:**196, 1966.
8. Karle, I. P., Blehler, R. E., and Ohlson, M. A.: Nutritional status of cerebral-palsied children, J. Am. Diet. Assoc. **38:**22, 1961.
9. Culley, W. J., and others: Calorie intake of children with Down's syndrome (mongolism), J. Pediatr. **66:**772, 1965.
10. Culley, W. J., and Middleton, T. O.: Calorie re-

quirements of mentally retarded children with and without motor dysfunction, J. Pediatr. **75**:380, 1969.

11. Pipes, P., and Holm, V.: Weight control of children with Prader-Willi syndrome, J. Am. Diet. Assoc. **62**:520, 1973.

12. Mertz, E. T., and others: Protein malnutrition in mentally retarded children. In Food and Nutrition Board: Meeting protein needs of infants and children, Publication No. 843, Washington, D.C., 1961, National Academy of Sciences, National Research Council.

13. Eddy, T. P., Nicholson, A. L., and Wheeler, E. F.: Energy expenditures and dietary intakes in cerebral palsy, Dev. Med. Child Neurol. **7**:377, 1965.

14. Kruse, R.: Osteopathien bei antiepileptischer. Langeitherapie (Vorlanfige Meheilung) Monat sch. Kinderheilko **116**:378, 1968. Cited in Borgstedt, A. D., and others: Long-term administration of antiepileptic drugs and the development of rickets, J. Pediatr. **81**:9, 1972.

15. Jubiz, W., and others: Plasma 1,25-dihydroxyvitamin D levels in patients receiving anticonvulsant drugs, J. Clin. Endocrinol. Metab. **44**:617, 1977.

16. Lifshitz, F., and Maclaren, N. K.: Vitamin D-dependent rickets in institutionalized mentally retarded children receiving long-term anticonvulsant therapy. I. A survey of 288 patients, J. Pediatr. **83**:612, 1973.

17. Silver, J., and others: Prevalence and treatment of vitamin D deficiency in children on anticonvulsant drugs, Arch. Dis. Child. **49**:344, 1974.

18. Medlinsky, H. L.: Rickets associated with anticonvulsant medication, Pediatrics **53**:91, 1974.

19. Borgstedt, A. D., and others: Long-term administration of anti-epileptic drugs and the development of rickets, J. Pediatr. **81**:9, 1972.

20. Hahn, T. J.: Bone complications of anticonvulsants, Drugs **12**:201, 1976.

21. Teotia, M., and Teotia, S. P. S.: Rickets precipitated by anticonvulsant drugs, Am. J. Dis. Child. **125**:850, 1973.

22. Norris, J. W., and Pratt, R. F.: Folic acid deficiency and epilepsy, Drugs **8**:366, 1974.

23. Reynolds, E. H.: Folate metabolism and anticonvulsant therapy, Proc. R. Soc. Med. **67**:6, 1974.

24. Chanarin, I.: Effects of anticonvulsant drugs. In Botez, M. I., and Reynolds, E. H., editors: Folic acid in neurology, psychiatry, and internal medicine, New York, 1979, Raven Press.

25. Hommes, O. R., and others: Convulsant properties of folate compounds: some considerations and speculations. In Botez, M. I., and Reynolds, E. H., editors: Folic acid in neurology, psychiatry, and internal medicine, New York, 1979, Raven Press.

26. Eastham, R. D., Jancan, J., and Cameron, J. D.: Red cell folate and macrocytosis during long-term anticonvulsant therapy in non-anemic mentally retarded epileptics, Br. J. Psychiatry **126**:263, 1975.

27. Chien, L. F., and others: Harmful effect of megadoses of vitamins: electroencephalogram abnormalities and seizures induced by intravenous folate in drug treated epileptics, Am. J. Clin. Nutr. **28**:51, 1975.

28. Klein, G. L., and others: Multiple vitamin deficiencies in association with chronic anticonvulsant therapy, Pediatrics **60**:767, 1977.

29. Illingworth, R. S., and Lister, J.: The critical or sensitive period with special reference to certain feeding problems in infants and children, J. Pediatr. **65**:839, 1964.

30. Scales, H. E.: The application of operant conditioning to establish self-help feeding patterns in two mentally retarded children, unpublished Master of Nursing thesis, University of Washington, 1966.

31. Bosma, J. F.: Structure and function of the infant oral and pharyngeal mechanisms. In Wilson, J., editor: Oral-motor function and dysfunction in children, Chapel Hill, N.C., 1977, University of North Carolina, Division of Physical Therapy.

32. Burpee, B.: Effect of oral stimulation in premature infants. In Heriza, C., editor: The comprehensive management of infants at risk for CNS deficits, Chapel Hill, N.C., 1975, University of North Carolina, Division of Physical Therapy.

33. Evans, C.: Muscles involved in oral-motor function. In Wilson, J., editor: Oral-motor function and dysfunction in children, Chapel Hill, N.C., 1977, University of North Carolina, Division of Physical Therapy.

ADDITIONAL READINGS

Crosley, C. J., Chee, C., and Berman, P. H.: Rickets associated with long-term anticonvulsant therapy in a pediatric outpatient population, Pediatrics **56**:52, 1975.

Finnie, N. R.: Handling the young cerebral palsied child at home, New York, 1975, E. P. Dutton & Co., Inc.

Gauge, A. L., and Ekvall, S. W.: Diets of handicapped children: physical, psychological, and socioeconomic correlations, Am. J. Ment. Defic. **80**:149, 1975.

Hahn, T. J., and others: Serum 25-hydroxycalciferol levels and bone mass in children on chronic anticonvulsant therapy, N. Engl. J. Med. **292**:550, 1975.

Springer, N. S., and Fricke, N. L.: Nutrition and drug therapy for persons with developmental disabilities, Am. J. Ment. Defic. **80**:317, 1975.

Tolman, K. G., and others: Osteomalacia associated with anticonvulsant drug therapy in mentally retarded children, Pediatrics **56**:45, 1975.

15

Management of mealtime behaviors

Sally M. O'Neil

It is apparent that parent/child interactions are important determinants of children's acceptance of food and attitudes toward eating. They often are responsible for difficulties presented to health professionals. Parents, anxious about their children's nutrient intakes, sometimes urge, nag, or pressure children to eat, and children often assume control of the feeding environment. The battle for control may become so intense that the children's nutrient intakes may be compromised. The conflict may result in a variety of problems including failure to thrive and overweight or obesity. Difficulties in achieving adequate nutrient intakes because of inappropriate parent/child interactions during the preschool and early school years have been observed clinically in children who have histories of allergies and oral motor difficulties during infancy and in children who are overweight and obese. Inappropriate parent/child interaction is that which, in the struggle for control over child behavior, results in high levels of tension and parental reinforcement of child behaviors that interfere with adequate nutrient intake. Children may be inadvertently reinforced for disruptive activities (e.g., tantrums and throwing food) as well as for eating exceedingly large amounts of food. Parent/child interaction is a complex reciprocal process. Events occur in sequence on an interaction continuum be-

tween parents and children in which each response to an action can become the cause of future behaviors. It is by this interactive process that both parents and children learn new behaviors. The interactive process includes parents' expressions of attitudes, values, interests, beliefs, and their care-taking behavior as well as children's individual growth patterns, learning potential, and ability to incorporate increasingly complex experiences into their current stages of thinking and functioning.[1] Behavior is both the cause and effect of other behaviors. All parent/child interactions are both elicited by the child and impinge upon the child. For instance, the cries of an infant who is hungry can become the stimulus for the mother to respond by feeding him or her.

The purpose of this chapter is to focus on parent/child behaviors, to examine their effects on feeding and nutrition, and to explore methods of changing behavior, which in turn may effect changes in food intake patterns.

BASIC CONCEPTS IN BEHAVIORAL ASSESSMENT AND MANAGEMENT

Behaviorists have determined that behaviors are increased, maintained, or decreased by the consequences that immediately follow them. These consequences can be reinforcing or punishing. Since reinforcers and punishers are defined from an individual's point of view, what may be reinforcing to one person may not be to someone else; the determination of what is reinforcing or punishing is made by the effect of a particular consequence on the behavior that preceded it. To be a reinforcer, a consequence must increase the behavior that it follows.

Reinforcers are of two types: positive and negative. Positive reinforcement is a consequence in which something desirable to the subject is added or applied to his or her environment as a result of a specific behavior. A smile, praise, hug, food, and money are examples of positive reinforcers. Negative reinforcement, on the other hand, is a consequence in which something aversive or unpleasant is subtracted, that is, removed or terminated. For example, a person who is annoyed by loud static on the radio may turn down the volume or turn off the radio. The silence, or absence of static, is a negative reinforcer for turning off the sound, and the person is likely to do it again if static recurs. All reinforcers must increase the behavior that they follow. The important distinction between these two concepts is that in positive reinforcement something pleasant is added as a consequence and in negative reinforcement something unpleasant is removed as a consequence.

Punishers decrease the behaviors that they follow. They are defined operationally in two ways. One definition includes consequences in which something aversive is added or applied, such as a spanking. This is generally termed punishment. The second definition includes those consequences in which a positive reinforcer is removed, for example, the withholding of adult attention (ignoring) during a child's temper tantrum, or withholding eye contact when someone else is talking. This is generally termed extinction.

Interaction processes between positive and negative reinforcement and punishment

In order to examine positive and negative reinforcement and punishment as interactive processes, it is important to analyze the various parts of interaction. Peterson has suggested that one way to do this effectively is to consider interaction in terms of A (antecedent events), B (behavior), and C (consequences).[2] Consider the following example in which the ABC analysis is used: A mother takes her preschool son into a grocery store. The child immediately begins to ask for candy, then whines and cries when the mother refuses to give him any candy. After several minutes of loud crying and repeated looks from other shoppers, the mother gives the child a piece of candy. The child immediately stops crying.

A diagrammatic analysis of this situation is presented below. From this analysis one would correctly conclude that in giving her child candy the mother had reinforced her child for crying. Also, because he was reinforced, it is highly likely that the child will repeat this behavior during future trips to the grocery store. The consequence that the mother received when she gave the candy was one of negative reinforcement because the crying ceased after the mother gave the child the candy. By giving candy, she terminated something that was aversive to her—the child's crying. In this interaction both mother and child were reinforced for their

A (antecedent)	B (child's behavior)	C (consequence)
1. Entering grocery store	2. Asks for candy	3. Mother refuses
	4. Cries and yells	5. Mother gives candy
	6. Stops crying	

CHILD BEHAVIORS AT MEALTIME

Noneating behaviors

	Meals observed					
	1	2	3	4	5	6
Arguing						
Complaining						
Crying						
Hitting						
Noncomplying						
Not sitting at table						
Teasing						
Yelling						
Pouting						
Whining						
Moving hands nonpurposefully						
Talking back						
Throwing food or utensils						
Spitting						
Gagging						
Refusing certain foods						

Eating behaviors

Using fingers for finger foods						
Using utensils appropriately						
Sitting at table						
Accepting variety of foods						
Socializing as appropriate						
Complying to requests						

PARENT BEHAVIORS AT MEALTIME

Antecedents to child behaviors

	Meals observed					
	1	2	3	4	5	6
Commanding						
Requesting						
Questioning						
Prompting verbally						
Physically assisting						
Interrupting						
Positioning child appropriately						
Presenting food appropriately						
Presenting appropriate utensils						

Consequences of child behaviors

Commenting positively						
Commenting negatively						
Ignoring						
Touching						
Spanking						
Yelling						
Arguing						
Laughing						
Using same tone of voice						
Talking irrelevantly						

behaviors. The child was positively reinforced (candy was added) for crying, and the mother was negatively reinforced (crying was removed) for giving the candy. Both are likely to repeat their behaviors next time.

What if, in a similar situation, the mother decided to ignore the child? What would the mother's consequences be if ignoring stopped the crying? As before, her consequence is that of negative reinforcement if she successfully stops the crying. Because the mother will be negatively reinforced for whatever she does that stops the crying, it becomes important for her to consider her behavior in the light of the kinds of behaviors she would like her child to learn. She has to consider his stage of development and reinforcers that fit his particular stage as well as the effects of the child on her own behavior. It is easy for parents to become trapped by their responses to their children's behavior and thus become unable to see those aspects that are ineffective for mutually pleasant interactions.

Assessment of mealtime behaviors

Initial assessment consists of identifying the patterns of parent/child mealtime behaviors. The observation checklist on p. 296 is a useful recording guide that pinpoints problem behavior as well as desirable behaviors. This tool can be used by professionals who are recording their direct observations or by parents who are recording the mealtime behaviors of themselves and their children. Behaviors can be tallied for each meal.

Once problem behaviors are identified the most frequent eating and noneating behaviors and their consequences can be identified in ABC sequences. Parents are helped to identify those child behaviors that they wish to change as well as the appropriate eating behaviors that they wish to foster in their children. The next step is to determine appropriate consequences for all of the behavior categories.

As we noted earlier, parents generally behave toward their children (reinforce, punish, or ignore) in certain ways because of the reinforcement they receive from their children. For instance, they may reinforce a crying child with a cookie, because they know this will stop the crying. Thus the parent is negatively reinforced for giving the child the cookie. Frequently, in order to help parents change the consequences they provide their children, it is necessary to look at what reinforcers the parents are getting for their own behavior. One way to do this is to help them identify the subsequent child behavior step to the ABC pattern. In order for parents to alter their antecedent cues to the child, they need to be aware of these behaviors and their part in the entire ABC pattern.

The brief case studies that follow illustrate a variety of parent/child ABC patterns that relate to mealtimes.

1 □ *Laura refuses to drink milk.*

A	B	C
1. Mother pours milk into glass	2. Child starts crying	3. Mother says, "Drink your milk"
	4. Child cries	5. Mother removes milk and gives child soda
	6. Child stops crying and drinks soda	

In this instance the mother was negatively reinforced. She successfully terminated the crying by giving the child soda, which, in turn, positively reinforced the child's crying when milk was presented to her.

2 □ *Billy, a toddler, writes his own menu.*

A (mother)	B (child)	C (mother)
1. Presents applesauce to toddler in highchair	2. Cries and whines, points to the refrigerator	3. "What do you want?"
	4. Cries, points to cupboard	5. "Do you want a cracker?" Gives him a cracker
	6. Cries, points to cupboard and refrigerator	7. "What do you want? Here is some cereal."
	8. Cries, points to refrigerator	9. "No you can't have ice cream."
	10. Child screams	11. "OK, here is some ice cream."
	12. Stops crying	

In this situation the child keeps his mother going in circles in an effort to stop his crying. A management plan was developed with her in which she would leave the room and when the child would stop crying she would return and praise him for eating so nicely. The ABC looked like this:

A (mother)	B (child)	C (mother)
1. Presents applesauce to toddler in highchair	2. Cries, points to cupboard	3. Leaves room (can see child but he can't see her)
	4. Slowly stops crying, starts eating applesauce	5. Returns and says "My, what a big boy!"
	6. Child laughs and keeps on eating	

3 □ *John, a school-age child who has a hearing impairment, wanders at mealtimes.*

A (parents)	B (child)	C (parents)
1. Announce dinner	2. Sits at table with parents	3. Talk to each other, ignore child
	4. Gets up and wanders around house	5. Yell, "Come back here, John."
	6. Approaches dining room	7. Ignore John
	8. Wanders away from dining room	9. "Come here, John." Father goes and leads him to table
	10. John sits and looks at food	11. Ignore John
	12. John leaves table	

In discussing this ABC with John's parents they decided that they had been reinforced by John's absence at the table since prior to that time, he had had tantrum behavior at the table. They believed that he should eat with them, but it was more comfortable to eat without him and to feed him later. A management program was developed with them in which they agreed to reinforce him for sitting at the table, using signing as well as verbal praise, and to try to include him in the general conversation. A subsequent ABC looked like this:

A (parents)	B (child)	C (parents)
1. Announce dinner	2. John sits at table, starts eating	3. Talk and sign to John
	4. Leaves table	5. Ignore John
	6. Approaches table	7. Talk and sign to John, discussing day's events
	8. Sits down, starts to eat	9. Eat, yet continue to socialize with John
	10. John talks, signs, eats, and remains seated during meal	

The importance of antecedents. While consequences are of importance in maintaining behaviors, the antecedent events frequently tell a child or parent that certain behaviors will be reinforced. As discriminative stimuli, antecedents set the occasion for reinforcers. For example, when the mother in case 1 poured the milk, the child knew that if she cried at that time she would be likely to get soda instead.

Frequently, in an attempt to get control of such a situation this parent may have suggested as she poured the milk, "You have to drink milk, you will not get soda this time." However, the child cries anyway, even louder and longer than before. To terminate the crying the parent generally gives in and replaces the milk with soda. Instead of discouraging the child, the parent has only made the discriminative stimulus even stronger by adding the verbal reminder when pouring the milk.

Another example of important antecedents is demonstrated in case 4.

4 □ *Suzi, a preschooler, uses cues supplied by her mother to control her mother's behavior.*

A	B	C
Meal 1		
1. Mother presents food	2. Child eats	3. Mother sits with book, does not talk to child
Meal 2		
1. Mother presents food	2. Child gags and spits up food	3. Mother attends, cleans up child, then finishes feeding her the meal

In assessing this situation, it was found that Suzi did not vomit every meal. Yet somehow she was getting cues as to when to vomit. In an attempt to further identify these cues, the mother's meal preparation was observed as part of the antecedent behavior. Surprisingly, the typical ABC pattern for vomiting and nonvomiting meals looked like this:

A	B	C
Vomiting meal		
1. Preparing lunch, mother says, "Suzi, you have carrots today. I hope you don't vomit them."	2. Child starts eating, then gags and vomits carrots	3. Mother attends, cleans her up, and feeds her the rest of the meal
Nonvomiting meal		
1. Preparing lunch, mother says: "Oh good, Suzi, you have macaroni today."	2. Eating well	3. Mother sitting with book, ignoring Suzi

For the vomiting meal mother was cuing Suzi to the fact that if she vomited she would get attention, be cleaned up, and be fed her lunch. For the nonvomiting meal no such cue was given, so Suzi ate her lunch as expected.

These ABC patterns were discussed with the mother and a strategy was developed in which she would not read at mealtime, would reinforce Suzi for eating by talking with her at mealtime, and would only provide antecedent verbal cues such as in the nonvomiting meal.

A later ABC pattern looked like this:

A	B	C
1. "Suzi, we have egg sandwiches today."	2. Child eats, smiles, and talks to mother	3. Mother attends to Suzi by smiling and conversing

ADDITIONAL CONCEPTS IN BEHAVIOR MANAGEMENT

There is no doubt about the importance of food as an effective reinforcer for most people. Since it meets a basic biologic need, it is considered to be a primary reinforcer. Secondary reinforcers such as affection, praise, and touch are said to derive their reinforcing qualities from having been paired with food during the early infant period. Later, money becomes reinforcing when used to buy a wide variety of reinforcers such as food, shelter, clothing, and other desirable items. Food is a potential reinforcer for a wide variety of activities; it is frequently paired with or follows attendance at outings, movies, sports, and social events.

The decision to use food as a reinforcer is made after a careful assessment process in which a variety of reinforcers are tried. Reinforcers are *individualized*, as discussed earlier. What may be reinforcing to one individual may not be to another, depending on biophysiologic factors within an individual and his or her history of experiences.

For some children social praise may be reinforcing, for others food may be reinforcing. For still others neither social praise nor food is reinforcing, and parents must seek other kinds of reinforcers. Children who have developmental delays may not be able to utilize the usual things that most children find reinforcing. Because of sensory deficits or problems in neuromuscular development and/or because experiences have been limited, these children may need specialized reinforcers such as vibration, flickering lights, or even music. The point here is that an effort must be made to determine what kind of reinforcers is effective for any given individual. In some instances food is the only reinforcer with which a child can learn appropriate behaviors. If this is the case, then food should be used and other reinforcers (e.g., affection and praise) can be paired with it

until they also become reinforcing for this particular individual and food no longer needs to be used.

When it has been determined that food will be the most effective reinforcer for a particular child, several considerations are important. The first factor is the kind of food to use. Again, this should be individualized according to the child's tastes, and care should be taken to use food with high nutrient value whenever possible. In many instances potato chips and candy are used when raisins or cheese might be just as effective. Any food reinforcement should be considered as part of the total nutrient and calorie intake for the child.

Another factor to consider is the timing of food reinforcers. If one is concerned that the child eat adequate meals, then training programs that utilize food reinforcers should not immediately precede a meal. Likewise, if success in the training program is important, then a program using food reinforcers should not directly follow a meal. Any individual may become satiated by food unless adequate time has elapsed between intervals of food intake.

Satiation can also occur when too much of the same food is given. If particular foods are used during a training program, they should not be available to the child at any other time of the day to ensure maximum effectiveness of the reinforcer. For instance, a child may be given a dish of ice cream daily at home. If a decision is made to use a dish of ice cream in a program at school, the ice cream should no longer be available at home.

Another factor to consider when using food reinforcement is the pairing of another potential reinforcer with food. Because it is important for the child to be able to use other reinforcers, it is necessary to provide reinforcers such as praise at the same time that food is given. After it is determined that the combination of food and praise is reinforcing to the child, the food can be given less frequently, whereas praise will still be provided every time the desired behavior occurs. The food is gradually eliminated, and praise will have become a reinforcer for the child.

Consistency is another important factor in applying reinforcers. As children learn an increasing variety of behaviors they learn about new and different reinforcers. Food and feeding habits may be incorporated into behavioral repertoires designed to gain adult attention. Throwing utensils and/or food may cause a variety of interesting adult reactions. A parent may laugh at one such incident, respond with anger at another, and at a third may feed the child in exasperation. In the effort to keep up with the child, parents may respond inconsistently, depending on their mood at the time. Consistency means that desirable behaviors generally are reinforced, whereas undesirable behaviors are not reinforced and may even be punished. What is important is that the child knows what desirable behaviors are expected by his or her parents and, in turn, what consequences can be expected for certain behaviors.

When food intake is the major concern, experience has indicated that reinforcers other than food are more effective for managing feeding behaviors. For instance, if a child must be on a special diet for a biologic reason such as allergy, parents and professionals usually become concerned that the child may not eat adequate amounts of acceptable foods. In this instance the child receives mixed messages if he or she is reinforced with food yet perceives that the parents will not allow certain other foods. The child quickly learns that by refusing foods that are allowed he or she can gain a great deal of attention and may even receive the forbidden foods as parents become upset by the child's refusal to eat. The use of nonedible reinforcers such as outings, toys, and games following meals generally helps to refocus the parents' and child's attention to other activities.

TEACHING SELF-FEEDING BEHAVIORS

In addition to the use of reinforcement, *shaping* and *fading* techniques are useful procedures for teaching new behaviors and skills. Both of these procedures are useful for teaching feeding behaviors and are frequently employed by parents and professionals.

Shaping is the reinforcement of successive approximations to a desired behavior. In this procedure the behavior is broken down into its component steps. The type and number of steps are determined by the task to be learned. The first step is reinforced; when that step is learned, the next step is added and the reinforcement is shifted to the second step in the chain of responses that lead to the desired behavior.

Teaching spoon-feeding by shaping

1. Desired behavior: independent spoon feeding
2. Changing steps in child responses:
   a. Child looks at spoon
   b. Child moves hand toward spoon
   c. Child touches spoon
   d. Child picks up spoon
   e. Child puts spoon in dish
   f. Child scoops food
   g. Child brings food to mouth
   h. Child takes food off spoon
   i. Child returns spoon to dish

3. Reinforcement: bites of food or other reinforcers as each step is accomplished

Fading is a different procedure in that the entire behavior is utilized each time for reinforcement. Instead of requiring the child's responses to proceed through several steps, the trainer's cues are changed as the child's skill develops. For example, the trainer holds the child's hand around the spoon and puts the child through the motions of scooping food onto the spoon, bringing the spoon to the mouth and returning the spoon to the dish. As the child gradually assumes independent movement, physical assistance is decreased, and the trainer only provides assistance as needed to complete the task. The number and type of trainer cues needed will depend on the task to be learned and the abilities of the child.

Teaching spoon-feeding by fading

1. Desired behavior: independent spoon feeding
2. Steps:
   a. Holding child's hand around spoon, scoop food, bring arm, hand, and spoon *to* mouth. Allow child to take food off spoon in mouth, then (still holding child's hand around spoon) return to dish.
   b. Holding child's hand around spoon, bring it *toward* mouth and allow child to complete movement to mouth if possible. Assist through rest of cycle.
   c. Assist child in holding spoon and scooping food. By touching arm slightly, provide cues that assist child in completing movement to mouth. Also by touches, assist child in returning spoon to dish.
   d. Provide only as much assistance as child needs to pick up spoon, scoop food, move spoon to mouth, and return to dish.

The actual number of steps delineated for any given individual depends upon the developmental level and skill that the individual possesses prior to employing either of these procedures.

GENERAL CONSIDERATIONS IN THE USE OF BEHAVIOR MANAGEMENT TECHNIQUES

Behavior modification is generally easy to utilize as a method of therapeutic intervention. The difficulties lie in the behavioral analysis, which is necessary to pinpoint specific behaviors and their consequences. Frequently, the relationships between behaviors and their consequences (particularly when two or more persons are involved) are diffi-

cult to discover, and care must be taken to delineate them with accuracy and reliability. Behavior is not simple and becomes increasingly complex when viewed within a framework of human interaction. Yet to try to remedy behaviors in isolation is to treat them outside of the context of their everyday occurrence. This, in turn, leads to unsuccessful programs.

The preceding examples have been assessed by direct observation of mealtime behaviors, yet there are more complex situations that would preclude direct observation or that would be greatly altered by the presence of an observer. In-home videotaped recordings (if available to the professional) frequently work well for these situations. Parents are usually quite willing to allow several meals to be videotaped to pinpoint difficulties. These tapes are analyzed according to their ABC patterns. Important segments of tape are then played back to the parents, who frequently are able to discover the problems themselves. Frequently, this is an impetus for them to discuss their feelings and concerns about the situations and to generate alternative ways of behaving with their children.

Professionals must be concerned about all of the possible effects of the techniques prior to implementing them and should secure assistance while learning the procedures involved. Collaboration of nutrition, nursing, and other disciplines will assist in continually refining observation and recording techniques and management procedures. Successful programs require that the role of each discipline in the analysis, program design, and implementation be well defined.

During nutrition and feeding evaluation, observations of parental and child behaviors by two or more disciplines can help to identify more reliably the cause of a specific problem. Programs should be designed jointly with parents by a member of one discipline primarily relating to the family. Changes in physical growth, nutrient intake, and behavior should be monitored on an interdisciplinary basis in order to direct attention to both psychosocial (behavioral) and physical parameters.

REFERENCES

1. O'Neil, S. M., McLaughlin, B. N., and Knapp, M. B.: Behavioral approaches to children with developmental delays, St. Louis, 1977, The C. V. Mosby Co.
2. Peterson, L. W.: Operant approach to observation and recording, Nurs. Outlook **15:**28, 1967.

ADDITIONAL READINGS

Becker, W. C.: Parents are teachers: a child management program, Champaign, Ill., 1971, Research Press.

McLaughlin, B. N.: Learning and social behavior, New York, 1971, The Free Press.

Patterson, G. R.: Application of social learning to families, Champaign, Ill., 1974, Research Press.

Sears, R. R., Maccaby, E. E., and Levin, H.: Patterns of child rearing, New York, 1957, Row, Peterson and Co.

Index